DEAR FRIEND:

The correspondence of
Hildred L. Cress &
Charles W. Husband, M.D.

OCTOBER 1913 - OCTOBER 1914

Compiled & Edited by
Hildred Corbett

Lynda —
a dear friend, herself
Hildy Corbett
June 2014

DEDICATION

Glenn and June Corbett,
who found the letters and knew their worth

Charles G. and Judith Thom,
whose quiet and unfailing belief and encouragement kept me on
task when my energies flagged

Eric M. Johnson,
who writes a fine letter himself, for his love and support

Hildred & Charles

ACKNOWLEDGEMENTS

This book would never have been possible in its present form without the help and assistance of the following:

Karen Fitzpatrick - Clerk, Main Branch, Detroit Public Library

Terri Thomson - Manager, Edison Branch, Detroit Public Library

Carole Hovsepian - Friend and Fearless Adventurer

Gail Campbell Schulte - Genealogist

Minnesota Historical Society Library

White Bear Lake Area Historical Society

The letters were legend.

Growing up, my mother told us the stories behind the letters this way: Her mother, Hildred Cress, lived in St. Paul, Minnesota. Her father, Charles W. Husband, M.D., of Detroit, Michigan, was visiting a relative in St. Paul, who was Hildred's employer. She was asked to take Charles on a tour of the city, and when his time there was concluded, they agreed to write one another. After a year, they married in St. Paul and settled in Detroit, where Charles had a thriving medical practice.

"Your grandparents only saw each other in person twice before they were married," she told me. "When they met and when your grandfather came to St. Paul to propose were the only times. The next time they saw each other was on their wedding day."

"They wrote to each other for a year," she said. She was sure the letters survived somewhere.

I had seen the letters once as a child, while I was exploring the vast attic in my grandparents' house on Argyle Crescent in the Palmer Woods section of Detroit.

The attic held many secrets: World War II memorabilia, portions of a human skeleton (Grandpa and Uncle Ray were surgeons, after all), milky cat eyes preserved in formaldehyde. We grandchildren couldn't get enough of the attic. Every visit was a terrifying and exhilarating adventure.

One afternoon in the attic, I remember glancing at yellowing letters, with postmarks from St. Paul, Minnesota and Detroit, Michigan, jammed in a dresser drawer; a dresser which belonged to my great-grandmother Emily Turner. It now rests, restored, in my bedroom less than three miles from the house on Argyle Crescent. I didn't pay them attention then. The cat eyes were infinitely more interesting.

In 1985, Hildred and Charles had both passed away. As part of that final rite of passage, their children, Raymond C. Husband, M.D., and the twins, Roberta Emily Thom and

Hildred Loretta Corbett, took on the task of preparing the Argyle Crescent house for sale.

Sometime in this process, my brother, Glenn Corbett, and his wife, June, visited the old house. As they entered the side yard, they noted the household trash accumulating in the garage. Sitting on top of a pile of discards were two long boxes of letters...THE letters. Glenn, bless him, plucked the letters from the trash and took them home, where they remained safe in a bedroom closet.

About 10 years later, while visiting Glenn and June at their home, my brother looked at me with a mixture of humor and seriousness and said: "I have something for you." He left the room and when he returned, he had two long boxes of yellowing letters, which he plopped in my lap. "You're the writer in the family, do something with these," he said.

It's taken another 15 years or so, but at last the letters have been catalogued and their place in history fixed. I've chosen to begin each month with a montage of newspaper headlines from the St. Paul Pioneer Press and the Detroit Free Press, two leading newspapers of their day, both of which still are in operation.

During my grandparents' youth, women, minorities and immigrants were not treated well. The world could be a dangerous place for those who were not white, male and upper-middle class. There was little mixture between groups; everyone had their place and understood the order of life. Perhaps what they knew about one another came from the newspaper – whose editors understood that sensation sold.

The headlines reveal a world that was as intemperate and fast-paced as it is today. World War I was brewing. Women were seeking their rights as suffragettes while the working man was seeking better pay and working conditions through the labor union process.

Automobiles were quickly supplanting horses as the primary means of transportation, and the new mobility meant the demise of a rural economy and the birth of an urban one.

But in the midst of this international change, were the letters between two young people: Hildred Loretta Cress, age 18; and Charles William Husband, M.D., age 25. Their letters show a growing friendship that deepened to an abiding love, with little regard to the changing world around them. Perhaps they didn't recognize they were living in a time of historic revolution. Perhaps it didn't matter.

All that mattered was each other and the life they would build, together.

-- Hildred Corbett
   October 2013

CONTENTS

SETTING THE SCENE

———◆———

In October 1913, Charles W. Husband, M.D., was a 25-year-old surgeon, setting up his medical practice in Detroit, Michigan. Graduated a year earlier from Detroit College of Medicine, Charles served his medical internship at Detroit's St. Mary's Hospital.

He was one of three sons born to William A. and Emily (Turner) Husband in Petrolia, Ont. He had an older brother, Leonard, and a younger brother, Sydney. Sydney died at age 21 of appendicitis.

It is unclear if his brother's death influenced his decision to become a doctor. Even as a child, Charles said he knew he wanted to practice medicine. After graduation from the University of Toronto and medical school, Charles remained in Detroit, setting his shingle outside his newly-built home at 320 Manchester, on the city's west side.

Sometime during the early fall 1913, Charles took the train to visit his uncle, C.W. Turner, in St. Paul, Minnesota. The treasurer of Booth Fisheries and Cold Storage, Turner helped oversee a thriving concern that bought and sold fish from locations along the Mississippi River. The St. Paul headquarters was a large building located along the teeming river, with openings covered by rolling doors along the back to accept and disburse its product along the Mississippi.

There, he met Hildred Loretta Cress, Mr. Turner's secretary. Just 18 years old, Hildred was the daughter of Henry A. Cress, a Booth Fisheries manager, and his wife, Rose Mary Cress. Hildred had a younger sister, Claribel, and a young brother, Addison. In 1910, Rose Mary died of breast cancer at the age of 38. Hildred was 15 years old; Claribel, 14 and young Addison, seven.

Henry Cress appears to have married not long after Rose Mary's death, approximately 1911, to a woman named Ellen S. Schmitt. She was 26 years old; Henry, 39. Despite being only 11years older than her eldest step-daughter, it is Ellen to whom Hildred refers as "mamma" in the letters.

Marrying quickly after the death of a spouse was not an unusual occurrence for a young widowed father in turn-of-the-century America. Henry was needed at work, and the children were still too young to manage by themselves.

Records indicate that by 1911 the family was relocated from Ashland, Wisconsin to St. Paul, where Henry again worked as a manager for the fishery company. In 1913, his eldest daughter, Hildred, was working at Booth, as well, as secretary to company treasurer C.W. Turner

That year, Charles Husband, visiting his uncle, C.W. Turner, would meet the young secretary who would become his wife.

Family history tells us C.W. Turner asked Hildred to show Charles around St. Paul during his week-long stay. And, from the first letter, it was clear they liked each other right away.

In all, there are 336 letters which survive, nearly all of them written by the pair. Several were written by key participants, and are incorporated in this book. The first is postmarked October 4, 1913, from Detroit. "Dear Friend" is the way Charles began his correspondence. There are seven in that first month. They peaked in July 1914, when 65 letters traveled the approximately 680 miles between Detroit and St. Paul.

They end with a letter postmarked October 23, 1914, just as Charles was readying for his trip to St. Paul to be married. "Sweetheart Hildred, Dearest Ever" is Charles' salutation. There are 40 letters that month.

The letters chronicle a love story; from its tentative beginnings to the discovery of whom each would become: Charles' tenacious pursuit of success in the field of medicine, Hildred's joy of life, itself. Their hopes and dreams and their plans for making them come true.

The correspondence reflects their roles as young adults in a changing world. Their support of each other would remain constant as they matured and grew as individuals, and as a couple.

At two-cents a letter, it is the story of life.

HILDRED & CHARLES

---◆---

PHOTOGRAPHS

Hildred L. Cress

C.W. Husband, M.D.

Hildred Cress' home on Ashland Ave.
in St. Paul, Minnesota

Charles Husband's house on Manchester St.
in Detroit, the address was later changed to
Northwestern

Booth Fisheries Building

Charles' parents, Emily & William Husband

Cress Family, about 1905

St. Paul Auto Club in White Bear Lake, Minnesota

Henry A. Cress, Hildred's father

Charles and his brothers Leonard (left) & Sidney (right), Sidney died of appendicitus at age 21

Rose Mary Cress & her children (from left) Addison, Hildred and Claribel

Katherine & Leonard Husband

Ernest & Claribel Groenig, about 1960

Hildred & Charles shortly after they were married, Note Charles' straw hat

Mr. and Mrs. Henry Addison Cress

will give in marriage

their daughter

Hildred Loretta

to

Charles William Husband, M.D.

Monday evening, October the twenty-sixth

nineteen hundred and fourteen

at half after eight o'clock

1847 Ashland Avenue

St. Paul, Minnesota

Your presence is requested

Wedding Invitation for Hildred & Charles

ary; Frank

ett's "Mile-
esented the
· by the
as follows:
nan; Ger-
'uttle; Mrs.
ey; Samuel
tose Sibley,
ym, Albert
Miss Ora
liam Rock-
ss Bonnie
rst, Elmer
uriel Pynn,
ard Sibley,
in, Herbert
c Matzner
ie pledging
Mountain
, '17, Min-

e St. Paul
will coach
iduction of
has chosen
in Paulton,
erex, Earle
ott; Adrian
man; Wat,
on Balch;
ilivan; El-
: Leonard;
ed; Elinor,
rriet, Miss
s Margaret
cCoy.
was chosen
ie Spanish
Miss Edna
uell is sec-

ed the fol-
esa Maier,
eness, vice
npson, sec-
illis, treas-

l hold open
after the

, has been
f the Tri-

party in the Armory Friday evening.

Merriam Park.

Miss Donna and Miss Nannoe Mur-
phy, 2069 Marshall avenue, entertained
at a beautifully appointed bridge party
yesterday afternoon at their home in
honor of Mrs. Homer Ward Rugg of
Minneapolis. The decorations and ap-
pointments were carried out in orange
and black, suggestive of the Halloween
season. Cards were played at six
tables. Mrs. Rugg, who is a recent
bride, was formerly Miss Dorna Butsch
of Owatonna.

The wedding of Miss Hildred Loretta
Cress, the daughter of Mr. and Mrs. H.
A. Cress, 1847 Ashland avenue, to Dr.
Charles W. Husband of Detroit, Mich.,
will take place tomorrow at 8:30 P. M.
at the residence of Mr. and Mrs. Cress.
Miss Claribel Cress will be her sister's
maid of honor and only attendant.
Leonard Husband of Duluth will be his
brother's best man. Rev. Dr. Alexander C. Stevens, pastor of Trinity
Methodist Episcopal church, will offi-
ciate. An informal reception will follow the ceremony. Dr. Husband and
his bride will be at home after December 1 at Detroit.

Miss Cress has been the honor guest
at a number of pre-nuptial affairs.
Tuesday evening, Miss Ethel Crosby
was hostess at a "handy" shower for
Miss Cress at her home on Selby avenue. Last Wednesday the Misses Alice
and Harriet Miles gave a parcel shower for the bride-to-be and recently Miss
Gladys Porter also was a hostess for
her at a parcel shower. Miss Celia
Brown, Selby avenue, entertained at
luncheon on Tuesday for Miss Cress.

The Woman's Home Missionary society of Trinity Methodist Episcopal
church held its annual meeting and
election of officers Friday afternoon in
the church parlors. Mrs. Vincent F.
De Vinny gave an interesting story of
"A Frontier Minister's Family." Mrs.
W. O. Hillman was elected president
of the society and the other officers

Miss Julia Connors,
entertained at a B
Tuesday evening.

The Merriam Park
meet November 2 wi
L. Strong, 1921 Dayt
Raymond Phalen of t
Minnesota will talk
Tax." The class met
home of Mrs. I. E. V
shall avenue. Mrs. A
a report of the stat
cently held at Roches
Pollock will present a
rent Events."

Miss Winifred Mur
avenue, has returned
by her sister, Mrs.
Fargo, N. D.

Mr. and Mrs. H. I
Laurel avenue, left V
month's visit in Mil

The Rector's Aid of
copal Church will gi
party Saturday eveni
rooms of the church,
be for all the younger
church.

The Woman's Guil
Episcopal Church has
for its annual Christ
will be held this ye
1 in the guild rooms.

The Roblyn Park I
will have an all-day n
the residence of Mrs
horn, 2071 Carroll ave
Miss Stella Harff, 17
will entertain Saturd
the members of the A
sorority.

Miss Vera Ladner of
is the house guest of
Rueth and the Misse
avenue.

The Misses Donnell
avenue, entertained i
nesday evening at th
The Merriam Park
will be entertained at
public library Wednes
tha C. Wells will give
has chosen for her su

Wedding Notice, St. Paul Pioneer Press

The Husband home on Argyle Crescent in the Palmer Woods section of Detroit

Hildred & Charles at the home on Northwestern

Anniversary Card with photo of ship where Charles proposed

Hildred & Charles in the living room of their home on Argyle Crescent sometime in the 1960s

Hildred & Charles entering 50th Anniversary Party

Dr. and Mrs. Charles William Husband

request the pleasure of your company

for Dinner

in honour of their

Golden Wedding Anniversary

on Saturday, the twenty-fourth of October

at seven o'clock

The Detroit Golf Club

R. S. V. P.
Argyle Crescent Drive   No flowers or gifts, please

50th Wedding Anniversary Invitation

Descendents of Hildred & Charles, 2003

OCTOBER 1913

Newspaper Headlines

Detroit Free Press

CIRCULATION: Unavailable

- Quote Constitution against Alien Law – Jap. Government sends third protest to U.S.
- Earthquake shocks rock Panama, fate of Canal unknown
- Michigan men will shine at Road Congress
- Depot loop to be portion of Michigan line
- Declares Detroit united ignores 16 hour labor laws
- Surgeon describes radium emanation
- Cites menace of racial problems
- Acquit doctor of illegal operation – Dr. Albert Bennett of Detroit, freed on third similar charge
- Rowley terms Wilson policy "Idealistic" (Mexico)
- Thousands lost by Detroit in alleged Standard Oil fraud
- Ferris urges necessity of better roads

- Germans bitter against Foreign Legion of France
- Wilson wedding sways Washington (eldest daughter)
- Mammoth found in cave stirs science
- Negro's "Insult" to three Virginians causes near riot
- NY suffragette now public taxi chauffeur
- Dike removal brings (Panama) Canal opening near
- Adolphus Busch, St. Louis Brewer, dies in Germany
- Is Detroit Prosperous? Billions being expended in all kinds indicate general belief in city's future as well as the present
- What dreams are made on – this Viennese psychologist says that our mental excursions are caused by wishes
- St. Mary's nurses will have home
- New York architects will meet to combat skyscraper evil
- Jack Johnson is down and out in Paris (first African-American World Heavyweight Champion)
- City proposes new plan for depot route
- Girl drinks acid when lover fails to write
- Moving pictures taken of cross-country tour

𝔖𝔱. 𝔓𝔞𝔲𝔩 𝔓𝔦𝔬𝔫𝔢𝔢𝔯 𝔓𝔯𝔢𝔰𝔰

CIRCULATION: 118,087

- French aviator flew two miles a minute
- Clarence S. Darrow – Says strike is labor best and just weapon of defense and that capital is labor's eternal enemy
- Quake is opportune test for the (Panama) Canal
- Depot burns with $250,000 loss – means new station
- Narrow neck of land to be blown up this week, completing the Canal
- Motor trucks are supplanting horse
- Minnesota will spend $3 million on good roads during 1914 & 1915
- World Series – New York Giants and Philadelphia Athletics features Connie Mack (The A's win the series)
- Pure Milk law sought
- Atlantic & Pacific are joined; boats enter gap in Panama Canal
- Kerosene to lower cost of gasoline
- Horses are fast being discarded
- Do you enjoy your full rights as a woman?
- Great crowd sees start of flights – half million people gather near Paris to witness international areal competition
- Advertisement – White Star Lines New Olympic Nov. 15 – Dec. 13
- Machine gun used on coal strikers; one killed, four hurt
- Lincoln Memorial to rise in Capital - Cost: $2 million
- World travelogue opens Kodak show
- Minnesota teachers uniting in plan to better conditions of profession
- Serum treatment for Typhoid
- U.S. Car exports have increased 100 % in three years
- Drop of 20-degrees (in temperature) is predicted today
- Wireless spans Pacific – Nome to Asia for Russian government
- Marooned 10 years, Eskimos are saved

OCTOBER 1913

◆————

LETTERS

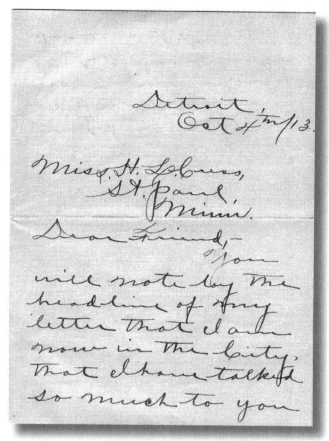

Postmark: 5:30 p.m. October 4, 1913

Miss H.L. Cress
c/o Booth Fisheries Co.
Third & St. Peter Sts.
St. Paul, Minn.

Detroit, Oct. 4th/13

Miss H.L. Cress,
St. Paul, Minn.

Dear Friend, -

You will note by the headline of my letter that I am now in the City that I have talked so much to you about [religiously], further more I do not know that I can stop telling you about Detroit until you come and see things as they are. (Next summer) if not before, by the way do not forget that you are saving ten cents a day and that I too am keeping tract [sic] of it. Will expect to hear from you on this subject.

Had a dandy trip home, weather a little cloudy on our arrival, but cleared up the following day, it is now just like the best day of summer.

I purchased my office furniture this morning, also have my order in for signs, but am strictly up against it in regard to getting a telephone installed. There is such a demand for service that the company can not meet it, therefore I do not know just when I will be able to get a telephone installed.

Before I forget (my fountain pen is sick), there is one thing that I was going to ask you before I left St. Paul but neglected, so I am going to take the liberty now. You remember the morning I spoke to you in regard to what I am doing now, you said something about what a lot of nurses etc. that I had or kept company with in Detroit, I was wondering what made you think or say that, or in other words what promoted that idea. I never thought enough about it at the time to make you any answer. If you will be kind enough would like to hear from you in regard to this matter.

Tell Uncle Chas. that we will be looking for him one week from to-day, and that we would be pleased to have him arrange to stay over Sunday.

Let me know how your Sister, Addison and everybody are getting along. And to answer my question I will say this that as long as I write you I would not be guilty of any attention to any one else; I do not know how you will take, or what you will think of me after making such a statement, but I hope you will take it in a kindly attitude of mind. I am not demanding an answer from you but how many pills will you need for the coming week, not fish or oysters but pills.

If I go any farther I will telling you something about the city, which I will do later.

Kindly let me hear from you at your earliest convenience. (8 pages)

Best Regards.

Sincerely Yours,

Chas. W.H.

(Gnd River Stat.) 320 Manchester

St. Paul, Minn.
Oct. 9th 1913.

Dear Friend:

Received your
letter, also your card, and
glad to know you arrived
in the "Big City" all O.K.
I suppose you are so glad
to get back that you will
never want to leave again,
at least for so long a stay
and in such a place as
I know you think St Paul
is.

As to my little bank,
I have been putting away
my ten cents religiously,
every day, but I think when
next summer comes, I

Postmark: 7:30 p.m. October 9, 1913, St. Paul, Minn.

Dr. Chas. W. Husband
320 Manchester Ave.
Detroit, Mich.

St. Paul, Minn.

Oct. 9th 1913

Dear Friend:

Received your letter, also your card and glad to know you arrived in the "Big City" all O.K. I suppose you are so glad to get back that you will never want to leave again, at least for so long a stay and in such a place as I know you think St. Paul is.

As to my little bank, I have been putting away my ten cents religiously, every day, but I think when next summer comes, will hate to spend so much money at once. That is, for a trip, but just the same it will come in handy.

I suppose by this time you have your office all fixed up in grand style and ready for big business. If it will do any good, I hope you will have a large number of patients, in fact more than you can take care of.

As to your question regarding the nurses, etc., nothing was meant by it at all, only Mr. Turner on his return from a trip to Detroit, made the statement that he had you and a lady friend to dinner one evening (maybe the one he gave the lecture to on promptness) and said what a pleasant time you had had together so I naturally didn't want to interfere but outside of that, nothing was meant at all.

By the way, I haven't received my package as yet and I have been anxiously waiting for it. If I do get it, I will surely send you a sample so you can help me enjoy it.

You ask how Claribel is getting along. She is doing very nicely but I guess I give her pretty strenuous exercise every once in a while. I think you got me into the habit of taking a walk in the evening so I am now trying to get her to do likewise. The only trouble is that she can't walk fast enough as yet to suit me but she is improving rapidly.

This evening one of my girlfriends and I are going to chaperone a number of seventh and eighth grade students on a "Roast" down at the river. Papa thinks it is a great joke, me acting as chaperone, says he thinks I need one pretty near as bad as they do but I assure you I am not going to be real easy with them the good advise that I always get, "go to bed early tonight."

Mr. Turner is over at the Dentist's this afternoon so have taken this opportunity to write you but guess I had better get busy as I have a report to make out on one of the Branches.

I hope to hear from you again, maybe you can tell me something more of Detroit. Also let me know how much you think I should have in my bank by this time.

Kindest regards, and wishing you every success,

Sincerely,

Hildred

P.S. How many pounds have you lost or gained?

H.C.

———————◆———————

Postmark: 12:30 a.m. October 14, 1913, Detroit, Mich.

After five days return to
Dr. Charles W. Husband
320 Manchester Ave.
Detroit

Miss. H.L. Cress,
c/o Booth Fisheries Coy.
St. Paul, Minn.

Oct. 13th/13.

Dear Friend, -

Your favor of the 9th Inst. To hand, kindly accept thanks for your good wishes contained there.

May say that my anxiety to get home was only due to my feeling of duty to get back to work. Further more I would far rather been in St. Paul than a great number of places that I have visited but at the same time Detroit suits me far better.

Please do not forget about the ten cents you are saving each and every day, Up until the day of my writing you should have about $1.20 in the little vault. You I hope already realize that you will have or be given no peace until you say "hurrah for Detroit with Mrs. Turner next summer, if your money by that time you will have to tell your troubles to me and see what I can do for you.

In regard to the package I do not see what has happened to it, I think we will have to fix things up again with Mr. Horlick, he does not seem to realize just who the order was to be sent to, otherwise he might have sent it, also that I was to share owing to your generosity a part of it.

Trust that you will continue with the walking habit that you credit me with starting. All I have to say is don't over do yourself, exercise with the power of development.

Glad to hear that Claribel is doing nicely, but you want to keep the upper hand on her.

By the way I would have liked to have been one of those eighth grade students that you chaperoned on a Roast down at the river. Did you get lost? Or roll down the embankment? Let me know how you made out.

Am already for business now except for electrical sign will have to be installed this afternoon, it cost me considerable money to furnish my office, but they show for it. If you were here I would have somebody to practice on, what do you think about it.

You did not say what time you go to bed and get up in the morning, & how about the washing & ironing and whether or not Mr. Turner gives you any more of those little morning talks.

Please tell Mr. Turner that I have our telephone fixed and what was wrong with it was that the man who installed it had it ring on L. instead of J. Our correct telephone No. now is Walnut 374 J.

Have not had time to sign [sic] myself.

Best regards to all.

Sincerely,

Chas. W.H.

Postmark: 7:30 p.m. Oct. 16, 1913, St. Paul, Minn.

St. Paul, Minn.

Oct. 16, 1913

Dear friend:

Received your letter and was very pleased to hear from you. Can only take a little time to answer as I am very busy today account of Mr. Turner being gone so long.

Mr. Turner had quite an exciting time at his house this morning. He intended going to Mpls. [Minneapolis] this morning and went out to crank his machine before Mr. Lucius got there. He just gave one turn and it backed-fire or something of that nature and caught fire. Mr. Turner hurt his right hand quite badly, it is all swollen up and he is pretty nervous today from the shock. The whole front of the car is burned also the top and the paint is all burned off. It doesn't look at all like the nice car we used to ride home in every evening.

We had a real good time at the Roast the other evening and nothing startling happened. We did have to look for the right path coming home but did not have much trouble in finding it.

By the way, I received my prize package this morning and Mr. Turner, papa and I sampled its contents and the rest I am forwarding to you as a sample. I think they would be a good thing for you to have in your office and then when you are too busy to eat your dinner, you can simply take a few tablets.

Mr. Turner has told me about your offices and from the description I should judge you have a very nice place and you surely should get lots of patients but I don't think I should care to be one as I don't like to take medicine unless it is the kind of pills you sent me with Mr. Turner. They were certainly fine and I thank you very much. I took the box home and treated the folks and Addison can't do enough for me because he knows I have some left.

I have been real good lately, have gone to bed not later than 10:30 and have not done any washing and only my own ironing so guess I haven't any scolding coming this time. I guess you are keeping track of the ten cents all right because you guessed about right. I have got pretty near $2.00 now and that will take me to the outskirts of St. Paul if not all the way to Detroit.

Was up to see a girl friend the other evening and she had just returned from Detroit. I didn't know she had been there at all. She says it certainly is a pretty city, so guess there is some truth in your statements.

I think I shall have to get busy again but be sure you do not over work or Mr. Turner will have to give you the lectures instead of me in the future.

Kind regards and trusting you have lots of business,

Sincerely,

Hildred

P.S. Let me know how you like the tablets. Mr. Turner says he thinks it would be better to send some of the mail addressed to him and as I open it all, it will be O.K.

H.C.

———————◆———————

Postmark: 8:30 p.m. Oct. 20, 1913, Detroit, Mich.

Addressed to Mr. C.W. Turner
Booth Fisheries Comp.
St. Paul, Minn.

Oct. 20th/13.

Dear Friend, -

Pleased to receive your favor of the 16th Inst.

As requested I will address all my letters to Mr. Turner, as a distinction between my letters to you and those to Mr. Turner, and in case Mr. Turner is out of the City, I will place a little dot or period mark in the upper right hand corner of the envelope, that is on the back of the envelope, as you will see in looking over the envelope of this letter.

Thanks for your good wishes in regard to business, it is always a slow and tedious course for a young Doctor when he starts out for himself, but I think things will pan out alright in the end.

You surely are a busy girl, but there is nothing like it. I wish I was worked to death, I know I would then be happy all the time.

Sorry indeed to hear concerning Mr. Turner, please find out if I would have received $5.00 for first aid had I been present. I believe I like money just in the same proportion as yourself.

Very anxious indeed to receive the tablets, I hope you have sent them by special delivery. Mr. Horlick at last woke up. How do you like them? Glad that you enjoyed the candy, Addison is wise no doubt in regard to getting around you.

I spend quite a lot of time teaching in the Detroit College of Medicine, also considerable time taking care of the surgical free clinic at St. Mary's Hosp.

How about that chronic sore throat of yours, don't you think I could fix it up for you, I think you had better let me try. I can also put you up an eye opener, to avoid inquiries as to what time you retired the night before.

Kind regards to all,

Sincerely,

Chas. W.H.

◆

Postmark: 6 p.m. Oct. 26, 1913, St. Paul, Minn.

Saturday afternoon

October 25th, 1913

Dear friend:

I received your welcome letter and among other things noted the dot on the back of the envelope. Hereafter I will look for it when your letters come.

Mr. Turner says you surely would have received $5.00 for first aid had you been here when he hurt his hand. There were two other accidents here in the building that same week so if you had been visiting here then, I would not have been such a bad weeks business. I think if you were here today I would be willing to pay $5.00 for first aid myself, providing you would cure the awful cold I have. Mr. Turner has been giving me those famous little white pills of his all day yesterday and today so presume I will be feeling fine again in a day or two.

You certainly must be a busy person taking care of your patients, teaching etc. but I know you like to work so hope you get a great deal of it.

Tomorrow, providing it is nice, Gladys and I are going to go for a good walk. We are going to start out early in the afternoon and stay out until supper time and then go to church in the evening so you see I have a busy day before me.

I hope you have received those famous tablets before this and that you liked them so well that you sent for a large size package.

We have had real wintry weather the past week, among other things had a nice snowfall and it stayed on the ground for several days. I thought Addison and I could go out sleigh riding pretty soon but guess we will have to wait a while for that.

By the way, if you can fix up anything that will avoid inquiries as to what time I retire, be sure and let me know as I think I need something like that as I am asked that question about every morning.

With kindest regards,

Sincerely,

Hildred

◆

Postmark: 12:30 a.m. Oct. 29, 1913, Detroit, Mich.

Addressed to Charles W. Turner – dot on envelope flap

Oct. 18/13th

Dear Friend:

Pleased to receive your favor of the 25th Inst. Note you found the dot, but you did not say how you liked our system.

In regard to your cold, and provided that you have a little cough, I am going to ask you to get the inclosed [sic] prescription filled, I know it will do you good, I supposed you will not tell me about the next cold that comes your way.

Tell Uncle Chas. that during my morning office hours today I had three of my old patients come in to see me all in a bunch. I wish they would keep it up.

Look here Young Lady if you were here, instead of playing around in snow you would be strolling around in sunshine and in the midst of delight.

As to inquiries regarding your time of retiring, I will give you a sure cure, which is as follows – go to bed any night at 8:30 (my old bedtime) for a whole week, then if Mr. Turner does not ask you next morning what time you retired the night before remind him of it. Finally he will take it for granted that you retired at 8:30 the night before and won't bother asking you any more.

You forgot to tell me anything about your little bank account, also whether or not you are still losing weight.

I am going to ask you to do a favor for me. I trust you will not try to find any excuse to take the place of the favor, but that you will comply with the request. The request is this, that you send me a photo of a Young Lady who lives on Ashland Ave. in St. Paul, works for Mr. Turner, gets an occasional early morning scolding, providing that she looks tired in the morning. I believe she has a cold at the present time. I trust you will get my meaning even if I am a little timid about it. She also bites at the tips of her fingers she gets nervous. Now do you know?

By the way I enclosed the tablets, kindly accept thanks, you sure are generous, you will be getting lots of mail before long, in all probability they will annoy you to death, if they do let me know and I will do my best to beat them up for you.

How is Claribel and your Daddy getting along.

Kindest regards to all.

Sincerely,

Chas.

P.S. Did you find the dot. - CWH

NOVEMBER 1913

◆

Newspaper Headlines

Detroit Free Press

- "Les Miserables" to be presented on screen
- Sees Belle Isle as a speedway for Vanderbilt Cup
- Palace of Versailles threatened with ruin
- French uniforms to be invisible; That is: They'll be of material difficult to be seen from an airship
- Care for tires says expert; is important
- Suffragists near Era of Militancy
- Private soldiery is being trained to crush strikes
- Auto parking good for city – great advertisement for city
- New income tax still perplexes Detroit bankers
- Titanic survivor is hurt in accident (automobile accident in Kalamazoo, MI; later proves fatal)
- Detroit Nursing Society formed
- Pension for teachers, say Suffragists
- Many Detroiters visit Belle Isle flower display

- Anti-saloonist to plan national fight on liquor
- The Castle Walk (dance) is simple, but heaps of fun
- Judge frowns on juries of women
- Scientists seek ways to measure enormous heat – Modern industrialism is developing some new problems
- Fenders needed on pleasure cars
- Surgeons work on bones in public – Operating amphitheaters crowded in Chicago, while new methods are shown
- Ulster exhausts revolver market
- Compulsory saving for women, Judge Lay's plan
- Urges prizes for designs of Fountain – City plan commission approves proposal for James Scott Fountain (on Belle Isle)
- Small Pox scare rouses Lansing
- Royal Austrians visit England – Archduke Francis Ferdinand and Consort guests of king at Windsor Castle
- (Women's) trousers the fashion in ten years
- Plans ready for Detroit Athletic Club's new home
  - Architect Kahn finishes work of eight months
  - No expense or pains spared on structure
  - Building will be eight stories in hight [sic]; cost about $1 million, ready Dec. 1, 1914
- Hall of Fame for American Women who deserve Immortality soon will be erected in New York
- Titanic appeal is in Supreme Court – Steamship company wants its wreck liability limited to $91,000 total

𝔖t. 𝔓aul 𝔓ioneer 𝔓ress

- Methodists urge Bibles in schools

- Either of these may be the Princess of Wales
  - Grand Duchess Tatiana [of Russia, second child of Czar Nicholas. Murdered along with her entire family by revolutionaries in 1918 at the age of 21]
  - Princess Elizabeth of Romania [married King George of Bucharest in 1921 and later divorced. Died 1956]

- Organization will aide Negro People – Branch of national association (for the Advancement of Colored People) to be formed in St. Paul Nov. 9

- Fusion sweeps Tammany to defeat in New York City, Democrats elect three governors and one senator

- Wife who works is called goose

- Moscow is full of drug fiends

- Ape descendent of man – theory to be reversed by finding of skull, said to be 500,000 years old

- Lifeboats fitted up with wireless (in response to Titanic sinking)

- Dr. Direon bearer of American flag to 189 Indian tribes describes suffering of fragments of conquered people

- First Patent for ice making plant

- Emigration bill to restrict flow to United States

- Czar Nicholas of Russia, whose son, Alexis is a victim of tuberculosis, and who fears the latter's death may result in the end of the present dynasty (father and son killed by Russian revolutionaries July 1918)

- Teachers may be mothers (U.S. Supreme Court Ruling of New York lawsuit)

- Future of Indians is huge problem – General Creel, supervisor, says he has real affection for red skins

- St. Paul man makes effort to prevent extermination of buffalo

- Auto license law unconstitutional (tax legislation in Ohio)

- Plan to welcome the Crown Prince and his Princess – Popular son of Kaiser Wilhelm is preparing for a visit to America

- Crucial Battle of Mexican struggle will begin today

- $8 minimum wage for girl workers (per week)

- Ireland's Potato Disease a menace

- $50,000 to the aviator first to cross the Atlantic

- How Americans have cut off China's pigtail of Paganism

NOVEMBER 1913

---·---

LETTERS

Postmark: 7:30 p.m. Nov. 1, 1913, St. Paul Minn.

Saturday afternoon

November 1st 1913

Dear friend:-

I was glad to receive your favor of the 28th and noted the dot on the back of the envelope. It is quite a system how did you happen to think of it?

I received your prescription, many thanks for sending it but my cold has disappeared so will surely try that next time. By the way, it is the first of the month so suppose you will be sending in your bill in a day or two for services rendered but if it is going to be a $10.00 charge, just let me know and I will send the prescription back first mail as I am too poor to go to such a high priced physician for aid. I think I shall have to try and catch cold, then have this prescription filled and see how it works.

You surely have a good prescription as to inquiries regarding the time I retire but think that is pretty hard medicine namely going to bed at 8:30. It may be all right for one night but hardly for a week.

As to your request, I have spoken with the young lady whom I think you mean but she says she has no photo just at present but expects to have one in the near future and if you are real good she may send you one providing she gets one in return. Is this answer from the young lady satisfactory?

I surely am keeping up my daily deposits and now have over $3.00. A person wouldn't think it would count up so fast.

You will pardon a suggestion on my part but it is just a passing thought. I notice on your letter heads, which by the way are very neat, that your office hours in the evening are from 6-7:30. Is this not rather early for the working class of people? It hardly gives them time to get dinner and get to your offices before closing time. Of course, this way you have the evening to yourself while if your hours were later, it would break up the entire evening. I hope you will take these remarks in the kindly way they are meant.

Tomorrow afternoon Gladys and I are going out for another long walk and I am going to her place for supper. Last Sunday she was over to our place. We certainly had a fine walk last Sunday, from our house within a couple of blocks of Lake Calhoun, Mpls. [Minneapolis] I certainly was tired that night.

Everybody here feeling fine. Claribel is just about a [sic] lively now as she ever was. Be sure you don't work too hard or you will have to take the rest cure again.

Kindest regards,

Hildred

P.S. – Got a big package of dates from Mr. Turner today. Doesn't that make you hungry? H

Postmark: 12:30 a.m. Nov. 5, 1913, Detroit Mich.

Addressed to Mr. Chas. W. Turner (ink dot on back of envelope)

Nov. 4th/13

Dear Friend, -

Pleased to receive your favor of the 1st last. Note your cold is better, I suppose the only thing left for you to do is to save the ppt. and have it filled some time if perchance the occasion happens to present itself, then pay me in accordance to what it is worth to you. Do you think I am square?

Your answer in regard to the photo which you plan on having in the near future, meets my approval, I will return one as requested.

By the way I always take suggestions in a kindly spirit and do my best to profit by them, my reason for having my evening office hours from 6 p.m. to 7:30 p.m. is that if patients know that my office hours end at 7:30 they will make an effort to be there at that time, and if a number happen to come in, I will be there at 8:30, whereas if I had my office hours until 8 or 8:30, it would be 9 or 9:30 when I got through, and providing I had an outside call to make I would be pretty sleepy before I got through. I never leave my office before 8 o'clock even if my office hour ends at 7:30.

Note you profited by my lessons on walking, but you do not want to over do it, nature has provided a limit to all things.

Doing all I can to get business, [illegible word] in to see an insurance man last evening think I can get some business from him, everybody I meet ask them out to see my offices, a Doctor does well starting in a city if he makes his expenses the first year, in about 8 yrs. from now if I am not clearing at least $1000 to $1200 a month I am going to jump into the Detroit River. Don't you want to jump in with me and end some of your troubles, it is far easier to die if you know you are going to have company. Will be very much pleased if you deliver a message to Uncle Chas. for me. Kindly tell him I received notice this a.m. from the American Exp. Cpy. [American Express Company] in Detroit, that they have the clock in their possession. We live two short blocks over the Boulevard, they will only deliver out to the boulevard, so I am going to have them deliver it out as far as they will, then say would not deliver it out farther for any money. As soon as I receive the clock will write to Uncle Chas. concerning its condition.

Eat two or three extra dates for me and don't forget the bank acct. & the photo.

Sincerely,

Chas.

Postmark: 5 p.m. Nov. 8, 1913, St. Paul Minn.

St. Paul, Minn.

November 8th, 1913

Dear friend:

Was very pleased to receive your letter and note what you say in regard to paying you for the prescription. It no doubt would do me a great deal of good but I think I prefer you making out the bill as you know I might accidently overpay you and that would be quite serious especially for my pocketbook although maybe not for yours.

As to your office hours, I guess your idea is better than mine all right and by getting through earlier you can get to bed sooner. I have sort of an idea you like plenty of sleep. Guess I get that from some of your teachings.

Regarding business, I hope your plans or wishes come true because I should hate to see you jumping into the Detroit River about eight years from now. You don't want to plan on doing anything like that, you want to plan on what you are going to do when you get all of that money you speak of.

As to the clock, I wish I were in Detroit with a Kodak about the time the Express Company delivers it as far as the boulevard so I would have a picture of you wheeling it the rest of the way or carrying it on your back. Which?

Mr. Turner bought tickets for Claribel and I to go to the Orpheum this afternoon so I get a dandy Holiday today. I think I am getting terribly spoiled and if I had to change my position and work in some offices I would never by satisfied.

If you should happen into St. Paul today, you would surely have to have your heavy overcoat on as it is awfully chilly. Everybody has a red nose today.

Tomorrow Claribel, Gladys and I are going to the Symphony Concert at the Auditorium. We are planning on walking down town as it does not start until 3:30 p.m.

It is now time to go to the Orpheum so will close as I don't want to miss any of the show. Take care now as I don't want to be reading of the tragic death of Dr. Husband who jumped into the Detroit River.

Kind Regards,

Sincerely,

Hildred

———————◆———————

Postmark: 12:30 a.m. Nov. 12, 1913, Detroit, Mich.

Addressed to Chas. W. Turner (envelope flap missing; black dot inferred)

Nov. 11/13

Dear Friend, -

Pleased to receive your favor of the 8th last, glad to note that you are having an occasional good time.

In regard to the inclosed [sic] slip from the so called Optoma Company I am unable to pass an honest opinion, as I do not know what is contained in the rules set forth look fairly good. May say that I personally would not recommend anyone to use a preparation not recognized by the United States pharmaepia, which means that the preparation contains some narcotic and in time no doubt would cause some injury to the eyes.

As to your inquiry concerning business may say that two patients just left my office, more over they were still living when they left and I trust they will live to come again.

How is it that you tell me everything but Mr. Turner's favorite question to you every morning, that is in regard to the time you retired the night before. Mr. Turner has certainly got me interested in this sleep proposition.

Business is looking a little brighter all the time, generally manage to keep busy at some time or other. Had two patients this afternoon, know of two more who are coming to see me tonight.

The grocery man was very good to me, he took it upon himself to deliver the clock, so you would not have been able get the picture of me carrying it had you been here.

Please do not send any more cold weather along with your letters, we had a little snow on Sunday, but as long as it makes people sick, alright.

I suppose you have to take the street car to & from the office now that the car is out of commission.

I am going over to take Dr. Howard's practice Wednesday eve. I also give quite a few anesthetics for him.

I am including an announcement card to you, a copy of which I am going to mail to the people living in my vicinity. What do you think of it. Kindly show it to Mr. Turner.

I have been interrupted about twenty times, but have finished my letter even the Preacher had the nerve to call on me this afternoon, he too went out alive. Please do not count the mistakes I have made writing this letter, I believe there must be one wheel out of place in my upstairs, will do better next time.

Sincerely Yours,

Chas.

DR. CHARLES W. HUSBAND
ANNOUNCES THE OPENING OF HIS OFFICE
AT
320 MANCHESTER AVENUE
CORNER GRAND RIVER
DETROIT, MICHIGAN

---

*Walnut
374 M.*

DR. CHARLES W. HUSBAND

320 MANCHESTER AVE.

OFFICE HOURS { 8-9 A. M.
1:30-4 P. M.
6-7:30 P. M.
SUNDAYS, 9-11 A. M.

DETROIT

PHONE

DR. CHARLES W. HUSBAND
320 MANCHESTER AVE.
DETROIT

HOURS:
8-9 A. M.
1:30-4 P. M.
6-7:30 P. M.
SUNDAYS, 9-11 A. M.

DATE *Nov 11/13.*

TO *Miss F. Laws,
St. Paul,*

ACCOUNTS RENDERED MONTHLY

To Services rendered $ 100.00

*Please do not send the bill
on ppt book, all I want is
the money. By the way I would
like to thank it by next monday*

Postmark: 2:30 p.m. Nov. 17, 1913, St. Paul, Minn.

St. Paul, Minn. / Nov. 17th, 1913

Dear Friend:

Received your letter and was very pleased to hear from you. Also note enclosed your statement for $100.00 and that you wished to have it by Monday. I must say your charges are very reasonable (?) but I thought I would ask if I was not entitled to at least 10 % discount if paid in thirty days.

May say that I used pretty near a whole bottle of that medicine last week. I certainly had an awful cold but am feeling fine again (thanks to the medicine). Then is when I got my scoldings, one every morning regular from Mr. Turner.

I thank you very much for the announcement card you enclose [sic]. It certainly is a very neatly arranged card and hope you will have lots of callers now. Mr. Turner thought it was a very good idea to send it out. By your letter I should judge your practice is picking up ad hope it will continue to do so but don't stay up too late nights or you will soon have to take some of yur own medicines.

As to the Optona, I showed Mr. Turner what you had to say and guess he has decided not to use it. Thank you for the information.

Claribel and I were real good and went to church last evening. Just think, next Sunday is our last Sunday in the Tabernacle and then we go into our new church. It certainly is going to be awfully pretty. Claribel is down at the office this morning helping to fold circulars. She is real pleased about it because she says it will give her a little extra Xmas money. Think she is going to be another close one though, like myself.

Note you were interrupted about twenty times while writing your letter. If you charged $100.00 for each interruption the way you charged me why my goodness you will be a millionaire before you know it.

I am not going to send any cold weather with my letter this time as it is just like Spring today. Does that suit you any better?

Think I will get busy and help fold circulars now as I am "Jack-of-all-trades" this week, Mr. Turner being gone.

Be sure and let me know about that 10% discount.

Kind regards,
Sincerely,

Hildred

———————◆———————

Postmark: Nov. 20, 1913, Detroit, Mich.

Addressed to Mr. Chas. W. Turner, black dot on back of envelope

Nov. 20th/13.

Dear Friend, -

Pleased to receive your favor of the 17th last. Note that my bill amounting to $100 left you rather shy of breath. If you are unable to pay it hand it over to Claribel, for I need must have the money, However, if Claribel thinks the bill unjust we will rule it out. You are not permitted to buy candy for Claribel to win her over. I will give you 20% discount if you wish it. This is my birthday so I almost feel inclined to give you 50% discount. [**Editor's Note:** November 20 is Charles' 26th birthday.]

By the way the ppt. sent you was not supposed to be used for so severe a cold as Mr. Turner told me that you had, I might have given you something better had I known the condition existing, am pleased that you give the medicine due credit.

If you were here I am afraid that I would walk you to death, I am too poor to travel around like most people, not that I do not make money, but that I find so many, many things to buy with my money, surgical instruments, appliances, etc. Some day I hope to have all these things then I will be able to finish paying for my house. I have to pay taxes next month. Everything a Doctor needs in his practice costs like the dickens. If you promise not to laugh I will tell you something, be sure and promise. I'll tell you – I have only been to the theatre once since I was in St. Paul and that was only to a ten cent show with Mr. Lucius, otherwise I would not have been there, you may think I am a miser but I do not think so. I just want to get into a position to make money. You can laugh at me if you like, but I'll bet you that in two years from now, I will not need to kiss my dollars good bye. I was out to see a Doctor Friend of mine the other evening he said he hated to look a poor person in the face because when he did it made him think of his own condition when he started out into the practice of medicine. This Doctor is now clearing $1500 to $2000, a month. I hope to do that some some [sic] sweet day.

Well I have succeeded in telling you my troubles, I don't want to tell you these things, but when I don't relieves me and I feel better, did you ever feel that way.

Business is getting better all the time, a Doctor gets patients in a mysterious way, oftimes [sic] I wonder how I do get them. I finally find that they have been referred to me by some one else I treated a long, long time ago.

I sure do feel better now that I have told you my troubles, you can laugh at me if you wish.

Sincerely,
Chas.

———————◆———————

Postmark: 7:30 p.m. Nov. 24, 1913, St. Paul, Minn.

Dear friend:

Was pleased to receive your letter also want to wish you many happy returns of the day (Nov. 20th) as I note you say you had a birthday on that day. I hope that day brought you a lot of good luck and that you will continue to have luck throughout the year.

I was very glad to note you are willing to give me 50% discount on my bill but would like to ask a favor, and that is that you will kindly hold this until after Christmas. I know this is strictly against your rules but would kindly ask you make an exception in my case as I am very short of ready cash just now.

You certainly ought to get rich quick if you keep up your good habit of saving. I did have a good laugh over the show deal but all the same think yu deserve credit for being able to hold on to your money. That is my chief trouble. It certainly does relieve one's mind to tell their troubles once in awhile and guess Mr. Turner hears about all my troubles.

Mr. Turner said you wanted to buy me a box of candy while he was in Detroit and while I appreciate it very much, at the same time am glad he wouldn't carry it home because if you want to be a millionaire before long, you will have to start saving your pennies right away. Let that candy money go towards something for the office instead.

Yesterday papa took our whole family for a drive in the country, and we certainly did enjoy every minute of it. We may have looked like "rubes" but at the same time we enjoyed it. That night when we got home, we ate like a bunch of woodchoppers. I think if we did that several times a week we would be so healthy we would never need to go to the doctor's.

Thanksgiving we are invited over to Mr. Turner's for dinner. I told him I was going to save lunch money this week so I would have a good appetite for Thanksgiving.

Glad business is getting better for you and hope you will be able to find a goodly share of the sick people in Detroit so that you will feel you can afford a little more pleasure. About the only time I go myself, is when daddy pays the way.

Gladys is coming out to spend the evening with me and is going to stay all night so I see where I get but very little sleep as we usually talk half of the night; and tomorrow I will get a scolding.

Kindest regards,

Hildred

◆

Postmark: 9:30 p.m. Nov. 27, 1913, Detroit, Mich.

Addressed to Mr. Turner, black dot on back of envelope

Nov. 27, 13.

Dear Friend, -

Pleased to receive your favor of the 24th last. Thanks for your good wishes in regard to the 20th. May say the more business increases the younger I feel. Every new patient I get increases the density of my smile, so much so that I believe Everybody who sees me must know that I have a new patient, when I get called out my feet want to go so fast that I can scarcely hold them back. Then when I get back Mother and I waltz, much against Mother's will, being a good Methodist.

Yesterday I was called out to see a young fellow with plastic pleurisy, through this patient I met a woman with two sons one 37 the other 39 yrs. old, the sons were imbeciles due to thyroid insufficiency. They also had an inherited lunatic condition, they were two of the funniest looking and acting fellows that I ever met. I will try and draw a little sketch of them for you, oh, I wish you could see them you would laugh your head off. Here they are, -

[left figure described as 39 years old]: A little bump, showing look of intelligence, shining white [hair], a little hair, long neck, half-developed arm

[right figure described as 37 years old]: A little bump, shiny white, hair

Two Brother do they look like it.

Which one of these two Brothers would you care to have for a Husband. Now while they are amusing, nevertheless their story is a sad one, they are wholly and always have been dependant [sic] on their mother for a livelihood. You will no doubt think me to be a poor artist, but they look like that to me.

We are all going over to my cousins place for dinner tonight, then I think I will journey back home and keep my evening office hours. I am going to stick right to business until I get things coming my way as much as possible, then I may loosen up just slightly.

The weather is real warm to day, but quite cloudy, with a little mud here and there.

Well I suppose you will have another laugh at both my business and myself.

Tell Mr. Turner I will write him in a few days.

Sincerely,
Chas.

HOURS:
8-9 A. M.
1:30-4 P. M.
6-7:30 P. M.
SUNDAYS, 9-11 A. M.

DR. CHARLES W. HUSBAND
320 MANCHESTER AVE.
DETROIT

they also had an inherited leaky condition, they were two of the funniest looking and acting fellows that ever met. I will try and draw a little sketch of them for you, Oh I wish you could see them you would laugh your head off. Here they are,

Which one of these two Brothers would you care to have for a Husband. Now while they are amusing, nevertheless their story is a sad one, they are wholly and always have been dependant on their Mother for a livelihood. You will no doubt think me to be a poor artist, but they look like this to me.

DECEMBER 1913

◆

Newspaper Headlines

Detroit Free Press

- Another Sicilian shot; slugs and shotgun are found in Mafia hang out
- Officer shoots son of director of Belle Isle Aquarium during row
- Club women study servant problem
- Women detectives to protect girls
- Ulsterites defy royal arms embargo; 90,000 ready to launch war
- Michigan Indians seek $200 million – Ottawa and Chippewa contend 1833 treaty faulty; to enter claim against U.S.
- Rebel sweep toward Mexico City checked; flank attack feared
- France will regain stolen picture (Mona Lisa)
- How new $2.5 million Hotel Statler will look
- Thinks earth will last 15,000,000 years more
- Detroit Athletic Club completes $1.1 million fund at enthusiastic meeting
- Horses can drink at new fountain
- Women warned of handbag danger – Inspector advises carrying purses in muffs; several robberies reported

- Packard Motor Car Co. opens hospital for its employees
- 74 killed in Calumet as false alarm of fire throws hall in panic
- Chinese have Clissmass? You Bet! Fong ting is it
- Perugia says "Mona Lisa" was offered to Morgan – tells of efforts to sell picture; magistrate amazed police were not notified
- Radium used in Detroit to fight cancer
- Blind genius (Helen Keller) to speak in Detroit
- 50 years of public service – Harper Hospital will this week observe its Golden Anniversary with the dedication of the J.L. Hudson and Theodore D. Buhl Memorial Buildings
- Jews' challenge to Christianity sounded by Rabbi
- Race betterment program issued
- Mayor-elect of New York selects woman to head city department (Commissioner of Corrections Dr. Katherine B. Davis)
- Having adopted men's minor vices, women might join them in New York "Swear Off" Resolutions - Tango teas, slit skirts, cocktails, cigarettes and even profanity suggested superfluities

St. Paul Pioneer Press

- Wolves eat two men
- Would use oil as fuel for the Navy
- Paderewski is dead
- Suffragists won't use word "Please"
- General strike is Teamsters' scheme
- Volunteer army is aim of House bill
- St. Paul leads in savings accounts
- Day of peace is dawning
- Money and people turn Florida-ward
- Archduke Francis Ferdinand on friendly mission
- Uses varnish in surgery - method does away with use of rubber gloves
- Finds three new tribe of Indians; Amazon expedition penetrates into unknown regions of Brazil
- Explorer wires he's safe, though his ship is gone (the Karluk)

- Plans protection of wild animals
- Dry zones around schools proposed
- Rebel Army loots churches, robs nuns, and banishes Spaniards (Chihuahua Mexico)
- Indians' treatment disgrace to nation
- Panama hats, rolled up sleeves and river swims mark December summer
- Elevator service in high buildings
- Limit building heights (New York City)
- Indian becoming defective race
- Clarence Darrow's bribe indictment finally dismissed
- St. Paul Beer is famed for quality
- Carnegie gives library to White Bear Village
- 3,000 families on Goodfellows list
- Man's false cry of fire in crowded Calumet Hall fatal to 58 children
- Radium found in PA
- Japs discuss the suffrage question
- Schools not ready for sex education
- Col. Bevins is dead; saw Booth shoot Lincoln

DECEMBER 1913

◆

LETTERS

Postmark: 11 a.m. Dec. 2, 1913, St. Paul, Minn.

St. Paul, Minn

December 1st 1913,

Dear friend:

Was glad to hear from you and presume by your letter that you will soon be wearing a perpetual smile, that is if your smile broadens every time you get a new patient. Mr. Turner told me about waltzing your mother around and I guess you must have some great times.

You certainly are a most wonderful artist. I never knew you were gifted along that line, why didn't you tell me about it before? I had quite a time figuring out what was the matter with them, but think I have it all straight now. It certainly is awful to think of anybody in that condition. Are they at all harmful, or are they allowed to be free, that is at home? I should think they would have then in some asylum where they could teach them something.

My scoldings are getting worse right along. You know it is getting near Christmas so I have quite a bit of sewing to do as I am not rich enough to go and buy them all so sometimes in the morning I look rather sleepy. Guess what Mr. Turner told me this morning! He said that as I disobeyed him so much he thought he would have to tell me the truth or rather his reasons for not wanting me to sew evenings. He said if I continued, in time I would get cross-eyed! Did you ever hear anything like it? I have had more fun over that to-day, every time I think of it I have to laugh.

Dec. 2nd

Second edition: Was quite busy yesterday afternoon so did not have time to finish my letter.

Last evening I started making some clothes for a little doll. It is for little Helen (mamma's niece). It makes me wish I had time to play with them again. I enjoy eating chocolate ice-cream and playing with dolls so guess I am still a good play mate for the little tots.

Claribel and I were awfully good last Sunday, went to two services and are going again tonight. You know we are in our new church now and it is real pretty.

Hope that between now and the time you write again that your smile will broaden still more as that seems to be a good sign.

Kindest regards,

Hildred

P.S. I showed your beautiful sketch drawing to Mr. Turner and don't know when I heard him laugh so heartily. He compliments you on your good work.

H.C.

———————◆———————

Postmark: 12-midnight Dec. 5, 1913, Detroit, Mich.

Addressed to Mr. Charles W. Turner (dot on envelope flap)

Dec. 4th/13.

Dear Friend,

Your favor of the 1st to hand, pleased to hear from you. Had I have known that you & Mr. Turner were going to kid me about being, as you say a wonderful artist, I would have taken more pains with my two sketches, However I am glad that the sketches amused you, May take a notion to draw you some more one of these days. For instance, before and after treatment, the two fellows under discussion, are not harmful in the least, why they would not or do not know enough to kill a fly when they see it, much less a human being. Therefore your office would be no place for them in the summer time (flies).

Now in regard to your sleep, may I take pleasure in advising you if possible along those lines, probably you will think that you know better but in the face of it let me say this, that in a person of your caliber, shade of hair and color of eyes, if you stay up later than 10 pm. night after night, one of your eyes will turn in and the other one out, then what a predicament, you might as well come down here and join the ones who prompted my sketches. Therefore all I have to say is beware.

Pleased to note that you are going to church real often keep it up.

Last week was my best week so far, all that is worrying me now is whether it will keep up or not. There are not very many people sick in Detroit at present, all the Doctors say it is dull here at present the weather has been so nice. Just like the opening days of spring.

Let me hear from you in regard to your changed bedtime.

Sincerely,

Chas.

Postmark: 1 p.m. Dec. 11, 1913, St. Paul, Minn.

St. Paul, Minn. / Dec. 11th, 1913

Dear friend:

I hope you will pardon me for my seeming neglect in answering your last letter, but I will not attempt to make any excuses only that I have been pretty busy and will try to do better next time.

As to my bedtime, it is simply impossible to change the time until after Christmas (11 p.m.) and then will promise to be good. Even if I do stay up late, I haven't started to see double as yet and am not losing in weight so guess there is no immediate danger.

About the latter part of next month or the first part of February, I think St. Paul will be in need of several more physicians. Mamma is planning on leaving about the 15th of January with her father for a trip out west and will be gone about three months so that will leave Claribel and myself as chief cooks and I am very much afraid of the after affects. [sic] I am afraid we will all have indigestion before many days. Mamma has decided that a change would do her a great deal of good as she has not been well at all lately. Papa says she has to stay out there until she weighs 146 lbs. but I think she will be homesick before she is there thirty days.

What do you think! Claribel and I have been asked to join the choir at our new church. There were about forty in the choir so it does not matter so much if there are one or two poor ones. I guess they want someone to help fill up the seats more than anything else. Claribel is going to join but I haven't quite decided yet as it will take up so much time and then another thing if mamma goes away I will have pretty near enough to do with my office work and then the work at home.

Am awfully glad to hear you are doing so nicely and hope you will be kept real busy. How about your smile? Has it grown any since last week? You know it is supposed to grow every time you get a new patient.

Sincerely,

Hildred

———————◆———————

Postmark: 9 p.m. Dec. 16, 1913, Detroit, Mich.

Addressed to Mr. Chas. W. Turner, dot on envelope flap

Detroit Dec. 16/13

Dear Friend, -

Feeling so good these days that your pardon is granted at first sight; just had another waltz with Mother, you know what that means; just called over to see a lady four blocks away, last Saturday she ran a nail in her foot so they poulticed it. Today they became frightened and sent for me. Her husband tried to open it up, but they all got nervous, she also said he run [sic] a little knife in it but it did not bleed, and hurt her terribly. While I was getting everything ready the husband put the daughter out of the room so she would not faint, he also stationed their son just at the entrance to the room giving him instructions to run after the ammonia bottle if his mother fainted, I proceeded, mother began to feel faint, Father yelled for the ammonia bottle, son ran after it, returned, handed to bottle to his father, who turned the bottle up to pour out the ammonia, found the bottle empty, he threw it down on the floor, got more frightened, ran and picked it up, poured some water into the empty bottle, shook it up, poured it out and trembling gave it to Mother, all the while the mother was telling him where the full bottle was, but they were so frightened they did not hear her, when I left the father was instructing the son to on the alert the next time anything happened, father wrote my telephone number on the outside of the telephone book so he could get me in a hurry after this without looking it up. They are very nice people, he the father is Editor of the Detroit Free Press. [**Editor's Note:** possibly Philip J. Reid, managing Editor] Tell Uncle Chas. my funny experience, I nearly split my sides laughing after I arrived home. It did not seem so funny at the time.

Got an operation lined up for tonight, that is after my evening office hours. Have been changing to the announcement of $10.00 to $15.00 per day. Why I say charging is because they are nice people and I feel that I can string them along more by doing this, various ones have wanted to pay, but I would not take the money, the fellow today that I had the fun with wanted to pay me but I would not take the money, because by not taking it now I eventually can get twice as much, am going to send my bills out January 1st.

If I stay in this business long I will be able to tell you all kinds of funny happenings, but I do like the money, if it keeps going the way it has been the past week I will be making about $50.00 a day before many years go by. Of course I have a place for every cent just at the present time buying instruments, appliances, drugs, paying taxes etc. but some day I will have everything, and then $21.00 bonus to St. Paul. Then I will sing My Country Tis of Thee.

Let me know how you enjoyed the story of my experience, and maybe I will tell you something else.

Got a little package by mail, thought it was your picture, but it wasn't.

Sincerely,

Chas.

———————◆———————

Postmark: 5 p.m. Dec. 20, 1913, St. Paul, Minn.

St. Paul Minn. / Dec. 20, 1913

Dear friend:

Was very pleased to receive your letter and must say you have some funny experiences in your line of business At least a great deal more than in the fish business. I wish I had some of that wonderful medicine I could take to make myself invisible and then follow you for just one day.. I imagine I would have a pretty merry time though trying to keep up to you because I imagine you pretty near fly around now that you are so busy. You are certainly doing fine and I hope the good work will continue but you don't want to get so busy that you over work or forget to go to bed nights because if you do, you might have to take some of your own medicine.

Mr. Turner says I should tell you how naughty I have been this week, not been to bed before 11 o'clock all week but after Christmas I am surely going to do better.

Tonight mamma and papa are coming down town with me, or rather I am going down with them, and I will finish my shopping tonight.

It started to snow a little this morning so guess we will have some snow after all for Christmas. I can hardly wait, guess I am worse than Addison. We are going to have an old-fashioned Christmas dinner and expect to have several of mamma's friends over to the house. On New Years Mr. and Mrs. Turner are coming over for dinner.

Note you thought the little package you got was my picture. I have had it taken but can't get them for a while as they are so busy with their Christmas work but possibly you will get one pretty soon.

Mamma just got home from the farm, was there about a week and has now decided not to go West for about two months as then her mother can go along.

Mr. Turner just came in the office so will have to start and get busy. Let us hear some more of your funny experiences. Mr. Turner thought it was pretty good.

Wishing you a Very Merry Christmas and Prosperous New Year.

Sincerely,

Hildred

———————————◆———————————

Postmark: 11:30 p.m. Dec. 22, 1913, Detroit, Mich.

Addressed to Mr. Chas. W. Turner – dot on back flap

Dec. 22nd/13.

Dear Friend, -

Received yours of the 20th last. I believe that you are beginning to like my profession, or at least some of my funny experiences.

I am sending to you under separate cover a photo that I had taken some little time ago. I will address it to Mr. Turner. As soon as I commence to take in more money, I am going to send you a more recent one. So kindly pardon me for sending you this one. However I believe my looks have not changed.

If you do not keep better hours I am going to send you some sleeping pills, requesting Mr. Turner to insist that you take them and then you will be glad to go to bed.

Pleased to note that you are going to have a big time Xmas. I suppose you will hang up your stocking. All my patients are getting better, I am stringing the old ones along and looking for new ones, I have not put a soul in consultation with St. Peter so far I believe he will think that I am not on the square with him.

I have to go to take a trip into the city, and I want to get the photo out tonight so I will wind short on my funny happenings and tell you all the news next time.

Wishing you a Merry Xmas and Happy New Year.

Sincerely

Chas.

———————◆———————

Postmark: 5 p.m. Dec. 27, 1913, St. Paul, Minn.

St. Paul, Minn.

Dec. 27th, 1913

Dear friend:

I received your letter, also Xmas card and thank you kindly but best of all, your photo came today. I was surely pleased to get it and think it is a very good picture of you. I am sending mine on Monday but I don't think it will come up to yours, think I am getting the best of this deal. Mr. Turner says next time I get one taken, he is going along with me.

I guess you are right, I am beginning to like your profession but not so much for the funny experiences as the money end of it. I think that would appeal to me more. I have to live like a miser for several weeks now to catch up again since my Christmas expenses. They were rather hard on my sized pocketbook.

I think next time you write you better scold Mr. Turner for a change. He caught cold the other day and went home sick this morning. He said if he felt better, he would come down later in the afternoon. He certainly has an awful cold, can hardly talk.

Was Santa good to you this year? He certainly was good to all of us and we had a dandy time Xmas. Gladys got a chafing dish for Christmas so she is going to have me down some evening to stay all night and during the evening we are going to make something good to eat. Will tell you later if we had to call a doctor or not.

Let us hear from you again with some more funny happenings.

Thanking you again very kindly for your photo and wishing you all of the good things for 1914,

Sincerely,

Hildred

———————◆———————

Postmark: [time obscured] a.m., 1913, Detroit, Mich.

Addressed to: Miss. H.L. Cress
c/o Booth Fisheries
(c/o Mr. Turner)

Dec. 30th/13.

Dear Friend, -

Pleased to receive your favor of the 27th Inst. You ought to have received my photo on Wednesday instead of Friday. Note you think it is good. Will send you a more recent one when circumstances permit. Will be on the look out for your photo.

Who do you think lives in the house, the picture of which I am inclosing [sic] to you. [**Editor's Note:** No photo was in the letter, but it was found with other family photos]. What does the electric sign in front say. Can you read the sign in the front bay window. Can you see any lettering on one of the front doors, if so what do you suppose it says. My patients go in one front door and out the other. The house is built of dark red pressed brick with block mortar and slate roof, the rest speaks for itself in the picture. Let me know how you like it.

Business is a little slower to-day than usual however I can not complain about the way things are going. So far this month I have charged $160.50 and taken in $77.50, I have not sent out any accounts so far. Quite a few have offered to pay me but I always refuse the money in order to keep them under obligation to me.

Had a quiet but pleasant time Xmas. All I do is try to work. The Doctor I used to chum with, has a steady girl now so I do not have him to take up much of my spare time. When you come to Detroit (next summer) I will make you acquainted with him he is a dandy fellow, I know you will like him.

Best Wishes for the New Year.

Sincerely,

Chas.

JANUARY 1914

◆

Newspaper Headlines

Detroit Free Press

- New Year gives promise of greater prosperity for Detroit industries
- Socialistic despot now rules Chihuahua for "the people's benefit" (Pancho Villa)
- Bank pass book develops thrift
- Autoists forced to have two tags – Police nab owners who await license laws test before buying number plates
- New York show is dominated by Detroit motors
- Tribal life of Five Nations near extinction
- "Mother" Jones seized and driven from coal strike district of Colorado
- Dr. Wiley condemns American women as worst cooks in the world but excepts his wife
- New industrial era is marked by Ford's shares to labors (they share a $10,000,000 bonus from Ford)
- Government upholds right of mine men to belong to unions
- Ulster unionists raise $5 million in war insurance
- More babies urged among upper class

- Men owning jobs and homes, says Rose Pastor Stokes, will not kill capitalism
- Police repulse Ford job hunters with icy streams
- Prosperity in Detroit never up to present
- Tango-maniacs get Tango face; with triple chins deep wrinkles, sloping shoulders, says physician
- Tyrus R. Cobb, world's greatest baseball player, tells how he learned to hit lean; calls Joe Jackson great natural batter, who could improve his average many points if he would mix a little science with innate ability
- Nearing the half century mark – Detroit College of Medicine surgery only institution of its kind in the city, has recently undergone complete reorganization along broader lines
- Detroit to turn out 395,000 autos in year
- Auto Show attended by 25,000 Tuesday
- Council considers ordinance to limit skyscrapers size – measure restricting structures to 10 stories sent to committees
- Once rich head of Siegel stores says he's broke
- Automobile Show closes; new Ford Car in limelight (Cycle Car) – Creation to sell for $350.00 or less it is said; exhibitors move on to Chicago
- George M. Cohan really retires from the stage
  - Playing his last act in Detroit next Saturday night (Broadway Jones). He will devote himself thereafter to playmaking
- Cadillac Square plan is sought
- Salary increase to be asked for school teachers

𝔖t. 𝔓aul 𝔓ioneer 𝔓ress

- Turkey Trot and Tango grew into popularity
- Christian ethics gaining on Islam
- Anti-Trust fight not likely under President Wilson
- Our schools are dismal failures declares J.J. Hill
- "Der Rosenkavalier" will not make popular appeal
- Tossing immigrant kids into the melting pot – how neighborhood associations are transforming youngsters of foreign parentage into lively, intelligent American kids
- The onward march of women in 1913; in every brand of activity the so-called weaker sex has progressed during the year just ended – Woman has taken part in public affairs, she has governed cities, fought in armies, headed banks and served as a "policeman"
- Women shouldn't bother husbands in office hours
- Henry Ford, head of Ford Motor Co., who will direct $10 million of the company's earnings each year as his employee's share of the profits. 2,500 men will be affected
- Dr. Howard A. Kelly, who declares the X-Ray machine invented by Dr. William David Coolidge may supplant even radium in treatment of cancer
- Wright Brothers victorious (as recognized inventors of aero plane system)
- Shackleton hopes to reveal hidden polar mysteries; five million square miles of uncharted land; leaving October 1914, out March 1915
- Cancer's loss like 150 Titanic losses
- Wilson supports Alaska Trade Bill
- Government extravagance touches every tax-payer
- Skyscrapers over 20 stories do not pay, says New Yorker
- Fashions for 1914 to be extremely feminine and classic in outline
- Rabbi likes Tango; calls it beautiful
- East is aghast at St. Paul's plan to teach boys sewing
- Motion pictures to replace the (photo) album

JANUARY 1914

◆

LETTERS

Postmark: 5 p.m. Jan. 2, 1914, Detroit, Mich.

Addressed to Mr. Chas. W. Turner – dot on back of envelope

January 1st/14.

Dear Friend, -

Just a line to let you know I received your photo. I certainly think it is dandy. Mr. Turner probably thought you were a little self conscious at the time, The majority of people are a little too self conscious, when they want to appear at their best. You spoke about getting the best of the deal, I take exception, I think I got the best of the deal.

Was out to my cousin's place to-day for New Year's good things to eat, but thought I would come back and keep my office open, that is my afternoon and evening office hours, I would awfully hate to miss anything, it seems quiet to be alone, but I Want to make money, which is one of my greatest pleasures.

After writing you the other day I had three new patients, had two new ones yesterday.

I am inclosing [sic] you an envelope and a little slip of paper. You are not to open the envelope, which gives the results of my business for last monthly, until after both you and Mr. Turner, make guesses as to the results of my last month's business, writing them down as indicated on the inclosed slip which is to be sent back to me. I want to see what good guessers you people can be. I will be anxious to hear or learn the results.

Wishing you a Happy and Prosperous New Year.

Sincerely,

Chas.

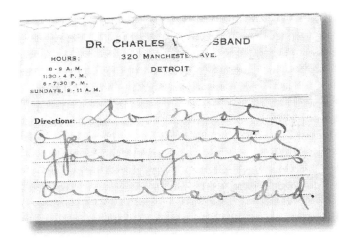

———————◆———————

Postmark: 2:30 p.m. Jan. 6, 1914, St. Paul, Minn.

St. Paul, Minn.

Jan. 5, 1914

Dear friend:

Was very glad to receive your letter of the 30th with picture of your house enclosed.

I should say I do know who lives there and must say I think you have a very pretty home. From your description I had it pictured a little differently but think the real thing better than the imaginary one. I was able to make out all of the signs with the exception of the printing above the office hours on your front door. Maybe you could tell me what that says. What I did notice was somebody standing in one of the front windows up stairs. Who do you suppose that is? I made a guess but do not know how real I am to being right.

Also glad to receive your favor of the first and to know my photo pleased you. I am not quite satisfied but guess it is because I have heard Mr. Turner and the folks criticise [sic] it so much. Mr. Turner thinks I should have worn a big "Teddy grin" [reference to Theodore Roosevelt (1858-1919), U.S. President 1901-1909; Bull Moose Party presidential candidate, 1912] in order to be natural.

Well, Mr. Turner and I both tried our luck at guessing and am enclosing you the results as you asked. [The guesses did not survive] I didn't take a peek at any of the figures you sent me at any time, just made a good honest guess but you will see we both underrated your accounts but it was all the more of a surprise when we opened the envelope. You certainly are doing splendid and making money fast. I hope you have as good success this month as last, but don't work too hard.

Best wishes for January,

Sincerely,

Hildred

———————◆———————

Postmark: 9 a.m. Jan. 10, 1914, Detroit, Mich.

Addressed to Mr. Chas. W. Turner, dot on envelope

January 10th/14.

Dear Friend, -

Pleased to receive your favor of the 5th Inst.

Am doing pretty good so far this month, but do not know whether to give you any more figures or not, I know I will feel ashamed of myself if I do not do as much this month as last, but I know you realize that it is a little different than the fish business, where you can talk them into buying fish. My last month's business so astounded me that I am sure I cannot do so much this month, this is worrying me considerably, but don't tell Mr. Turner. My last month's business was nearly as good as some doctors do their first year out in a city the size of Detroit. I will give you comparate [sic] results so far.

Dec. 1 – 10th - Charged $16.95   January 1-10th - Charged $41.60
                 Took in $25.25   Took in $61.50

I have paid my mother what I owed her, also Dr. Howard and have bought a score of things besides taxes, telephone and light bills, someday I hope to have all I want also bought three nilton rugs yesterday.

Am going to tell you something real funny, was called down street to see a woman, she had a headache and wanted a hypodermic injection to stop it so she could go out to a big feed with her husband that night. While there she asked me who massaged and manicured my wife's face and finger nails, I told her that there had been a woman around some time ago but I had not seen her lately, so there was, I know my face turned red, but she did not ask me whether I was married or not and she did not find out. I wish they would not ask me that question; they think I am on account of having my office in the house.

You certainly have good eyes in regard to the house, of course I had to peek out but I did not know enough to have the front window shade raised.

Note you are a professional guesser, but guess low this month, if you guess high you will be disappointed.

How are Claribel and all your people getting along.

Best Regards

Sincerely,

Chas.

———————◆———————

Postmark: 1 a.m. Jan. 14, 1914, St Paul, Minn.

St. Paul, Minn.

Jan. 14, 1914

Dear friend:

Was very pleased to hear from you but you should not be worrying over this month's business especially in view of the fact that you have taken in more this month than you did in the same period last month. You know if you worry you cannot do justice to your work and as you done so exceptionally well last month you could hardly expect a repetition for this month and you know people can't afford to be sick all of the time even though you would like it for your pocket book's sake. You certainly have had splendid success so far in January and I can't see where or why you should be worrying. Take some of the advice my "daddy" gives me, "Never cross the bridge until you come to it."

Regarding the lady asking who massaged your wife's face, I think possibly she was admiring your complexion and of course it was rather a delicate proposition to ask you who massaged your face so she inquired as to your wife, thinking of course you would engage the same party. That sure is some joke though and Mr. Turner and I had a good laugh over it. I wish I could have seen the expression on your face about that time.

You ought to be here to enjoy some of the good times we are having this winter. Claribel has now reached the required age and has joined the Sunday school class I am in which she has wanted to do for some time as we have so many parties etc. Thursday night they are going to have the first of a series of moving pictures at the church and Claribel has me spotted so guess I will have to be a good fellow.

Now whatever you do, don't worry about January because I have an idea you will do just as well as you did last month and if you do all of that worrying for nothing it would be terrible.

Sincerely,

Hildred

———————◆———————

Postmark: 7 p.m. Jan. 17, 1914, St. Paul, Minn.

Dear friend:

Thanks ever so much for the lovely box of candy you sent me. It certainly tastes good, you must have known I was candy hungry.

By the way, Mr. Turner says that you worry when the patients don't come fast enough to suit you. Now please don't do that because you are not going to gain anything by so doing. Glad to know you are working up a nice practice because I know that is what you want.

Will have to make this short as I have an awful lot of work to do. Thank you again for the candy. Just ate a nice creamy one with a cherry on top. Doesn't that make you hungry?

Kindest regards,

Sincerely,

Hildred

St. Paul, Minn.

Jan. 17, 1914

S T O P   W O R R Y I N G

◆

Postmark: 11 p.m. Jan. 17, 1914, Detroit, Mich.

Addressed to C.W. Turner; dot on envelope

January 17th/14.

Dear Friend, -

Pleased to receive your favor of the 14th Inst. I note you are being moulded into the words of my Uncle, you expressed yourself to me just the way he would had he have received my letter to you, anybody would be inclined to believe he worded it for you. I thank you for the encouragement, it did me good.

The whole trouble lies in the fact, that I am too anxious after money, if I made one million to-day I would want to make two million to-morrow. I told Mr. Turner I was getting to be a regular old miser, every night after I wind up the day's businesses I have to sit down and figure a little while to see how things are going. I have always been so close pressed for money. When I was going to public and high school I had to figure and work to get the $3,000.00 that it cost me for my college training, then when I saw my way clear to go to college, I had to work to get the money to have a Hospital training and build the House. Now it is expenses, getting an automobile Etc. But thank Heavens I do not have to shovel any more coal or wheel any more bricks.

Now I am not going to tell you any more of my troubles, just once in a while I feel this way.

Am losing a little ground Dec. 15th made $13.50. January 15th only $10.50. Dec. 16th made $22.75 Jan. 16th only $5.50. Was going to take a little kid's tonsils out to-morrow which would boost the day by $20.00 but the little kid took chicken pox last night so that will hold me off until next Tuesday. Have taken in $85.00 so far this month, where as last month I only took in $87.00 all month.

Spent last evening after my office hours with Mr. Lucius. Some of Mr. Hall's people are not feeling very well so he said they thought of coming out to see me.

Just got in some new medicine, am sending some of my little wafers to you, taste it and see how you like them, do you want me to send you some.

Well I must get busy.

Sincerely,

Chas.

———————◆———————

Postmark: 7:30 p.m. Jan. 21, 1914, St. Paul, Minn.

St. Paul, Minn.

Jan. 21st, 1914

Dear friend:

Was glad to hear from you and note you think I am beginning to use a great many of Mr. Turner's expressions. I think that is natural because I take so much dictation from him that I gradually start wording things the way he does.

I don't think you are quite a "miser" as you term it but rather it is your pride that makes you work so hard and try to get ahead. I am keeping track of my expenses too, since the first of the year but I don't deal in as large figures as you do.

I shouldn't think you would worry about your January earnings as long as your results are as good as they are, because you know you done wonderfully in December and could hardly expect to repeat in January. In every line of business people will show a decrease at times and you know you are not an exception to that rule. You must expect that too. You ought to be glad that little fellow got the chicken pox because now you can treat him for that as well as take his tonsils out. Think I better quit all of my lecturing.

I tasted a little bit of that medicine you sent and it does not taste bad at all, in fact is kind of good but I think I should like to know what it is for before I order any as I am not overly fond of taking medicine especially when I do not know what it is for and I think if you intend to prescribe you would tell me what you are prescribing for.

I think I will undertake a new line of business, namely that of a waitress. Monday evening the Business Men's Club at the church gave a supper and several of the girls helped serve and it was just loads of fun. After that was over our Sunday school class had a party so I had some busy times. Next week the choir giving a roller skating party at the Selby Rink. Don't know whether to go or not as I am afraid I will break a couple of bones. I haven't done any roller skating for about two years.

Mr. Turner is in Duluth today expect him back in the morning. Are you doctoring Mr. Hall of the Detroit Cold Stge, hope so.

Best wishes,

Hildred

———————◆———————

Postmark: 12:30 a.m. January 22, 1914, Detroit, Mich.

Addressed to Mr. Chas. W. Turner – dot on envelope

January 21st/14.

Dear Friend, -

Pleased to receive your favor of the 17th Inst. Glad to note you enjoyed the candy.

By the way I had a good day yesterday, made $28.00 in the one day. Am now ahead of last month, and think I can stay that way until the end of the month. Will give you my standings –

Dec.   1 – 20th - $116.93 - charged
           1 - 20th - $51.95 - took in

January 1 – 20th - $124.60 - charged
           1 - 20th - $109.90 - took in

Tell Mr. Turner that I will write to him in a few days.

I wonder what will turn up next month. This is anxious business.

Sincerely,

Chas.

———————◆———————

Postmark: 5:30 p.m. Jan. 26, 1914, St. Paul, Minn.

Jan. 26, 1914

Dear friend:

I wish to congratulate you very much on your increase of business, it is certainly splendid.

When I first came to work for Mr. Turner, he had little things come up that would worry me and he used to say to me, "Never cross the bridge until you come to it" also that it was not work that kills but worry. Possibly he has told you these very things but I am inclined to believe that this applies to you more than it ever applied to me because you surely do worry unless you are on the jump all of the time. From all you have told me about physicians in Detroit and their first year, I think your start is most wonderful and you really should congratulate yourself on what you are doing.

I am going to ask you to promise me something and that is that you will stop worrying and until I get your answer I shall consider that you have promised me this. Anytime that business is not coming as fast as you think it should come and you have a little time to yourself, think of the promise I consider you have made me and it will be purely for your own benefit.

In your letter you say you will not worry but just the same you wonder what is in store for you next month. Now, those two stories won't work together.

Yesterday we had a good old fashioned snow storm and we went to see some friends out on a farm near town. It seemed nearly like it did last summer only one day was quite enough although we did have a real good time.

If Mr. Turner goes to Florida next month as he is planning now, don't know what I will do to keep busy as he is planning on being gone for about three weeks. Think I will have to jump in Mrs. Turner's trunk and get a free ride.

Guess I shall have to get busy now. Kindly don't take any offence at the remarks in this letter as they are all meant for the best.

Best wishes for your success,

Hildred

Postmark: 7:30 p.m. Jan. 30, 1914, Detroit, Mich.

Addressed to: Miss H.L. Cress, c/o Mr. Turner – no black dot on envelope

[**Editor's Note:** The address of Dr. Husband has changed from Manchester Ave. to Northwestern Ave.; Manchester is scratched out in ink and the new street name written in by hand.]

Dear Friend, -

Please to receive your favor of the 26th.

Note your remarks in regard to worrying. I believe I have given you the wrong impression, I do not think I worry, I always was the way I am, that is I always worked and slaved to the best of my ability to get along. What am I going to do with my brains if I do not make use of them they will undergo fatty degeneration and become dusty. I like to have some thing to think about. Further more I eat and sleep alright and can laugh with the next fellow. When a person lets their business interfere with their sleep and appetite that is what I call worry. I have never felt better or younger in all my life.

It is true that I would like to have more business, and if there is any way of doing it, I am going to do it.

Sure I'll promise you that I will not worry, because I do not think I am worrying, of course I mean for you to adopt my meaning of the word worry to a certain extent. Now if you do not think I am right in regard to this matter let me know and may be I will see it your way, of course I have just explained it to you the way I see it.

Got two more patients Wednesday; Thursday nothing new, I do not know what is in store for to-day. Have gotten a number of new patients this month but nothing much has been wrong with them, last month the new ones seemed to have more wrong with them. February ought to be a fair and March a good month. I have gotten enough money saved up to pay all my debts, and also to pay my interest. I think I will try and pay off that $100.00 note. In March I want to buy $100.00 or invest that much in instruments pretty soon, and get a machine in the spring.

By the way you ask Uncle Chas. to get the name and address of the corp. that Dr. Beckley buys his rubber gloves from. (in Ohio) I had the address and have mislaid it. I am right out of gloves and must get some.

If the weather would only freeze up a little business would be brighter.

I am not worrying.

Sincerely

Chas.

FEBRUARY 1914

◆

𝔑𝔢𝔴𝔰𝔭𝔞𝔭𝔢𝔯 𝔥𝔢𝔞𝔡𝔩𝔦𝔫𝔢𝔰

𝔇𝔢𝔱𝔯𝔬𝔦𝔱 𝔉𝔯𝔢𝔢 𝔓𝔯𝔢𝔰𝔰

- New rim raises tire mileage
- "Service" keynote of Ford Motor Co.
- Ones who hold those five dollar (per day) jobs must fit them – how "Big Brother" movement inaugurated by the Ford Motor Co. in the distribution of $10,000 to its employes [sic] is being worked out
- Plan 90-day race around world in air
- "Go to Church" plans outlined by eight faiths
- Wilson raises embargo on arms to let Mexico decide her own future
- (U.S.) House Democrats against Suffrage
- Grandmother, 40 years old, six feet tall, anti-suffragist, is first policewoman candidate
- Literacy test for aliens is up to Senate
- Third meeting at the Haig called by U.S. – Peace Conference will be held June 1914
- First public discussion on women's minimum wage question in Michigan to be taken at Detroit Business Men's mass meeting

- Austria to tax people's income to uphold Army
- Rat kills cat in battle to death
- "Crook" movies in favor in Detroit
- Prohibition wave alarms Congress
- Asserts boats have polluted Detroit River
- Indians of Amazon ate Cramer-Seljan party, is explorer's report
- Highest tax rate in Socialist town (Granite City Illinois)
- Americans cry for action in Mexico by U.S.
- Plucky woman loops-the-loop in aeroplane
- Blizzard grips entire Middle West, suffering intense over wide cold
- Vast coal bed in Antarctic region, declares Mawson
- Largest British-built steamship is launched (Brittanic, White Star Line)
- Detroiters rush to avoid penalty on income taxes

𝔖𝔱. 𝔓𝔞𝔲𝔩 𝔓𝔦𝔬𝔫𝔢𝔢𝔯 𝔓𝔯𝔢𝔰𝔰

- Crucial time for organized labor
- Trust Bills ready in another month
- Method, not intent, modern dance bane – majority have no thought of vulgarity
- Heat high school with electricity – is the only one of kind
- Germans to honor the Kaiser tonight
- Advertisement – The Electric Car – "Quiet as silence itself" furnished by the St. Paul Gas Light Co.
- Tight skirts bugaboo of all women autoists
- Chemistry and Bacteriology make it possible for citizens to pump water from germ-infested rivers and yet have purer drink than some from wells
- Lunches for children in schools now practiced in 75 cities – originated in Germany
- Working girls get too small wages
- Trust in Radium declared unsafe
- Illiterate adults national disgrace
- Helen Keller hearing and seeing a play
- Ordinary kitchens have wasted space
- Earth trembles in eastern part of country; costs life, results in minor damages
- Editorial – danger for all from keeping gun in house
- Smoke from volcanos in Japan may be visible in St. Paul this week
- World end in 2022, so begin to worry
- The Britannic Liner afloat, newest launched today is said to be equipped with safety devices to prevent a replication of Titanic disaster

FEBRUARY 1914

---◆---

LETTERS

Postmark: 7:30 p.m. Feb. 2, 1914, St. Paul, Minn.

[**Editor's Note:** This letter was typed and the envelope used had a return address to Booth Fisheries.]

St. Paul, Minnesota,

February 2, 1914

Dear Friend:

Will you pardon me for writing you on the machine but truly, I have been so busy lately account of Mr. Turner going South this week that I hardly know what to do first. Saturday I didn't have a minute to write and Sunday was out of the question as we had company at the house so will steal a few minutes today and promise to write in long hand next time providing you will excuse me this time.

I am very pleased that you promise me you will not do any worrying also that you have a good appetite but please remember that when you are in your office waiting for customers, don't sit tapping your pencil on the desk thinking, as that is usually a sure sign of nervousness; instead, take out one of your medical books and read something in that to get your mind off of whatever you are thinking of.

Glad to know you are getting new patients right along, that is fine and even though there is not much the matter with them, at the same time it means a new patient and naturally if they ae favorably impressed with the first call it means they will come again. Possibly you cure them too fast, how about it?

How did you come out for January? Think you must have been quite a bit ahead of December and presume you have that all figured up by this time especially when you are thinking of doing so many things this Spring, getting a machine, buying instruments etc. I wish I could make the money you do but poor me, I can't make $8.00 one day, $10.00, I just get my little $15.00 dollars at the end of each week and can never expect more or less that is, just now.

You should have some of the cold weather we had yesterday, if it would help business. Today it is not so bad but yesterday everybody was hustling to get to their destination and last night we had a good snow storm.

I have told Mr. Turner of your request regarding the name of the Company that handles those rubber gloves. He has tried to get Dr. Beckley several times today but has not been successful so far. He intends to ask the Doctor tonight and will drop you a few lines tomorrow, giving you the name and address of the firm.

Regarding those black pills, when Mr. Turner wrote the other day, that wasn't any of my doing because I supposed you would agree with him anyway but truly, I don't need any pills, I just had a little cold that day and I had to take about a dozen different kinds of medicine more or less that day and you know how I dislike taking medicine. Tell Mr. Turner they are not good for the kind of colds I have. Think you ought to agree with me for a change anyway.

Kindest regards and remember your promise,

Sincerely,

H i l d r e d. [typed signature]

———————◆———————

Postmark: 9 p.m. Feb. 4, 1914, Detroit, Mich.

Addressed to C.W. Turner, back flap missing

Feb. 4th/14

Dear Hildred, -

Pleased to receive your favor of the 2nd Inst. Every word of your letter reads Mr. Turner, I would not know whether the letter came from Mr. Turner or yourself by reading it providing I did not see the beginning and end. He is a pretty shrewd advisor, so you better continue in the same path.

I wish I was as busy as what you are I would be making $100.00 per day. As it is the most I have made in a single day since I started is $28.00. However my hopes are still in the future and I can see where things are looking brighter all the time. My January results are as follows –

Charged up - $178.00

Took in - $133.00

You can make comparison with the other months. Have made more money so far this month than what I made last month.

Thanks for your trouble in regard to the gloves.

I have made you a promise now I am going to ask you to make me one, I am planning on you visiting Detroit this coming summer, although you have not said positively that you would, now I want you to promise me that you will, in fact if you say no I will not be able to accept your answer, and you do not know how disappointed I would be. Aunt Lizzie will be here and take care of you. And if you can not or have not the money I will send it to you, and the money part of it will be sub Rosa [sic]. Kindly think it over and make me the promise.

Have decided to buy a Ford car, as soon as I feel I can afford it, as they are the most economical machine on the market, then later I can get a better car, I also have to build a garage.

It seems a little quiet here this afternoon Mother is in to the city doing some shopping and I have had no callers so far (2 pm.)

Now I am going to close the same way that you did, that is I will consider that you have made me the promise until I hear from you. And I know that you will say that Detroit is the prettiest and nicest city you were ever in.

Sincerely,

Chas.

Postmark: 5 p.m. Feb. 6, 1914, St. Paul, Minn.

St. Paul, Minn.

Feb. 6, 1914

Dear Friend:

Was very glad to hear from you also to know that you are doing so nicely. I don't see how you get so many new patients all the time, how do you do, stand outside and hail passers by or what?

Note you made $28.00 one day, that is just about equal to my two weeks salary. I used to think $15.00 was pretty big but since your reports have been coming in I realize how little I am making. You certainly done fine in January and hope you break the record again in February but remember that is a short month so you can only figure as against the 28 days in January. How do your charge patients pay? Have you any delinquent debtors as yet or have they all A No1 credit?

As to my going to Detroit this summer, I could surely ask for nothing nicer but really don't see how I could promise because if I promise anything I want to keep it and you know so many things could happen before then. I would have enough money saved by that time because I am still saving my 10 cents each day (thanks to you) so that would not worry me so much and I am going to try awfully hard and go. I will promise you though that if I go any place this summer it will be Detroit and if I can't go I won't go any place. I have heard so much about Detroit that I surely would like to see the city also know I would have a nice time. Does my promise suit you or not? I suppose if I go to Detroit you would give me a ride in your new machine if you had it by that time, wouldn't you? Haven't had an auto ride for so long, forget what it is like.

Have not had much to do since Mr. Turner went away but today we are quite busy with circulars.

Thank you again for your kind invitation to visit in Detroit and I am going to try mighty hard and accept.

Best wishes,

Hildred

———————◆———————

Postmark: 8:30 p.m. Feb. 10, 1914, Detroit, Mich.

Addressed to C.W. Turner – black dot on back flap

Feb. 10th/14.

Dear Hildred, -

Was going to answer it this a.m. but was called out then when I arrived home I found a surgical instrument agent waiting for me. I hate agents selling instruments to call on me because they always have so many nice instruments to see that I really need and almost must have. It stirs up trouble within me, my heart says that I must have certain things, my conscience and pocket book say no, wait a little longer. However the man this morning sold me a pair of forceps for $4.75. I have to have them and with care will last me all my life. An agent yesterday sold me 100 yds of gauze for $3.50. I cut it myself sterilize it and put it in packages, I also roll all my own adhesive, whereby I save on the average about 30 cts. a day. Now you know some of the things I do after office hours. You should see me wash dishes and see how fast I can wring clothes for mother. She jumps when I strike her funny bone.

Had 8 patients in my office yesterday. You asked me about my collections. Yesterday I collected $18.00, Sunday 50 cts. Saturday $11.75, Friday $10.25, Thursday $7.00, Wednesday $0, Tuesday, $0, Monday $14.50, Sunday $0.

Pleased to note what you say in regard to Detroit. That is when you promise anything you want to do it. Also that if you go any place it will be to Detroit, and that you are going to try mighty hard to accept. I do not want to do anything that is not right, but along with these other things I would like you to promise me one more thing, that is if there is anything that turns up which you think might interfere with your coming here that you will immediately let me know, so that if possible I may be able to help you out.

As soon as I collect in $20.00 I will have enough money to pay all my debts with the exception of what I owe for the house, also enough to pay my interest and the $100.00 note that you made out. My note is not due until seven weeks from now. Buying drugs, and what you have to spend moving into new house takes lots of money.

It has been pretty cold here the last few days night before last it was 5 degrees below zero, but it is considerably warmer to day.

I trust my Detroit scheme will be favorable to you.

Sincerely,

Chas.

———————◆———————

Postmark: 10:30 a.m. Feb. 13, 1914, St. Paul, Minn.

St. Paul, Minn.

Feb. 12, 1914

Dear friend:

Was glad to hear from you, also to know you are kept so busy and I would like to peek in the window some day to find you washing dishes or wringing out clothes. You will be a specialist in housekeeping some day as well as medicine.

As to my going to Detroit: I will let you know right away if anything should turn up whereby it would interfere with my going. Supposing I couldn't go, do you think you could come to St. Paul? Of course I know it would be pretty hard for you to leave your practice during the first year but maybe the rest would do you good.

What would you say if I should go out West the first of next month with mamma? If I went I would stay for three or four months. Mamma has practically made up her mind to go but would like to have a partner and has picked me out as such. I suppose you will say that I promised to go to Detroit if I went anyplace and that I will have to stick to it. I have been thinking this over for about a month and have about decided to stay at home and keep Claribel company because if I went it would leave her all alone with the work and she is not very well. Yesterday she had something injected into her like Mr. Lucius did as she is troubled with boils lately. Poor girl if it isn't one thing it is another.

Notice you think you had cold weather when it was 5-degrees below. You should be in this part of the country. It has been 20-degrees below all this week that is in the morning. In the afternoon it would go up to about 15-degrees below.

Did you know Mr. Hogstad's little boy? He was an awfully cute little fellow and so full of life all the time. Last night papa got a telephone message that they had lost their little boy. He caught cold about two weeks ago when they were visiting in St. Paul and the morning after they got home they found out he had Scarlet Fever. It was their only child so they take it pretty hard.

Guess I will close now as it is 4 P.M. The office force got up a petition today saying they wanted to go home at 4 P.M. account of Lincoln's Birthday and my dear "daddy" agreed so off we go at 4 P.M.

I think I envy Mr. Turner just now as it is pretty near 15-degrees below and he says the roses are blooming where he is.

Kindest regards and best wishes,

Hildred

P.S. Are you keeping your promise?

———◆———

Postmark: 2:30 p.m. Feb. 17, 1914, Detroit, Mich.

Addressed to C.W. Turner; envelope flap missing

Feb. 17th/14.

Dear Hildred, -

Pleased to hear from you glad to know you are not frozen to death, do not let any of those polar bears eat you up.

As to house work, there is only one person who ever sees me into it, that is Mother, I beat it if I hear anyone coming.

I thank you for your promise in regard to Detroit. It would be very nice if you could go west and come to Detroit also this summer, but at the same time, if you can only go one place, you will no doubt remember that I have that little promise, by the way I have the letter saved in my little private till. And another thing should you go West and be taken sick there would be no one there to take care of you, whereas in Detroit I could fix you up. Last Summer you were out on the farm and you were glad to get back home. Therefore you better try the City this time. Another thing I am pretty sure about getting a machine this spring, and there may not be any machines out west where you are going. You must also remember that there are not such places as Belle Isle Etc. out west. Another thing if Claribel should go West instead of you, the change might make a new girl out of her, and then she would be better able to do the work while you are away. As far as I am concerned in regard to me going to St. Paul, I may say that I will not need a rest, I am better off both physically and financially while I am working. I trust you will see things as I do, and come to Detroit.

Sorry to hear concerning Mr. Hogstad's little boy. It seems as though he has lots of trouble with his family.

I am keeping my promise, and know or at least feel sure that you will keep yours and will have no reason to regret it if you do. You better promise me that you will come to Detroit this summer and then the matter is settled.

Business has been fairly good lately, but I do not think that I will make as much money this month as what I did last month.

Now I am going to consider that you have made me the promise until I hear from you.

Sincerely,

Chas.

———◆———

Postmark: 7 p.m. Feb. 18, 1914, St. Paul, Minn.

Dear Friend:

Mr. Turner expects to be home in the morning and thought that if I wanted to write a letter this week, I had better do it right away because I know how busy we will be for the next few days. I am going to bed real early tonight so I will be able to do a good day's work tomorrow.

How are your patients and are there many new ones coming? I hope so but remember you are not to do any worrying. I have your promise.

You should have been with us last night. One of the girls gave us a sleigh ride party, there were between 25 and 30 that went and we had just a great time. It is the first sleigh ride I have been to this winter and I surely did enjoy it and the weather was ideal for the occasion.

Saturday night our class (Sunday School) is going to have a "Washington Supper" for the members of the class only. There are about forty members and we have some real good times together.

That is two nights of celebrating this week. If I should tell Mr. Turner I can just about imagine what he would say, that I looked as if I did not get enough sleep and that I would have to go to bed earlier nights but I am surely going early tonight as I admit I am tired.

Kindest regards, and remember not to work too hard.

Sincerely,

Hildred

———————◆———————

Postmark: 7 p.m. Feb. 20, 1914, St. Paul, Minn.

St. Paul, Minn.

Feb. 20, 1914.

Dear Friend:

Was pleased to hear from you. Did not think I would have time to write this week but Mr. Turner went to Minneapolis this morning so I am not very busy.

You don't know what you missed by not being here yesterday. Mr. Turner brought some oranges with him from his fruit farm and I had the privilege of eating one of them. My! but it was delicious. They taste all together different from the ones up here. The skin is so hard you can't peel them, you cut one end off and suck the juice out. They are simply great!

Mr. Turner is looking fine since his short vacation. Mrs. Turner stayed in Chgo. for a few days longer.

Regarding Detroit, I would surely like to go and if some friend chances to be going that way I will try awfully hard and go along. Your mentioning Belle Isle, machines etc. sort of makes my head whirl and I know I would have a splendid time if I did go.

As to any possibility of my getting sick while out West as against Detroit, I have no doubt but what you could cure me but I don't know if I could pay the bill and there I would be in a terrible fix, first thing I know you would be commencing suit against me to get your money.

Am awfully glad to hear that business is good and hope it will continue so.

I think you ought to let me play Doctor for a while and tell you what I think ails you. I have decided you have a very serious case of "Americanitis." Have you ever doctored anybody for that? Probably you have not got the prescription for that. If not, let me know and I might be willing to give you the prescription. Of course if you can treat it yourself, you are so much ahead as I am rather an expensive doctor. This "Americanitis" is rather serious if not treated carefully so take care!

Kindest regards and good luck,

Sincerely,
Hildred

———————————◆———————————

Postmark: Feb. 23, 1914, Detroit, Mich.

Addressed to C.W. Turner – envelope flap does not survive

Feb. 23rd/14.

Dear Hildred, -

Pleased to receive your favor of the 20th Inst. Note you say that I have a very serious case of Americanitis, it's as an offense of course meaning inflammation, therefore you have diagnosed me as an American with an inflammation but you do not say what part of me is involved. I take it that you mean my cerebellum and I sure want the cure regardless of the price. However, let me add this that I do not believe that I have as much mind as the ordinary person suffering from Americanitis – therefore you can leave one ingredient out of your ppt.

Would that I had one of those oranges, can't you send one. Tell Uncle Chas. that I will write to him as soon as I think he has caught up with his work.

Regarding Detroit Aunt Lizzie comes here every summer, and I know will be only too pleased to have you come along with her, the only easy way out of this is to say you will come I'll take chances on you not coming, if you will only make the promise. Besides having you see Detroit I have a number of friends here that I would like to have you meet and get acquainted with, I know you will like them. Now if you do not make me the promise I am going to draw up a little statement and send it to Mr. Turner, to have you sign it, and I know he will do all he can for me. I expect your promise in the next letter to me.

I am doing a little business every day. My cash receipts up to the present time are a little ahead of last month but I am about $25 behind on my charge account, I wish I had some money to buy real estate, I paid $1050.00 for my lot last May, now they are selling lots around us for $1500.00. A contractor told me I could get $2000.00 more for my house that what it cost me.

Sincerely,
Chas.
(Look at top)

[Editor's Note: the final entry refers the reader to the top of the page to read: Don't forget that promise, be sure to make it. I'll have you arrested if you don't. The notation is accompanied by a drawing of a woman being pushed from behind toward a jail.]

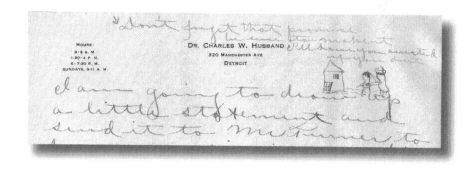

Postmark: 7 p.m. Feb. 27, 1914, St. Paul, Minn.

St. Paul, Minn.

Feb. 27, 1914

Dear Friend:

Was very pleased to hear from you and I guess you have about diagnosed your case right. I think Americanitis is about as good a name as you could give it. You see, one of your Sarah (Cere) sisters is working too hard, namely "Cerebrum" and you must not overtax her because if you do, she might go back on you some day and not work quite so readily. This is what you should do to relieve her: After working hard all day, from 6:30 A.M. until possibly 7:30 P.M. you should find some change of work, something that has not as much brain work to it (for instance washing dishes) as a change is as good as a rest they say. Another thing you should not worry or get nervous if patients don't come quick enough to suit you as that is a bad thing to do. Last but by no means least, do what Mr. Turner tells me to do, namely go to bed early.

You see you need no medicine to cure your case at least not as yet and if you follow some of these suggestions you will not need any.

As to Detroit, if Mrs. Turner goes of course it would be different but even then I could not go unless she would ask me or on her invitation, and don't forget something else, I am a young lady alone and I cannot do as Vanderbuilt said when he was asked what he thought of public opinion [businessman Wm. Vanderbuilt: "The public be damned."]

*Another feature, what would your good mother say if I should walk into her house
uninvited. It is very true Mrs. Turner could come and stay there and I know she would be
welcome but the question regarding myself is so entirely different that I know if you think
a few minutes you will realize that I might not be a welcome guest and I would not want
to come under those conditions. You have asked me to promise I would come but how can
I promise you with these things in my way? I think when you think of this in your own
mind you will say I am right. I have a good deal of faith in you and I do not think you
would ask me to do anything that would prove objectionable to me because it would be very
humiliating to me also to you if I should arrive in Detroit and found I was not welcome.
Your good self of course would be an exception to the above rule. I hope you don't take
any offense at these remarks, but you asked me to promise and I feel I shuld tell you why I
haven't promised.*

Kind regard,

Sincerely,

Hildred

Put yourself in my place and then think.

H.C.

MARCH 1914

◆

Newspaper Headlines

Detroit Free Press

- Fenkell asks support of garbage reduction plan
- Scott Memorial (proposed for Belle Isle) interests many
- Propose looping cars at Grand Circus
- Russian State seeks to create money monopoly; Czar is to become a financial dictator if plans carry
- British polar explorer party carries airship – Stackhouse expeditions purpose is chiefly mapping, goes out in ship late Capt. Scott used
- "Moderns must be amused to be saved" says Battle Creek Pastor; Runs Church "Movies"
- Original Svengali, assisted by Miss Elsie Terry – All new show (theatre advertisement)
- "Kiss your wife once a day" Tom Marshall's advice if you want to escape divorce mill
- Wilson realizes that Mexican situation is near crucial point
- Medical Society takes action to stop Diphtheria
- Post Office receipts grow

- Calls machines bad for genius
- Surgeon grafts organ of dead youth to self (a gland, in effort to find a remedy for Bright's disease)
- St. Paul railway "doctored" books, says U.S. report
- Spread praise on Michigan apple
- Mongol race is dying out quite rapidly
- Ice fishing flourishes – Saginaw Bay thronged
- Pneumonia and grip cutting wide swaths
- Millions at stake in auto patents war opened in Detroit; three companies join to secure royalties from over 150 concerns for alleged infringement (Packard, Peerless and American Ball Bearing were the complainants)
- Fourteenth White House bridal couple to-be - Eleanor Wilson to marry M'Adoo (Treasury Secretary Wm. Gibbs M'Adoo); Word from the White House
- Poisoned own father to win bridal home (Cheboygan, MI)
- Ford to have new Polish Catholic Church
- Accidents are cut down 73 percent in Cadillac plant
- Would you send your daughter to college?
- Chinese mandates offer freedom in religious worship
- Building of ships important among Detroit industries
- City water free of Typhoid says health official
- Dodge brothers open attack upon income tax before courts; assert enactment gives competitors unfair advantage – content Act discriminates against individuals and partner ships in plain favor of corporations
- City death rate from pneumonia has no parallel
- Methodist divine assails modern dance and dress
- Public light fund cut by alderman on economy bent
- Ulster waits signal to begin revolution; 200 arrests planned
- Banks will offer system to foster thrift in pupils
- "Wizard" smiles and naturalist and automaker join him (Photograph of Edison, Burroughs and Ford in Ft. Meyers Fla.)
- Britons toast Ulster declaring they will not coerce province
- (Pancho) Villa escapes federal trap, battle rages
- While exports of autos increase, imports slump
- First dirt turned on new Receiving Hospital grounds
- Women's whims count in auto manufacturing
- Schools will play baseball on D.A.C. lot

St. Paul Pioneer Press

- Northwest swept by snow and winds
- Woman Labor Law is valid (limiting a work day to 10 hours)
- She teaches Tango to Chinese Princes
- Killed editor who criticized husband
- Building of scenic highway assured
- America behind in Child Labor laws
- Unemployed Army plots revolution
- Women's suffrage loses in Senate
- Ulster volunteers hastily summoned to headquarters
- Immigration growth heavy
- Discover Earth is mighty hot inside
- Cornea of pig's eye brings child sight

MARCH 1914

◆

LETTERS

Postmark: 1:30 a.m. March 3, 1914, Detroit, Mich.

Addressed to Mr. Chas. W. Turner (envelope flap missing)

March 2nd/14.

Dear Hildred, -

Pleased to hear from you. I thank you very much for the inclosed [sic] pens and clipping. In regard to the pens I do not see why I did not happen to think of that little extra turn they have added to them. I certainly have the time to think about these things, I must try to be more watchful in the future. Also read the clipping, do not think that there is much danger of me ever getting one of those [dance] hearts.

In regard to Detroit there was a few things that I was not going to tell you but it seems as though I must before you will make me the promise. In the first place I appreciate the fact that you are a girl just as well as you do, and would not for all the world have you do anything wrong. And am not going to. Nor would I even think of such a thing. I trust you will only have confidence enough in me, to believe that I will get everything without exception fixed up alright, not only to look alright, but to be alright, if you promise me. What I was not going to tell you is this, that when Mrs. Turner was here last fall I asked her if she would invite you to come to Detroit with her this coming summer, she said she would only be too pleased. As far as my people are concerned I have lived with them for years and feel sure I know them and know them well. And if they do not make you feel welcome and also feel that your presence was O.K. I will never ask you to believe anything else I say. Furthermore I have told my mother a certain few things and she takes it for granted that you and Aunt Lizzie are coming. All I ask of you is this that you promise me you will come to Detroit providing that I make everything O.K. for you coming. Now if you think I have overlooked anything let me know. What you told me in your letter is just what I believed of you. You can not know whether my condition is improving or not unless you see me.

My February earnings are a follows.

Charged up $140.00
Took in $142.00

My charge a/c is nearly $40.00 short of last month, and the other is the best yet. What March will be I have not the slightest idea. Got one new patient to-day so far. Am batching it for a few days as Mother is out of the city attending the funeral of an old Friend.

Now I have written the letter, put myself in your place and thought it over and think I would make the promise if I were in your place.

Sincerely,

Chas.

———————◆———————

Postmark: 7:30 p.m. March 5, 1914, St. Paul, Minn.

St. Paul, Minn.

March 5, 1914

Dear Friend:

Was very pleased to hear from you and to know you got the pens and clipping O.K.

As to my coming to Detroit with Mrs. Turner. It is all right the way you have it fixed or since you explained to me but you see I did not know anything about these previous arrangements you had made for me which was very nice of you. Of course I believed you would fix things all O.K. but I could not promise until I knew. Mrs. Turner has not said anything so far but I presume that will all happen in due time. I asked papa last night if he had any objections to my going to Detroit this summer with Mrs. Turner and he said, "Absolutely none" so I guess it is up to me now. Now that I have permission to go and know everything is all right, I am just like a little youngster, can hardly wait until the time comes. Therefore, unless something unforeseen turns up you will see me in Detroit and tickled to death that I can go. Does that promise suit you?

Mr. Lucius met with quite a severe accident on Monday morning. He was running to catch his car, he slipped and fell on the ice and pulled his arm or shoulder out of its socket. He had to have two doctors and has not been out of the house since. Mr. Turner says he may be able to go to work next week but not do any actual work for several months.

It is pretty near 6 P.M. so guess I will close this time rather short.

Thank you again for your kind invitation to come to Detroit and you can consider I have made you the promise.

Think you have done fine during the month of February because remember that is a short month. Hope you will do equally well in March.

Kindest regards,

Hildred

Postmark: 9 p.m. March 7, 1914, Detroit, Mich.

Addressed to: Mr. Chas. W. Turner (envelope flap missing)

Mar 7th/14.

Dear Hildred, -

Pleased to receive your favor of the 5 Inst.

I knew I would frighten you if I drew some pictures, but leaving all jokes aside, I am more than pleased with your answer, if everything is not fixed up alright, or if anything does not suit you, all you will have to do is to let me know, and it will be so. May say that if you ever liked anybody in this world you will like my Mother, because my Mother treats everybody in such a way that they can not help but like her. What I want to do now is to find out what time Aunt Lizzie is coming to Detroit and then I will let you know. I am thinking about writing Uncle Chas to-day, probably I will mention to him in regard to Detroit. May say that you had better not figure on being back home for four to six weeks at least.

Sorry to hear in regard to Mr. Lucius, had I have been there, I might have had another patient.

Business is moving along slowly this week, nothing exciting, getting an occasional new case, but the trouble is they have nothing much wrong with them. Most all the Doctors say that it is dull just at present, contrary to other years.

Sincerely,

Chas.

[**Editor's Note:** Another hand-drawn picture follows Charles' signature – a police officer standing behind a woman with his hand on her shoulder. The caption reads: "The cop looks disappointed his charge is (illegible) sulky. The jail is a long way off see if you can find the jail."]

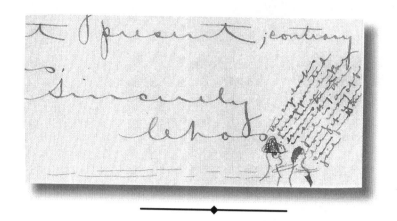

Postmark: 1 p.m. March 11, St. Paul, Minn.

St. Paul, Minn.

Dear Friend:

Was awfully glad to hear from you and thank you for fixing everything up so nicely for me concerning Detroit. I guess though, according to the way Mr. Turner talked yesterday, I better not make up my mind too much that I am going because I might be disappointed, although I hope not.

As to liking your mother, I am sure I would as I have heard many nice things about her. If there is such a thing as my not being able to go to Detroit, do you think you could come to St. Paul for a short visit? I don't dare say a long visit because I know we would have to consider ourselves lucky to have a short visit from such a busy person.

As to your business, glad you are getting along so nicely but as to one poor week, cheer up those are to be expected once in a while in all lives of business and we have had more than one in the fish business. I hope though, that in March you will make more than any month heretofore.

3/11/14

I started this last evening but got so busy could not find time to finish. Have been awfully busy lately. The building next to our new Cold Stge. Building in Mpls. burned (the Company owned it) and there has been two different fires in the new building so that makes three fire losses Mr. Turner has had to adjust and it has kept him hustling for the last week.

We are having just dandy weather here now don't think you can beat it in Detroit this time – just like Spring.

Kindest regards,

Sincerely,

Hildred

———————◆———————

Postmark: 12:30 p.m. March 13, 1914, Detroit, Mich.

Addressed to: Mr. Chas. W. Turner (dot on back envelope flap)

Mar. 12th/14

Dear Hildred, -

Pleased to hear from you. In regard to Detroit don't let Mr. Turner discourage you in any way, I don't want you to think for a minute but that you are coming here because you are, may say that I always have trouble when I first try to do any thing, but it seems as though everything always pass out alright. Therefore make up your mind that you are coming. For instance I had loads & loads of trouble to get an individual telephone line, I got it today it is Walnut 3314. If everything else fails I have a big suit case, I will arrive in St. Paul on some mysterious road, put you in my suit case and beat it for Detroit in other words I will smuggle you.

You did not say anything about your cold in the letter, is it getting better or worse, I don't blame you for not wanting to soak your feet.

Business has been pretty good so far this week, have made $10.00 so far today have $3.00 more in sight today, and trust something else will show up.

We are also having dandy weather.

Be sure and let me know if Mr. Turner discouraged you in anyway in regard to Detroit.

Sincerely,

Chas.

◆

Postmark: 1 p.m. Mar. 17, 1914, St. Paul, Minn.

St. Paul, Minn.

March 17, 1914

Dear Friend:

How do you like shaking hands by wireless? I hope it worked all right because I got a good scare with it and I like to pass it along. I handed it to Mr. Turner the other day in an envelope and I wish you could have seen him jump. I suppose by this time he has visited with you and gone on to Toronto.

As to my going to Detroit, don't think I don't care about it for I surely do, would like nothing better than to take a trip to Detroit this summer. But in talking with Mr. Turner, he thinks I better not make up my mind too strongly for fear of being disappointed. There is a possibility of Mrs. Turner not going until late in the Fall on account of other trips she has planned and again it is hard to tell what mamma will say. Of course, papa has no objections to my going at all but mamma is not here now and it is very doubtful as to what she would say. Guess I better not plan too much on going to Detroit, will have to trust to luck.

As to your big suit case, don't think you better try it because it would be pretty heavy and you might drop it by the wayside.

Am glad to know you at last have your telephone fixed, you surely had your share of trouble with that.

Note you expected to get about $15.00 the day you wrote. My goodness! You are beginning to make me feel dissatisfied, that is all I make in a whole week but I hope you can keep it up every day and you will soon be a rich man (your ambition).

Claribel and I are going to a Hard Time Party a week from tonight. We are supposed to be among the unemployed who are marching to Washington or rather to the "I.W.W." (I Want Work) Society. Imagine we will have a real good time.

Kindest regards,

Sincerely,

Hildred

———————◆———————

Postmark: 8:30 p.m. March 19, 1914, Detroit, Mich.

Addressed to: Mr. Chas. W. Turner [envelope flap missing]

March 19th/14

Dear Hildred, -

Pleased to receive your favor of the 17th. The thickness of your letter made me rather suspicious, then when I opened it the letter part was so tight in the envelope that I rather spoiled the joke. However I got it on Mr. Turner again.

When I asked you to come to Detroit, I am going to tell you that I had a second reason in mind. First of all I wanted you to come because I wanted you to. Secondly I wanted to see whether you thought enough of me to want to come yourself. I think you have shown me that you want to visit Detroit. Now being that you have been so nice to me I am going to try to accept your invitation to go to St. Paul and spend one week with you may be in June then later on possibly in August or the first part of September you can come to see me. I would like you to see what I have here and to meet my people. I trust you will not think any less of me for what I have told you in fact I think you will think more of me for being frank with you.

Business has been great the last two weeks, one new yesterday, one the day before, 4 the day before that, one before that, one the day before that, skipped a day, and one the day before that Etc.

Do you suppose you could get a week off if I go to St Paul in June, then we could enjoy ourselves more. Let me know what you think in regard to this matter.

Sincerely,

Chas.

———————◆———————

Postmark: 8:30 p.m. March 20, 1914, Detroit, Mich.

Addressed to: Mr. Chas. W. Turner [envelope flap lost]

March 20th/14.

Dear Hildred, -

I wish you many happy returns of the 22nd [**Editor's Note:** March 22, Hildred's 19th birthday], kindly decorate your neck accordingly, which through the kindness of Mr. Turner has made it possible, If the present does not altogether suit your wishes I will change it for you. It is always hard for me to buy a present for anyone, that is I do not know just what to buy.

I am also going to offer you a position as my private secretary at $20.00 per week, I am awfully busy and need some one to answer my telephone and keep my books. Got these new families today. Made $12.00 so far and looking for lots more business before the day ends. Kindly let me know in regard to the position, because I certainly will need somebody if business keeps good.

Say I am all bound up in my work, if business keeps up, I see where money in years to come will never worry me.

Let me hear from you in regard to the position, of course I would not pay anybody else such a large salary.

Sincerely,

Chas.

———————◆———————

Postmark: 4:30 p.m. March 22, 1914, St. Paul, Minn.

St. Paul, Minn.

Mar. 22, 1914

Dear Friend:

I don't know how I can thank you for the beautiful necklace. It is certainly fine and I thank you ever ever so much. I couldn't imagine why Mr. Turner was so anxious for me to come to the office this morning because we finished up the work pretty well and this morning thought there would not be much to do but now of course I can see through it all. It is just what I wanted and is the prettiest necklace I have ever had, only wish you were here to see it. Next summer when you are here you can see it, see what a good choice Mr. Turner made.

Also want to thank you for the box of candy you sent, it is just fine. Seems to me everything is coming my way the last day or two.

As to your offering me a $20.00 position, it sound awfully good but don't think I can accept for several reasons and another thing I think you made the offer without thinking or figuring very hard. If you had to pay out $20.00 every week it would soon eat up all your profits and if you should have a couple of dull weeks, I think when Saturday night came you would wish you did not have that burden on your hands of paying out $20.00. I am more than pleased to hear you are doing so nicely in business and every time I hear you have some new customers I can imagine about how you feel.

As to your coming to St. Paul I am so pleased to hear you are coming, it is almost more than I expected but don't change your mind whatever you do. As to my getting a week's vacation, Mr. Turner thought I could have it so I will be real good until then and possibly I will be granted the request. Don't forget now, will be looking for you some time in June.

I want to thank you again for that necklace and I am so pleased with it and it was such a surprise and a pleasant one too.

Kindest regards and trust business is real good. According to your reports this should be a record month for you.

Sincerely,

Hildred

Sorry that joke didn't work but you can rest assured it will next time.

———————◆———————

Postmark: 12:30 a.m. March 26, 1914, Detroit, Mich.

Addressed to: Mr. Chas. W. Turner [flap missing]

March 25th/14.

Dear Hildred, -

When I commenced to write to you I was wondering what I was going to do next, just then a patient walked into the front offices, he would like me to go out to the country with him to see his kids. I am going in a few minutes. All my old patients are getting well, so I am getting just a little anxious, although I made $18.75 yesterday and $8.00 so far today. So far this month I have charged up $185.00 I want to charge up over $200.00 before the month is over, as I say I have nothing in particular in sight, therefore I wish you would put a little extra word in your evening prayer for me, I can do it in a few hours if I can only get busy. Got one new patient so far today.

Pleased to hear you liked the necklace, I venture to say knowing what I now do that

I got more pleasure out of giving it to you than you got by receiving it. You are the most appreciative person I ever met. I only regret that I did not make Mr. Turner buy a better one.

In regard to the candy I know I am head over heels in love with chocolates and I think every body else is. I never buy any for myself, but I get Mother to buy them for me. (I of course diby [?] up to her.)

Tell Uncle Chas. that I hired a wash woman and we tried her out last Monday. She is pretty good so far, I have lost my job.

I would be pleased if you would ask Mr. Turner what size he thinks I ought to build my garage, I am figuring on building it of frame, shingle roof and cement floor, buying a Ford first, then a larger car as the occasion demands it.

March 25th/14.

I also wish you would give the inclosed [sic] check to Mr. Turner. I wish you would hold it until the first of April as I always like my account to show up well at the end of each month.

I have certainly got to make lots of money if I am going to go to St. Paul, buy a machine etc. but it won't be my fault if I do not do it. I am going to do my best.

Sincerely,

Chas.

Postmark: 7 p.m. March 27, 1914, St. Paul Minn.

St. Paul, Minn.

March 27, 1914

Dear Friend:

How did you like your trip to the country? Also how did you get there. Did the gentleman take you with him? There is a time your machine would have come in handy.

I surely will put in an extra few words of prayer for you tonight and hope it will do some good but I certainly don't think you should complain, instead of asking for more patients you should say how thankful you are for those you have.

I understand that one of those foolish fellows you doctored up, is now drumming trade for you in return. How about that? That's pretty good.

As to the necklace, really, I like it so much, like it better every time I wear it. Mr. Turner says he guessed I should not have got it until summertime because he never will be able to make me keep my coat buttoned up. You can't blame me though can you, when I have something nice I like to show-off as well as the rest.

Mr. Turner is in Grand Forks today but expect him again in the morning when I will ask him regarding size etc. of your garage, also give him the check. I rather hate to give the latter up, wish I was so rich that I could afford to make out my own checks like that, especially such large ones. I suppose you are real busy now, looking up figures regarding your automobile also the building of your garage. Look out for the lamp-posts when you start running your machine.

Tonight is choir practice again and I am so tired, wish I could stay home. It seems every night this week there has been something to keep us out late or rather I should say up late. Tuesday night we had just a fine time at the "Hard Time Party," more fun than I have had in a long time and you should have seen some of the awful looking specimans [sic] there were there, real hard time looking.

Mamma is coming back next Thursday, that will make five weeks she is gone. We have had a pretty good siege of housekeeping this time. Good luck for the rest of this month so you make all the money you want.

Hildred

———————◆———————

Postmark: 4 p.m. March 31, 1914, Detroit, Mich.

Mar 30th/14

Dear Hildred, -

Pleased to receive your favor of the 27th Inst. As to your inquiry regarding the country trip may say that I walked.

May say that your little prayer has been answered, so far today I have made $19.75, and I do hope something more will turn up. I have broken my old time record all to pieces. May be a few more little words would not do any harm, next time I write will let you know concerning this month's business.

That foolish fellow when he hears of anybody being sick in his neighborhood he goes to them and tells them they better send for me. As far as his looks go, his advertisement is not the best.

If you catch cold owing to the wearing of the necklace let me know and I will send you some tablets. I would kind of like you to take some of my medicine anyway.

My Brother's Wife and her little Chas. W. arrived here from Duluth today, I wish you could see the little kidlet.

Glad to hear that you are having a little enjoyment, better not look tired out in June else I will be leaving you some pills.

I think possibly I better not learn to run a machine until you come, and then we can have some fun together.

Sincerely,

Chas.

APRIL 1914

Newspaper Headlines

Detroit Free Press

- Lodge would curb Detroit liquor sales
- Britain may extend Home Rule scheme (in Ireland)
- 64 perish when sealer is caught in drifting ice floes
- Detroit may get new Post Office at Michigan Central terminal
- Detroit's Receiving Hospital will care for emergency cases
- Chinese art leaking away to America
- Mexican refugee lays carnage and property loss at Wilson's door
- Newspapers and union employees at peace
- Americans now in full control of quiet Vera Cruz
- 203 miners entombed in two W. Virginia pits; believed dead in flames
- Addition for hospital cut from budget (Receiving Hospital)
- Tax rate to be $19.89; budget is cut $1,847,176 by Board of Estimates

𝔖t. 𝔓aul 𝔓ioneer 𝔓ress

- Coal mines close; 50,000 men idle; Ohio operators refuse to renew contracts under new state law

- Hobo Army (of unemployed) Chief on trial

- Three airmen are killed at Rheims – Emile Vedrines falls to death and two are consumed by gasoline explosion

- State will build scenic highway

- Thinks Jap would make a good American citizen

- Silly fashions are all men's fault

- Calls $9 a week the minimum wage. Secretary of Commission thinks this is the least woman worker can live on; Father Ryan's figure less; $7 weekly for board and clothes leaves little for incidental expenses

- High taxes scare some politicians

- Chicago Jew to lecture (at the Anti-Defamation League)

- Women put saloon on the run in Illinois with first votes

- Women candidates beaten in Chicago

- Says selling papers on street by small boys is becoming national problem

- Blames cancer on meat and cooking

- Columbia warships get (Panama) Canal rights

- Panther hunt is Yellowstone sport – 18 mountain lions are bagged in 15 days

- Umpires to enforce new rules strictly (infield fly, balk, third base coach prohibited from touching third base runner)

- Many silk street costumes are seen, but almost as many chic cloth frocks

- A new portrait of Crown Prince George of Greece, who will marry Grand Duchess Olga, eldest daughter of the Czar of Russia (who, with her family, was murdered during the Russian Revolution)

- Ulster cry to uphold George termed fraud

- Minnesota richest state in America

- Wilson seeks permission to take over Mexican ports

- Negro municipal judge (Robert H. Terrels)

- (Professional dancers Vernon and Irene Castle) Castles uplifting Tango; yes, Press Agent says so

- Opening of White Bear Yacht Club

APRIL 1914

❖

LETTERS

Postmark: 3:30 p.m. April 3, 1914, St. Paul, Minn.

St. Paul, Minn.

April 3, 1914

Dear Friend:

Was glad to receive your letter yesterday, also to know that my prayer has been answered. Think I shall have to keep up the good work. You have certainly got my curiosity up to know how you came out this month because you say you have broken your old time record all to pieces. That sounds good!

Have not caught cold from wearing the necklace as yet, that seems to be sort of a lucky piece. Why are you so anxious for me to take some of your pills? Do you think I need some? I have taken several of those little red pills that you gave to Mr. Turner. I don't know what they are for but every few days Mr. Turner says I look as if I needed another pill and that ends it, I have to take it whether I think I need it or not but just so they are sugar coated it is not so bad.

Mamma came home last night, she had been gone five weeks. I am glad she is home again because I can have more time to sew again. We have been doing double duty at church too lately, account of Easter also a wedding the day before Easter. One of the girls in the choir is going to be married and she has asked us to sing her wedding march. We have just loads *of fun practicing. The choir is going to give her a large rug as a wedding gift and two of the other girls and myself are to make the selection and collect the money. As far as collecting money is concerned, guess I can do that but as to picking out the rug that is quite a joke. I haven't any idea as to prices, etc. and imagine I will be rather a poor judge but the best I can do is to try anyway.*

Bought my spring coat today, it is between a tan and mustard shade and trimmed with just a touch of green. Mamma liked it real well and think I do but I thought more of my poor $25.00 than the coat. That is quite a big sum for me to pay at once.

I suppose you will be spending all your spare time playing with the big boy you have with you now. I know when there are little youngsters at our house, I never see anything to do but play with them.

I think possibly you better learn to run your machine before I get there because then if you run into anything I can bail you out otherwise we might both be put in the lock-up for ten days and I would rather have something else to eat beside bread and water. I imagine though that it would be great fun to be with you when you learn to run your machine. Claribel and I were with Mr. Turner the first time he ran his machine but were pretty near scared to death.

Think when you come this summer I will have to try and lose you again but I will be sure I know where I am first and not do like last summer. I have never said anything to Mr. Turner about it, think I will some day.

Sincerely,

Hildred

P.S. Mr. Turner has the Grippe and it has settled in his back. He has not been at all well the last few days but better again today.

◆

Postmark: 2:30 p.m. April 7, 1914, Detroit, Mich.

Addressed to: Mr. Chas. W. Turner [back flap missing]

April 6th/14.

Dear Hildred, -

Pleased to receive your favor of the 3rd. I am going to give you some figures, as I know you are interested in my business..

Results for month of March   {Charged $243.00
                                                {took in cash $130.00

This ought to be a good month for collections, I sent out statements this month amounting to $127.00, my people are all good. Now I will give you comparative results so far this month –

Nov – 1 to 6th - $8.50
Dec – 1 - 6th $12.00
Jany – 1 - 6th - $20.00
Feb – 1 – 6th - $24.00
Mar – 1 – 6th - $17.00
Apr – 1 – 6th -$65.00
              Up to 7 p.m.

May say that it seems as though as a rule my business starts off a little slow at the beginning of the month, then increases toward the end of the month.

I guess your little payer [sic] helped me out immensely, for my business certainly did spruce up.

I am anxious for you to take some of my pills because I know they will do you good. I am inclosing [sic] you a ppt. which you had better give Mr. Turner the next time he has the La Grippe, you save it and see that he gets it filled when he needs it. [Ed. Note – the prescription remains paper clipped to the letter]

You had better not work too hard because if you do you will get old quicker, I think possibly you are staying up sewing when you should be in bed. You ought to make a rule to go to bed at 10 o'clock every night, then you will never get sick.

I think when you collect the money for the rug you will hate to spend it, what you said about your coat and the $25.00 amused me. I am glad you described it to me. I imagine that it looks real pretty. You will have to buy a new hat now to wear with it.

If I have my machine when you come, I will give you the fastest possible ride to be sure you had better take out an accident policy.

Kindly give the inclosed [sic] envelope to Mr. Turner. [Ed. Note: no envelope was found]

Sincerely,

Chas.

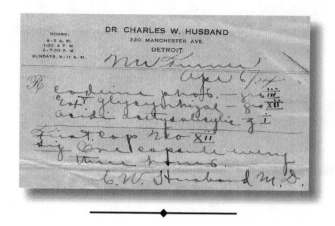

Postmark: 3 p.m. April 10, 1914, St. Paul, Minn.

St. Paul, Minn.

April 10, 1914

Dear Friend:

You cannot imagine how glad I was to receive your March figures. You are certainly doing wonderful for a beginner and Mr. Turner is mighty proud of you too. I can't understand how you get so many patients and do so much business. Your figures from April 1st to 6th are more than double of any previous month covering the same period. I can hardly wait until the end of the month to see what happens because if your business increases toward the end of the month as you say, April will sure be a record breaker.

Don't think I am working too hard for really I am not. Of course the practicing has meant quite late hours the last few weeks account of the wedding and Easter but that is just about over with, tonight last night to practice and tomorrow night the wedding. I am anxious for the time to come as I imagine it will be quite a swell affair.

Mr. Turner just about over the La Grippe now but I have told him next time he has an attack I am going to have the prescription filled. Thank you for sending it.

I got a new hat the other day but they cost so much all ready trimmed that I bought a shape and trimmed it myself, last night. I have got some ribbon on it just about the shade of my coat, also one big flower the same color. Don't know as this interests you though very much.

A week from Sunday if it is nice, a bunch of we girls are going out taking pictures and if they turn out good, may send you some. It is getting nice and warm now so we are planning long "hikes" for Sunday afternoons.

I told Mr. Turner about the fast automobile ride you had promised me if I go to Detroit and you should have heard him talk against it. He knows my failing (fast automobiling) and *he certainly warned me against it. I have only had one <u>real</u> fast automobile ride and that was about a year ago when Sidney Lankester took me home from the office one evening. We went so fast that I had to hang on so I would not fly out because you know how bumpy Summit Ave. is. That surely was great fun but of course as Mr. Turner says, if a wheel had came [sic] off, I wouldn't be here to tell the story.*

Mr. Turner says to ask you how Katherine is? I asked him Katherine who? but he would not say, said she was a friend of yours and to ask you. Who is it?

Am waiting real anxiously for the end of April to hear how things are turning out.

Sincerely,
Hildred

P.S. Have delivered the little envelope to Mr. Turner

———————◆———————

Postmark: 5:30 p.m. April 11, 1914, St. Paul, Minn.

St. Paul, Minn.

April 11, 1914

Dear Friend:

I want to thank you ever so much for the lovely Easter gift you gave me, through the kindness of Mr. Turner. It was certainly very nice of you to remember me and I appreciate it very much. It is a lovely box of Mrs. Gregory's chocolates, the best made in St. Paul, and they taste simply delicious. Only wish you were here to help enjoy them, am sure they would taste still better if you would help enjoy them as I know candy is your long suit.

Thank you again, very very much.

Sincerely,

Hildred

*P.S. I have found out who Katherine is, think it real mean of Mr. Turner to tease me that way but he sure had me guessing for a while. [**Editor's Note:** Katherine is Charles' sister-in-law.]*

Happy Easter!

H.L.C.

———————◆———————

Postmark: 1:30 p.m. April 14, 1914, Detroit, Mich.

Addressed to Mr. Turner; no envelope flap

April 13th/14.

Dear Hildred, -

Pleased to receive your letter of the 10th & 11th Inst. More pleased still to note, what you had to say in regard to my business, a little encouragement does me a world of good.

Sunday (Yesterday) was a little slower than usual only made $5.50, today is a great deal better so far, have gotten three new office patients so far today.

Always glad to hear in regard to your hat, coat, etc. by the way month after next I will be able to see them. I am getting anxious for the time to come. I ordered a new suit today a sample of which I am enclosing to you.

I am going to tell Mr. Turner he must not tease you, as in regard to Katharine, my Brother's Wife. She comes to Detroit from Duluth every Summer for a visit with us. I took her to church last night the preacher got through his sermon about a dozen times and started again. He finally got on our nerves. I like them to preach quick and let us out.

I wish you would send me some of the pictures you are going to take next Sunday. It does not matter whether they are good or no, send them anyway.

Thank you for delivering the little envelope to Mr. Turner, glad you enjoyed the chocolates.

Now in regard to this month's business, do not let me deceive you. I admit that it is far ahead of all other months but I do not know any more about the rest of the month than you do. However, my hopes remain high. I have averaged about $12.00 a day so far, that is including Sunday etc.

I am stalling off in regard to the machine as long as possible, I rather hate to spend so much money. I may wait until after I get back from St. Paul.

Are you still making your little daily deposit, you must have quite a bit saved by this time.

Best Regards,

Chas.

Postmark: 5:30 p.m. April 16, 1914, St. Paul, Minn.

St. Paul, Minn.

April 16, 1914

Dear Friend:

Was glad to hear from you and to know you have done so nicely this month. By the way things look, April will be still better than March. There is only one thing I am afraid of, you will be making so much money when June comes, that you will hate to leave Detroit and come to St. Paul but don't let that happen.

As to my daily deposit, you are right, it is growing quite fast. I now have $20.80 in the safe and Saturday, 70-cents more is added. I usually put in 70-cents every Saturday, because then I am sure not to spend it. Thanks to that little stamp you put on my desk. It is still there to remind me.

I must say I think I will like your suit very much. It certainly is beautiful material and again, I am very partial to blue. If it looks as good on you as your grey suit did last year it certainly will be fine because I admired that very much.

I don't know just yet whether we will take pictures Sunday or not, all depends on the folks. I think they have something planned for Sunday and if they have of course we will have to postpone our little trip until some other time but just as soon as we have them taken, will forward the good ones to you.

Expect two of my girl friends from Ashland in about two weeks. They are going out West to live and if they can they are going to stop over and visit with me for a day or two.

Claribel hasn't been very well lately, now that it is getting warm it doesn't seem to agree with her. Grandma Cress wants her to come and visit with her this summer to get rested up and I think she is going some time in June. I think it will be the best thing for her because she hasn't been herself since her operation.

Good luck to you for April.

Sincerely,
Hildred

———————◆———————

Postmark: 12 p.m. April 13, 1914, Detroit, Mich.

[**Editor's Note:** This postmark appears to be in error; likely, the letter was placed in this envelope in error by a later reader]

Addressed to Mr. Turner; flap not attached

Apr 18th/14.

Dear Hildred, -

Pleased to receive your letter. In regard to St. Paul I am certainly going and as I said before can hardly wait until the time comes, I plan on leaving here Saturday June the 6th arriving in St. Paul around 10 a.m. Sunday June 7th. Will you be down to meet me. Now if you would rather have me come at a little different time let me know and I will make other arrangements. I am going to send notices to all my patients to the effect that I will be out of the city from June 6 to 15th. Now when I say I am going to be there you can depend on it.

June as a rule is one of the slack months for a Doctor, there by leaving on the sixth I will have ample time to get my statements out. By the way Hildred I feel younger than I ever did and I would like you to be ready for a race on foot with me, you know that I have had some good stout practice the last few months, I think we better run a mile instead of one hundred yards, in regard to a machine I think I will get a touring car instead of a roadster, I really could or can afford to buy a car now but I am trying to hold off as long as possible, I am saving all the money I can to pay for it, and have half the price of a touring car now saved, then again if I had a touring car I could take out some friends if I wanted to, or cart a patient to the hospital what do you think about it.

My business by tonight will have ammounted [sic] to, that is as I see it now 3:30 p.m. to about – charged $200.00 took in $133.00 that is so far this month. Now I would like to run it up to about $300.00 this month, when I get making about $2,000 a month I think I will be satisfied.

I am inclosing [sic] to you a card, which speaks for itself, I am intending to send a copy to all my patients have you any suggestions in the way of improving it to offer.

Do not forget to be at the Depot seven weeks from tomorrow a.m., about 10 o'clock if the train is on time.

Sorry to hear about illness of Claribel. You will have to send her down this way.

Sincerely,

Chas.

Enclosure: Card announcing the opening of Dr. Husband's office –
(over) written in by hand – back of card reads: Dr. C.W. Husband 320
Northwestern Ave. Detroit announces that he will be absent from the city
from June 6th to 15th/14. inclusive.

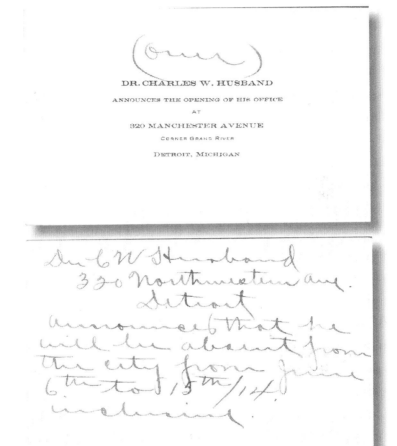

Postmark: 8 p.m. April 21, 1914, St. Paul, Minn.

St. Paul, Minn.

April 21, 1914

Dear Friend:

You don't know how glad I am to know you are coming to St. Paul and will arrive in the city June 7th. The time is perfectly satisfactory to me, any time it is most convenient for you to leave your practice as that is most important.

As to my coming to the depot to meet you, the machine doesn't breakdown, car run off the track or something else happens, I will surely be there and on time. Just think, it is not seven weeks any more.

*As to the card you enclose, I think that is a splendid idea but don't you think it better to have the street address in the lower left-hand corner, something as per enclosed. [**Editor's Note:** No enclosure found] Of course where ever you have them printed, they are able to show you so many new ideas, that I think it would be advisable to look over some of the cards they have printed. Yesterday, while talking with the lady in the Stationary Dept. at Fields, she said most Doctors just have a card sent out when they return but I don't think that is the best plan. This way you announce when you leave, also return and it sometimes saves patients a long trip to your office only to find you out of the city.*

You certainly are to be congratulated on the good work you are doing, it is simply great. Each month that your final statement comes in, I think you surely can't beat the record next month, and sure enough if you don't but it is always a pleasant surprise.

As to your machine, if as you say, you think you can afford it, I would surely say get a touring car as I think you would find it a great deal more handy than a roadster account of patients etc.

Yesterday afternoon my friend Margret and Evelyn were in the city. They are from Ashland. They left last night 10:30 for Tacoma. Of course only being here for such a short time they went to their cousins for dinner. They have a dandy big machine and their three cousins and the two girls called for me about eight o'clock and we were out riding until train time. Only stopped once and that was at Smith's to get some ice cream. We certainly had the grandest kind of a time and we were only sorry that they couldn't stop over a little longer.

Don't forget June 7th!

Sincerely,
Hildred

P.S. Mr. Turner suggests having your telephone number put in the lower right hand corner. What do you think. Of course, these are only suggestions maybe they would not suit. H.L.C.

———————◆———————

Postmark: 8:30 p.m. April 23, 1914, Detroit, Mich.

Addressed to Mr. Turner, black dot on back of envelope

Apr 23rd/14

Dear Hildred, -

Pleased to receive your letter glad to hear from you. I guess we have the St. Paul question settled, In regard to the notices, I thank you for suggestions made I think they are good.

By the way you write I take it that you stay up pretty late nights, kindly let me suggest, that nothing makes people get old faster than keeping late hours. Mr. Turner goes to bed about 9 p.m., he holds his age well and another thing it will make you nervous.

I have some pretty sick children under my care just at present, one of them is just hovering between life & death it certainly keeps me guessing to keep their heads above water.

My results up until last night Apr 22/14 have been

Charged	$230.00
Took in	$170.75

so I guess I am going to run ahead of last month, I wish I could raise the $230.00 up to $300, and the other up to $200.00.

I am supposed to get my new suit today the next thing will be a new hat. Do they wear straw hats in St. Paul in the month of June. I am going to try and hold out in regard to a machine until after I get back from St. Paul.

Sincerely,
Chas.

———————◆———————

Postmark: 6 p.m. April 25, 1914, St. Paul, Minn.

St. Paul, Minn.

April 25, 1914

Dear Friend:

Was very pleased to hear from you and imagine my surprise on my return from lunch when I opened the drawer of my desk to put my purse and gloves away, I found a very very lovely box of candy with your note on as sent to Mr. Turner who had made the purchase while out to lunch. Now friend Charlie, I really don't know how to thank you I appreciate it very much and certainly will enjoy every piece of it but don't you think you will spoil me? I have a very sweet tooth as it is and as Mr. Turner says you make it more desirous for candy therefore would kindly ask that you do not buy any more until you come to St. Paul and then will let you buy another box. Please do not think me ungrateful because I truly enjoy it very much but you as a physician should know I am right.

I am awfully glad to hear you are doing so splendidly but do hope those children recover because I imagine it would mean so much to you. If they should not get better do not worry over it because you know you done [sic] all you possibly could for them and those things are to be expected.

Mr. Turner got his machine the other day and it seems quite a treat to have a ride again in preference to the old street car.

Claribel and I went to the dentist the other day, haven't been there for two years and I imagined I would have to have a lot of work done. Claribel has eleven cavities but he said he guessed I done [sic] him out of a job, didn't have one. Maybe I wasn't happy. Of course I had to have them cleaned but that is all.

Surely the men wear straw hats here in June. You will be right in style if you have one the first of June. I would like to see you in that new suit of yours but I will have patience and see it in June. Thank you again for that candy, very fine but hope you have not taken any offence at my remarks,

Sincerely,

Hildred

———————◆———————

Postmark: 12:30 a.m. April 28, 1914, Detroit, Mich.

Addressed to Mr. Turner; flap is missing

Apr 27th, 1914

Dear Hildred, -

Pleased to receive you letter, glad to hear from you. Just got through unpacking a new supply of drugs. I do mostly all my own dispensing it takes more time and means a little more work, but I make more money by doing it; if you write a prescription they go to the drug store repeatedly and get it refilled otherwise they half [sic] to come back and see me and also pay me.

Now in regard to the candy, glad to hear that you enjoyed it. I surely appreciate your remarks in regard to it immensely, but feel as though I am doing or buying a quarter as much for you as I ought to, I know too much candy is not good for your teeth, stomach or general health, but what am I going to do, I am not there to take you any place, and to buy you a box of candy seems about the only thing I can do, and as I said before I take more pleasure out of giving it to you than you do by eating it. May be you think I need the money, while I can use all the money I have to good advantage at the same time I am making good money, this month so far I have made $295.00 and taken in $198.00. May say that $275.00 is half of $550.00 which is the price I will be paying for a Ford five passenger touring car. Of course I am going to put about $200.00 more into a garage. Then again I am always adding a little to improve the house and my offices, in two or three months more I hope to be able to get down to business and see what I can do to that $2,000. Note I expect May & June and possibly July to be rather quiet months, and Aug & Sept. to be good months, I guess I have wandered away from the candy questions, now just let me send you one more box before I go and we will call it square.

Forty more days and I leave for St. Paul. Now be sure and get lots of sleep because I am as you know a rooster, then again there is that race.

Sincerely,
Chas.

Postmark: 5 p.m. April 30, 1914, St. Paul, Minn.

Thursday

Dear Friend:

Last night I really took some advice and went to bed early. I was good and tired and right after dinner Claribel and I got busy with the dishes and I was in bed by 8 P.M. and asleep by 8:15. I certainly had a good nights rest and would feel fine only I have quite a sore throat but not near as bad this afternoon as it was this morning. I think the week before you come to St. Paul, I will go to bed 8 p.m. every night so you can't say I look as though I needed some sleep, also so I will be ready for that race. I think I shall have to do some practicing because I am pretty near out of practice.

As to the candy: Don't think for one minute that I do not appreciate it, because I most certainly do; and as to your thinking that you don't do enough for me, I don't see how anybody could think that because you know you are a long way from St. Paul and again if it were not for Mr. Turner's kindness in purchasing it for you here, I could not even expect the candy because you would be too far away to send it, so please do not think that you are not doing enough for me, because you really are. Don't you think you better wait until you come to St. Paul to get the next box and then we can enjoy it together because I think you are about as fond of candy as I am.

I am anxious to see your final statement for this month because you are already away ahead of last month.

A week from tomorrow night, one of the gentlemen from our church and his wife are going to give the choir a banquet. That sounds awfully good to me and I am hungry already. There certainly is a dandy crowd of young people in the choir and in our S.S. class and we have some mighty fine times. Mr. Turner is in Duluth today; expect him home tomorrow morning. Mrs. Turner is visiting in Leavenworth, Kans.

Kindest regards,
Hildred

MAY 1914

Newspaper Headlines

Detroit Free Press

- Jury says tent town fire set by militia men [**Editor's Note:** The Ludlow Massacre was an attack by the Colorado National Guard and Colorado Fuel & Iron Company camp guards on a tent colony of 1,200 striking coal miners and their families at Ludlow, Colo. April 20, 1914.When workers at Colorado mine went on strike, company guards fired machine guns and killed several men. More battling followed, during which two women and 11 children were killed. John D. Rockefeller Jr., the chief mine owner, was pilloried for what happened. Source: Wikipedia]

- Wayne County is proud of 150 miles of good roads

- Popular bathing refrain this summer will doubtless be: "But don't go near the water!" [swimming costumes were made of delicate material]

- Shocks from Mt. Etna kill many in Italy

- Famous surgeons will hold annual clinic in Detroit

- Railroads attack Anti-Trust bills

- Weight loss in jungle but strenuous still [Theodore Roosevelt]

- Billion dollar loans and protectorate in Mexican peace plan

- Mercury hits 96 while Detroiters hunt cool spots
- 50 firemen overcome by billows of dense smoke in big Union depot fire; Ladder Co. 2 House transformed into temporary hospital – others taken to St. Mary's
- 954 perish as Empress of Ireland is sunk; 61 Detroit passengers reported victims
  - Liner vanishes 14 minutes after crash; 433 saved – crowds besiege Detroit offices in quest of news
- Karluk crew, ship crushed, is marooned (steam whaler off the Siberian coast)
- Plan for new tunnel under Detroit River
- Carranza assumes Mexico presidency; forestalls envoy

St. Paul Pioneer Press

- Violence to young John D. (Rockefeller, Jr.) threatened
- Railroad travel is cheaper today
- White Bear Yacht Club formal opening today (Saturday, May 2, 1914)
- Urged by his own supporters, Huerto expected to quit
- St. Paul is "movie" mad, managers say
- The commercial possibilities in land of naked men (Philippines)
- Wilson completes new Bank Board
- White House busy for wedding today; (daughter Eleanor Wilson) marries Wm. Gibbs M'Adoo, Treasury Secretary
- Collection of war news is carefully regulated
- Fuller skirts for women
- Flowers and letters home mark Mother's Day
- Calls for fund of $20,000 to finance St. Paul Orchestra
- Women kneel in prayer – now skirts won't let them
- Take heart – lilacs bloom this week
- Envoys plan elimination of Huerta, giving rebels hand in running Mexico
- Negro rewards kindness – Mill City high school teacher is left big sum by former slave
- Prospects for fall elections worry Wilson
- Rivers of diamonds and free gold tales of Roosevelt Party (Brazil)

- Drinks beer; falls 90 feet (fatal accident)
- Increased pay for college teachers; gain from $80 to $350 in five years
- New comet is observed
- Americans second in divorce court – report says only Japan higher in broken homes; propose stricter laws
- Mayo (Clinic) attends Czarevitch; Rochester surgeon in St. Petersburg said to have been summoned by royal family
- Ate Peyote and saw God and the devil Indian testifies in trial of man accused of selling drug
- America leads in number of autos
- Latest disaster unlike Titanic's spectacular end – no ship's band to play near St. Lawrence River

MAY 1914

◆

LETTERS

Postmark: 12 p.m. May 2, 1914, Detroit, Mich.

Addressed to Charles W. Turner; envelope flap missing

May 2, 1914

Dear Hildred –

Received your letter of the 30th. Note that you are keeping better hours by the way I have been feeling pretty tired the last few days. I ought to have a machine right away, if business keeps up I'll soon half [sic] to do something, everybody tells me how thin I am getting, I feel good, but walking so much keeps me in weight. I not only got to buy a car but to build a garage, and I am waiting until I get the where with.

Comparative business

April 1 – made $14.00 –	May 1 made $24.25
April 2 - $8.75-	May 2 $16.75
	Day not over 5 p.m.

May as you see is starting in all O.K. What the remainder of the month will bring forth I know not but my hopes are in the right place of course. Doctors figure on May and June as being rather slow but here's hoping.

I presume you have made the guess in regard to the last letter so I will quote to you last month's business.

Charged up $336.00 which is the money I made last month, collected or took in. $215.00 remainder outstanding but all good do you understand me.

I am enclosing you a ppt. which is good for sore throat, I trust it will be better by this time.

Am going to get my vacation notices printed in a few days. The time is getting pretty close.

I am wondering who is going to win that box of candy.

Sincerely,

Charles

(How do you think my business will be this month.   C.W.H.)

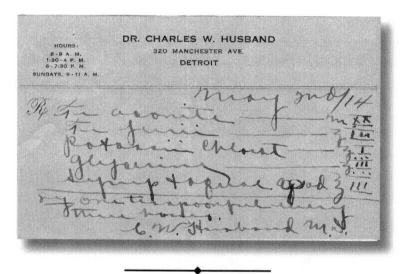

Postmark: 6 p.m. May 2, 1914, St. Paul, Minn.

St. Paul, Minn.

May 2, 1914

Dear Friend:

I want to thank you very much for the box of candy, even though it did come to me indirect. You certainly are pretty foxy to send it that way. At first I wanted Mr. Turner to take it anyway but he wouldn't think of it, said you knew he never ate candy, etc. and knew you meant it for me. It certainly was foxy and no wonder you make so much money, when you can think of so many stunts every day. You asked before if you could buy one more box before coming to St. Paul so this is the one and if you send any more you are disobeying orders so be good.

As to guessing how much you made in April, my guess is just to the "Charge" Column not on the "Take In" Column at all. You certainly are doing fine and I suppose you have a surprise for us or you would not have us guessing as to the result.

Thank you again, very very much for the candy and I will surely enjoy it.

Kindest regards,

Sincerely,

Hildred

Postmark 6 p.m. May 2, 1914, St. Paul Minn.

Typed

St. Paul, Minn.

May 4, 1914

Dear Friend: -

Will you pardon me for writing on the machine? I am very busy today and it takes so much longer to write in longhand, thought you would not mind a typewritten letter for a change.

Was very glad to hear from you but awfully sorry to hear you are getting thin. That is very very bad and I think you deserve more scolding than I get because even if I do stay up rather late nights at the same time I hold my weight and am not getting thin. If you are so busy that you need a machine, why not get it before you come to St. Paul. You know you can't afford to get all run down simply because you have not got all the necessary money to pay spot cash. I suppose you figure if you have the cash you will get a discount which would be very good but at the same time if you are going to get thin chasing around to your different customers, you should get a machine right away.

I was telling Mr. Turner about this and guess I got quite excited and he said if you needed your machine now, you should not hesitate but let him know and he would gladly send you the required money. Now if you need your machine, be sure and let him know because I know he would be only to glad to loan you the money and it would be so much better than holding off until you get enough enough [sic] of your own to pay cash. Don't you think Mr. Turner and I are about right? Of course I will not be able to give anything towards the check but my good will, wish I had more but maybe that will help some. Now don't you get thin, eat more, stop worrying, and don't walk so much or do something to prevent getting thin.

As to April business, you certainly done fine. Don't you think I made a pretty good guess because I really didn't know what I was guessing about, Mr. Turner got me all mixed up. He figures that part of your months profit is in the "Take In" column, that is "Charge" plus part of the "Take In". Who is right? I think by your letter today that I am right. But the way you are starting out, May will be a record breaker.

Thank you very much for the prescription you sent but I do not need it just now but will surely use it if I get a sore throat again. I had quite a cold for a day or two but it is much better, Mr. Turner made me take "White Pine Cough Syrup" and put some kind of a plaster on my chest at night. I told him I think he should have been a Doctor, he is so good and giving medicine etc.

Yesterday – Sunday – Mr. Turner took us out for a drive and the roads were simply terrible, pretty near turned turtle in the mud once or twice but enjoyed it just the same. Mr. Turner was over to our house for supper, also to spend the evening.

Mr. Turner is waiting for me to get through, time to go home so will have to cut this letter short. Now remember, we think you should get that automobile and also that you should get it right away so don't be bashful, if you need the money let Mr. Turner know and he will gladly send it.

Kindest regards, and GET FAT not THIN!!

Sincerely,

Hildred.

Postmark 12 p.m. May 5, 1914, Detroit, Mich.

May 5, 1914

Dear Hildred, -

You are a pretty good guesser, why didn't you add $1.00 more on to your guess, may be I'll give you another chance this month, what do you think about it or don't you like to guess about these things. Business is good so far, am sending out my monthly statements today, could not get at them before.

Glad you enjoyed the candy, supposing I take a notion to send some more, all you can do about it is to eat it and injoy [sic] it. In a hurry to catch the mail collection.

Sincerely,

Chas.

———————◆———————

Postmark: 12:30 p.m. May 7, 1914 - Detroit, Mich.

Addressed to Mr. Turner; dot on envelope flap - Note in upper right-hand corner:
(Will write to Mr. Tuner Tomorrow curt.)

May 5th/14

Dear Hildred, -

Received your letter, I surely appreciate your remarks regarding the machine. It is
certainly kind of you to think of these things.

As to me getting thin I rather hate to talk about it, but at the same time, I never felt
better in all my life, you write in regard to me eating if you had to see my food bill or
grocery bill you would think I eat of quantity sufficient.

In regard to business as compared to my first month, last month and present month
up to the 6th,

	Charged	Took in
To 6 Nov.	$6.16	$2.00
" " April	$66.25	$40.50
" " May	$122.00	$89.00

Of course I am expecting business to let up a little most any time as it always does
according to other Doctors at this time of year, but it seems to be increasing with me
how long it will last I do not know.

Yesterday I certainly needed a machine, I was busy in my office when a call came
in to go out one mile father than we live on the car line, then go one mile back in
the country and take care of an accident case, a man had fallen from a building. I
finished in the office, another call came in, and I knew of some people coming to
see me in a very short time, I made the call out in the country, sewed up a lacerated
wound in a man's face, and was back to the office in one hour. I run from the end
of the car line all the way to the house and run back again to the car, how is that for
going and had to wait about 10 minutes in all for a street car.

I almost feel tempted to do as you say borrow the money. I have a little over $300.00
saved myself and all by accounts paid for this month, then there is a garage to build,
and my trip to St. Paul to think of. I expect to take in about $300 this month. I
could store my machine in a garage near here for $10.00 a month. I have got to do
something pretty soon that is sure but I always like to do these things on my own
resources. The interest however would not mean much to me.

Sincerely,
Chas.

———————◆———————

Postmark: 7:30 p.m. May 8, 1914, St. Paul, Minn.

May 8, 1914

Dear Friend:

Awfully glad to hear from you and your letters contain good news, that is to business. You certainly are going ahead every month and so far it doesn't look as though May, June and July would be slack months for you.

As to guessing what your results will be, why no, I don't mind it at all, in fact like to providing I can guess anywhere near right.

Now, after quoting the little incident which happened the other day, I really think you should get a machine. If you would have had one then, you could have made the trip in just about half the time, easily, and besides not hurry as much as you did and possibly lose a pound or two. You know you can't afford to do that. Mr. Turner will gladly give you the money necessary for the purchase. I know that positively. Of course I know you would like to wait until you personally had the money but maybe it would pay you to get it now because you would save so much time on all of your trips, especially those long ones and then you could put more time in your office. What do you think?

Mr. Turner is in Duluth today but expect him in the morning. Tuesday morning the "America" went on the rocks at Burlington Point (near Two Harbors) in a very heavy fog so of course Mr. Turner left for Duluth that evening. They sent the SS "Easton" also two tugs up to pull her off but they had to call for another tug because the boat was on good and hard, amidship. She was leaning pretty bad and they did not get to Duluth until late Thursday. That surely will be expensive because besides paying for tugs etc. she has to go to the dry dock.

By rights, I ought to go to bed early tonight because there is just loads of work tomorrow but tonight is the banquet and of course I can't miss that. One of the girls just called up and asked me if I was hungry and of course I always am that.

Kindest regards,

Sincerely,

Hildred

Postmark: May 12, 1914, Detroit, Mich.

Addressed to Mr. Turner - dot on envelope flap

[**Editor's Note:** Letterhead changes from 320 Manchester Ave, Detroit to 320 Northwestern Ave. Detroit]

May 11th/14

Dear Hildred, -

Pleased to hear from you, in the first place would be pleased to know if you note any difference, between my letter of today and others previously sent, if you do not notice anything different let me know and I will tell you.

This afternoon it is raining and I took the opportunity to address envelopes to certain parties which will contain the notices of my absence from the city about three weeks and I will be a la route, and remember Young Lady if you look sleepy and all tired out, I'll strap all your movable joints together to keep you quiet, further more I am a rooster and have had good practice all winter, therefore store up strength, get a hump on your back, I may be a little on the lean side, but I could not feel better, a week goes fast and we have got to make good use of it while it lasts. May be I'll get a little excited if so will you dance a jig with me. I always like to know these things in advance.

Business is still keeping up pretty well so far this month as follows

10 days – May 1-10 –
Charged up $182.25 – {Made on average $18 a day
Took in $221.75 – {Better than any full month so far. Average only $22.17

At this rate I do not think I would notice the expense of running a car very much furthermore, if I do not get a car before long I will be losing business by it if business increases all the time and I don't see why it will not, some day I hope to make $2000, to 3000 a month. After I get everything paid for I am going to work real estate on the side.

As soon as I hear from Mr. Turner, I will make up my mind definitely in regard to a car.

Now go to bed early nights, may say that I am very much interested in you and do not want to see you looking all tired out on Sunday A.M. June 7th/14.

Sincerely,
Chas.
(P.S. Let me know what you think in regard to these things. (C.W.H.)

———————◆———————

Postmark: 9 a.m. May 15, 1914, St. Paul, Minn.

St. Paul, Minn.

May 14, 1914

Dear Friend:

I should say I did notice something different in your last letter, somebody has bought some new stationary. Did I notice the difference or not? I did not know what it could be at first but after looking at your letter a second time I saw "Northwestern Ave., right away.

You seem to be feeling pretty good by the way you write and I surely will have to rest if I want to keep up to you when you come. Today I am home nursing a cold. Mr. Turner left last night for Leavenworth to meet Mrs. Turner, expects to be back Sunday morning so told me to stay at home and doctor up. I don't know if papa will let me go down to the office tomorrow or not. I have been doping up all week with pills, hot lemonades, hot mustard foot baths, plasters and almost everything imaginable. It is quite a bit looser today so suppose I will feel O.K. in a day or so. I want to be over it by the time you come or perhaps I would be in line for a good scolding.

As to your business, don't know as I can say anything more than what I have said, that it is just "great" and I hope it keeps getting better right along.

As to your car, I will be glad when you get it because it will save you so much time also those terrible tramps that you have to take across the country. Don't figure on learning how to run a car from me, because when you go driving with me you will have to take out an additional life and accident insurance policy. I am all right when somebody is there to tell me to "change to second" "change to third" etc. but as far as running it and giving you lessons I should say not.

There is one thing I would like to ask you. Mr. Turner and I were talking about it yesterday. Do you tell any other doctors what your income is, that is how good business is and if so do you think it a wise plan?

Of course, maybe I shouldn't ask you this but Mr. Turner told me to. We were thinking if you tell others, they may want to move into your neighborhood and that would make competition so much keener.

As to the jig, surely I will jig with you, that is providing it is not one of the new fangled jigs.

Guess I will hop to bed now as everybody else is sleeping tight with the exception of daddy.

Sincerely,
Hildred

———————◆———————

Postmark: 12 p.m. May 16, 1914, Detroit, Mich.

Addressed to Mr. Turner; dot on envelope flap

May 16th/14

Dear Hildred, -

Sorry to hear that you are sick, I trust that you have received the box of tablets that I sent. I feel sure they will do you good, better keep me posted as to how you get along. You better take good care of your self, try to avoid taking more cold. I thought probably that you were over doing things a little and would get sick. May be I will need to bring my medicine case along. Three weeks from tonight, or this a.m. finds me I trust on my way.

You are right in regard to the stationary. I give you credit for being very observing, I also have been observing, as for instance in regard to you making the letter D. On time make it like this – D. [**Editor's Note:** a short top flourish) and again like – D (note – a long top flourish ending below the letter]

Business is slightly slower today, but not too bad at that, in regard to the machine, am going to try to hold off until after I get back from St. Paul but I am sure going to get it then.

I make it a point not to tell other Doctors in regard to my income. When they ask me how I am doing, I tell them that I can not complain, of course I would not say that I was not doing anything, and I do not think my answer means so very much to them (Thank you for the suggestion).

Sincerely,

Chas.

———————◆———————

Postmark: 7:30 p.m. May 18, 1914, St. Paul, Minn.

St. Paul, Minn.

May 18, 1914

Dear Friend:

Received the tablets yesterday morning and really, thank you very much. I guess usually I am not very grateful for medicine given me because I don't like to take it but this time I really am thankful because I believe it has helped me at least I feel a great deal better today but am still taking them regularly. I think Mr. Turner must think I am getting to be a regular grouch because I know I have been awfully cranky the past week or two but I lay that to my cold and am going to try and be better natured hereafter. Don't you bring that medicine case of yours with you because if I see you first and you have the case with you, don't think you could ever catch me, I would run so fast.

Tomorrow night, providing it is warm and my cold is better, I am going to a roast down at the river. Our Sunday School class is going to take their supper, leave about six and get back early. I hope I can go because I think it great fun to go to a roast.

I notice there is a letter here for Mr. Turner from you. He is in Chicago today and said if things were such that he could get away he no doubt would go on to Detroit so possibly he is with you by this time.

Well, it is time to take another pill, 4:45 P.M. so better get busy. Thanks again for sending them.

Sincerely,

Hildred

———————◆———————

Postmark: 8:30 p.m. May 20, 1914, Detroit, Mich.

Addressed to Mr. Turner; dot on envelope flap

May 20th/14.

Dear Hildred, -

Pleased to hear from you, glad to know you are getting better, also to know that you are taking your tablets regularly. I know they will do you good but be careful not to take any more cold. You simply will have to take better care of yourself in the future lest St. Peter, will have some dealings with you.

In regard to that grouchy feeling you speak of, if it still persists, let me know and may be I can send a remedy for that. May say that while I am great for giving other people medicine I never take any myself, I never take time.

I am still sticking to business, up until last night the 19th I have made and taken in as follows:

Taken in -	$282.50
Made -	$280.50

so you see if I make about $60.00 more this month this will be my best month all the way around. I have already taken in more money than any month previous. Before I leave here expect to have enough money saved to pay cash for my machine and also enough to cover my trip. Of course I got to build a garage & pay taxes before long which will amount to about $80.00 (spring taxes).

Katherine and the baby are going back to St. Paul with me and my brother Leonard is going to meet her there. They will stay in St. Paul until Monday and then go back to Duluth.

You better tell your Daddy that you are going to be busy all the week of the 7th. Think you won't be scolded for being away from home so much in such a short time. However you know how to fix it up better than I do. Mr. Turner said he would give you a week's vacation.

Now don't forget to keep me posted in regard to your cold.

Sincerely,

Chas.

◆

Postmark: 7:30 p.m. May 21, St. Paul, Minn.

Thursday

Dear Friend:

Mr. Turner arrived here this morning and with him he brought a box of candy which he says is from you. Thank you ever so much for remembering me. Mr. Turner bought the candy from Kranz in Chicago and it surely is delicious.

Mr. Turner thinks it is pretty good too and every once in a while he says "Long time between drinks" and of course I know what that means. It surely is fine though wish you could have some of it and thank you ever so much.

My cold is about what you might say well and I must say those pills were fine because I guess I tried everything else under the sun without helping. Papa had a touch of a cold so I gave him some of the pills and they fixed him up in no time. He thinks they are the best he has ever taken. Sure as fate if I get another cold I will take one of those pills and nobody will have to tell me to take it either.

Two weeks from Sunday will see you in St. Paul but don't bring your medicine case along that is to use on me.

Sincerely,

Hildred

———————◆———————

Postmark: 12 p.m. May 23, 1914, Detroit, Mich.

Addressed to Mr. Turner; envelope flap missing

May 23/14

Dear Hildred, -

Received your letter very pleased to hear that your cold is getting better, glad to note that you enjoyed the box from Kranz.

Have something very important to tell you that is I have enough cash on hand to purchase a Ford touring car $550.00. Now don't you realize that I am going to get that long talked of car. Now I have got to make or take in enough money to build a garage and to meet my trip. I lost $8.00 this morning by not being able to get around in a hurray (sic.), so I do not think I can stand to go much farther without a car.

My results up to noon today for this month are as follows, -

| Made or charge - | $330.00 |
| Took in - | $316.00 |

I ought to be able to make $400.00 this month what do you think. But I suppose if I don't I ought to be partly satisfied at least.

You better take good care of yourself from this out, or I certainly will have some pills for you to take.

Sincerely,
Chas.

———————◆———————

Postmark: 7 p.m. May 23, 1914, St. Paul, Minn.

Dear Friend:

Real glad to hear from you and think I can now say my cold is all well although Mr. Turner says it is not. Last night Claribel and I started off for choir practice without any hats and when we got about half a block from the house, we met Mr. Turner. Suppose you know what happened — anyway when I got to church I had a hat on. Yes, and that grouchy feeling is gone to (sic.), so you don't need to send a cure for that.

It is certainly nice that your sister and the baby are coming to St. Paul with you, it will make the trip so much more pleasant to have company but you want to look out for the baby, because I might steal him.

Have been awfully busy since Mr. Turner got back. Don't know whether he told you or not but he is taking charge of six more branch houses in addition to what he has, namely Omaha, Kansas City, St. Louis, Denver, Lincoln and Salt Lake City. It surely means a lot of work and correspondence because he intends to change the management in pretty near all of the houses.

I told papa you were coming or expected to come on the seventh to stay a week so thought I would be going out quite a bit and asked if he objected. He said "not at all" so guess there won't be much said this time although I haven't said much at home.

Mr. Turner just came back so will have to get busy and take some more dictation.

Sincerely,
Hildred

———————◆———————

Postmark: 8:30 p.m. May 26, 1914, Detroit, Mich

Addressed to Mr. Turner; dot on envelope

May 26/14.

Dear Hildred,

Pleased to hear that your cold is better, maybe Mr. Turner saved you from getting another cold by seeing to it that you wear your hat also note that the grouchy feeling has worn away.

With the extra work Mr. Turner is taking over, no doubt a vacation will seem good to you. No doubt you will notice that my hand is none to steady today, had an operation at that, but it taxed my right hand just about to the limit, so much so that it feels a little unsteady at the present moment.

I almost roasted this morning it was so hot, how about it in those Northern Regions?

Business is going along nicely, am not going to give you any more satisfaction until the end of the month in regard to my earnings, so here's for another guess with the chance of winning a box of chocolates.

Tell Mr. Turner that I let the contract to build my garage last Sunday price $130.00 frame shingle roof, concrete floor size 10 x 15 ft. I plan on ordering my car for June 15th. You better come back with me and have a ride in it.

Sincerely,
Chas.

———————◆———————

Postmark: 11 a.m. May 26, 1914, St. Paul, Minn.

St. Paul, Minn.

May 26, 1914

Dear friend:

Glad to hear from you and to know your splendid results for this month. I should say, if you keep on the way you have started this month you will surely make $400.00 but if not you will at least beat last month and that is sure fine. I imagine somebody was provoked to lose $8.00 the other morning, and can't say I blame you either.

As to your machine, Mr. Turner thinks it would be a good idea for you to look over the "Saxon" car. It is made in Detroit, Mr. Turner says, by automobile men who are working for a reputation and I believe their selling price is $395.00 F.O.B. Detroit. I suppose this would be a runabout although Mr. Turner did not say. He spoke of seeing one on Summit Avenue Sunday and said it looked like a fine machine however as we expect to see you soon you can talk it over personally with him.

I am going to be what you might say a lady of leisure this week. Mr. Turner left last night for a week's business trip, Sioux City, Omaha, St Louis and Kansas City, expects to get home next Sunday morning but then it will mean get busy again.

Sincerely,

Hildred

———————◆———————

Postmark: 12 p.m. May 28, 1914, Detroit, Mich.

Addressed to Mr. Turner; dot on envelope

May 28th, 1914

Dear Hildred, -

Pleased to hear from you while you are not busy in the office. I am going to keep you busy reading and writing letters. You know you might get out of practice, which is a bad habit.

I have got quite a surprise for you, may say that I have surpassed my aim, but do not let me make you or lead you to guess to high, you better guess low, in other words go easy and be on the safe side.

By the way I have about all my notes ready to mail. Quite a stack of them, tonight I am going through my Ledger and make out some accounts.

Now in regard to a machine, as you know I have had my mind made up for some time to buy a Ford Touring car, However if I can see a better car, as for instance a Saxon car which would suit me better, I will sure change my mind, nearly everybody says that the Ford car is the best buy for the money. Will you kindly ask Mr. Turner whether or not I should notify the city (illegible) of the Ford before I leave so I could have prompt delivery when I return or wait until I arrive home.

Sincerely,

Chas.

———◆———

Postmark: 7 p.m. May 28, 1914, St. Paul, Minn.

Thursday afternoon

Dear Friend:

I can't imagine it any hotter in Detroit than it is here. It is simply terrible, especially after the cool weather we have been having right along. The mosquitos also, are getting far too lively to suit me. I guess I am too particular but I do hate those mosquitos. If you attempt to sit on the porch in the evening, it helps keep you busy killing mosquitos.

How near must I guess to your earnings this month? I will take the last figures you gave me and add about an average of $15.00 a day (my week's salary by the way) but maybe put in a little more account of the operation the other day and then do you think I would guess anywhere's near right? This is just a feeler so I will know about what to guess.

I should say I will enjoy that week's vacation. I will be all ready for good hard work after that as a result of the vacation. Too bad you won't have your machine, that is here in St. Paul. We could cover more ground. Think we will have to steal a Ford that week and then you will know how to run yours when you get home. Imagine that will be a nice garage you are going to get, will tell Mr. Turner as soon as he gets home. The man next door is going to build one, expects to start this week but don't know what kind he is going to build.

Sincerely,

Hildred

◆

Postmark: 9:30 p.m. May 30, 1914, Detroit, Mich.

May 30th/14

Dear Hildred, -

Since writing you last I have gotten a time table and planned out just what time we will arrive in St. Paul. We are going to leave Chicago Saturday night June 6th at 10 p.m. on the North Coast Ltd, which arrives in St. Paul at 10:30 a.m. the next day which will be Sunday morning.

In regard to mosquitos we do not have those treacherous little animals in Detroit, at least I never see any, so have them all killed by the time I arrive in St. Paul, as I know just about what their bite means.

In regard to my earnings this month, do not guess too high, as I have not been quite so busy the last two or three days. By the way I am running for Sec. Treas. of the Alumni Association of the Detroit College of Medicine, the election takes place next Wednesday but I do not figure on being elected as there are so many competitors.

I certainly will be glad when I get a (illegible) so I will not have to parade around in this hot weather.

Are you all better now.

Sincerely,

Chas.

JUNE 1914

---◆---

𝕹𝖊𝖜𝖘𝖕𝖆𝖕𝖊𝖗 𝕳𝖊𝖆𝖉𝖑𝖎𝖓𝖊𝖘

𝕯𝖊𝖙𝖗𝖔𝖎𝖙 𝕱𝖗𝖊𝖊 𝕻𝖗𝖊𝖘𝖘

- Hospital – City had expected still private (Detroit General Hospital, at Hamilton and West Grand Boulevard)
- Dodges resist income tax in second action
- Racing balloons feared wrecked in storm and fate of crews unknown
- Income tax will fall $21 million below estimate
- Appeal to force in Ulster seems almost certain
- Physician shows need of correct food for infants
- Beet sugar men see end of industry
- Austrian heir and his wife slain by student in capital of Bosnia
  - Death of Francis Ferdinand brings new Austrian heirs apparent
- Liner strikes rocks in fog off coast of Ireland
- Rebel split growing and mediation once more seems doomed (Mexico)

𝔖t. 𝔓aul 𝔓ioneer 𝔓ress

- Wilson would give increase to roads

- Inheritance taxes end at $1 million

- Over-study is cause of girl's downfall

- To build $46,000 harness factory

- Sounds a warning against cigarettes

- Put fire out with beer

- Bare heads at all business sessions – rule laid down for delegates in general federation of women's clubs

- Federal boats are ordered to begin blockade (Mexico City) – Cuban steamer carrying arms for rebel garrison expected to arrive Wednesday; Washington silent as to whether hostile actions will be suppressed

- Actors forming big union (1,400-member Actor's Equity)

- Edison predictions (at 37th annual convention of the National Electric Light Association) – Electricity will be derived directly from coal, bypassing steam and future of aviation will be found in wings of bumble bees that beat wings 300 times per second. Plane with wings that beat the air 200 times per second will solve being airborne

- Ford to finance workers hospital - $3 million

- Women of today simply press the button and do housework without backbreaking labor of our mothers

- Asserts Tammany voted four dead men

- Club women protest plans to bar décolleté gowns

- Prohibition vote due soon in House – nationwide embargo on liquor to undergo ballot within a few weeks is prediction

- First picture of craft which may fly across ocean – daring aviator will attempt to make flight in 72 hours - $50,000 prize offered by London Daily Mail (Lt. John Cyril Porte, Royal Navy, in a Rodman Wanamaker Aeroplane)

- Irish volunteers spreading rapidly – National movement now serious reality in home rule question

- Wilson to attend opening of (Panama) Canal

- To save elephant and rhinoceros – Powers interested in Africa take action to prevent extinction of animals

- (Pancho) Villa quits rebel chief; takes over government

- Doctor tells TR (Theodore Roosevelt) he must be quiet – Brazilian trip causes affection [sic] of larynx that will prevent campaigning

- Capt. Scott's trip to South Pole will be related in picture form
- Ex-slaves can't inherit
- England and France dying; war is needed for new life
- Ask Negro speaker at NEA (National Education Association) program
- College presidency offered to woman
- Remove 12,667 gallstones (new surgical record – all from one farmer)
- Oil King (Rockefeller) gives $2,550,000 to medical research
- Jack Johnson remains heavyweight champion of world – black wins easily; Moran at his mercy near end of contest
- Assassin kills heir to throne of Austria and wife on street – Archduke Francis Ferdinand, heir presumptive of the throne of Austro-Hungary, who with his wife- Duchess of Hohenberg, was assassinated at Serajevo by Servian [sic] student

JUNE 1914

◆

LETTERS

Postmark: 1 p.m. June 1, 1914, St. Paul, Minn.

June 1st, 1914

Dear Friend:

Six days more and the seventh you will be here. That surely is not very far off and I am glad. Think I will go to bed early every night this week. My cold is all well again but I lost about five pounds, weigh 123 this morning. I am not worrying about that though, glad I lost a couple of pounds but suppose I will gain it all back again in a few days.

Just worked half a day Saturday account of Decoration Day but made up for it Sunday, worked Sunday morning for a while. In the afternoon papa took us all out in the country. We left about one o'clock and did not get home until 7 p.m.

We surely had a fine time. Papa got a rig, we took our lunch with us and had a good old fashioned time.

I do hope you get elected on Wednesday, that sure would be great. They ought to let everybody vote whether they belonged to the Alumni or not and then if I were in Detroit I would do a little cheating to make sure you get the office.

As to the machine, Mr. Turner says it is o.k. to order your car before you leave so you have it as soon as you return. However, he would kind of like you to look over the Saxon car before you fully decide. The Saxon car is made by several people one man was headman of the Ford company etc. I do not know much about it, just what Mr. Turner has said he would like it if you would look it over.

We are going to be without a daddy all week. He leaves tonight for St. Louis on a business trip for Mr. Turner and it sure will be lonesome as we are so used to having him with us all of the time.

I guess this will be the last letter I can write before you come to St. Paul. I figure you will get this Wednesday and possibly I will get an answer Friday so you would not get another letter before you leave. Therefore, so long! until Sunday morning. Be sure now that you don't miss your train.

Sincerely,

Hildred

(over)
By the way, I forgot to mention Mr. Turner says there are excursion rates from Detroit to the West commencing with June 1st. You might inquire about this and possibly St. Paul might be included in the list of Western Cities.

———————◆———————

[**Editor's Note:** The lapse in letters corresponds with Charles' trip to St. Paul. During that week, they became engaged.]

Postmark: 11:30 a.m. June 15, 1914, Chicago, Ill.

Addressed to Miss H.L. Cress, c/o Booth Fisheries

Monday 8 a.m.

Amongst the skyscrapers once more. Arrived on time, had breakfast. My train leaves at 9:05 AM. Going to call up Mrs. Turner and tell her something. CWH

14706 - The Heart of CHICAGO, Ill. From Photograph, Copyright 1900, by Detroit Photographic

Postmark: 12 p.m. June 15, 1914, Detroit, Mich.

June 15th/14.

My Dear Hildred, -

Arrived home all O.K. I certainly extend my most hearty thanks to you for the manner in which you entertained me while in St. Paul, my only regret is that I was not a little more hasty, then probably I would have you with me now, next time I go, somebody by the name of Hildred goes too.

Have had three patients in so far this morning, one I am going to do a little minor operation for on Wednesday which will amount to $20.00 clear for me. Have four calls to make so far tomorrow.

I told my mother and father; my brother thought for a minute or to (sic.), it seems as though they expected it, Dr. Moon called me up, he finally got it out of me by promising he would not tell.

By the way I had a dream about you while on the pulman (sic.) Sunday night, I will tell you about it some time.

Now I only have a few minutes to get this letter out, so will close, be sure and let me hear from you, because I am anxious to know how you are getting along.

With Love and Best Wishes,

Sincerely,

Chas.

(They are going to deliver my automobile at 4 p.m. tomorrow)

◆———————

Postmark: 7 p.m. June 15, 1914, St. Paul, Minn.

June 15th, 1914.

Dear Charles:

Of all the days I have written you, this is the worst, don't know when I had so much work to do. It is 6 P.M. and Mr. Turner is waiting for me but will sure write you first thing in the morning. I promised to write so hope you will excuse this note. Have loads to tell you in the morning.

Lots of love,

Hildred.

◆———————

Postmark: 10:30 a.m. June 16, 1914, St. Paul, Minn.

St. Paul, Minn.

June 16, 1914.

Dear Charles:

Presume you are real busy learning to run your "Ford" today but just look out that you don't get in a smash-up and don't forget about the insurance you promised to get.

You should have been here yesterday to help me bear the brunt of all the teasing, it was awful. Mr. Esch of course was the worst and he started in again first thing this morning. I suppose it will be all over church by Sunday because Celia Brown, one of the girls from church came over to see me last evening and I couldn't bluff her about buying it. I think I will write to Dr. Moon so you get your share of teasing. I have also gained an enemy, namely Mr. Lucius. He was in the office yesterday and didn't have a thing to say. When I saw him coming I took off my ring so he wouldn't see that but guess he is wise just the same. He always used to be so friendly, had so much to say, quite a difference from yesterday. Ethel called up last night and said it looked rather suspicious for us to be running away so quick Sunday morning but I wouldn't give her any satisfaction at all.

I mailed that package to your brother yesterday morning but why did you leave a quarter? To tell the truth I was too excited Sunday to notice you left it, otherwise I surely would not have taken it because it only cost six cents to send it. I tell you what I will do though, I will make a batch of candy for you some fine day and then use that money for the postage.

I didn't cry Sunday night, but pretty near did. The last thing Mr. Turner said was that he was going to ask me if I cried in the morning and of course I would let him tease me about that too – I did cry just a little but didn't count that, didn't say anything to Mr. Turner about it.

Be sure and write often and give me all the news.

With loads of love and best wishes,

Hildred

———————◆———————

Postmark: 12 p.m. June 16, 1914, Detroit, Mich.

Addressed to Mr. Turner; dot on envelope flap

June 16/14

My Dear Hildred,-

Just a line to let you know I am a man with an automobile, it will rest in my garage over night, a man is coming here at 4 pm this afternoon to give me a lesson, and I will have to make out a check amounting to $550.00 which is the largest I have ever made out on myself.

Say do you know that it has not rained in Detroit since before I left on my trip, everything is almost dried up.

Hildred I do not know how I can wait until Oct or Nov. It did not seem so long when I was in St. Paul, but now it seems an awfully long time to me. I want to give you plenty of time of course. Had three or four Doctors call me up this AM. to see whether or not I got married while away. There were also a couple who called up last night, I told them I would like to be able to say yes, all my patients are putting the question to me in an off handed way. I might as well wear an engagement ring, I don't see how these people have gotten such ideas in their heads.

Don't forget to write to me Hildred,

With Love,

Chas.

———◆———

Postmark: 1 p.m. June 17, 1914, St. Paul, Minn.

June 17th 1914

Dear Charles:

My! I was so pleased to hear from you, only it made me feel quite blue for a while, wishing you were here instead of away off at Detroit but then, the time will pass before we know it.

Real glad to know you were busy your first evening at home. I suppose you are in your glory now that you are home again and can make some money. How is your indigestion? Are you still bothered by it?

From the way mamma talks, I don't think she is planning on giving me any money because she said from now on she would lay a few dollars away every week towards getting things for me and get them gradually. I wouldn't like that at all, because maybe sometime there would be something I would like to get and she would think I didn't need it and anyway I would rather spend my own money but I am not going to worry about that until after "dad" gets home this week.

Mrs. Turner has asked me to go to the matinee with her tomorrow afternoon at the Shubert. I really should stay home and accomplish something but guess I can spare that much time. I am invited to an excursion next Wednesday, just a bunch of young people from the Park are going but I have declined going to quit everything like that for the time being and keep busy.

Won't you tell me what your dream was? You have my curiosity aroused and think you might tell me now instead of later. Be good now and let me hear about it.

Mr. Esch was just in the office and when he saw I was writing a letter maybe he didn't tease me. He was in here about 15 min. kidding life out of me. I was so angry I could have fired the ink bottle at him and still he is so comical you can't help but laugh at him.

With love,

Hildred

P.S. Imagine a kiss enclosed

———◆———

Postmark: 8:30 p.m. June 17, 1914, Detroit, Mich.

Addressed to Chas. W. Turner – dot on envelope flap

June 17th/14

My Dear Hildred, -

Pleased to hear from you, you had better slow down a little, do not over do your self, you will make yourself so nervous that you will not be able to run my car next fall.

The demonstration took me half a block then we changed places and I took him all over the city, down on the busy streets, Cadillac Sq. and all over. I stalled the engine once, I went to slow down instead of letting the clutch down into neutral I pushed it over into low power at the same time pressing on the foot brake, stalling the engine, we were in tight corners with lots of automobiles, street cars and people around, I do not think I would get excited in St. Paul. I wish you were here to go for a ride with me tonight. Today I have spent nearly $600.00. So far, however, I made $20.75 this morning in about one and a half hours, made $10.50 yesterday.

Last night I helped mother pick a crate of strawberry's, I have told her all about my Kid Wife, and I know she will be glad to see you.

Write me a big long letter.

With love,

Chas.

———————◆———————

Postmark: 12 p.m. June 18, 1914, Detroit, Mich.

Addressed to: Miss. H.L. Cress, c/o Booth Fisheries

June 18th, 1914

My Dear Hildred, -

I am enclosing to you a pamphlet from the American Automobile Insurance Coy. which speaks for itself. (Ed. Note: no enclosure found). Would be pleased if you would show it to Mr. Turner, and let me know what you both think of it, the policy can be made to include everything or only certain things that you wish to be protected against. In a way it looks good to me but I hate to spend too much money for something that may not do me any good.

Business is rather on the slow side today. Up until last night I have averaged $13.75 per day for the days I have worked so for the month, I have worked 7 days.

I received a letter from you yesterday, and rather expect to receive one this afternoon, sorry they are teasing you so much, but do not pay any attention to them and they will soon get tired of it.

A woman called me up this am regarding some medicine and asked me to leave it with my wife and she would call later on for it. My mother thought she was slightly on the hasty side.

It is trying to rain for the first time in three weeks. Drove my car almost 50 miles this am.

With love & XXX,

Chas.

———————◆———————

Postmark: 1:30 p.m. June 19, St. Paul, Minn.

My dear Charles:

Just as happy to hear from you as can be.

You surely did fine for your first lesson in automobiling. Wish I could have been with you. Didn't it pretty near break your heart to make out such a big check at once?

I have something to confess to you. I broke my promise. You know you made me promise to go to bed at 10 P.M. Well, last night it was later. I washed several of my waists, done my weeks' ironing and then started to sew. Claribel and mamma were also busy sewing and we never gave the time a thought. After we were through, guess what we did, we each ate a big piece of lemon pie and when we looked at the clock, it was 11:30. Maybe we didn't hustle to bed. We were so busy that truly we never thought of the time and didn't notice the clock strike. But you will forgive me this time, won't you?

I have got a good place to keep my ring now, I put it in the case, and then slip it way to the bottom of the pillow case and put the open end of the case to the center of the bed so nobody could get it without first waking me. What do you think of the little stunt? Pretty near every day Addison wonders why I don't hurry up and get married. I think he has advertized it pretty well too, because actually everybody I meet knows more about it than I do myself.

I think I shall have to quit saving my 10-cents a day now because I need the money. I have $25.00 dollars in my little bank and $15.00 besides that, but papa says not to spend that keep it for a starter. He just got back from St. Louis today and had quite a talk with him re: money matters. Don't know just how it will all turn out, will let you know though as soon as I do.

Just loads and loads of love from,
"Your Kid Wife To Be"
Hildred

———◆———

Postmark: 2:30 p.m. June 18, 1914

June 18, 1914

My dear Charles:

Have not got time to write you very much today. Mr. Turner just got back from Kansas City so of course there is plenty to do and besides I was going to be a lady this afternoon, going to the matinee with Mrs. Turner.

Real glad to know you have your automobile. Now promise me that you will be real careful because if you only go fifteen miles an hour, it will still be ten miles faster than heretofore so you can afford to be a little slow at first.

Do you notice any change in your business since you are home? I mean do you think you have lost any patients by going away?

I would hate to have you say "yes" and still would like to know.

Spent the evening with Mrs. Turner (last evening) and we had a very nice visit and she gave me some valuable information. She has offered to buy my table linen when she is in Toronto this fall, isn't that dandy? I told mamma and she didn't say a word, don't think is overly pleased but I can't help that.

I am glad they are giving you your share of teasing but I know I get a great deal more than you do.

As you say, Nov. does seem a long way off now that you are not here, but at the same time it will pass before you know it and then we won't have to count the number of weeks until we see each other.

With lots of love,

Hildred

P.S. I wanted to finish this before Mr. Turner came back from lunch because if he saw me writing he would tease again.

H.C.

———◆———

Postmark: 8:30 p.m. June 19, 1914, Detroit, Mich.

Addressed to Mr. Turner; no dot on envelope

June 19th/14.

My Dear Hildred, -

Just a line to let you know I am alive and that I received your letter of the 17th Inst.

In regard to the Lucius affair, don't let that worry you, if he is provoked at you, how do you suppose he will feel toward me.

As far as the money business is concerned, there is only one thing to do that is to handle it yourself. Otherwise in all probability there will be trouble in the near future, you earn it and therefore have every right to its use, now what I would do if I were you, is to stick up for yourself and I don't doubt what you will win out.

My Dream – Sunday night on the sleeper of course I went to sleep with you on my mind, when I woke up I was reaching out for you, but instead of having hold of you I was pulling on the window shade, disappointing nevertheless true. I don't like to dream like that.

I did not drive my car this morning as it was raining and the streets were pretty slippery.

Don't forget to write to me.

With Love & XXX

Charles

———————◆———————

[**Editor's Note:** This letter from Chas. W. Turner, enclosed with this letter from Hildred]

No Postmark

June 20th, 1914

Dear Charlie: -

Yours of the 16th to hand and note you got home all right and feeling fine, also that you dropped the nervous tension, which is I suppose, excusable under certain conditions but as a physician you should know that the high strain or nervous tension is not healthy and you must always advise your patients as well as yourself to put on the safety valve.

Regarding your visit to us, you were certainly welcome and we are glad to have you with us at any time.

I am very pleased you spoke to your father and mother that they said they thought you were old enough to know your own business, that is very nice. I hope by this time you have got that personal matter between yourself and mother adjusted because you certainly ought to do that.

Regarding automobile insurance as per printed matter enclosed [**Editor's Note:** No enclosure survives]. I have read the same and respectfully return. This may be a good proposition and it may not. The question is, who are the American Automobile Insurance Company? Of course, they show their names and directors but I do not know what standing they have got, I have never heard of these people before. I should think your friend in the Ford Company would be able to tell you more about it. You should certainly have some insurance, this is not very expensive, why not take this for a year. It does not state the amount of money it will pay but I suppose however, it pays the loss of whatever it may be up to the value of the car. In the writer's judgment you cannot run an automobile without insurance and as this is a very light policy, $42.50, I think possibly you better try it.

Trusting everything is moving along with you and that you did not lose any patrons by coming here,

Sincerely yours,

Uncle Charlie (hand-signed)

Dr. C.W. Husband,
Detroit, Mich.

———————◆———————

(This letter enclosed in the envelope with the letter from C.W. Turner)

June 20th, 1914.

Dear Charles: -

It is now 3:15 P.M. and have not got time to write much today as I have a date at 3:30 with a very dear friend of yours, namely, ------- Guess!! By the way, the telephone message says to be sure and bring some money with me. That sure doesn't sound good to me but suppose I should take it good natured.

Will answer your letter Monday, so goodbye for tonight. Lots of love from,

H i l d r e d.

Postmark: 12 p.m. June 20, 1914, Detroit, Mich.

Addressed to Mr. Turner; dot on envelope flap

June 20th/14.

My Dear Hildred, -

Your letter to me of June the 19th 1:30 p.m. so amuscd me that I just had to sit right down and answer it. This expression in particular "Your Kid Wife To Be" is the one I have reference to so please don't forget it how do you like it.

Tomorrow is Sunday why aren't you here to go auto riding with me Sunday afternoon, I am going to take Mother & Dad out for a spin. I tell you Hildred while I want to have all the money I can get together by next fall at the same time I do not see how we can afford to lose so much time in waiting. If I just had one thousand beans, I don't think I could wait any longer, I would steal up to your room, put you in my suit case, ---Detroit –

In regard to your ring supposing they would cut your pillow case with shears or a knife what then. I would wear it at night if I were you and always be careful not to lay it down when washing your hands anyplace, have a certain place to put it on your person and always in the same place.

To answer your question regarding patients may say I lost four or five new calls while away, but instead I got a life long patient in St. Paul. There is a great deal of difference between St. Paul and Detroit, here you have to meet them from all sides and corners. My Kid Wife will be a little nervous at first I am afraid. My mother says (illegible). I will forgive you for staying up late this time. Don't forget to write often.

With Love & XXX

Chas.

Postmark: 3 p.m. June 22, 1914, St. Paul, Minn.

Monday morning

My dear Charles:

I was so pleased this morning when I got to the office and found two letters from you. You see one came in yesterday and I didn't get that until this morning. After this, how would it be to address your Friday letter to me and then papa can bring it home to me on Sunday morning or would you rather not?

As to the money, you know Saturday mamma called me up and asked me to meet her at 3:30 and *to be sure and bring some money along as well, instead of my meeting her she came to the office and got some from "dad" and while we were out shopping she didn't ask for my money and I didn't give it to her. They haven't asked for it as yet so I still possess fifteen whole dollars. I feel it in my bones though that something will happen today.*

Claribel is leaving this morning to Phillips, expects to stay about three weeks and then go to Ashland for a week. I sure will miss the girl because we always tell each other our so-called troubles as it were.

Saturday afternoon Mr. Turner was called away unexpectedly to Duluth and Harriet was up the river on an excursion so I stayed with Mrs. Turner over night. It stormed quite hard until about 10:30 so I broke my promise again, couldn't go to bed when it was storming so hard. You should have been here and had Sunday dinner with us. I was chief cook and nobody got indigestion either. We had chicken noodle soup, potatoes, cabbage salad, buttered beans and lemon pie and I did every bit myself, the folks were all to church. Possibly that is why Claribel made up her mind so quick to go to Phillips when she found out I was going to be cook Sundays.

As to my ring, I am going to sure get a chamois tomorrow and make a little pocket to wear pinned on. I never thought of them cutting the pillow case, now I won't know what I will do tonight.

There was a young man over to the house yesterday, he is minister of the "Dutch Church" as Mr. Turner calls it and his father owns a Ford Car, has had it a year, run it over 7,500 miles and has only spent $1.95 for repairs all the while he has had it. Of course he has had to buy gasoline, oil etc. but that sure is a good record I think.

I am getting so absent minded lately, think you will have to send me some pills. The other evening I meant to ask for the radishes at dinner and instead I asked them to pass me horseradish. Maybe they don't tease me about that. I have done things like that several times lately and think you are to blame!

Isn't your mother going to run your machine now? If she is scared out presume I will be too.

Received your (XXX) as you call them, while I love to get them, they aren't near as good as the real. Just imagine a whole lot sent with this letter.

Lots of love from your K. W. -----------------Be,

Hildred

<hr />

Postmark: 12:30 p.m. June 23, 1914, Detroit, Mich.

Addressed to Miss H.L. Cress, c/o Booth Fisheries Coy.

June 22nd/14

My Dear Hildred, -

Received your favor of the 20th Inst. In regard to that very dear friend of mine whom you had a date with in St. Paul, you got me, unless it be Aunt Lizzie or Uncle Chas. so please do not forget to tell me when you answer.

Did some auto riding Sunday took my Dad around the boulevard, then took my Mother over to the Cemetery, to (illegible) out Woodward Ave., home, made a hurray up call etc. Machine working fine. I wish you were here to take a ride with me, Hildred you know I left the time when with you, so you will just look over the calendar we will fix things up to a certain extent between us, and not give anybody outside any satisfaction as to any definite time, all on the Q.T. of course it will take me two or three months to recover from last month's business. May say I have spent nearly $1,000.00 in the last Twenty days. If we know something in regard to the time we will be able to make better arrangements and we will have something more definite to work for. But remember we cannot afford to wait too long. My Brother waited nearly a year, he said he did not know what married life was or else he would not have waited so long.

It rained this am, (please do not tell Uncle Chas) I was driving over some muddy slippery roads I commenced to slip and slide just thinking I knew my car was turned at right angles to the road. I stopped, started, and was tickled to death when out of the neighborhood. I would like to have that insurance but hate to pay out so much money. You know how that is. Let me know how you made out at church Sunday. Lots of love & XXXX

Chas.

{I wished I was in St. Paul Sunday. How many more Sundays let me know!}

———————◆———————

Postmark: 11 a.m. June 24, 1914, St. Paul, Minn.

Sunday evening.

Dear Charles:

Not a very long letter tonight because it is past my bed time but I will not be able to write tomorrow, going on an excursion down the river with mamma. I wouldn't consent to go at all at first but I was given a complimentary ticket so can't get out of it very well. Mamma wouldn't go unless I went along and I wouldn't pay fifty cents and now that I have the ticket I can't get out of it very well but I can't say I care to go the (Dutch Church) is giving the excursion and both Mpls. and St Paul churches are going. They certainly are working hard to get Claribel and I to go to their church, one of the ministers called at the house Sunday and another one at the office this morning and he was the one that gave me the ticket. I didn't want to take it at all, said I didn't think I had time, too much to do at the office and, of course, dad had to remind me that Mr. Turner would be in Winnipeg tomorrow and that he had given me Wednesday as a holiday. I was provoked but guess I am doomed never the less.

It is storming something fierce tonight, pretty near like a cyclone, so windy. I think it has rained pretty near every day since you left.

By the way, Charles, have you taken out any insurance as yet? You know you promised and I really don't think you should delay this for your own good and another thing, how fast do you drive your car? Be sure and don't exceed the speed limit.

How is business going? You haven't given us any figures since you are home or are you waiting until the end of the month and then have us guessing again?

Tonight I had the same job you did the other night, helped pick over a crate of strawberries. Also made a batch of fudge for tomorrow and it turned out pretty good.

It is getting late so will say good night and I sends lots of 000 and xxx to you. Know what an "0" means?

Lovingly,

Hildred

P.S. Will tell you about the money next time I write but will say I am not at all satisfied. Will you excuse the blots, etc.? [**Editor's. Note:** *refers to ink blots on the stationary, the result of using a fountain pen*]

Postmark: 9 p.m. June 24, 1914, Detroit, Mich.

Addressed to Miss H.L. Cress c/o Booth Fisheries

June 24th/14.

My Dear Hildred, -

Was tickled to death to receive your letter of the 22nd. Can hardly wait to hear from you, so write often, because I feel better when I hear from you.

Think I will have to send my Mother up to tease you for a change she kids the life out of me.

Will address Friday letters to you, don't be afraid to tell me about these things, because I will do all I can for you.

In regard to the money proposition, assert your rights. I am going to be a tight wad now for two or three months until I can get a nice little bank c/e. This automobile garage business took quite a lot of money, I am glad they are paid back for I rather hate to pay out $45.00 for insurance, to tell the truth I try to be very careful, Dr. Moon does not carry any insurance, Do not say anything to Mr. Turner but what do you think I better do.

By the say I was over to see Dr. Moon Saturday, he told me that he was a very busy man while I was away, busy in as much as he is figuring on getting married in Sept. I told him that he did not have anything on me, and we enjoyed ourselves together so he is also pinching the simmolians too. He will have to rent a place.

In regard to your ring you had better get a chamois bag and pin it on the inside of your gown at night time. I think you will be safe the main thing is to be careful about laying it down anywhere when you wash your hands always put it in the chamois bag and pin it inside your waist.

We got some wash woman, she comes to work dressed in silk clothes, Mother had her house cleaning she thinks the woman is surprising eggs etc. her purse fell on the floor and a chew of tobacco came rolling out. Pretty soon you will have to deal with these people, do you want her when you come. Mother is almost peeved at the woman, I tell her to keep cool, don't worry, be sure your right, go ahead.

Had an accident case this a.m. My car came in very handy. You are certainly going to run it even if mother won't.

Let me know how you are getting along. I am get more anxious every day to see you. If you write often I don't worry so much.

With all the love & XXX in me.

Chas.

Postmark: 12:30 p.m. June 25, 1914, St. Paul, Minn.

Thursday morning.

My dear Charles:

Was certainly pleased to hear from you but surprised you could not guess who I meant by that dear friend of yours. I sure thought you were a better guesser than that but maybe if I had said "Old Lady" you would have known. Now do you know who it was?

You didn't wish you were in St. Paul Sunday, anymore than I did, I was really lonesome, didn't know what to do with myself all day. I didn't go to church all day Sunday so haven't had much teasing from there but just about every morning when I go down in the street car I meet someone I know. It is beyond me how they all find out. I know I never said anything. This morning I met one of the boys from our Sunday School class he never said "good morning" or anything, simply said, "Well, I suppose you are real busy getting ready for the big event" and the worst of it is every time they say anything my face flushes up. I wish it didn't do that.

As to when we should be married. I have done a little figuring this morning and how would the first or second week in November suit you? Or, would you be willing to wait a little longer? I would like to get some idea from you too, and then I can see how that time would suit me. I agree with you, we ought to settle on an approximate time and then can arrange accordingly.

There is something I would like to ask you too. Would you like to have me married in white or just in my suit. I have an idea of what I would like now let me see how we agree or disagree on this. Do you think your mother can come to St. Paul. If you can possibly arrange it, I would just love to have her come.

I won't tell Mr. Turner how you skidded the other day, but do be careful and you should take out insurance. Of course I know how big that money looks to you but how much bigger it would be if you had an accident so open your heart just a little and be on the safe side. Don't you think that is the best way?

How is business. You sure must be making a lot to be able to spend $1000.00 in twenty days.

Lots of love, from your

Hildred

———————◆———————

Postmark: 12 p.m. June 25, 1914, Detroit, Mich.

Addressed to Miss H.L. Cress, c/o Booth Fisheries

June 25th/14

Dear Hildred –

I'm looking over your letter of Tuesday June 23rd I note in particular that your are worried about something in fact your letter read as though you are down hearted over something. The way things are, (illegible) and pretty near to each other, I don't like to have you feeling that way and I wish you would confide in me in as much as you tell me what is wrong, May be I can do something for you. Is it in regard to your money if so be independent [sic] and let (me/her) know.

Getting along very nicely with my car, I don't know that I could get along without it now.

Business has been a little slower the last two or three days, but June is always the slowest month of the year. In the fifteen days I have worked this month I have charged $62.75 & taken in $220.50.

To be frank with you I feel worried about you, so write right away and let me know what the trouble is.

In regard to those "O"s I don't know as I ever have seen anything like that in print before but I imagine that it means a hug, if so it looks good to me. Have you any more.

With Loads of 000 & XXX's.

Chas.

———————◆———————

Postmark: 1:30 p.m. June 26, 1914, Detroit, Mich.

Addressed to Miss H.L. Cress c/o Booth Fisheries

June 26th/14

My Dear Hildred, -

Why I was a little slow in guess was because I did not think that party to be any dear friend of mine, in fact I always have had another impression as to what I believed they thought of the Turners and their relations.

More in regard to the time when I am going to offer you a definite suggestion and let you comment on it say Monday November the 9th. If you would rather wait longer, let me know your reasons as I told you before I will do all I can for you. However, it is going to tax me pretty hard to get along all this time without you, I am getting more anxious every day when I don't hear from you every day I feel worse still, I don't know what is wrong with me, when I left St. Paul I left with a feeling that I ought to be satisfied, and contented when I would get home but I now realize that I won't be until you come.

I asked my mother in regard to what I would suggest for you to wear and she thought it would be nice if you were married in white then changed to your travelling suit before you left the house. If we were married on Monday we could go to the Hotel Monday night and leave St. Paul at 7:30 a.m. Tuesday get in Chicago at 9:00 am Wednesday and be in Detroit Wednesday evening.

Got a fairly good day lined up for tomorrow.

By the way my Mother is going to write you some day, then you can ask her about going.

Now don't be afraid to let me know what you think in regard to these things, as you are the one to be suited.

If there is any money to be gotten I am going after it.

With piles of Love & Kisses.

Chas.

Ps, {My mother just caught sight of this letter she certainly is a tease}

———————◆———————

Postmark: 5:30 p.m. June 27, 1914, St. Paul Minn.

Saturday afternoon

My dear Charles:

My I was so pleased to hear from you, and such a nice long letter too, those are the kind I like.

No, you needn't send anybody here to tease me, I get more than my share as it is. I did another crazy thing the other evening at dinner but Addison did the same thing although they didn't say anything to him but they sure teased me. In one set of salt and pepper holders, we have paprica in one and cinnamon in the other. Well, it happened we had both on the dinner table the other evening. They are just about the same color and I wanted some paprika on my steak and if I didn't dope it up with cinnamon. Honestly, anything like that makes me so mad because I get enough teasing as it is.

As to your insurance, really I don't know what to say. Have you any accident insurance for yourself? I think that is more necessary than on the machine and if you are really careful I don't imagine it will be necessary and the first year $45.00 looks pretty big and then another year, when you are better fixed financially you could take out insurance on it. There is hardly any chance of it burning up like Mr. Turner's did because yours is a new car and if you ae careful and go slow there is hardly any danger of getting in a serious smash-up. To tell the truth if you are careful I really don't think that the insurance is absolutely necessary but if anything happens don't tell Mr. Turner I said this. Why not see what your folks think? Mr. Turner asked me today whether your machine was trimmed with nickel or brass and I told him nickel as that is the way I understood it. Am I right?

Was surely surprised to hear about Dr. Moon's intentions, thought he was such a fickle fellow. It looks as though he was going to beat us, doesn't it?

I made a little chamois bag last night and now that I have it, think it is about the only thing. Wherever it is a little cool and I am typewriting my ring slips around and the stone being underneath my hand would bother me so now when it does that I have some place to put it and it is both handy and safe.

You sure must have a classy washwoman. I would like to catch her stealing eggs, I would take and fire them at her and make her get out no matter what she happened to be doing. We had a girl one time and my mother missed so many things, linen, silver, dishes etc. and she sort of suspected the girl of taking it so one day when she was downtown mother searched her trunk and found just loads of things she had taken. She never got another meal for us, mother made her pack right up and "get."

If your mother has backed out and will not run the car, maybe I will be scared out too when I see your crowded streets but I will make a big attempt at it anyway.

Had an awfully busy day today, in fact everyone seems busier than the one before and Mr. Turner's blood pressure is up again, 40 points more than it should be.

Dad leaves for Omaha tomorrow night and Mr. Turner leaves for the same place Monday or Tuesday night.

Just loads of love and kisses from

Your Hildred

———————◆———————

Postmark: 9 p.m. June 28, 1914, Detroit, Mich.

Addressed to Mr. Turner – dot on corner flap

Sunday A.M.

My Dear Hildred, -

Did not write to you Yesterday so am going to make up for it by writing you this am.

Am just wondering what "My Little Kid Wife to be" is going to do today. About twenty more Sundays and I figure you will be in Detroit and if the weather permits may be we can go auto riding.

Just interrupted by a patient, he has a sore throat, if it is will imagine by Wednesday July 1st I am going to take out his tonsils that will be a little starter for the month of July. This month's earnings will run a little over $200.00 which is not too bad for the month of June and also being away for 10 days. So far I have taken in $231.00

I am inclosing a piece of glass to you which I found buried in my left rear tire the apex of the pyramid run straight in, why I did not get a puncture I do not know, the glass was in so deep I could hardly pick it out with my knife. I was almost afraid to take it out for fear the air would start coming out to.

With lots of 000 & XX and another great big 0 & X.

Chas.

PS. It is raining so I don't know whether or not I can go auto riding this afternoon.

CWH

Postmark: 4 p.m. June 29, 1914, St. Paul, Minn.

Monday

Dearest Charles:

Was awfully glad to get two letters from you this morning. I guess the one letter that was supposed to come Sunday was delayed.

I am real sorry if I said anything in my letter to worry you. I wouldn't do that for the world knowingly. I admit I did have a little wrangle regarding money etc. and don't know as yet how it will come out but please don't be worrying about me because Mr. Turner will help me at this end and I will let you know how things turn out. You have a lot to attend to there at Detroit and it won't pay you to be worrying or thinking about me, you can't do justice to your work if you do. I will promise, if anything serious comes up to confide in you first thing.

Thank you very much for remembering me with a box of candy but as Mr. Turner says, don't you think you should have those one dollar bills because they can be used almost to better advantage buying gasoline, etc. Of course, don't think I don't appreciate it or like the candy, you know better but wait until I get to Detroit and then we can enjoy it together. What do you say?

You guessed what the 000 meant all right and surely I have lots more for you. I send them with every letter.

Glad that your business is as good as it is, thought it wouldn't be so good because I had not heard anything about it for so long and I will be anxious to hear about it at the end of the month.

Mr. Turner is leaving the city tonight so have not got time to say more today but will write you a good long letter tomorrow answering the other letter I received. Now don't worry about me please because I think everything will be OK.

Lots of x x xs and xoo from your sweet ♡ Hildred.

Postmark: 8:30 p.m. June 29, 1914, Detroit, Mich.

Addressed to Miss H.L. Cress, c/o Booth Fisheries

June 29th/14

My Dear Hildred, -

Thanks for your long letter of Saturday p.m. I too like long letters. If the people are going to tease you all the time find something to tease them about and may be they will quit.

I sure was lonesome yesterday, I like to have the time go fast but don't like Sunday to come. I get the blue willies on Sunday. I took my people and Mr. and Mrs. Menges out Woodward and all around Belle Isle yesterday, drove about 75 miles in all, the wind was so strong it nearly blew us to pieces, I think I will love you to death the next time I see you. I do hope the time goes fast, all I am doing is saving all the money I can, but I missed a call while out driving yesterday.

By the way my Mother told me to tell you not to bother sewing too much as you would have lots of time after you come here.

In regard to insurance, as you know I have none. I figure this way if the insurance Coy. can afford to take the risk for $45.00 why can't I it would be different if I were a reckless driver, then again it is the people insured who keep up the insurance Coy, the company does not keep up the people insured, they only pay money out to a very small percentage of the people insured, another thing it is not as though my car was a very inexpensive affair and another thing I will in all probability have a car all my life and if I keep paying insurance it is bound to cost me money, otherwise, it may not cost me a single cent, let me hear what you have to say. Then again when the car wears out (dies) I won't get any money anyway.

My car is trimmed with brass. I forgot to speak for one of the nickel trimmed ones.

Did you get the keeper for your ring?

Guess I commented on our wash woman too soon, her daughter was taken sick in Toledo last week and she has gone to Toledo to live but she came back and washed for us today. Mother was getting pretty leary [sic] of her anyway. I think I will call up the Salvation Army and get another one. You sure are going to learn to run my car, I run it and so can you.

I took my blue suit back to the taylor [sic] today they did not give me a good fit, I will have to try another place next time.

You did not tell me what Gladys had to say to you after she found out.

Just loads of Love & Kisses, from

Chas.

P.S. {It will take a big long letter to answer these questions}

CWH

———————◆———————

Postmark: 2:30 p.m. June 30, 1914, St. Paul, Minn.

Tuesday

My dear Charles:

I just wish you were here today as I do not have to work this afternoon. It is raining but think we could enjoy ourselves anyway. Really it has rained pretty much every day since you left. You never saw such weather.

I am enclosing a little clipping of the announcement the folks had put in the paper Sunday morning, in with the list of other announcements. Is it O.K.? As to the date you suggest, yes, that is satisfactory to me now, but if something should turn up in the meantime that I would have to postpone it for a week, would you be willing? I guess I feel about the same as you do, namely don't know how I can wait so long to see you but then again when I think of all I have to do yet, the time really seems short so cheer up, it will pass before we know it.

I am glad you asked your mother as to what she thought would be nice for me to wear and her opinion surely pleases me very much. I myself prefer to wear white but thought possibly you had some other idea and of course I would like to please you.

I surely will be delighted to hear from your mother but when she writes will you suggest that she address it to the office? You can guess why can't you? I will be on the lookout for a letter from her.

Your Sunday morning letter came in this morning and Sunday all I did was to wish you were here. In the afternoon we went to visit some of mamma's friends in South Park. Two girls my age were visiting there from out of the city and there are two girls living there so the five of us managed to have a pretty good time. In the evening they took us out for an auto ride.

That surely was some piece of glassware you found in your tire and it is a wonder you did not have a puncture. Do you carry an extra tire with you or not? By this time I bet you are an expert chauffeur, think I will have to call you my "chauffer to be" seeing you call me your "Kid Wife To Be."

Just "oodles" of love from

Hildred

"Oodles" is a new word not found in the dictionary. H.C.

> Mr. and Mrs. H. A. Cress, 1847 Ashland avenue, announce the engagement of their daughter, Hildred Loretta, to Dr. Charles W. Husband of Detroit, Mich. The wedding will take place in the fall.

JULY 1914

◆

Newspaper Headlines

Detroit Free Press

- Wilson offended at questioning; curtly quits Suffragists
- Democrats in Senate vote to act on Trust Bills at this session
- Bombs to kill Archduke obtained from Servian [sic] arsenal, says assassin
- Street vendors are allowed to sell fire works
- Output next year will exceed auto production record
- Autos carried on backs of mules to interior
- Michigan sixth in corporation and income revenue
- Dodge brothers incorporate with $5,000,000 stock
  - New motor car firm may become rival of Ford
- Ways greased for U.S. warship
- Scott Bequest to transform west end of Belle Isle (Scott Fountain)
- Ulsterites depend on England's fairness in Home Rule outcome
- Wales alarmed as U.S. takes coal trade
- Vatican anxious about Archduke

- "Advertise physician's work, not physician," said Detroit doctor, who hates publicity
- Little tours bring car owners closer to country life
- From 1 to 4 out of every 100 scholars in state public schools are feeble-minded, say authorities of Lapeer Home now conducting course for teachers of backward children
- Heiress and papa's chauffeur eloped (Boston, MA)
- Huerta resigns, leaves Mexico City; (Francisco S.) Carvajal is sworn in as president – Wilson blamed for helping rebels to win
- Oil war is likely to keep Detroit price at 11-cents
- (Windsor, Ont.) Mayor will urge tunnel to Detroit
- Veterans of 1861 may occupy Fort Wayne for week
- Naked dancers with carnival fined $10 each – entertainment so popular that police are attracted to scene
- Owners of house boats fight plan to remove them (from Belle Isle)

St. Paul Pioneer Press

- Wilson signs bill for three battleships

- Curb women's garb says Boston "prof" – then teach her importance of home life

- Men teachers are needed to make schools more efficient, NEA (National Education Association) secretary says

- Bomb in one hand, poison in other – slayer of Austrian Royal pair and accomplices planned tragic deaths for selves

- Minnesota's climate is most healthful in the world

- Ford cars in the making – motion picture at local theatre show big auto factory at Detroit in operation

- Don't write love notes/telegraph – it's likely to make trouble later when breach of promise suits or divorce cases are being heard – the written word is best evidence (feature)

- Shackleton expects to reduce hazard of Polar exploration to minimum by motor sledges rather than dogs; dryer for clothing

- Negroes test ordinance – three file suit attacking Constitutionality of Louisville Segregation Law

- Pledges Ulstermen to never give up (Irish Rebellion)

- Auto license law upheld – South Dakota Supreme Court says fee is for roads that cars tear up

- Mississippi's fall rapid – drops 27 inches in a week

- Guests at Auto Club – include Mr. and Mrs. C.W. Turner (July 21, 1914)

- (Panama) Canal open to the nations August 16

- Servia [sic] refuses Austrian demands; both countries begin war preparations

- Austrians receive Declaration of War with spirit akin to religious fervor

- France quietly preparing for war

- European war may be general in a few hours; Austrian Army reported repulsed at Belgrade

JULY 1914

——————◆——————

LETTERS

Postmark: 1:30 p.m. July 1, 1914, St. Paul, Minn.

Wednesday, July 1st

My Dear Charles:

Was surely pleased to get your nice long letter, that is the first thing I look for every morning. I wish I had been in Detroit Sunday to enjoy that drive you had, I bet it was simply great. As to loving me to death when you see me, mercy on us don't do anything rash, while I want a good big love, still wouldn't want it quite that hard and besides don't want that to be the last one I have.

Gladys was surely more than surprised when I told her because I never said very much to her. She didn't tease me but pretty near smothered me with kisses and good wishes. She also let me in on a secret that nobody knows, not even her own mother. She and Henry (her friend) have had sort of an understanding, not really engaged, that if inside of two years they still think as much of each other, they also expect to be married. Account of the money end of it thought it better to wait a while. I don't think I would like that very well but she has been going with another young man quite steady of late and guess he got scared.

Now as to your insurance I really don't think it is an absolute necessity. If you drive real careful as you say then you are safe and if somebody should run into you then they would have to make good your loss at least I should think so. As to that $45.00 policy, how much damage must be done before they pay anything or will they pay any amount no matter if it *is only $25.00? Again, didn't the policy say that providing the loss was $200.00 or over, they would include the tires? By that I thought that they wouldn't get new tires for you, only on condition that your loss was $200.00 or more and I don't think that is right, they ought to include those anyway if they are damaged. As to yourself, I really think you should have accident insurance because it is always the least expected that happens. Whatever you decide, get accident insurance for yourself, whether you do on your machine or not.*

Note your machine is trimmed with brass. Will have to tell Mr. Turner as I said nickel and he might think I was getting absent minded.

You should see the beautiful flounce Mrs. Turner made for me, don't know as I told you about it. I have seen pretty near every one she has made but truly I like mine the best. She also gave me two beautiful linen towels that she got one time while in Toronto. She embroidered my initial in one end. If you are real good you can have the privilege of using them some time.

Say guess what dad did. He just got back from Omaha this morning and when he saw me writing he wondered if I got two letters Monday morning. I told him I did and then he said that they come in Sunday morning and he meant to be good to me and bring them home and what did he do but carry them in his pocket all day, never noticed it until he got to the depot Sunday night so he stuck them in the mail box again. Isn't that the limit? Just look what I missed Sunday.

I think I have written a pretty long letter this time, don't you?

Lots of love and kisses and a Big Hug but not hard enough to love you to death, although pretty near.

Yours,

Hildred

———————◆———————

Postmark: 9 p.m. July 1, 1914, Detroit, Mich.

Addressed to Miss H.L. Cress, c/o Booth Fisheries

July 1st/14.

My Dear Hildred, -

I sure was pleased to received your letter, and note that I will get another one tomorrow, which looks good to me.

I think if I could send you just a few tablets for you to give to somewhere that the money business would pass out all O.K.

In regard to last month in the twenty days I worked I charged up $216.00. Took in

$267.00, of course move into our slack season but here's hoping. (Just interrupted patient came in and paid me $25.00. You ought to see me smile) I have nearly $400.00 on my books and I sure am going after it this month, some I am going to see personally. You see there are only three months left. Aug, Sept. & Oct., then I have got my Little Kid Wife to take care of so I am putting all my pennies away. Next winter I expect my business will amount to half as much again. And I may be double. And I sure will feel like working when I have a Little Wife to love. This month I have got taxes to pay, also water rates, etc. And I will have to get the House decorated before long, all our walls are white.

We sure are having lots of rain, my machine got a little muddy this am. so I am leaving it out this afternoon in front of the house for the rain to wash off the mud. I drove over an unpaved street this Am.

Thought I had an operation lined up for this Am. But the fellow disappointed me. He may show up for Saturday, but otherwise I would have a pretty good day. Only made $5.25 this Am.

In regard to the candy I take pleasure in giving it to you, the way you write makes me think I can't afford it, however it is very nice of you to look at it the way you do if you would rather not have me send it, I will only send it once in awhile.

Lots of OOO and XXX wish I had a real one.

Chas.

Postmark: 8 p.m. July 2, 1914, St. Paul, Minn.

July 2, 1914

My Dear Charles:

Just a little note before I go home. Was a little disappointed not to hear from you today don't think I am selfish, though because I know you are a busy man and tomorrow I will appreciate your letter all the more, if such a thing is possible.

Mr. Turner will be home in the morning. He has been gone since Monday.

Papa and Mamma expect to go to Phillips, Wisc. for the Fourth. If they do, Addison and I will be alone Friday night, Saturday and Sunday. Think I will have Gladys come out and stay with me. Of course papa won't know if he can get away until Mr. Turner gets home.

I forgot to tell you that I got my new keeper and it fits just dandy.

Loads of love and all the XXX imaginable from Yours,

Hildred

———————◆———————

Postmark: 8:30 July 2, 1914, Detroit, Mich.

Addressed to Mr. Charles W. Turner c/o Booth Fisheries – dot on envelope flap

July 2nd/14.

My Dear Hildred, -

Always tickled to death to hear from you, always look for a letter every day. May say that I will soon have to find another secret spot, the old one is pretty near filled up.

I have something very funny to tell you. My sides ache from laughing. May say I took that man's tonsils out today had Dr. Moon give the anesthetia, before we started the anesthitia we tied the man down on the table with bandages, because he was a big bruit of a fellow and we knew when he reached the stage of excitement he would be hard to hold, everything went along fine for about ten minutes, I was holding the fellow as tight as I could lest he should stir, all of a sudden he became semi conscious yelled that we were trying to arrest him, made a big lunge, tore the bandages loose, sent me flying, and before I could collect my thoughts had Dr. Moon on the floor laying on top of him, and for the life of me I could not pull the fellow off Dr. Moon, the fellow did not know what he was doing of course, finally we got him woke up and some man off the street to help us out. Dr. Moon lost a bunch of skin, the fellow was real sorry when he woke up. We got his tonsils out before we finished, may say the fellow's wife got scared rolled down the back steps and another Lady on top of her. I operated this Am, I feel a little sore this afternoon.

The announcement suits me fine, now in regard to the time when I want you to be suited, but at the same time if my work is such that I could make more money by us being married say the latter part of Oct. say Oct. 26th would this be suitable to you, I really think we both ought to be ready this far ahead of time anyway Mother says you do not need to do a great deal of sewing because you will have lots of time when you get here, however as far as I know now Nov. the 9th is O.K. I will do all I can to suit you in this respect, but life is short, and to wait too long is throwing that much time away. Let me hear from you along these lines.

I think in all probability I will bring some new inner tubes tomorrow in case I get a puncture, I have a patient in that business so I think I can get some whole sale prices. My car is running fine. Thanks for much for your "oodles" of love. I send loads of oodles back. Wish I had something real.

To my Dear Little Wife To Be.

Chas.

P.S. Have you seen Mr. Lucius lately. - C.W.H.

———————◆———————

Postmark: 9 p.m. July 3, 1914, Detroit, Mich.

Addressed to Miss H.L. Cress c/o Booth Fisheries

July 3rd/14.

My Dear Little Sweet ♠, -

How does that suit you, I am surely going to squeeze You tight when I see you if I don't love you to death, but I'll bet anything somebody will be around and then I will sure lose my nerve. Here's hoping Nobody is present.

I rather agree with you in regard to the insurance business, so I think I will chance it a little longer, what do you say. By the way I bought an extra inner tube for both back and front this Am. Also an air gauge, so I think possibly I can take care of a puncture on the road side if necessary. My car is running fine tell Uncle Chas. that I wish he would soon find some thing to come to Detroit for then he could look things over. Think it was real nice of Aunt Lizzie to give you those things.

I have the Spring Fever this afternoon, I am unable to think of anything which would be very interesting to you.

Business was pretty good yesterday, have only made $4.00 so far today, have a little more in sight for tomorrow.

July is passing by, but (illegible) to it passing fast.

With Lots of O's, X's & squeezes how do you make the squeezes part.

Write me Sunday.

Chas.

———————◆———————

Postmark: 5 p.m. July 4, 1914, St. Paul, Minn.

July 4, 1914

My Dear Charles:

I will celebrate the Fourth by answering your always most welcome letters. I have two to answer today because I could not find time to answer your yesterday's letter.

Papa and mamma have gone to Phillips for the Fourth, will not be back until Monday sometime so that leaves Addison and I alone for three whole days. Mrs. Turner simply wouldn't have it that we stay in the house alone or have Gladys with us either so we will have three nights lodging at the Turner home. Truly I am kind of glad but at the same time I can't help but feel we are putting them out to a certain extent but they can't see it that way say we simply have to come so we do.

Your months' earnings sure look good to me for twenty days expecially it being an off season as it were. I sure will try and boost business along because your Kid Wife will not be satisfied unless her percentage keeps up.

As to the candy, I sure do enjoy it but perhaps you better wait until I get to Detroit, put those extra dollars towards your fare to St. Paul.

You should have seen me laugh when I read your letter, it sure struck me funny. Wouldn't I have liked to see him flying around at you Doctors. I bet Dr. Moon won't want to give an anesthetic again in a hurry. Mr. Turner says you should have had a hose handy when you performed that operation, that cold water will bring them too right away. That stunt would have made a good comical moving picture, too bad there wasn't a machine handy.

As to the great event, I can't say just about the 26th but if I have anything to do with it the money making stunt why think I would be willing to give in to a week or so sooner however, will we let it go at the 9th for the present?

Had to work half a day today and it is now twelve o'clock time to go home but will write you more along this line tomorrow.

Just loads of love from

Hildred

———————◆———————

Postmark: 9:30 p.m. July 4, 1914, Detroit, Mich.

Addressed to Charles W. Turner c/o Booth Fisheries; dot on envelope flap

July 4/14.

My Dear Little Wife, -

You sure are going to be my little wife from this out, no more of the "To Be", Business for me. I am surely lonesome to see you, I love to get those ooo & xxx, but they do not hit the spot, they are too far fetched and narrow. Just let me say this Hildred what do you say if we figure on Oct. 26th, November not only is a harder month to get away than Oct. but you understand we would be together two weeks sooner. I have told you what my Mother said, then again if you send some of your sewing down this way, I'll help you out. Think it over and let me hear from you.

I will give you my daily figures (illegible) for this month of course my accounts have not started to come in as yet, to speak of.

July 1,	July 2,	July 3,	July 4 –Just to 2 p.m.
Charged	Charged	Charged	Charged
$7.50	$15.50	$9.00	$12.50
Took In	Took In	Took In	Took In
$22.75	$14.25	$4.00	$9.00
			(which is a part day only)

Next Winter I hope to make from $20.00 to $30.00 every day.

Enclosed you will find a little statement from the Mommiers[sic] people ask Mr. Turner if he does not think I got a pretty good price on my inner tubes.

Sorry that I missed waiting to you that day; that is just my way when I feel I do not hear from you. OOO upon OOO, XXX upon XXX

Chas.

{will look [sic] you a long letter next time}

———————◆———————

Postmark: 8 p.m. July 5, 1914, Detroit, Mich.

Addressed to Miss H.L. Cress, c/o Booth Fisheries

Sunday Am

My Dear Little Wife, -

Just got through in the office, had more office patients than usual for Sunday Am. Am going to get my machine out as soon as I write this letter, have got to make a trip over to Harper Hospital. If you were here we could make the trip together, getting anxious to hear from you in regard to Oct. 26th, this date strikes me better every time I think of it.

Had you have been here last night you would have had a sick Hubby to take care of. I blame it all on to the machine, I never walk any more, and my diet is just about the same as when I used to walk. The result is that I sure did get indigestion last night. I had to get up at 2 am and dope up. This is the first time I have felt sick in Years and when I do get sick, I sure think I am going to die. Those lines I used to have in my face have nearly all disappeared, I believe I have gained about 10 lbs. Since I do not have to walk often times I used to tease Mother about her food giving me indigestion, when I felt fine, so may be the Good Lord punished me last night.

Just myriads of OOO & XXX and a great big Hug.

Chas.

———————◆———————

Postmark: 5:30 p.m. July 6, 1914, St. Paul, Minn.

Sunday afternoon

My Dear Charles:

Just a little letter to my sweetheart. Mr. Turner brought your letter home this noon, didn't carry it in his pocket all day the way dad did. The heat is something terrible this afternoon, a little over ninety on the front porch. Addison is asleep in the hammock. Mr. Turner is in Minneapolis. Mrs. Turner and I are upstairs in the South bedroom, the coolest place in the house. Now you know what we are all doing. I have been so lonesome all day, yesterday too for that matter. Sundays and holidays sure are blue days for yours truly.

Say Charles, there is something I am going to ask you to do. You know if we just have a small wedding, there will be announcements to send out and they should be mailed from here I think, the morning after we are married. It will mean quite a little work to make out your list and addresses, so when you have any spare time, will you make out your list and send it to me? We really have to figure about a month to get them back from the printers and we should have our lists made out before we have them printed so we can figure accordingly. I really don't think it is too early to figure on this because there will be so many things the last minute. So get busy dear and make up your list. Have you any suggestions to offer along this line because I surely would like your opinion as well as mine, you are to be considered as much as I am.

*By the clipping [**Editor's Note:** No clipping found] you sent, Detroit surely is coming to the front, suppose you will be showing me those buildings some day in the near future and I sure will be happy when the time comes.*

Now think up all your school and college friends, relatives etc. that you would like to send announcements to. The way I am doing, I take each town we have lived in and the friends in those places. I put down their names as I think of them.

Mrs. Turner sends her love to your people and says she hopes you ae all well even though she would like you to get all the patients possible. Of course, it goes without saying I send my love, all you can possibly accept. I am glad there are not many more Sundays. I like yourself don't like them.

This is the way I make a squeeze (small circle inside a larger circle) and I send lots of them. That means a double hug. Lots of ◎ X and O's

From Hildred

I am wondering if I will get a letter tomorrow. Hope so. Am using the telephone book for a desk so please excuse my scribbling. H.C.

———————◆———————

Postmark: 3:30 p.m. July 6, 1914, St. Paul, Minn.

Charles Dear:

They were kind of late bringing the ten o'clock mail this morning so I went out and reminded the office boy of the fact. Not that I wanted or needed more work, but I was pretty sure I would get a letter from my "Hubby To Be" in Detroit. How's that? I look for a letter first thing in the morning and if I don't hear from you, I feel kind of disappointed and can't work as well.

Dad came home this morning but Mamma liked it so well, decided to stay a week longer so I will be chief cook until Mamma gets home. Don't know as yet whether they will pull through the week or not but I am afraid it will "not" especially if they get serious cases of indigestion every day the way you did. Was surely worried about you that day and if it hadn't been for your good constitution, don't know what would have happened.

I am afraid when I go to Detroit you will find out all my secrets. Last night Mr. Turner wasn't feeling well so he slept in my room and I slept with Mrs. Turner and guess I told her pretty near everything I knew. Maybe they didn't tease me this morning. I also had a crying spell in my sleep but don't know what it was all about. I sure do funny stunts.

As to the 26th of October. Charles, as far as I am concerned personally, yes, and wish it was only a week off but don't know just how things will turn out yet. If it will be more convenient for you to leave in October, I will surely try and fix it so it is convenient for you. Mr. Turner has asked me when we expect to be married and I told him I thought, some time the first part of Nov. and he insists that is too early, we should wait until the latter part of Nov. or Dec. I don't know whether he is joking but he seems real serious about it so I didn't dare say anything about October. Really I don't know what to do, but if it is more convenient for you, should we decide on Oct. some time? You know Mr. & Mrs. Turner are planning on going to Denver in Oct. some time and we sure want them to be at the wedding so we must sort of plan on that too.

I didn't ask Mr. Turner about the price you got on your inner tubes, he was too busy this morning but will let you know tomorrow. Don't I wish I could have a ride in that automobile though. Your comparative figures look good, did you have any accident cases on the Fourth?

Will write a big long letter to my sweetheart tomorrow as Mr. Turner will be in Chicago. I do wish you were here so I could talk to you instead of just write. Here are some more of those far fetched OOO XXX and ☺☺☺. You remember what the last is don't you?

Lovingly
Hildred

———————◆———————

Postmark: July 6, 1914, Detroit, Mich.

[Editor's Note: Despite its postmark, the letter appears to have been written June 5, 1914, shortly after Hildred and Charles became engaged. The letter is from Charles' mother, Emily Husband]

June 5th, 1914

Dear Hildred

I feel I must introduce myself to you, not being (illegible) in having anyone else to do so for me. It seems harder to write to one I haven't met but I am looking forward to the time when I shall have that pleasure. The time seems long to look forward to it but the months pass so quickly. I often look back and wonder where the time goes.

While it was a little surprise to me still I feel those things are to be, something we expect in life. No doubt when Charles gets married his business will increase. Some people think a Dr. must be married to be any good.

I hope you will never have any regrets at the step you are taking. I want him to make you a good Husband, as well as a good provider. If he is as successful in the future has [sic] he has been in the past there isn't any doubt but that he can give you a good home in the short future. I want to to feel (illegible) with me and I hope to feel the same with you and that we shall both be united in love one towards the other.

Yours lovingly
E. Husband

———————◆———————

Postmark: 5:30 p.m. July 6, 1914, Detroit, Mich.

Addressed to Chas. W. Turner, Booth Fisheries; dot on envelope flap

July 6/14.

My Dear Hildred, -

Received your letter of July 5th, guess I lost out on the 3rd, didn't I but if you were busy, you sure had a good excuse.

Note you had a good laugh, in regard to the experience of Dr. Moon and myself. I was quite sure you would not have laughed had you been there, I think in all probability you would have rolled down the back steps with the fellow's Wife. We might have called on you to have helped us out.

Lost a patient yesterday because I am not married, don't see why that should make any difference, but I guess it makes lots of difference with certain people, which I think is another pretty good reason to hurry a little what do you think, then again Nov. is a busier month than Oct.

I think I will close a little before time today, because while I feel better today than yesterday at the same time I feel pretty punk yet I suppose I ought not to have taken the people out for an auto ride Yesterday feeling the way I did.

Loads of OOO & XXXX and a Big Hug, from

Chas.

Postmark: 6 p.m. July 7, 1914, St. Paul, Minn.

Tuesday afternoon

My dear Charles:

I was awfully sorry to hear you were sick the other night. You want to be good now and not get sick again or you will find me in Detroit trying to find what is the matter. I surely hope you are better and won't ever have another attack like that. Probably it would be a good thing to take a little exercise every evening, take a good brisk walk.

As to the 26th of October: Yesterday I told Mr. Turner I wanted to ask him something but I wanted him to be serious about it and not answer in a joking way because really, I don't know when he is joking or when he is in earnest anymore. I told you could get away better in October and another thing would like it if we could make it in October. He said he didn't see that two weeks should make any difference, said he thought it would be a good plan as long as it is more convenient for you. He says when I leave him he is going to paint the office black but guess that is another joke.

Glad to know you are getting fat, keep up the good work. You could stand to gain quite a bit before you have too much. I weigh 125 again, guess I gained that playing lady at Mrs. Turner's. It doesn't agree with me to be idle, I gain too quick to suit me.

Charles, I just received a letter from your mother and I surely appreciate it with all my heart. It certainly was very kind of her to think of me and I know I will not feel near as strange now. Some how I feel like having a good cry over it, it pleases me so much. That letter surely will be a prize letter and kept with yours. I will answer it tomorrow.

I feel so good just wish you were here so I could give you a big hug. I would give you such a hard one you would have to tell me to let go.

It is just about 5 o'clock so will have to hustle home and get dinner. Was home this morning so have everything pretty near ready to put on the stove.

Just loads and loads of love from your lonesome kiddie,

Hildred

Postmark: 8 p.m. July 7, 1914, Detroit, Mich.

Addressed to Miss H.L. Cress, c/o Booth Fisheries

July 7/14.

My Dear Little Wife, -

Was sure pleased to receive your Sunday letter, if you miss a day I am disappointed. I try not to feel that way but I do. You may need to save all the pennies you have but some long sweet day when we get squared away, why such things won't bother us. (I am going down hill) [references a downward dip in his writing)

I will do as you say in regard to the addresses let me know that exact date you want them and I will hand them in ahead of time. The way you are planning is O.K. so go ahead. The only thing don't forget that Oct. 26 is going to be a nice day and Nov. 9th will be a stormy day.

Business is a little quiet today only made $6.00 so far but there is quite a bit of the day left.

Feeling quite a little better today, I was beginning to think of my troubles when your letter came after all those 6, X, O, I feel better, so send some more.

Am in a little hurry to-day going over to see Dr. Moon, promised to be there at 4 p.m. and I also have to put some water in my radiator.

Myriads of 6 6 6, XXX and plain ones as OOOOOO and a big Hug.

Chas.

Postmark: 5 p.m. July 8, 1914, St. Paul, Minn.

Wednesday

My Dear Charles:

Really I am so sorry to hear you are not well. I thought you would be all well by this time and it surely must be something more than indigestion. Now try and use some of your good pills on yourself because I am a bit anxious about you. I thought surely when I heard from this morning you would be feeling fine again. Mr. Turner says possibly you do not button up your coat when you are driving which you should do.

I myself am not feeling as spry as I might, I have another of my famous colds again and my head feels about as big as a bushel basket. I kind of suspected I was getting cold though my throat has been scratchy for several days. I think this must be what you call a sympathetic cold. You see I know you were not feeling extra well so I had to catch cold to keep up with you. I don't think it will last long because I have taken some of those famous pills and they should fix me up if anything does.

That surely is the limit to have to lose a patient because you were not married. I bet somebody felt blue for a few minutes. I shouldn't think that would have to make any difference, you would have to better work after we are married, will you? I think if your patients are going to do such stunts, we possibly better plan on the last week in October. Do you realize Charles how near at hand that is? Won't I be happy when the time does come though.

I haven't had time to do much sewing this week, it keeps me pretty busy just with the office and housework.

I don't fancy cooking meals when I get home at night but guess if the rest can stand it I can. Don't know just yet when the folks will be home, guess Claribel is coming back with Mamma. They plan on staying with grandma for a while yet and then go to Ashland for about a week. They may not stay that long though, don't know positively what they will do. Tonight papa is going to take Addison to the circus, the youngster can hardly wait. I expect to play circus with the ironing tonight, but you bet I didn't tell Mr. Turner that.

As to your inner tubes, Mr. Turner will write you about that and I will send your receipt back then.

Now, be real careful and get well. Maybe it is as dad says, people who are in love need a guardian all the time, that's what he tells me.

All kinds of OOO, XXX and ☺☺☺ to my sweetheart and a few extra kisses to make you all well again.

Lovingly,

Hildred.

P.S. Don't think I will have time to write to your mother today. Mr. Turner just got back from Chgo.

◆

Postmark: 5:30 p.m. July 8, 1914, Detroit, Mich.

Addressed to Miss H.L. Cress, c/o Booth Fisheries

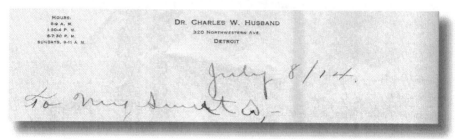

Always look for your letter every Am. The first thing I do every afternoon is to write to you that is if I get a letter every morning. Wish I were in St. Paul to help you out on that housekeeping stunt, I'll bet I could give some body indigestion without trying to.

Note you tell things in your sleep, [illegible] when somebody's Hubby isn't awake nights, I'll have a piece of paper and a pencil along with me too and if you happen to say anything about me I will bite your ear. Of course I will want you to say something.

Now in regard to our big day I sure want Mr. & Mrs. Turner to be present, but at the same time I would be delighted if you would tell Mr. Turner that I asked you to tell him that we were going to be married Oct. 26th if he says anything tell him the reasons I had for requesting it be on that date, think we will say just what he had to say. They would not stay in Denver over one week in all probability and possibly they would go a week earlier to be back in time. I think in about a week we will have the day settled of course I want to have it satisfactory to you. But you know the way it is I want to be living with my little Wife as soon as possible. Another thing in December cold weather starts in, and there just is no pleasure auto riding then. May say that I did not have any accident cases on the 4th although I had a pretty fair day.

This is about the stormiest time of the year in the practice of medicine, Next winter I hope to make up for it. And I ought to feel like working when I have a little Wife to love. I am glad you told me about the night business may be I do the same things.

With loads of OOO, XXX, and 𝟔 𝟔 𝟔, I am unable to make those squeezes as good as what you do but I send them.

With a big Hug

Chas.

Postmark: 7 p.m. July 9, 1914, St. Paul, Minn.

Thursday afternoon

My dear Charles:

I surely was pleased to hear from you, but that of course goes without saying.

Now as to the list of names you are getting up, and time you have that finished, send it along but try and have it here the latter part of September anyway. I no doubt will have some names on my list that you will have on yours so I will have to check it over and then don't you think we better figure about a month for the printer?

Of course it won't take that long but after we get them back they have all got to be addressed. I think it is a perfect shame you can't be here and help me, it would be so much more fun to do it together.

Note you say the 26th will be a nice day while Nov. 9th will not. You surely are a good weather profit, funny the U.S. Weather Bureau hasn't found you are this. I guess we will make October 26th that will be two weeks sooner and will please me just dandy now that I have thought it over. Just think only August and September and then October and we are married and I will be your really truly wife. Sometimes it seems almost like a fairy tale to me but then I just have to look at my ring and think of the pleasant week I had when you were here and I realize it must be true.

Yesterday we sent that desk pad to you, Wells Fargo express, prepaid so hope it reaches you safely. Maybe you won't like the odor of the burnt cork, then give it to some good friend, like Mr. Turner did, or fire it.

The choir is going to have their picnic Saturday, you know most of them got cheated out of it that rainy Saturday. Don't know whether I should go or not, think they will have a good time but I almost need all of the Saturday afternoons I can scrape together.

Awfully glad to hear you are feeling quite a bit better but what I would like to hear still more, is that you are all well again. It surely is too bad you had to get sick that way. My cold is about the same today, am going to try a hot mustard foot bath tonight.

Just loads of love and kisses [followed by a phrase in German],

Hildred

How is this, can you guess my little German ending here. If you can't guess what it is, I will have to tell you next time.

H.C.

◆

Postmark: 9 p.m. July 9, 1914, Detroit, Mich.

Addressed to Chas. W. Turner, c/o Booth Fisheries – Dot on envelope flap

July 9/14

My Dear Hildred, -

I sure do appreciate hearing from you every day. I will be tickled to death, if your work is only so that you can keep it up. Sorry I am not there to receive that big hug, I am surely lonesome for it. We will have some lost time to make up for.

As far as my Digestive apparatus is concerned I feel pretty good the warm weather and then again business being a little on the slow side makes me have rather a dull languid feeling.

My business for the 1st Eight days has amounted to –

Charged $72.00 Taken in $116.25

Now supposing, between ourselves we let our minds rest on Oct. 26th and tell our friends next fall, I will get more names and addresses for you in the near future.

If you get so fat I can't get my arms around you I will have to give you some anti-fat [illegible]. How will you like that. But you do not want to work too hard.

We will soon have to get our house decorated, which will mean about $300.00 for the two rooms, then there will be the cloths [sic] cubbys [sic]. I would like to get it done before you come, but if we don't get it done this fall we may be able to get the work done more reasonable next winter, when business is slower for those who do that work.

In about three years time if everything keeps going the way it has in the past, I believe we will have a pretty good home of our own, which will be rated at about $9000.00, then we have an auto and a garage. My Mother asked me this morning what was next. It seems as though I have always been striving for something, first it was getting the dough to study medicine, getting through getting into a Hospital, building a house, getting a practice, Best of all My Dear little Wife, then my automobile, now I suppose it is decorating, buying furniture, paying debts, getting another lot.

OOOOOO & XXXXXXX ⑥⑥⑥⑥⑥⑥⑥

Chas.

———————◆———————

Postmark: 7:30 p.m. July 10, 1914, St. Paul, Minn.

Friday afternoon

My dear Sweetheart:

I was surely glad to hear from you, and I wish the days would go twice as fast if I would get a letter that often.

You should have been here about fifteen minutes ago. Honestly Mr. Turner is the limit when it comes to teasing. He had some of the Fry girls from Omaha, and a Miss Cosgrove from Mpls. to lunch this noon and when they came back to the office, he introduced me as the young lady that was going to run away and get married and he kept it up for about ten minutes. I was so rattled, I believe if anybody had asked me my name I wouldn't know it. I had never met the girls before and maybe I didn't color up but I ought to be used to it by this time. I am only wishing you would get some of it.

Glad you told me you would stay awake nights to see what I said in my sleep. I will see to it now that you get to sleep before I do and then there won't be any chance of your hearing my secrets. That is where my hubby will get left and I will have the secrets instead but I won't bite you if you talk about me, I will give you a kiss instead.

Am sorry business is slower this month but cheer up, you must expect that in all lines of business it is bound to be slow once in a while. I will have to offer a little extra prayer in your behalf tonight to help the cause along.

As to telling Mr. Turner, you have no doubt have my letter telling you I have already asked Mr. Turner. He says he has only been teasing me and that we should go ahead and make whatever arrangements we want to, that we might as well get married one time as another so should we decide on the 26th? I wish it was the 10th of October all ready instead of July.

Elizabeth Goodjohn was over to the house last evening, she and her mother are visiting with Mrs. Turner. Edith C. and her cousin are coming to St. Paul this coming Sunday so they will surely have a house full.

We expected mamma home tomorrow but she has decided to go to Ashland for a little visit so possibly will not be home for a week or more. I surely would welcome you to do the cooking this week whether we got indigestion or not. By the way, you did not say in your letter today how you are feeling. I hope my "hubby to be" is all well by this time.

I send you some more "oodles" of love, kisses, hugs, etc. Have you guessed what my German was?

Lovingly,
Hildred

Mercy it is hotter than hot here today.

Postmark: 8:30 p.m. July 10, 1914, Detroit, Mich.

Addressed to Miss H.L. Cress, c/o Booth Fisheries

July 10th/14

To My Dear Little Kid Wife, -

Thanks for your sympathy in regard to my little sick spell, feel all OK, now. But Hildred you be sure and take those tablets and let me hear from you every day. I will be anxious about you until you are back to normal, you better write and tell the people you are sick and may be they will shorten their trip and help you out.

When I arrive in St. Paul you better have a whole lot of people around if you don't want to be loved to Death, because I know I just will squeeze you to pieces if there are no spectators.

Business seems slow now to what it did before I went away. Yesterday I just made $6.00, today so far $4.55, but we will give them the dickens this winter won't we. Nothing less than $400 to $500 per month will do.

Some of these days later on I am going to figure with you in regard to what part of my business belongs to My Dear Little Wife. If you have any suggestions to offer I wish you would make them known. I am planning on giving you a certain percentage, with certain things to pay. Or else having a joint bank a/c, possibly you would be more interested if you got a certain percentage what do you think.

I am inclosing [sic] to you a sample of tread gumm made by the Mommier [sic] Auto Supply Coy, Detroit, which I would like you to show Mr. Turner. All you do is to clean out the hole in your casing with a little gasoline and put a little cement in, then pack it with this tread gumm. I packed the hole made by the piece of glass I sent you, and now you can't find the spot, 25 cts worth goes a long way.

I used to like Sunday to come, I like it to come now in order that the time pass quickly otherwise it is a lonesome day. If you were here I could enjoy an auto ride Sunday.

From someone in Detroit who loves his little Sweet ♤ .

OOO, XXX, ۩ ۩ ۩ ۩ ۩ ۩

Chas.

———————◆———————

Postmark: 2:30 p.m. July 11, 1914, St. Paul, Minn.

Letter is typed, with Booth Fisheries envelope

Saturday noon

My Dear:

I hope you will not be disappointed if I do not write you much today, but I have decided to go to the choir picnic out at Tonka but will surely write you a dandy long letter tomorrow. I have promised Mr. Turner not to go in any rowboat and to stay out of the sun as it is something terrible outside, the hottest day we have had this year, over ninety in the shade. Don't you work too hard in this hot weather, take it a little easy so you don't get sick again. I surely was a little worried for a few days.

Lots of love from

H i l d r e d.

———————◆———————

Postmark: 8 p.m. July 11, 1914, Detroit, Mich.

Addressed to: Chas. W. Turner, c/o Booth Fisheries; dot on envelope flap

July 11th/14.

To My Dear Little Wife, -

Received your Thursday Letter, had a letter every day this week which I surely appreciated.

Sorry I am not there to help you out, but go easy and every thing will turn out all O.K. I will have those names and addresses for you in due time. As I said before I surely will love you to Death when I see you, I suppose if I had some sisters I would not be quite so much inclined that way. Therefore I might be a hindrance to you when you get so busy.

Received the desk pad in good order, kindly accept thanks, am writing on it this afternoon.

You better tell me just how that cold of yours is acting, and may be I can send you something more suitable for the occasion. As far as I am concerned I feel fine and dandy.

You got me on that little German stunt. I will be giving you some Latin or French the first thing you know, if you don't tell me what it is pretty soon I will have to take the letter to some friends of mine and have it translated.

By the way another Doctor is going to build across the street from me and locate there, but I don't know as that will make any great difference with me. This Doctor is located about 1-1/2 miles from here at present, but says business has been very quiet with him lately. Loads of OOOOO-XXXXXX, and ⒢ ⒢ ⒢.

Chas.

Postmark: 10 p.m. July 12, 1914, Detroit, Mich.

Addressed to H.L. Cress c/o Booth Fisheries

July 12th,/14

My Dear Hildred, -

Another one of those Sundays, one week nearer to my Little Wife. I think it too bad that you couldn't have lived in Detroit instead of St. Paul. If you were here today we would be out in our machine looking over the country.

It is just 9:30 Am. I already have made a trip out in the country to see a fellow who owes me $16.00. I didn't get anything but think I have stirred him up a little. I told him I had taxes to pay and certainly needed the money and that I did not feel I could hold him up any longer. He promised to come and see me July 18th.

Have just been looking over that little German expression of yours, think probably it means From your little Sweetheart.

Saturday afternoon after my office hours, I washed my car from top to bottom think possibly I will shine brass to-morrow. Next car I get I am going to have it trimmed with nickle[sic] instead of brass.

I surely hope you are feeling better by this time. I trust you are writing to me today, concerning your condition, as far as I am concerned I feel great and wish I could say the same about you, and know it to be right.

Just interrupted had two office patients in. Every patient I see makes me that much more anxious to get you here.

What you want to do Hildred is to plan on being all ready by the 19th then you will have a whole week to sleep before Oct. 26th comes, because I know you will be all tired out by the time you get to Detroit. Just the excitement alone will be enough for you.

Before closing I am going to send you the biggest Hug, Kiss and Squeeze that I have sent you so far compare them O, X, (§), and some little ones – OOOOOO XXXXXX (§) (§) (§) (§) (§) (§)

Just Loads of Love,

Chas.

Postmark: 9:30 a.m. July 13, 1914, St. Paul, Minn.

Sunday evening

My own dear Charles:

I do hope you get this letter Tuesday as I get one on Thursday, but possibly it will be a little late as I can't mail it until the morning.

My goodness, I have had such a busy time since Saturday noon, on the go pretty near every minute. You know I was in such a hurry to get away Saturday, I actually forgot to eat any lunch and never gave it a thought until we were coming home in the car that night. Four of we girls met at Ethel Crosby's home and started for Mpls. together; when we got there the rest of the crowd met us, - about 35 – and we all went to Minnetonka together. We took the Deephauen car and got off at Groveland Station. It certainly was a pretty place and only about three blocks walk to the beach and picnic grounds. I didn't intend to go in bathing so didn't take any suit along but Ethel knew some of the people living there and got me a suit. I surely had a fine time enjoyed every minute of it and only wished you could have been there. When it come to eating supper is when they teased me, of all the things they thought to say to me, it sure was the limit and Mr. Dane the choir director was as bad as any of them. I will have to tell you all about it some time. After supper we walked about a mile and a half to the dock and took the boat over to Excelsior to get the car. Excelsior Station is where we had dinner that day my sweetheart and myself were over at Tonka. Can you imagine who he was? Somebody pretty nice! When we got home it was just about nine o'clock so Ethel invited the crowd over to her house to have some music and finish up the sandwiches, cake, etc. Most all of them went and the boys got some ice-cream, so that sure was some busy day, don't you think so? I was so tired when I got home, papa didn't wake me this morning and mind you, I slept right through until 8:15 without waking. Isn't that laziness for you? I had to hustle around then, get breakfast, do dishes, dusting, get dinner and then this afternoon Gladys, a girl by the name of Serena and myself went to Lake Calhoun, Mpls. (where you and I were one evening) and we went in bathing again. It surely is just a splendid beach and what do you know dear, I am learning how to swim. Of course I can't go all alone as yet but Serena says I get the strokes just dandy and all I need is a little more confidence. She sure is a fine swimmer, can do diving and everything imaginable but she has just about lived in the water. Her home is on Puget Sound, Wash. so she sure has all the water she wants. Next time you see me, I hope to know how to swim that is something I have always wanted to learn. Next Sunday afternoon papa says if mamma isn't home he will go with us. This evening we were out for an auto ride with Mr. Turner, and surely enjoyed every minute of it. We were home by dark and then spent the evening up at Mr. and Mrs. Turner's. They have quite a bit of company now, Mrs. Goodjohn, Elizabeth G. and Edith from Duluth. Isn't that a dandy housefull [sic]?

Am awfully glad to hear you are all well again, you should have had me their [sic] to play nurse. I sure would have given you pills and a kiss after each one so they wouldn't taste so bad.

Now as to your business, if it is not as good as you would like it to be don't worry about it because this winter we will get out and boost it along and will sure reach the $500.00 mark or know why.

Don't worry about my getting so fat you can't get your arms around me because I will have you give me anti-fat before I get that big. Don't weigh 125 now, weigh about 123, guess this hot weather don't [sic] agree with me but I always go up and down from 120-125.

As to having your house decorated, if you can get it done cheaper this winter, why don't you leave it be? A couple of months won't make much difference in time but it might your pocket book. Sure, leave it go. And again, do you intend to have the whole house decorated at once? That will be pretty expensive won't it. I should think it would be a good plan to just have the downstairs decorated the winter and the upstairs next Sring or Fall. Of course, this is just a little suggestion and you will take it for what it is worth, possibly you would rather have it all done at once.

As to what my proportion of the earnings, or rather credits and debits will be, I will leave that you, whatever you think best. That percentage stunt surely seems good but I don't just know what you mean about the joint bank account.

If business isn't good next winter I will sure go out and put something in people's coffee to make them feel sick so they will have to call Dr. Husband.

Well dear, how is this for a lengthy epistle? I am about all talked out now and besides it is quite a bit past my bedtime. Let me have a good, big letter from you real soon but I have no kick coming you sure are a faithful Hubby for such a busy man as you are.

My cold is just about all well again, thanks to those wonderful little tablets. They are the best I have ever taken.

Just millions and millions of kisses and hugs to my dear sweetheart from

Hildred
S.W.A.K. – Guess!

2:30 p.m. July 13, 1914, St. Paul, Minn.

Monday afternoon

My dear Charles:

Quite a nice surprise this morning, got your letter in the early mail.

Trying to swim yesterday surely stiffened me up for today, I can hardly move any way but what I feel are ache or pain somewhere but that will not stop me from going again because I am determined to learn how to swim this summer. Gladys knew how last summer but can't stay up at all this summer.

What does that doctor mean by building right across the street from you? You just tell him he better get out of there right away because if he doesn't we will run him out of business this winter. Is he an elderly gentleman, or is he just starting out? Maybe some of your friends have told him how well you were doing and he is going to try and get some of your customers. We will lead him a merry chase this winter though, won't we?

As to that tread gum, Mr. Turner says he has never tried it but as long as it does such good work and is reasonable, thought maybe it would be a good thing to get a little. Mr. Turner has a great big hole in one of his filled tires and has to take the machine to Minneapolis to be fixed. It is about half the size of a tea cup.

Mamma and Claribel are leaving Phillips today for Ashland. Don't know just how long they will be there but now they say a week. To tell the truth, I will be glad when they get home.

If you should see me today, you would have to ask where your Hildred was, you would think I was some Indian girl running around. I surely got pretty well tanned up yesterday, hope I will get bleached out by October.

Tomorrow I am going to tell you something the lady next door told me, a little would-be advice as it were. Have not got time today.

That little German phrase translated simply is "From your dear future" or "dear wife." That is the way you would say "From your dear wife to be."

Just loads of love from your Indian girl.

Hildred

Just imagine a big hug.

◆

Postmark: 8:30 p.m. July 13, 1914, Detroit, Mich.

Addressed to Chas. Turner c/o Booth Fisheries; envelope flap missing

Monday 4 p.m.

My Dear Hildred, -

Pleased to hear from you. You better tell Mr. Turner if he does not stop teasing you we will get married in Sept. instead of Oct. Then you in all probability will scare him.

Pleased to note that you have decided on Oct. 26th. But I just know I will get terribly anxious before that time. My if you were only here now. I know too that I will feel much freer to get away in Oct.

Have just made $6.00 so far today, which according to what other Doctors tell me is pretty good for my first July in practice, but I believe times will soon be a great deal better and my business will also be busier, I have made $100.00 this month so far and taken in $140.00 of course this amount will keep my Little Wife and I but I want to make about $30.00 a day. We have not found a wash-woman so I was back to my old job this A.M. The lady next door laughed at me and invited me over to her house, she saw me through the basement window. My Mother and I picked over 10 boxes of red currants this afternoon, then I took care of the letter I had to do also. Of course I can travel around pretty fast in the Machine.

Last night we had such an electrical storm that none of us could scarcely sleep, I pulled my shades down and the lightening would reflect in the room even at that. I just thought if My Dear Little Wife were only here that she would have wanted to cuddle up pretty close to her Hubby. It rained so that the rain beat in under the door that leads out on our back porch upstairs, something it never did before.

You did not say how your cold is.

Just bunches of OOOOOO O, XXXXXX X, ⑥⑥⑥⑥⑥⑥ ⑥ , and a Great big Hug.

Chas.

———————◆———————

Postmark: 7:30 p.m. July 14, 1914, St. Paul, Minn.

Tuesday afternoon

My dear Charles:

I was surely pleased to hear from you today as I was sort of out of sorts with the world as it were. Don't be alarmed at all or worry either because I will be allright [sic] in a day or so but my cold is worse again and I sure have an awful headache in the back of my head since yesterday afternoon which is something unusual for me. This afternoon papa and Mr. Turner simply made me go to the Doctor's (Dr. Lankester) and the first thing he did was to feel my pulse and ask me if I stayed up late at night and did any work. I told him I did some but not very much and he said I simply had to quit it or else quit working at the office because my pulse was away too high and he could tell I was overtaxing myself. I laughed, really I couldn't help it because I know I am not doing too much. He gave me a tonic to take, nothing for my cold because he said if I were in good condition I would not take cold so easy. Mr. Turner told him some time since that you and I we're going to be married this fall and he surely spoke very highly of Dr. Husband. He says if I don't go to bed at ten o'clock every night and quit my working nights he is going to write to you so I guess I better be good when I come back to the office. I accused Mr. Turner of talking with Dr. Lankester before I went there but he says on his honor he hasn't seen him since yesterday.

Now listen dear, don't worry about me one bit because I assure you I am not working too hard and I never felt better in my life. If it wouldn't be for this little headache I happen to have. Last night I was in bed by ten o'clock and tonight I will do the same and by tomorrow I will feel like a top. Don't you go worrying about me now but you wanted to know how I was and if you do worry I won't tell you again, see!

As to being ready by Oct. 19th that is a good idea but that is what I want to write you about when I get a little more time have been awfully busy lately; Mr. Turner was in Mpls. this morning so I did not get to the office until pretty near noon, caught up a little at home.

Have not got that tonic yet (suppose it is real bitter) but will send you a copy of the prescription tomorrow so you can see if the medicine is all right. I just dread taking that stuff.

That great big hug, squeeze and kiss was fine, send some more like them. I am getting out of practice and we will have to make up for all this lost time.

XXXOOO⑥⑥⑥
Lovingly,
Hildred

S.W.A.K. means "Sealed with a kiss"

———◆———

Postmark: 8:30 p.m. July 14, 1914, Detroit, Mich.

Addressed to Chas. Turner c/o Booth Fisheries; dot on envelope flap

July 7th/14 – out of order?

My Dear Little Wife, -

I surely thought I was not going to get a letter today, but sure enough one came on the last mail;

Sorry to say that I will not have time to write you much today, as I have got to take a friend of mother's over to Palmer Park and be back in time for dinner.

You don't know how pleased I was to get that dandy long letter and I am going to make up for it tomorrow.

Awfully lonesome to see you. Just oodles of OOOOOO, XXXXXX, & ⓖ ⓖ ⓖ ⓖ ⓖ ⓖ and a great big hug.

Your Hubby,

Chas.

———◆———

Postmark: 3 p.m. July 16, 1914

St. Paul, Minn.

Typed

July 15, 1914

My dear Charles:

Just received your letter a little while ago. Mr. Turner is over at the Dentists and my work is finished so will take this opportunity to write you.

First thing I want to tell you is what our neighbor lady told me Sunday. She said she heard I was to be married this Fall etc. wished me good luck and then said, "Of course I do not know what month you are planning on getting married but whatever you do, don't get married in October." She pretty near took my breath away and I asked her why. She says both May and October are unlucky months to be married in, that she was advised against but was married in Oct. anyway and that she has had bad luck ever since and then started to tell me a string of her troubles. I was awfully provoked at her for telling me that, because while I didn't believe it, it makes me feel kind of leary just the same. Just because she had a lot of trouble isn't saying we will, do you think so? Maybe we better wait until the first of November or aren't you superstitious? I didn't let her know we wre planning on October, maybe she was just trying to find out something.

You surely must have been a busy man Monday doing a washing and picking over currants, you should have been here last night to help us with the raspberries. Papa and I put up two crates of raspberries. I tell you we are some cooks, between the two of us we manage to get things together somehow. I also dampened the clothes last night so that means get busy and iron tonight.

Did I tell you Elizabeth Goodjohn and her mother were visiting with Mrs. Turner? They expect to be here for several weeks. Thursday night Elizabeth, Gladys, Serena and myself are going down to the Wilder Baths to see what they look like. The rest of the girls want to go in but I am undecided, I want to see what they look like first.

I am getting awfully stylish lately Charles, don't know whether you will like it or not but I have a pair of slug pearl earrings. Sidney was out playing tennis and when he came home he found them in his pocket. Guess while his coat was hanging up some girl dropped them into the wrong coat. He said he couldn't use them so if I wanted them I could have them, isn't that great? Dad and Mr. & Mrs. Turner think they look fine so guess I will wear them once in a while.

I am enclosing that prescription to you. I think it is merely some water with something bitter in it to make me think I am taking something for my health. Let me know if it is going to kill me by inches or what? I sure hate to think of two o'clock, that is when I have to take it again. I feel a great deal better today and think my cold is better. My headache was gone this morning when I got up but my head feels kind of sore yet. I am feeling lots better though and know by tomorrow I will feel "Great."

You won't want to have any of those electrical storms when I get to Detroit because I sure am scared of them and would be apt to lock myself in some clothes closet until it was over with.

Just all kinds of love and kisses from your sweetheart, Hildred

P.S. Did you ever hear the song "I never thought I'd miss you as I do —oo-oo Each day seems like a year away from you-oo-oo

Think I will have to start singing that song pretty soon.

H.L.C.

———————◆———————

Postmark: 9 p.m. July 15, 1914, Detroit Mich.

Addressed to Miss H.L. Cress, c/o Booth Fisheries

July 15th/14.

My Dear Little Wife, -

You don't know how pleased I was to get that nice long Sunday Letter, It was surely dandy.

Glad you told me in regard to bathing. I would suggest that you be pretty careful, not to stay in the water too long, or to go in where the water is deep. Another thing I would suggest not to wear any bathing suit even though you know who it belongs to unless it has been boiled for 20 minutes. A Doctor as you know meets with those who are sorry too late. I would not wear one no matter who wore it before unless it was boiled for twenty minutes.

Now in regard to business, yesterday I had a funny day, did not make a single cent until 1:20 pm. yesterday, and before the day was over I made $8.00 In the morning I got my hair cut, drove over to the Ford assembling room, got my transmission filled with grease also my dope enps. [**Editor's Note:** medicine envelopes] and took care of the surgical clinic at St. Mary's Hospital. In the afternoon I took my Brother's old sweetheart over to Palmer Park to meet some party there about 20 miles in all, may say I made it in about 20 minutes, how is that for going, don't tell Mr. Turner.

In regard to decorating why I would like to have it done as soon as possible is because it makes the place look so much better, but I will leave it depending on business.

May say that a joint bank account is where the money is put in the bank under two names and either party can draw it.

You rather have me on that S.W.A.K. business, I rather imagine something but dare not say it for fear it be wrong. So will you tell me?

My right arm and hand is pretty low today on account of cleaning out my crank case. I drained all the oil out, poured in a gallon of gasoline, turned by hand to wash it, and refilled with fresh oil. I suppose I will have to be an engineer next.

Now Hildred supposing we got ready before Oct. 26th would you consider cutting the time a little shorter say by two weeks, now I am not asking you to do this just asking your opinion that's all.

I have just received your Monday letter. A year ago if anybody had told me I Was going to love a papoose I would have believed them not, but an accordance with your letter I do. Better wear a sun bonnet next time.

That Doctor has not started to build across from me as yet. I believe he has been considering it for a long time he may possibly flunk out. He is about 36 years old and has been practicing about a mile and one half away from here for the last 7 or 8 yrs.

Don't forget to tell me what the lady next door said.

I suppose you think that, that cousin Edith of mine is a regular tart, but I suppose she would have to quiet down a little being at Turner's. Last summer Ruth Schofield and Edith offered to give me lessons in loving for $10.00 apiece and suggested that I go to Isle Royal and take them, what do you know about that, or do you want that I go before we are married.

I just wish you were here so I could have a nice little kiss, a great big Hug & a tight squeeze.

Just loads of love.

Chas.

———————◆———————

Postmark: 4:30 p.m. July 16, 1914, St. Paul, Minn.

Typed; Booth Fisheries envelope

Thursday

My dear Charles: -

Was surely pleased to get your little letter this morning, because to tell the truth I hardly expected to hear from you today, did not think you would get my letter in time but am mightly [sic] glad you did.

Have not got time to write much today either because this morning I was checking up Mr. Turner's June balance at the bank, have not had time to do it before and I was out $300.00. It is the first time I have ever been out and I worked pretty near all morning and could not find the pesky thing. How I happened to make the mistake. I had an amount of $419.00 and in checking them this time I run a line through it like this (419.00) and it made the four look just like a figure one because they all have a little hook on them. I surely was glad to find it but now have to hustle and catch up with my work.

You should have seen papa help me with the ironing last night, he worked fine. He ironed all of the handkerchiefs and did pretty good even if he did get the initial away on the inside of the handkerchief in folding them but did not worry about that this week because there sure was quite an ironing to do in one evening and I was bound to get it done last night, did not want to start in again tonight. I did not get to bed until 11:30 last night but will make up for it tonight and go to bed early. I did not have time to press papa's trousers this week so got cheated out of my 25-cents a pair, I do that as a little side issue.

My cold is not better yet, about the same but my headache is all gone and I must say I feel better if he [sic] wouldn't be for the crazy cold but don't worry about me because I am coming along just fine.

Must get busy now so goodbye until tomorrow when I expect to get that nice long letter from you.

Your ever loving,

H i l d r e d

Just "oodles" of love.

◆

Postmark: 9 p.m. July 16, 1914, Detroit, Mich.

Addressed to Chas. Turner c/o Booth Fisheries; dot on envelope flap

July 16, '14

My Dear Little Wife, -

Was pleased to hear from you, but very sorry indeed to hear that you are not feeling good. There is just one thing I am going to ask you to promise me that is "Not to go in bathing next Sunday or not for ten days." I am going to take the liberty of considering that you have made me this promise until I hear from you. I think or have every reason to believe that the water business of last Sat. & Sunday has all to do with your present trouble. Just remember that inside of two weeks that my little love and myself will saying month after next and you know nothing must interfere.

By the way in regard to the wedding and your planning to have anybody stand up with us or not. I would suggest not of course if it were going to be a big affair I would suggest in the affirmative on that particular day. I would like to have my Brother and his Wife from Duluth maybe one or two of the country's then Mr. & Mrs. Turner, I do not know what my Mother will do. She seems to think she will either stay here to answer the telephone etc. seeing I will not be sending out any notices. However I am leaving all these things to you for final settlement. I suppose Mr. Turner will want to take us away from the house, do you think we better call a taxi of course almost have to let Mr. Turner know our plans, but I don't want everybody at the Hotel to know we just got married. Where had we better take our train to Mpls. or St. Paul then we will put up near the depot. Am train will leave Mpls. at 7:30 Am & St. Paul at 8:30 Am.

I'll tell you what to do get Mr. Turner to make you a promise that he will shield us, not let anybody in on our plans or whereabouts if we let him know otherwise nix. Then I would have to ask you to see about our tickets for the return trip. In all probability will not arrive in St. Paul until 10 Am of the big day and therefore will not have much time.

My business amounted to yesterday $7.75 took in $13.75 so far today 3 p.m. made $8.25 Took in $10.75

I heard mother say she was going to write to my sweetheart pretty soon. You surely wrote her a very nice letter, and your Hubby appreciates it, I pleaded with Mother to let me read it & she did. She held off quite awhile to tease me.

Don't forget to tell me what the lady next door said, also about Oct. 19th.

If you were here I could give you a good fast ride in my machine. I usually peak around every couple of blocks to see whether or not a cop is coming. Don't tell Uncle Chas. that because I am very careful.

Just look OOOOOOOOOOOOOOO OOO XXXXXXXXXX XXX

and a great big Hug.

Chas.

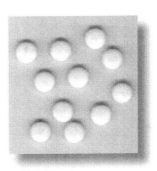

◆

Postmark: 3:30 p.m. July 17, 1914 - St. Paul, Minn.

Friday the 17th

My dear Charles:

I felt just fine when I came to the office this morning, got to bed at 10 o'clock last night but when I found that dandy big fat letter waiting for me I felt still better. See what good your letters do! After I finished reading it I was standing by the window, smiling at what you said regarding Edith and Ruth and was putting on my apron. Some fellow from the West Pub. Co. was just going to work and when he saw me smiling I guess he thought I was trying to flirt with him and he smiled back as hard as he could and tipped his hat. Maybe I didn't sober up pretty quick and get busy at my desk!

As to your taking loving lessons from Edith and Ruth, well I don't know about that, I think if it came to a show down you could show them a few things, at that. By the way, where did you get all your experience?

As to the joint bank account, that sounds rather good too, however either plan would be satisfactory to me. We can talk that over though a little later personally, maybe when we are making our trip home, what do you say?

As to the S.W.A.K. I told you the other day, no doubt you know by this time. I am real anxious to know what you thought it meant though so be sure and tell me.

Regarding getting married before Oct. 26th, you are getting kind of anxious it seems to me. Now really, don't you think the 26th is soon enough, you know there is really just a short time until then and I have hardly had anything made the past two weeks, have not had time as it has kept me pretty busy with the house since mamma is not there but she has promised to help me as soon as she gets home which I think will be Monday evening.

Write me another one of those big letters again, the boy that got the mail this morning said he had such a big one for me he had to come back on the truck, it was too much to carry.

As to some tablets Charles, could I ask you to send a few more of those brown pills, they are dandy. I finished taking what you sent, last Sunday and then Sun. I guess caught another dandy cold and have been taking some of Mr. Turner's couyza [sic] tablets but they don't seem to help me so much. You don't need to send many because it only takes a few of those to put me in shape again. This cold has hung on pretty long now and I am getting anxious to get rid of it. I feel just fine only that I have this cold.

Just loads of love and some of those far fetched hugs and kisses from

Yours,

Hildred

Postmark: 5:30 p.m. July 17, 1914, Detroit, Mich.

Addressed to Miss H.L. Cress, c/o Booth Fisheries

[**Editor's Note**: The return address on the envelope is now 320 Northwestern Ave., Detroit]

July 17th/14

My Dear Hildred, -

Received your letter with the enclosed ppt. Note what your neighbor lady told you. Don't you pay any attention to what she said, if she says any more about it to you, you tell her that I say she is an old witch, how could there be any truth in such things as that, married life is just what you make it, the trouble is she hasn't bad luck, her misfortune on her part, so forget it. As I told you before Oct. 26 is going to be a fine day and another thing look how much time we are losing now. Just think it is 14 weeks before I can actually love my little Wife.

In regard to the ppt., he sure gave you a large bottle, it costs me about 15 cents for six oz. of that Medicine. You better take it, it will not do you any harm anyway.

Your Hubby took a hunch and woke up just a little yesterday instead of making from $6 – to - $8. He made $16.00 and took in $10.00 See if you had been my little wife on Yesterday on the 30% business you would have made $4.80 instead of $2.50 and when your Hubby averages $30.00 a day that will be $9.00 a day for his little wife.

Have you been writing to my Mother in secret, she sure is sticking up for you already. You know I give my Mother her Morning rub, she does not like them in the warm weather any too well, she says they make her face smart. Mother got after me this morning and ticked my ribs, something that I can't stand very well, then I told her Hildred wouldn't do that, so she told me I would have to [illegible] myself when you come, else I won't get beat up. Would you help my Mother beat me up. Some doing if you wish I will demonstrate a rub to you. Rubs are my speciality.

Rub = _____

Just loads of _____ _____ _____

OOOOOO XXXXXX & 🅖🅖🅖🅖🅖
And a Big Hug.
From your Hubby
Chas.
P.S. Note my new envelope C.W.H.

---◆---

Postmark: 3:30 p.m. July 18, 1914, St. Paul, Minn.

Saturday

Dearest Charles:

Just tickled to death pretty near to hear from you and yes, you have my promise that I will not go in the water Sunday. Furthermore, this time I do not intend to go in until my cold is all well. I was pretty near over my cold last Saturday and then had to do the foolish stunt of going in the water. I had a dandy time but guess I am paying for it this week. Last night papa made me take a hot mustard footbath and a hot lemonade and get right to bed. I felt pretty near like a furnace inside after all that.

As to having somebody stand up for us, to tell the truth I was sort of figuring that way but if you would rather not have it that way, all right.

I asked Mr. Turner as to where we should leave from and he said St. Paul right away. He said at first he was planning on taking us to the hotel with his machine but since then thought possibly it would be better to get a taxi because if he went down with us possibly mamma would say she and dad wanted to go along down or something similar so they would think we were going to the train and I wouldn't want that, would you? As to the tickets, yes I will attend to that and see that we get the right tickets.

As to your mother coming, I surely wish she could make it but I hate so say anything about it to her because maybe for reasons of her own she would rather not come. However, let me know if you would like me to say something to her because I surely would love to have her here if she can arrange it.

What do you think we should do, just send a little note to our own relations that are coming and then have announcements sent out, or send a regular invitation to them? I think possibly grandpa and grandma Cress and my Aunt Louise and her husband will come and possibly Uncle Dan. I will write you more tomorrow.

Ever so much love and kisses from

Hildred

———————◆———————

Postmark: 8:30 p.m. July 18, 1914, Detroit Mich.

Addressed to Charles W. Turner c/o Booth Fisheries; envelope flap does not survive

[**Editor's Note:** This is an empty envelope]

———————◆———————

Postmark: 10 p.m. July 19, 1914, Detroit, Mich.

Addressed to Miss H.L. Cress c/o Booth Fisheries

July 19th/14

My Dear Little Hildred, -

Sunday again, and I am in a hurry as I have to be at the Depot in ¾ hrs. to meet Mrs. Turner from Chicago and want to mail this letter before I go.

I surely hope my little Wife is feeling better today. Because if you die somebody else will follow suit. And I am sure I want to live.

By the way that Mother of mine sure sticks up for Hildred, I told her that Hildred would go halves on the price of the fruixt [sic] she puts up. Mother will not hear to any thing, she says I have to put up or pay instead of you. So I tease her. What do you know about that. Business has been a little better the last few days. Seems something like old times. Made $11.50 this am. My wife and I will have money to take a trip to Europe some day, as it is I intend to spend a year in Vienna in study, when I get the money.

I just wish you were here today. I got Dad to wash my car and shine all the brass, and it looks fine for a ride, had two pretty long trips this AM. If you were here I would just have to hug you so hard, may be I would hurt you. Time is getting short, will write more to-morrow.

Just Loads & Loads of love and a big hug.

S.W.A.K. How's that

Chas.

Postmark: 9:30 a.m. July 20, 1914, St. Paul, Minn.

Sunday evening.

My dear "Best of All": -

How does that sound to you? Note by your letter you were not very well pleased at what the neighbor lady told me and I can't say that I blame you, think she says a lot while the day is long. I am enclosing a little clipping [Ed. Note: Does not survive] that Addison cut out of the paper and handed to me. He surely takes a lot of interest as to when we are going to be married. I don't believe a day passes that he don't ask me something about it.

As to the medicine I am taking, you surely ought to make money if you could buy all that for fifteen cents, that medicine cost a whole sixty-five cents, what do you know about it. I think that medicine business must be a "get rich quick stunt".

The sixteenth surely must have been a good day, they must have kept you busy cranking your machine that day. I am always pleased to hear when you have had a good day because I know that is what you like, and again the money looks good to me.

I am glad to know you are tickled, now I will know how to get even with you. I may not help your mother to "beat" you up but I sure will help her tickle you. That is the way we get even with dad, we can't beat him in a wrestle but if we once can get our fingers down his neck we have him beat because he simply can't do a thing.

I intended writing a nice long letter tonight but it is getting late and papa keeps telling me to turn out my light and get to bed so I will tell you the news in the morning.

By the way, what is a rub, that is something new, maybe it is like my dad gives.

Don't forget to tell me what you thought S.W.A.K. meant.

All my love, XXX OOO and ☺☺☺ to my sweetheart from,

Hildred

———————◆———————

Postmark: 7 p.m. July 20, 1914, St. Paul, Minn.

Hand-written; envelope from Booth Fisheries

Monday, July 20th, 1914

My Dear Charles:

Was real glad to hear from you, but don't see how I can keep from going bathing for a whole month you know I just got enough to want to go again but if you would rather that I didn't go in, all right I won't. After a month from yesterday though I think I will make another attempt, will that be all right? Of course I must take my dear Hubby's advice.

You should have been with us yesterday, we surely had a nice time. Gladys came out to spend the afternoon and evening with me, Henry (her friend) having gone to St. Peter Minn. over Sunday. About 2:30 Mr. Turner called for us and took us all down to Mr. Kochendorfer's farm. Isn't that a name? That is Mr. Turner's butter man. There was Mr. Turner, dad and Addison in the front seat, Mrs. Turner, Mrs. Goodjohn and Elizabeth in the back and Gladys and myself in the middle. We had just a dandy ride and after we got there we found three other girls there just about our age so maybe we didn't have a good time. About 4:00 Mr. Turner took the whole crowd of girls and Mr. K down to South St. Paul just for the ride and to see what it was like. We did not intend to stay for supper but when we got back they wouldn't let us go so we girls got supper and then dad washed the dishes and Mrs. Turner and Mrs. Goodjohn wiped them. We left quite early and then the folks spent the rest of the evening at our house. We surely had a dandy time, enjoyed every minute of it.

Say you can't guess what I got yesterday for my "Hope Box" as it were. Elizabeth gave me a lunch cloth and six napkins, the prettiest set you ever saw. Each napkin has a little basket of flowers in one corner, worked with cross stitch and the cloth has the cross stitch and their [sic] in another corner my three initials. It certainly is a little beauty and maybe I wasn't pleased to get it.

Mamma and Claribel are coming home this afternoon at 4:30 and then my duties as cook are at an end. I didn't mind it though, it was really kind of an experience. The only thing I didn't like about it was I didn't have much time to sew but mamma says she will help me as soon as she gets home.

What do you think Mr. Turner says, he says I am writing too many letters to you, that it interferes with your business and you have not time to read them. Is this a fact? He suggests we write about once a week but of course, I think he says this as a joke.

*The letter you enclosed [**Editor's Note:** Enclosure follows] was pretty good suppose you will get more than one of those. I have received all kinds of circular matter asking me to call and look over stationery for one thing, furniture and all kinds of things like that. Suppose they* got our names out of the paper. *All of the OOO XXX and* 🙂🙂🙂 *hugs imaginable to my dear sweetheart,*

*From
Hildred*

P.S. I forgot to mention your envelopes, don't think I would have noticed them, was so anxious to get to your letter. -HLC.

CABLE ADDRESS "REGANHOD"

Hotel Knickerbocker

FORTY-SECOND STREET AT BROADWAY

New York, July 15th, 14, 191

JAMES B. REGAN

Dr. Charles W. Husband,
Detroit, Mich.

Dear Sir:-

Your esteemed patronage is respectfully solicited should you contemplate a trip to New York City after your marriage. You will find that an air of refinement predominates in every part of the Hotel Knickerbocker, and you certainly will not make a mistake by spending a few days with us. We will care for your wants and look after your entertainment in a way that will make you feel at home.

Assuring you of our urgent desire to give you every attention possible, and trusting that we will have the pleasure of caring for you and that we may hear from you prior to your arrival, beg to remain

Yours very truly,

James B. Regan

Z/EBJ
Enc.

Dear Sir:-

Your esteemed patronage is respectfully solicited should you contemplate
a trip to New York City after your marriage. You will find that an air of
refinement predominates in every part of the Hotel Knickerbocker, and
you certainly will not make a mistake by spending a few days with us.
We will care for your wants and look after your entertainment in a way
that will make you feel at home.

Assuring you of our urgent desire to give you every attention possible,
and trusting that we will have the pleasure of caring for you and that we
can hear from you prior to your arrival, beg to remain

Yours very truly,
James B. Regan

Postmark: 10 p.m. July 20, 1914, Detroit, Mich.

Addressed to Miss H.L. Cress, c/o Booth Fisheries

Monday

My Dear Hildred, -

Just received your letter, note that cold is still with you, and I sure will get some
tablets right off to you, I trust you will let me know every day just how you are getting
along. Am very sorry it is keeping up so long. You know if it lasts too long you will
be getting hay fever, asthma or something like that, these things are very bad so be
careful.

You asked me where I got my experience in regard to what I told you about Edith &
Ruth, may say partly from Mother and the rest from loving Mother & Hildred. You
surely have told me things I never knew before, as in regard to what S.W.A.K. meant.
I was ten miles away in my guess, also as what (Ḡ) was. Now you will tell me where
you got your experience, won't you, fair exchange is no robbery. I just wish you were
here now. My! I just bet anything you would think I had been in training since I last
saw you. I would just squeeze you so tight.

I surely thank you for making me that promise in regard to bathing, I trust you have
received a later letter from me with something more in it along this line.

May say that I spoke with my Mother in regard to having some lady stand up with us
and it really was her suggestion that I quoted to you. The way Mother talked to me I
thought her ideas were pretty good in as much as it would have a tendency to make
the day quieter. However you are the one to decide these things, and if you would

like somebody to stand up with us, that settles it. I will tell you what to do you get everything arranged in your mind let me know and then I will tell you what I think about it.

In regard to my Mother going to St. Paul, the only thing if I have a number of sick patients at that time it would be fine for me to have her stay here as she knows more about my work than anybody else, you can write to her about it, we may be able to fix things up. Of course I will have to arrange to have my patients taken care of.

In regard to asking certain relatives to the big event, either way you have suggested is O.K. Have a little neuralgia headache today so am not any good on the think. But you go ahead draw up the plans and let me know.

By the way that Dr. started to build across the road today, but there will be a time when we all will have all the business we want. As long as we are able to take care of it.

I send you all the O's X's and ⓖ there are in me and the greatest Hug of all times. Your Hubby "To Be"

Chas.

PS.

Will probably write to Uncle Chas. tomorrow

CWH

Postmark: 6 p.m. July 21, 1914, St. Paul, Minn.

Tuesday

My dear Charles:

Was pleased to get your Sunday letter and surely glad to know that business is picking up again. Keep up that good work and we sure will be able to go to Europe some day.

While I enjoyed my ride Sunday, I know I would have enjoyed it a great deal more if you had been there or I had been in Detroit to ride with you.

As to being afraid I am going to die, I am a pretty live one as yet and don't expect to die for a long time to come. My cold seems quite a bit better today, think it will be all well by the end of the week and I feel fine. I think if I did not have this cold and you did not have my promise, I would be tempted to try and go swimming again. It is awfully warm here today, heard somebody say 98 and then I sure felt warm. Now, if my cold is better in a week, I can go bathing before a month is up can't I? You know that will be late in August.

Mr. Turner leaves tonight for Duluth and Port Arthur and is going to take Mrs. Turner, Mrs. Goodjohn and Elizabeth with him. They expect to be back here about next Sunday and then Monday night Mr. Turner leaves for Kansas City and St. Louis. I think during the next two weeks I will be getting lazy unless I can find something to do out in the other office.

You surely will have to be good when I get to Detroit otherwise you will have both your mother and myself after you and I think you will have to go some to get ahead of us when we are both after you.

I surely did miss Claribel when she was away and am glad she is home again. We got to bed by 10 o'clock but I wouldn't say what time we got to sleep, we had too much to talk about. I guess she had a fine time all right.

Just ever so much love and kisses from your sweetheart

Hildred.

P.S. Don't forget I am wondering what you thought S.W.A.K. meant. If you have not sent those pills, don't bother because I believe my cold will be all well in a few days. Thanks ever so much just the same.

"Wifie"

------------◆------------

Postmark: 8:30 p.m. July 21, 1914, Detroit, Mich.

Addressed to Charles W. Turner, c/o Booth Fisheries; dot on flap

July 21st/14.

My Dear Hildred –

Just received your letter on the last mail. I sure would have had the blues or felt lonesome had I not received it.

Hildred do you know had I have payed [sic] attention to what anybody and everybody told me and lived up to what they advised me to do I would not be worth anything to-day, the only way to accomplish anything is to carefully plan it and put all your energies into it, if you are a stickler nothing can stop you, there is nobody on earth who can keep you down, unless you give up to them, so do not pay any attention to neighbors, what the newspaper has to say, I Don't care what month we get married in regard as to how these storys [sic] read, if it is in us to get along we will, nobody can keep us down. I don't see any reason to fear, I have a good start and we are going to make good and live happy, so don't worry. $12.00 so far today, and I have another call to make and it is just 4 p.m.

My Rub I believe is something like your Daddy gives will show you when I see you.

Enclosed you will find a little envelope for Mr. Turner [Ed. Note – does not survive]. Will be pleased if you give it to him.

Will write you more tomorrow.

I surely send all my love to you and a Big Hug.

Chas.

———————◆———————

5:30 p.m. July 22, 1914, St. Paul, Minn.

Wednesday afternoon

My Dear Charles:

Thanks for the dandy letter, also for the tablets, it was real nice of you to send them so soon. I have taken two of them and it is pretty near time for the third and I know I will be O.K. in a day or two. My cold doesn't make me feel bad at all. I feel just fine so guess there is no danger of my getting anything else. As to yourself, I hope that headache didn't last very long, they are mean things to have. Had I been there, I should have given you a good massage, how would you like that?

As to your experiences along certain lines which you wrote about, I don't know Charles, but I think you were a pretty apt scholar by the time you started loving me and as to my experience, why I didn't have any, I merely saw mamma and dad spooning. You taught me all I know about such things. As to the ☺, I made that up myself. I sure wish you were here so I could get one of those famous hugs.

Saturday afternoon our S.S. [Sunday School] class is going to have a picnic out at Lake Harriet, Mpls. and in the afternoon they are all going in bathing. I would like awfully well to take that in, but can't see my way clear owing to the promise you have from me.

Now, I am going to ask you a few questions before going any further with our plans. As I understand it, you would rather just have a small wedding, that is relatives only. Am I right? So many of my friends here think we are going to have a large wedding and I know they are sort of planning that way. I haven't said anything to them, just let them think as they like and when they ask when, or any other questions, I simply say we expect to be married some time this fall and haven't made any definite plans as yet. I don't know, but in a way I think a home wedding would be nice, that is, invitte some of our best friends. It is something that we hope will happen only once in a lifetime and I kind of think it would be nice. Now don't think I am planning on this, I merely want to know your opinion and maybe it is only a passing thought of mine. Maybe you have reasons for just wanting a quiet wedding.

When I write to your mother again, I will ask her about coming to the wedding. Of course, you people know best how to arrange that, know whether she really can leave or not but I will mention it in my letter anyway.

There is something Mr. Turner asked me to write you about, that is not to say too much to Mrs. Turner about how well you are doing, let her see that for herself because naturally knowing you are doing better than her boys, she would feel a little sensitive on that point and if you say too much she might create a dislike for you which you would not want. I must say I think I agree with Mr. Turner on this. I hope you will take this, merely as a little suggestion.

We still have some of that hot weather, it sure is a fright. Don't know when we had so many hot days.

Just all kinds of love to you XXX OOO ☺☺☺ etc.

Anxiously waiting a real hug,

Yours as ever,

Hildred

———————◆———————

Postmark: 8:30 p.m. July 22, 1914, Detroit, Mich.

Addressed to Miss H.L. Cress, c/o Booth Fisheries

July 22nd/14.

My Dear Little Hildred, - It seems as though I can put twice the energy in my work when I hear from you every day.

By the way Hildred, I surely don't want you to think I am trying to hold you down in any way but at the same time Your Hubby hears things in ways that you do not know of. I Refer in particular to all the house work that you are doing at night. Also I am not going to ask you to make me any promise in regard to these things, but at the same time I just feel absolutely confident that you will not go in bathing for a month, and will not do housework at night if I do not think it good for you. That is other than drying the dishes. You are a Young Girl, who realizes that your future depends upon your present any more than a Doctor does. Supposing you come down here, health all impaired why Hildred my patients will run away. And I feel sure if a change does not take place that these things will be in reality. I trust you will take these few remarks in the spirit in which they are given, and let me hear from you.

Pleased to hear that you enjoyed yourself Sunday, and that Elizabeth thinks a great deal of you. It surely was good of her.

You tell Mr. Turner when I do not hear from you every day, business is punk simply because I do not feel right, if you people are contemplating a change make it twice a day instead of once.

Business is pretty good for this time of year made about $12.00 so far today. My auto I don't see how I managed so long without it. I suppose I drive about 40 miles a day. I cleaned my spark plugs yesterday.

The weather sure is warm don't forget to write me a nice long letter.

Just imagine all kinds of OOO, XXX, 🅖 🅖 🅖, from the One who Loves You and a Great big Hug.

Chas.

———————◆———————

Postmark: 7 p.m. July 23, 1914, St. Paul, Minn.

Thursday

My dear Charles:

Just a little letter before I go home. Have been working pretty steady today even though Mr. Turner was not here. Papa is getting out a circular this week and I have to help him check back the prices, copy it on the machine etc. I like to do that kind of work for a change.

Awfully glad to hear business is so good again, it seems more natural to be getting those dandy reports and certainly hope it will keep up.

As to the little envelope for Mr. Turner, he expects to get home Saturday night so I will give it to him, first thing Monday morning.

I am not going to be a bit superstitious about October, but just the same when she told me the big long string of her troubles it made me a little uneasy for awhile but it is all over with now.

Our Sunday school is giving an ice cream social tonight and Addison is selling tickets to of course dad had to buy some tickets from him so we all get a chance to go to the social. Addison has sold sixteen tickets and didn't start until after dinner last night. I think he did pretty good, sold every one he had.

Guess I better hustle if I want to go home with dad, will write more tomorrow. I sure am lonesome to see you and will be glad when I can talk to you again, it seems pretty near an age since you were here. All kinds of love and kisses from Yours lovingly,

Hildred

7:30 p.m. July 23, 1914, Detroit, Mich.

Addressed to Miss H.L. Cress, c/o Booth Fisheries

July 23rd/14.

My Dear Sweetheart, -

Hildred, when I arrived home this noon, I thought I was not going to hear from you, and to say the least I surely felt kind of funny, but it just happened that our Mail Man was a little tardy, and turned up a letter later with what I was looking for. "Thank You."

Last night I drove about 40 miles, and also made a call about 9 miles from the office, took Mrs. Turner, My Dad and Dr. Moon along with me. I surely hope Oct. 26th will hurry up, the last thing I think of at night and first thing in the morning is My Hildred, and what is she doing. I think there are just 13 weeks more, then you will be my truly wife, a funny thing, it always seems to me that I am nothing more than a Young Kid, not yet reached the marriage age. Does it seem like that to you, but I can not go any farther in fact how can I wait so long.

Pleased to hear that your cold is somewhat better will be glad when you are all better. Keep me posted.

In regard to any guess what S.W.A.K. meant I was so far off that I am ashamed to tell you.

I was just out dusting my car and drying it off after the rain. This AM. I have to make a 16 mile trip after my office hours this afternoon.

Now while Mr. Turner is away you better take life pretty easy. Eat, sleep, write a big long daily letter to your hubby, send lots of O.X.O. and figure just a little on the big event.

In a few days I am going to get down to business and get those names and addresses for you, if you want them right away just let me know and I will be ready. You will also have to figure on the time you want to be married.

By what you say you are getting just as warm weather in St. Paul as we are getting in Detroit, if it is not warmer.

I send all the OOO XXX & , to my Dear Little Hildred. A big long letter Hildred. Best regards to Claribel.

Lovingly,
Chas.

———————◆———————

Postmark: 5:30 p.m. July 24, 1914, St. Paul, Minn.

July 24, 1914

My dear Charles:

Your letter that I received today is really a surprise. What makes you think I am doing a lot of housework? Really I haven't done anything in that line since mamma and Claribel are home. All I do is help with the dishes in the evening and probably make my bed in the morning. Now surely, you can't call that doing too much can you? Of course when the folks were gone I had a little extra work but I didn't begin to keep it up as it should be kept because papa and Mr. Turner were always after me. They must think I am an invalid or something, I can't imagine what is the matter. To tell the truth, I kind of think Mr. Turner has written to you because he has threatened to do so several times and has written several notes that he wanted me to put in with mine but I always put him off. Now, didn't he write to you? I am going to ask him in the morning. He didn't intend to get back until Saturday night but he has made a days' time and will be here tonight.

As to changing our letter writing system I will sure have to tell Mr. Turner about that in the morning and then guess he won't object to our writing once a day. I know I look for a letter every day without fail because I have had one for so long.

On second consideration Charles I think I would rather just have a small wedding as we had first planned but I am going to wait and see what you have to say about it first and then will go ahead and plan. Just wish I could have some of those automobile rides you are having. This hot weather they would sure be welcome.

We have a new office boy, (Andy has been promoted to Bill Clerk) and this new one sure is a joke. He is only fifteen and the most inquisitive youngster you ever saw. He has been trying to find out my name and Sidney told him it was Hulda and I told him Mary so he don't know who to believe. He doesn't know dad is my father so he says he is going to ask the manager who I am so he will know what to call me.

I send all my love to you and hope I will get a dandy long letter tomorrow.

Lovingly
Hildred

Postmark: 8:30 p.m. July 24, 1914, Detroit, Mich.

Addressed to Miss H.L. Cress c/o Booth Fisheries

July 24th/14.

My Dear Hildred, -

I was a little doubious [sic] as to whether or not you would receive the tablets sent as they were in a letter were they in good order. If you wish any more let me know right away so that they will arrive in due time.

I would certainly like to see you enjoy yourself Saturday, but you know how these things work, they say a stitch in time saves nine, and I believe it. The majority of people who die kill themselves, through some inconsideration on their own part. As I said before I will not tell you not to go in bathing, but your Hubby would be delighted if you would not.

Now in regard to the wedding, make any plans you wish and go ahead the only thing we don't want anybody following us away from the house. Just imagine a whole bushel of rice coming down on your head in some conspicuous place. But if you can stand it I can. That Brother of mine and his Wife are two bad actors (Just interrupted a new patient). You will have to plan a little get away for us. But don't be afraid go ahead anything you do will be all O.K. Next month we will be saying month after next.

Thanks for the suggestion in regard to Aunt Lena, had some long trips this AM. Took Aunt Lena along with me we must have covered about 50 miles, have a 10 mile trip which I am going to make tonight to see a patient will take the family along with me Saturday and Sunday. I am going to help Dr. Hommand [sp?] out so I will cover a few more miles. I am afraid the shine will be worn off my machine before you get here better hurry up.

Made $10.00 so far today. Just 2:30 PM. now.

I believe you are getting hotter weather in St. Paul than we are getting in Detroit of course you are inland whereas Detroit is near the water.

Note you think I was a pretty apt scholar along loving lines, glad you think so, because if I had it to do over again I would not go home at 9:30 and 10 o'clock at night. Next time you see me you will think that I have been taking lessons because you have a whole lot of O, X & Ⓖ coming.

Just Loads & Loads of OOO, XXX, & ⑥⑥⑥, to my Sweetheart and a great big Hug.

Lovingly
Chas.

(PS) Write me a big long letter Sunday- C.W.H.

———————◆———————

Postmark: 5 p.m. July 25, 1914, St. Paul Minn.

July 25, 1914

Dearest Charles:

Mr. Turner just got home today so maybe we haven't been busy. He wants to go home in about ten minutes, 3:30, so it means hustle some more but will surely write you a dandy long letter tomorrow.

You bet you, I guessed Mr. Turner did write you, he couldn't get out of it, had to own up this morning.

Whenever mother used to find out naughty things we done she told us a little bird told her, but I have outgrown that age now, even if I do like chocolate ice cream. Mr. Turner really just imagines I am working hard because I am not. If I did any less, think I would get lazy.

I think of you Charles every night and morning, but I even think of you in my sleep because Claribel woke me up during the night since she is home and said I was hugging her for all I was worth. Just see what you missed. She is pretty good though and has promised not to tell any tales out of school so nobody knows anything about it.

I was pretty busy helping dad this week but Mr. Turner is going away Monday or Tuesday again and while he is away this time I am going to plan on our big day and will write you a whole history on it, possibly Wednesday or Thursday and then want you to pick it all to pieces and find all the fault with it you can and see if we can't improve it. I haven't started my list of names as yet so you need not be in any great hurry. If I get it in September some time, think that would be time enough. I don't suppose I will realize I am going to be married until I really am because every thing came in such a hurry "So sudden you know".

Just "oodles" and "oodles" of love and will write a dandy big letter to my sweetheart tomorrow.

Yours,

Hildred

Postmark: 7:30 p.m. July 25, 1914, Detroit, Mich.

Addressed to: Mr. Chas. W. Turner, c/o Booth Fisheries; dot on flap

July 25th/14

My Dear Hildred, -

Just a little line to-day, your letter was awful late in getting here should have arrived this AM.

Done quite a lot of chasing with my machine to-day. Mrs. Turner went along with me have also two or three long trips to make tomorrow, which will be another one of those Sundays but just think a week from to-day it will be month after next. Then I can love my little wife all the time can't I and I surely will. Aunt Lena says our house is too big for just two so we will have to keep my people with us or bring Claribel along. Of course when my Young Wife gets older and stouter which as a rule comes along in due time, she will help take up more space if I get squeezing you too hard I suppose you will go the other way, which is one good remedy.

You do not say how your cold is progressing. I surely hope it is better by this time.

Glad to hear that you are not going to be superstitious in regard to Oct. The Good Lord made the months and he made them with all the same intentions & purposes, so Oct. is one of the best months of the year to be Married in, if it is not we will make it so.

Will write more tomorrow had to hurry like everything to get this in before collection.

Loads of OOO XXX, ⑥⑥⑥, and a big Hug.

From your Hubby

Chas.

———————◆———————

Postmark: 8 p.m. July 26, 1914, Detroit, Mich.

Addressed to Miss H.L. Cress, c/o Booth Fisheries

Sunday 10 AM.

My Dear Hildred, -

Another week nearer to my little wifie, am just wondering what you are going to do to-day. As soon as I leave the office I am going to take my Mother over to the Cemetery make two calls on the way there, then come back home get or eat dinner, about 2:30 P.M. I will take Aunt Lena and my Dad around Belle Isle also making two calls on the way there, when I get back I am going to make another call, after that I will do something else. I hope to put the day in.

I think my business has been fairly good so far this month taking into consideration that July is one of the slowest months of the year. In 25 days or from the 1st to the 25th of July I have charged up $236.25 and taken in $225.75. How does that look to my little sweetheart. Do you think we can keep up on that amount of money. When the busy season comes we got to more than double this in 25 days.

Another thing what do you think of my buying the lot next door, do you think we can get away with it alright, because some day I will want 4 rooms in my offices in stead of having just two. I can buy the lot for $1500.00

The Doctor building across the street has just got his basement all excavated.

All kinds of OOO XXX & ⑥ ⑥ ⑥ to my Dear little wifie and a Great big Hug.

Lovingly,

Chas.

✦

Postmark: 9:30 a.m. July 27, 1914, St. Paul, Minn.

Sunday evening

My dear Sweetheart:

Was glad to get my Sunday letter, thanks. It sure must be hotter here than in Detroit because it is a fright here. Today we could not find a cool place on the premises. It was too hot to go to church this morning. This afternoon Claribel and I were going to sit and read in the basement but I knew if I did I would be laid up with another cold so instead we took two of the cots we had at the farm last summer and put them between the houses, took some pillows, each had a book and we read until we went to sleep.

There was quite a nice breeze there even though it was warm. Addison had the whole porch to himself and mamma and papa were in their room because it is a South facing and there is a dandy breeze there most of the time. Tonight we ate a little lunch on the porch and about seven o'clock Mr. Turner came and took mamma, Claribel and I [sic] for a ride, that was all he had room for because Mrs. Goodjohn and Elizabeth are still here. Tomorrow Myrtle Goodjohn from Chicago is coming. They surely have loads of company in the summer.

No, I didn't go to the picnic yesterday because they were all going in bathing in the afternoon and I didn't want to be the only one sitting and looking on and while my cold is about O.K. again I knew what it would mean if I went in. Glady [sic] called up today and wanted me to go to Calhoun with her today. It was mighty tempting but I said I thought I better wait a while. Now if my cold is better and it is warm next Sunday, don't you think it will be all right for me to go in again? I sure want to learn how to swim and I can't be watching the others. I won't stay in long, now be sure and say I can.

As to our wedding, I am not going to say anything definite until this next week but we sure will do our best to give the folks the slip. We will make them all believe we are going to leave that same night and leave in time to catch the late train. Also, as soon as we leave the room that our suit cases are in we will lock it so they can't steal anything. One of the girls up at chuch was married this month and they left for Isle Royale the same day and the boys stole Frank's (the groom's) light suit so he had to wear his brother's luckily they were pretty near of a size. We will have to guard against all this. I know if there is any way that brother of yours can play a trick he will do it.

The folks insist I come down stairs and give them a little music so will give you more news tomorrow.

Have just been down and done my duty, papa sure likes to have anybody drum on that piano. I tell him to get Claribel to play for him but he says she will get her share after I am gone and guess that is no joke.

I am going to ask a question of you. I have to get a trunk also a suit case or traveling bag before we go. Now in a way I would like a traveling bag because I will not mean so much to carry but if I get one, I could hardly get my dress and my trunk would be gone. Do you think you will have room enough in your suit case for my dress or should I get a suitcase instead of the traveling bag. Now don't be afraid to tell me because if you haven't the room I will get a suit case.

It sure is a job to write a letter here at the house, now Claribel is after me to get to bed so I won't waken her after she is asleep. I think I have written a pretty good letter thought because I have written pretty small.

I will be really delighted when I can have a really truly kiss again, these sent by mail aren't near as nice as the real ones but they sure are better than none.

Just all kinds of O's X's and ☺'s from yours,

Hildred.

Take a ride in your automobile for me. I am anxious to get a ride before all the shine is off. - H.L.C.

Postmark: 7 p.m. July 27, 1914, St. Paul, Minn.

Hand-addressed; letter is typed

July 27, 1914

My dear Charles: -

I have to resort to the machine again, have been pretty busy all day. Saturday was Mr. Turner's first day home and we only worked half a day and as he expects to leave tomorrow night for St. Louis and Kansas City to be gone the rest of the week it means hustle to catch up.

I hear you are taking a blonde lady out riding with you quite frequently, aren't you afraid I will get jealous? Well, I guess I wont [sic] this time seeing I know the lady in question and she surely must be having a good time going out auto riding every day. You certainly are some stylish people in Detroit, don't think we can keep up with you here.

You certainly have some encouraging remarks for me as to getting fat etc. but if I do, you will sure be kept busy squeezing me if that will make me thin again, because I don't want to get fat by any means. I weighed 138 once upon a time but I assure you I am perfectly contented with my present weight, 121 today. That 138 lb. weight may be all right for some people but I sure looked like a German girl when I weighed that much and I don't want to reach it again.

Addison is going to Ashland to visit with mamma's sister, he is going on Wednesday and maybe he isn't tickled. Mamma's sister expects to visit here the latter part of August and Addison will come back with her.

So long for tonight Charles, will sure try and do better tomorrow. I expect to get a good long letter tomorrow by the tone of your letter and that certainly sounds good to me. Mr. Turner told me how dandy you were doing again this month, that sure is fine. Don't forget to give me some figures at the end of the month because I can't fall behind in my little book.

Just millions of x's, o's and •'s from yours lovingly,

HILDRED.

*[**Editor's Note:** Next passage is hand-written] Couldn't make those squeezes very good on the machine so just put a dot there. It means just the same though. H.C.*

———————◆———————

Tuesday Afternoon.

My Dear Hildred, -

Have not received your Sunday letter as yet, expect it on the next mail about 4 or 4:30 PM. Therefore business has not been as good today, have just made $5.50 so far, Yesterday I made $18.50 so you see what a difference it makes, but I still have lots of time left today to increase my earnings, it is just 3 PM.

We have just struck a cool spot in the weather I feel a little cool.

Hildred what do you think I have been waiting for your letter until it is too late to get my letter out to-day. One of our neighbors just delivered your letter the Mail man left it at their house, the simmer [sic] of a Mail carrier.

Now Hildred in regard to going in bathing you may go providing your cold is all better and you feel all O.K. but do not go unless you are feeling all O.K. But you must promise me that will not go where the water is over 41/2 ft. deep. Then I will feel sure you will not get drown [sic].

In regard to you getting a suit case or a traveling bag, get a travelling bag Hildred because I will have a suit case and will be all able to take care of your dress, false hair, powder, chamois, pouche or what ever you call it. Can I put my false teeth in your travelling bag. Leaving all jokes aside buy a traveling bag. I see where all Hildred's money goes. Don't you hate to spend it. Glad you asked me in regard to the suitcase.

Business is still keeping on the slow side to-day, wish I had gotten the letter before and then I know everything would have been O.K.

Do you know I will be tickled to death when the time comes, and my Hildred surely has some loving coming to me, if I just had you here now my: how I would squeeze you.

I am going to take a ride for you to –morrow as requested, my Machine is sure working fine. Does Mr. Turner ever say any more to you about insurance. I hope he has forgotten about it.

All kinds of OOO XXX & ⓖⓖⓖ to my Dear little Wife and a Great big Hug.

From

Chas.

———————◆———————

Postmark: 7:30 p.m. July 27, 1914, Detroit, Mich.

Addressed to Mr. Chas. W. Turner c/o Booth Fisheries; dot on flap

July 27/14.

My Dear Little Sweetheart, -

Felt so good after hearing from you I turned right around and made calls to the amount of $13.75. Just see what a Dear Little Wifie can do. Took Mrs. Turner with me all the calls were quite scattered and I believe we covered fully 50 Miles.

So Mr. Turner told on himself, well I am glad he wrote to me anyway. You surely want to take good care of yourself else I will have to send you a guardian to watch over you.

Now in regard to the wedding, if you wish you could have a quiet wedding and have a reception after wards, but we have got to get away from these people at night, we don't want them following us with signs tin cans etc. but do as you see best. I can stand it if anybody can.

May say that I am getting rather jealous of Claribel getting all those hugs, I think possibly I will have to write Claribel and have her send all the hugs she gets to me. Don't make any mistakes, on the street and get hugging any telephone posts etc will you. People will think that you are drunk if you do.

Note you are going to plan on the big event go right ahead, everything you do I know will be alright.

It is a little cooler today, although I really believe I suffered more with the heat while I was in St. Paul than I have since coming home. I was just out and put my Machine in as it looks just a little like rain.

By the way you ought to see our new wash woman, I think you would run away if you did, she is a peach. Mother can say about two words to her and she is almost afraid to look at her. She is some toot see (unintelligible) – get that Hildred, our old wash woman was in to get back on the job last night, I believe she will.

All kinds of kisses, Hugs & ⓖⓖⓖ, to my Sweetheart and a Great big Hug.

As Ever,

Chas   (my pen slipped)

———————◆———————

[**Editor's Note:** Katherine is Charles' sister-in-law, married to his brother, Leonard.]

Postmark: 1:30 p.m. July 28, 1914, Duluth, Minn.

Addressed to: Miss Hildred Cress, c/o Booth Fisheries Co.

July 27, 1914

Dear Hildred –

Charlie wrote some time ago, the glad news that you have given him the privilege of changing your name to Husband in the near future and I have tried several times to write a few lines to express our pleasure and extend our very best wishes. Am sorry we live so far away for I would love to help you with your sewing for I know how much you are trying to crowd into these days.

Charles [Katherine and Leonard's child] is so cross these days with his teeth that I have to get my house work done before Leonard leaves in the morning or else leave it until after supper. The only way to keep him quiet is to keep him outside and he refuses to stay alone in the yard so I usually take him in his buggy or cart and before I know it the day is gone.

The last letter I started to you I wrote at least six different times and then couldn't finish it and it seemed to jumbled that I decided to try over again hence the delay.

We are hoping that you will take a day or two at least to run up here before the "big event" for when you once get to Detroit it will be harder to get away and we would love to have you here with us for a while.

With best wishes and many of them from both Leonard and myself, I remain

Yours Sincerely

Katherine R. Husband (signature)

722-10 Ave. E.

Postmark: 9:30 p.m. July 29, 1914, Detroit, Mich.

Addressed to Miss H.L. Cress, c/o Booth Fisheries

July 29/14

My Dear Hildred, -

Was just going to say my Dear Mary (you know why) but I changed my mind, I don't know as I care very much for the name. Many time I thought you might not like it. If you were not going to be my wife why probably I could call you that and not think anything about it. You better not teach me such things, how about it.

Business has been a little better today than yesterday. It must be because I received your letter this a.m.

Hildred if you except [sic] this little letter to-day will write a longer one tomorrow, have been called out.

All kinds of Love to my Sweetheart and a great Big Hug & Kiss.

Chas.

Postmark: 9 a.m. July 30, 1914, St. Paul, Minn.

Wednesday 8:30 p.m.

My dear Sweetheart: -

I am awfully sorry I could not write to you yesterday. I really started a letter but did not get back from lunch until pretty near one o'clock and Mr. Turner got back soon after I did and had a second bunch of letters to dictate and I simply could not get at it again. I am going to try awfully hard and not let it happen again. Hope you wrote to me anyway.

The reason I am writing so late was not down to the office today, Mr. Turner says I have to stay home and rest the rest of this week and if I don't look better when he gets home, will have to stay home until I do. Don't know what is the matter, I think he imagines I don't look well and pretty soon he believes it because I feel fine and my cold is well again.

As to getting jealous of my giving Claribel all the hugs, I told her about it and she says to just wait until you come to St. Paul and she will pay them all back to you doubly!! Now who should be jealous?

We have been entertaining a bride and groom today. One of mamma's brothers was married on the sly, nobody knew anything about it and early this afternoon they walked in on us. We don't know how long they expect to stay in St. Paul, they are just stopping here for awhile, on their way to No. Dak. I can't tease them very much because if I do they start in on me so I have to be good. Dad and mamma took them down to the show tonight. The bride is quite a good looking girl, real dark and French. Now you know as much as I do about her.

As to that lot next door, $1500.00 I hardly know what to say, that would make $3500.00 or nearly $20.00 a month interest. Of course, it would not be that much very long but we want to get that $200.00 paid as soon as we can. With any kind of luck at all though I think we should be able to carry it through, if we don't take a risk once in a while we will never get ahead. Is there anybody else figuring on buying the lot other than yourself? Also do you feel like paying taxes on that lot until such time as you would care to build again? Again, do you think we would have this all taken care of by the time you would want to have a lot for your folks and if you should wait and nothing now? Do you think you could get another lot in the same neighborhood later on which would be just as suitable? There are lots of things to think about before making a purchase amounting to so much money. Maybe you could buy it and sell for more money, that would not be so bad. You do just what you think best Charles.

I did a wise stunt tonight, when I was washing the dishes I put a paring knife in the dishpan and forgot about it until I run into it and pretty cut a slice right off the end of my middle finger, hence my beautiful scribbling.

*I got a lovely letter from your brother's wife today, also one from your mother yesterday [**Editor's Note**: letter does not survive]. It is surely kind of them to write me and I appreciate it very much. Mrs. Husband [**Editor's Note**: Charles' sister-in-law, Katherine] would like me to visit with her for a few days in Duluth but that I am afraid is impossible. It was very nice of her to ask me but I hardly have the time or the ---- ---- (you know)*

Papa is mail carrier now, hope he will bring me a good long letter from my sweetheart tomorrow. The best part of the day is when I get my letter.

Lots of loves and kisses from

Yours lovingly,

Hildred

P.S. Claribel says you sure ought to be satisfied with this letter, she just got a glimpse of the length.

———————◆———————

Postmark: 8:30 p.m. July 30, 1914, Detroit, Mich.

Addressed to Mr. Chas. W. Turner, c/o Booth Fisheries; dot on envelope flap

July 30/14.

My Dear Hildred, -

I guess my Dear little Wife's letter is among the missing today, however I am not going to wait any longer, going to write anyway.

By the way Hildred did you tell Uncle Chas. about me driving to fast. I asked Mother if she said anything to you about a swift ride I gave her Sunday she said she did and of course I at once thought that that was the way Mr. Turner found out. Be sure and tell me Hildred. But let me say this Hildred you will be doing the same thing your self before very long. Of course I will not want you to speed lest you meet with an accident, but it seems just a little different to me when I speed myself.

To-morrow is the last day of the month and goody, Saturday I will be saying, and waiting for month after next, then I can love my little wifie 24 hrs. out of 24.

Yesterday was a pretty fair day for business. Today is just a little slow so far, but I think August will be a little better than July although I have not done too bad this July.

I wish I was in St. Paul to help you sew get my Sunday dinner, see what I am missing.

This morning I got up at 5 p.m. [sic] and took one of the neighbor ladies to the market we bought everything imaginable, among other things 32 boxes of huckleberries so I had a joke after I arrived home. I told Mother to keep account of all the fruit and Hildred would pay half. Mother says I have to, I believe you are sure on the good side of Mother. I had the machine chucked full of all kinds of fruit and vegetables any body would have taken us for peddlers. The worst part of all a new office patient came I lost him because he would not wait. May say we were back home at 7 a.m., first morning in two months that a patient has come so early.

Just Loads & Loads of OOO, XXX & ⓖ ⓖ ⓖ to my sweetheart, write me a nice big long letter Hildred.

Lovingly

Chas.

Postmark: 9:30 a.m. July 31, 1914, St. Paul, Minn.

Thursday, 10 p.m.

My dear Charles:

I think you will have to give that mail man a few pills to wake him up so he won't be carrying yur letters to the wrong house. I know I wouldn't want any other Charles to get those letters. I surely will have to see that I write every day if it makes business brisker, glad everything is coming along so nicely.

As to the traveling bag, thanks for the suggestion, I will do as you say but as to the false hair, rouche [sic], etc. I don't know about that, think I would prefer carrying that because I imagine I would be rather timid about letting you see these false additions. As to the false teeth, think they would look better with your wearing them than stuck away in the traveling bag. What about your cork leg? Well I should say the money does go, it is simply a fright it is ten dollars here and ten there and before you know it you got to skimp to make it run to the end of the week.

Now as to the wedding, I have been thinking, planning and everything else the last few days, so has mamma. I am kind of on the fence as it were but this is about what we thought. If we just have the relations, really there will be hardly anything to it and again it is rather hard just to pick a few of your most intimate friends so we have decided to limit the number of guests at fifty. Remember this is all providing you approve of it. Mamma says no matter how few or how many are here, she positively will not do the cooking, she does not want the responsibility but says she is willing to get the caterers. We could be married in the evening, possibly 8:00 P.M. and then have the refreshments or reception. I also imagine I would like to have someone stand up for us and I know Claribel is anxious for the job. I was planning on Gladys at first but I know Claribel would be terribly disappointed if I did not ask her. If we did have someone, who would you like to stand up with you? After the reception we can get ready to skip but we sure will have a job to get away from the crowd. We will make them believe we are going to leave on the night train and if they follow us, we will simply have to do our best at trying to give them the slip. Lets not let anybody know where we stay over night though, not even Mr. Turner and then we can stay either in St. Paul or Mpls. as we like but we will register under a fictitious name. Claribel wanted to know where we were going to stay and I said we were going to leave the same night but she don't believe it and says she will call up every hotel in both cities until she finds us. Of course we will send invitations to the fifty and announcements to the rest. Have you any suggestions to offer and would this meet with your approval?

I have been thinking about that $1500.00 lot and don't you think we better let it go for the present. That $2000.00 looms up pretty big and I think the interest would look as good in our pocket as [illegible]. Think we better see how you get along with that first. Maybe you will have an extravagant wife and won't be able to make payments on the $1500.00. What do you think.

I intended doing a lot of sewing today but Mrs. Turner called up and said Elizabeth and her mother were going to leave Friday so wanted Claribel and I to take lunch with them and then go to the matinee. I really had a good time but I couldn't help thinking how much more I could be accomplishing if I were home and felt rather guilty spending my time that way.

No, Mr. Turner doesn't say any more about insurance, but how about it? I don't mind the machine but really think you should carry accident insurance. Have you done anything about this?

I just wish you were here for a big good night kiss and hug, I sure am lonesome for one of those but just wait a little while.

OOOXXX and ☺☺☺

From

"Wifie"

Postmark: 1 p.m. July 31, 1914, St. Paul, Minn.

Stationary reads: Reception Room
Field, Schlick & Co.
St. Paul, Minn.

[**Editor's Note:** Field, Schlick & Co. was a St. Paul-based department store]

◆

Friday A.M.

My dear Charles:

I don't know what is the matter with me but I think something bit me on the lowest joint of my thumb, right near my wrist. I didn't notice it until yesterday noon when Claribel and I were leaving to meet Mrs. Turner. It started to swell then but last night when I went to bed it didn't look very bad although it was a little puffed up so I painted it with iodine. This morning though, it is so swollen I can't get my glove on and dad made me come down to see Dr. Lankester. He says he can't say just what it is but he don't want to cut it until it is absolutely necessary, maybe he can prevent it. He has given me some kind of a tablet to dissolve in cold water (a quart) and says to bandage my hand and keep it wet with this cold liquid all the time and keep ice on it and then come down again in the morning.

It hasn't hurt me at all until this morning and now the swelling is about half way up to my elbow. I think it will turn out all right though so don't worry but I knew you would want me to tell you first thing.

I received your short but sweet letter, hope I will get a nice long one tomorrow. I sure would *be your little fat wife today.*

Please excuse this simply awful scribbling but will try and do better next time.

Just all kinds of love and kisses from

"Fatty"

How do you like that name, is it better than Mary? H.C.

Postmark: 3:30 p.m. July 31, 1914, Detroit, Mich.

Addressed to Miss Hildred L. Cress, c/o Booth Fisheries

July 31st/14

My Dear Hildred, -

Just an inquiry as to what is wrong have not heard from you for three days.

Thought surely I would get a nice long letter today being that Mr. Turner was away but am or was awfully disappointed.

If you are sick let me know and may be I can do something for you.

Trusting I will find out what the trouble is as soon as possible.

Lovingly

Chas.

P.S. Feel awfully worried about you.

C.W.H

AUGUST 1914

———◆———

𝕹𝖊𝖜𝖘𝖕𝖆𝖕𝖊𝖗 𝕳𝖊𝖆𝖉𝖑𝖎𝖓𝖊𝖘

𝕯𝖊𝖙𝖗𝖔𝖎𝖙 𝕱𝖗𝖊𝖊 𝕻𝖗𝖊𝖘𝖘

- Germany declares war on Russia; first shots fired; France to enter fight today
- Bryan urged to send ships for tourists
- Half of all autos made in America
- Emperor of Austria is reported slain – London, Aug 3
  - The Daily Chronicle has received an unconfirmed dispatch that the Emperor, Francis Joseph of Austria-Hungary, has been assassinated
- Four great European powers now at war; fighting follows first border invasions; all armies and navies moving to strike
- Sir Edward Grey commits Britain to aid of France
- Lusitania sails for England in spite of enemy
- England declares war on Germany; world's two greatest navies near battle; 18.6 million men in conflict; Britain brought into hostilities after Kaiser rejects ultimatum as to Belgium
- Mexico peace parley proves flat failure
- Wilson's Proclamation of Neutrality (printed in its entirety)
- Doll shortage threatened by war in Europe

- Mrs. Wilson at point of death in White House
  - Social and charitable activities contribute to breakdown
- China calls upon U.S. to protect Far East
- Confederates may march as guests in G.A.R. parade
- Café orchestras, composed of sons of warring nations, bar European patriotic airs
- Food soars as German crops rot in fields
- Olympic hastens home for use as army transport
- Bells toll white train; bears Mrs. Wilson to grave
- Irish patriot "practices" for war by fighting whole corps of Griswold German waiters
- Relief ships will provide room for 20,000 Americans
- Panama Canal opens to world's commerce today
- Beer imports cut only to give boom to home product
- Wright's Soul Mate and Scorned Wife
  - Mrs. Mamah Borthwick Cheney, the "Soul Mate"
  - Mrs. Frank L. Wright, the discarded wife
    [**Editor's Note:** Photographs of the women illustrate the story about the murder of Mamah Borthwick.]
- Later in the paper:
  - Negro ax slayer may be guilty of another tragedy; assassin at Wright's "love castle" suspected in Chicago mystery
  - Chef's insanity sham, believed prosecutors
  - Architect to rebuild bungalow as monument to woman who deserted all for him
- Pope Pius dies, heart broken by war, body wracked by ill health
- Austria's ruler, Francis Joseph, said to be dying
- Germans checked by Allied forces in great battle in Belgium; fighting now extends along 100-mile front
- City bathed in light to greet G.A.R. veterans
- Eating less hinted as one result of European war

St. Paul Pioneer Press

- Russia and Austria again open negotiations; England and France in new effort for peace

- Russia orders mobilization; Germany declares state of siege and England and France practically are under arms

- Diamonds of world in trust control – DeBeers Syndicate owns African fields and sets the price

- England faces danger of famine if German fleet is not held in check

- Throngs of U.S. tourists seeking refuge in London

- The Cape Cod Canal connecting Buzzards Bay and Cape Cod Bay, which opened to commerce today

- Car builders seek to interest women

- Ford Car owners to see profits (through reduced pricing)

- Great Lakes ships for ocean service

- American Red Cross offers its aid to relieve wounded of European armies

- Neutrality of U.S. presents grave problem to administration

- Death claims Mrs. Wilson; nation mourns

- Officials sure U.S. will take mediator role

- Dr. Mayo (Clinic) tells of thrilling voyage – Rochester surgeon passenger on Mauretania during record-breaking trip

- War halts tinker – kiddies' Xmas [sic] to be toy-less

- Mothers' clubs to join Peace Move

- State Board may rule against nuns – rule prohibiting teacher to wear Sister's garb expected this week

- A Siberian Russia's ruler attempted assassination of the peasant Monk Rasputin reveals the fact that the Czar goes to him for direction as to affairs of state

- Northwest milliners say war is America's gain (women no longer can purchase European-made hats)

- Lusitania wins in sporting chance and reaches port after dash across ocean which others feared to take

- St. Paul's citizens contribute to war's toll in the increased cost of food

- U.S. may establish cable censorship

- Open the (Panama) Canal today (August 15) – Steamer Ancon to be first ocean-going vessel through new waterway; run expected to be made in eleven hours

- Inheritance taxes to break a record

- Negro with ax slays five and injures four – sets fire to Spring Creek, Wis. Bungalow and hacks victims as they crawl from window; murderer escapes but later gives up to posse
  - Mrs. (Mamah) Borthwick, one of the dead, gained notoriety in recent Chicago scandal (by leaving husband for architect Frank Lloyd Wright, who also left his family)
  - Black planned slaughter, waited until all entered dining room before blocking door with flames
- Pope (Pius X) is dead after brief illness due to grief over war; Death of Pope is followed by that of sister
- Vote on war risk bill today (concerning insurance on ships)
- War puts American ingenuity to work
- Wisconsin has one-eighth of all cows in the Union
- The biggest family row of history (Russia, Germany, England) – When Europe goes to war it means close relatives, sitting on different thrones, must hurl javelins at each other to uphold so-called honor
- Paris is saddest place – all men of genius at front
- St. Paul Housewives League to issue cards on sanitary conditions in dairies of city
- Waxed paper milk bottle is endorsed as clean and not too expensive
- Many faults found in hospital system
- U.S. can end war by food embargo
- American will lose citizenship by enlistment in army of warring nations
- War hits bridal bouquets – Lilies of the Valley scarce
- Senators put on women's black list – Nine congressmen also named as being opposed to Suffrage Movement

AUGUST 1914

LETTERS

Postmark: 2 p.m. August 1, 1914, St. Paul, Minn.

Stationary: Reception Room Field, Schlick & Co. St. Paul, Minn.

Saturday A.M.

My dear Charles:

Just came from the doctor's office and he has my hand bandaged so tight I can hardly hold my pen. Maybe you will have to get somebody to help you read this. He says he thinks it looks a little better today, all he did was put an ointment on and bandage it up. That stuff he had me put on yesterday took down some of the swelling but it just like burnt my hand and it is all blistered. It sure hurts like everything.

Last night I did not get to sleep until after three in the morning. (That sounds awfully Dutchy but guess you know what I mean) I don't know when the time passed so slow as it did then and I sure wish you were here to be my really doctor. I have to come down again tomorrow to let him see my hand but he says it is getting better and won't have to be lanced.

Yes, I did say something to Mr. Turner about your driving fast and you know if you won't let me drive fast you should not because an accident could happen to you as well as to me. Just think, August and September and then we can have a drive together. We will go fast though then because if one goes over an embankment the other will go too.

As to those berries, sure I am willing to pay half but of course if your mother can get you to pay I won't object in the least. I owe your mother a letter and should have written before but now would like to wait until my hand is a little better. She may not be able to make out my scratching.

I hope I get a nice letter tomorrow, write me a good long letter. I suppose I was not supposed to go in bathing, hence my sore hand.

Just loads of love to my dear sweetheart, from,

Hildred

◆

Postmark: 8:30 p.m. August 1, 1914, Detroit, Mich.

Addressed to C.W. Turner, Booth Fisheries; dot on envelope flap

August 1st/14.

My Dear Hildred –

You don't know how much better I feel to-day in as much as I received a letter from you. I could not figure out just why I did not hear from you. If I don't hear from you again for so long I am going right up to St. Paul take any revolver along with me, force you to marry me at once, leave for Detroit. Then how will you like that, now I can say month after next and the big event. Wish it were next month, Hurry up Hildred.

In regard to those hugs tell Claribel she has to fix me up doubly as promised. I think Claribel will be pretty well experienced when she falls in love and that she sure will have it bad when she does. Maybe she will see a man coming along the street and start loving him up without thinking as to whether it is her hubby to be or not. Studied the matter over thoroughly as yet I wish Mr. Turner were coming to Detroit. I would explain and have him look the proposition over.

Sorry to hear you cut your finger, had you been here I could have fixed it up for you.

It would be nice if you could make a trip up to Detroit, By the way aren't you glad you saved that 10 cts. a day.

Now I suppose you are wondering how I made out this month, May say I made out better than I thought I would. Results as follows, charged - $297.50 why couldn't I have made $2.50 more so I could say $300.00 which would have sounded a great deal better. I took in $237.50 today so far I have made $8.50 it is just 1:30 p.m. this amount is more than what I made on July 1st.

We sure are having dandy weather not to [sic] hot, not to [sic] cold, just right. Dr. Howard is going away to-morrow for a week or so. And I am going to do all I can to help him out am going over to see him at 4 o'clock this afternoon.

Just Loads & Loads of Love to you and a great big hug. Give Claribel a little wee hug and tell her it is from me, and let me know what she says.

Lovingly,

Chas.

———————◆———————

Postmark: 11 p.m. August 2, 1914, Detroit, Mich.

Addressed to Chas. W. Turner, c/o Booth Fisheries; dot on envelope flap

Aug. 2nd/14.

My Dear Hildred, -

Surely sorry to hear in regard to your hand. Glad you told me about it and would be very pleased indeed if you keep me posted. But above all other things keep the ice on it constantly and you will not need to have it opened up.

Have had a very good day for Sunday have made $16.00 so far and it is now 5 p.m. Not only made a little money but got my first puncture must hurray [sic] up get my tires changed before dark.

Your plans in regard to the wedding are all O.K. You asked for a suggestion in regard to who I would like to stand up with us, Claribel to be sure, and then what do you think in regard to my Duluth Brother, otherwise you would have to make the choice, as my knowledge and acquaintance with people in St. Paul is very limited, but you will have a job giving all those people the slip at nighttime. I think it would be nice not to let even Mr. Turner know our whereabouts and we will go by some uncommon name as L'Esperance or something like that.

Will write to you more tomorrow Hildred but be sure and keep me posted in regard to that hand.

Just Millions and Millions of OOO, XXX, & ⓖ ⓖ ⓖ, from Your Hubby,

Chas.

Postmark: 9:30 a.m. August 3, 1914, St. Paul, Minn.

My dearest Charles:

I can't understand how it is you have not heard from me for three days, there is something wrong somewhere. Do you think I could forget or neglect you that long time? I have written every day with the exception of last Tuesday and I was so busy, could not possibly find the time. I have been home since Tuesday so have had to write to you in the evening and then papa would take your letter down in the morning and mail it for me. I asked him this noon if he had mailed all the letters I gave him and he said that was the first thing he did so he would not forget it so how is it you have not received them? I hope by this time your mail carrier has delivered them and am awfully sorry this has worried you. Maybe your mail carrier thought you were getting too many letters and is holding them off for a while because I know I wrote to you and papa says he mailed all I gave him.

Say Charles, if we have a little wedding at the house, I have another stunt planned to get away from the crowd, rather mamma thought of part of it and I the other. You know if I went up stairs to change my dress, they sure would be after us hot and heavy when we came down. How would it be to have the taxi come and stop a block from the house on Laurel and Dewey Ave. one block in back of the house? Then during the reception pick up and get out of the back door any time we get the chance, if we can't get out just together because none of the people will be coming out in the kitchen and for a bluff I could go out there once or twice before we slipped. We could take our suit cases and suits over to some kind neighbors and dress there. I know Mrs. Otis would let us take our things there and would not give us away either and if we had any kind of a wedding at all I would like to ask them so nobody would be at the house. We could take our things over there in the afternoon, take the streetcar if it is only a few blocks and then the people here would think you were going to the depot with them because my Aunt Louise (dad's sister) will be here and if anybody is up to tricks it is she and I know your brother and his wife are pretty good at those things too. This is about the best plan I can think of now because if we go out the front we will never get out alive, if the machine stops near the house they will have it all decorated up and if we change our clothes here at the house we will never get away without them seeing us but if we leave with our wedding clothes on they will not suspect that so quick and I think it is a pretty good plan. Now what do you think or suggest? You know anything you think of, just write it because it is the ideas we are after.

Really, you can't imagine how glad I will be when the time comes although I don't know when or how I can accomplish what I would like to. Here I took my weeks' vacation that was due me because Mr. Turner insisted on it and the very second day my hand got sore and haven't been able to do a thing since fancy work or anything and I had planned on doing so much. All I can do is little one handed jobs around the house and it certainly is more than disgusting.

It is pretty good today though and this noon I wiped the dishes again and played on the piano for a few minutes. Friday night and Saturday morning it hurt the worst. That liquid Dr. Lankester had me put on simply burnt my hand in great shape and it looks just as if it had been scalded and all kinds of little and big water blisters from my knuckles on my hand to about half way up to my elbow. It sure is the funniest thing how it all started, don't know if it was a bite or what; at first they thought it was a bite but they can't find any marks so guess it is a mystery. It feels fine tonight and tomorrow I am going to work again. Mr. Turner just got back from his trip this morning so imagine about a week's work piled up on my desk to start in on Monday morning.

I do hope my next letter will be good and long and newsy. Of course when you are busy, just so it is a word or two, I am satisfied and if you feel the same as I do I can imagine again how you felt when you did not hear from me for three days but I sure wrote so get after your mail carrier.

All my love, kisses and hugs to my dear sweetheart and "Hubby To Be,"

From yours lovingly,

Hildred.

P.S. Give my kindest regards to your mother and Mrs. Turner.

H.C.

Postmark: 9 p.m. August 3, 1914, Detroit, Mich.

Addressed to Chas. W. Turner, c/o Booth Fisheries; dot on flap

August 3rd./14/

To the Best Little Sweetheart in the U.S.A, -

Don't know when I was or how I could have been more pleased to hear from you than I was this a.m. Guess I was pretty anxious about your hand. Glad to hear it is a little better, keep me posted won't you.

Now Hildred I just wish we could be married next month, Oct, surely does not seem very fast in coming. Your Hubby just made $25.00 this a.m. and has three house calls yet to make. Which will bring it up more, when I get busy honestly half the time I feel too tired to do the posting with my Ledger, I am sure if you were here you would help me out. It is just 2 p.m. now, so in all probability I will make out pretty good today, also made, I think it was $17.00 yesterday which was Sunday. I will tell you how I got my first puncture was driving on 29th St. there was a bottle on the road. I went to turn out instead of running over it, & on to another piece I drove, [illegible] away I was, had to change inner tubes.

In two or three days I must get busy at those names. I have [illegible] going to get at that for some time.

In regard to the wedding, as I said before, your plans are all O.K. and as long as you can figure out a scheme to get away from the crowd at night.

Just all Kinds of OOOs, XXXs, & ⑥⑥⑥, From Your Hubby,

Chas.

———————◆———————

Postmark: 5:30 p.m. August 3, 1914, St. Paul, Minn.

August 3rd.

My dear Charles: –

I am awfully busy again today and making rather slow progress account of my hand being tied up but I was up to the doctor's for the last time this morning and he has taken quite a bit of the bandage off. I knew I had better write though because I was scared of that promised revolver. I think I better get permission to carry one on the street so I will be prepared when I see you coming.

As to that hug for Claribel I will have to see about it tonight. Don't let me see her giving all those hugs back to you doubly because I might get jealous, you better get them when I am not looking.

I asked Mr. Turner when he thought he would be going to Detroit, that you would like to see him and he says he can't tell a thing about it but maybe he could make it some time this month so have all your questions in mind.

I would like to spend a few days in Duluth if I could but I can hardly spare the time now, think I will have to wait until my hubby goes along some time. How about it?

As to your earnings for July, they sure look good to "Yours truly" and if you can only keep gaining like that every month it will be splendid.

*Mr. Turner has asked me to send you the enclosed, possibly you have seen this "Ford" clipping before. [**Editor's Note**: clipping did not survive] Don't suppose this will make you feel bad though, because you must have sixty dollars worth of use out of it by this time. As to the other enclosure, think that is pretty near the truth.*

Let me have a big long letter Charles but presume you are pretty busy if you are taking care of Dr. Howard's practice.

All the love and kisses in me from,

Hildred

Mr. Turner is waiting to dictate some letters.

———————◆———————

Postmark: 12 p.m. August 4, 1914, Detroit, Mich.

Addressed to: Miss H.L. Cress c/o Booth Fisheries

Tuesday Afternoon,

My Dear Hildred –

Just received your Sunday letter, may say that I believe I know just why I did not hear from you for three whole days. They changed mail men here so after that they seemed to get things mixed up once in awhile, however I believe I have received all your letters, and I sure like to hear from my little wifie every day.

In regard to leaving the house after the wedding I think your plan is good. Now supposing instead of having the taxi just a block away from the house, if you could make arrangements with some one a friend of yours about a block or so away from where you live to leave our grips there, some place where they have a telephone, then we could change our clothes, and lay low for a little while and later on call a taxi to come and get us. Of course we sneak out the back way as you planned on. Otherwise the only thing I see to do is to make the crowd believe we are going to stay at your place over night, then when they go home we call a taxi and make our departure. Another thing where do you think we better take our train St. Paul or Mpls. Of course I would not know my way to the Depot in Mpls.

Made $36.00 Yesterday $10.00 so far to-day and I think I can make a little more tonight, don't know what I would do if I did not have an automobile. Had Aunt Leana around with me this morning, tell Mr. Turner I would like to know when he is coming to Detroit.

I surely hope that your hand is all O.K., by this time, and "Oh" that big day I wish it were here, just think I will have a little wifie to love & hug day & night, month after next, won't that be great.

Another thing you think we better stop over night in Chicago or go straight through, and get home.

Just Loads & Loads of hugs & kisses and a great big hug.

Lovingly,

Chas.

◆

Postmark: 7 p.m. August 4, 1914, St. Paul, Minn.

Typed with Booth's Cold Storage mailing envelope

August 4, 1914.

My dear Charles: –

You sure had an exciting Sunday to make $16.00 and also get a puncture, how did you happen to do that? I suppose you were going along about forty miles and hour, one of those speedy rides. When I get to Detroit I want you to give me one real fast ride if we bust all of the tires. If you give me just one I will be satisfied to go slower after that, will you do this for me? By the way, you never answered me about that insurance for yourself, I suppose you thought if you let it go I would forget about it but remember I have not. This is just a reminder.

As to the wedding, you seem to be satisfied with everything but really, I thought possibly you would rather have Theresa stand up with us than Claribel but as to your brother standing up, surely that suits me, anybody you wish. If we can only keep from Mr. Turner as to where we are going to stay that night we will be lucky, I will have to invent all kinds of excuses I think because he will want to help me when it comes to getting our tickets and if we should stay in St. Paul we have to get our tickets from here or if we stay in Minneapolis we have to get our tickets from there, at least I suppose so.

Well I really can't write you more today although I would like to but Mr. Turner leaves the city again tonight for Sioux City, Omaha and Lincoln, guess I will take the rest of my vacation this week and see if I can possibly squeeze in a little sewing this time. Really this hand of mine has put me back terribly but it is getting along just fine now and I can use it for everything again but still have to keep it bandaged a little because some of the bubbles or blisters broke. Can't imagine what it all started from, thought it was a bite at first but guess not.

Loads and loads of love from your sweetheart,

H i l d r e d.

P.S. – Claribel says that hug was great but she will wait for the real ones.

C. W. T.

1:30 p.m. August 5, 1914, St. Paul, Minn.

Wednesday A.M.

My dear Charles:

So you were anxious to hear about my hand. Well, it is getting along just dandy, took the bandage off this morning but it looks fierce. I have to wear long sleeves, hot weather or cold, so as to cover the most of it up. The skin is all peeling off now so guess it will soon be O.K.

Now as to the wedding Charles, you just have a little patience and wait until October. My goodness, I really don't know where the time is flying too [sic] because I have so much to do before then and could not possibly make it before then. Just think it isn't three months anymore. Here I fall in love, become engaged and married all in six months time, that is going some and it means hustle.

So glad to hear your business is coming up so splendidly but sorry you are so tired at times. I know what that is like and when I get to Detroit I will help you all I can and with anything you think I can do.

Sorry about that puncture but of course that is to be expected and will have to expect more before the machine is worn out.

When yu make out your list, don't forget to keep the names separate, that is invitations in one and announcements in the other. No doubt there are some other than relations that you would like to send invitations to. I have all my list made out but have not got it divided or counted up as yet, expect to fix it all up slick on Sunday next. Will we decide definitely on the 26th of October now? Would that be more convenient for you than the 27th? I am not going to give any reasons for mentioning the 27th until I hear from you as to whether it would be convenient or not. Can you think of any other plan to get away from the crowd other than I have mentioned? If you can be sure and mention it.

I did not expect to come to the office at all today but I had quite a few letters to file etc. So thought I would clean up this morning and then not come down at all tomorrow unless mamma can go with me to do some shopping. Commencing with this week they are going to let me have my money but I pay $4.00 per week for board. I sure would rather have it that way but don't know what they are going to do with what I have given to them heretofore. You know beginning with the 1st of July they were going to spend my money on me but haven't spent any to speak of as yet, maybe I am out all that, don't know.

Just all kinds of love to you and don't go over working now and get all tired out, think you need some of the lectures I have been getting lately.

Lovingly,

Hildred

———————◆———————

Postmark: 8:30 p.m. August 5, 1914, Detroit, Mich.

Addressed to Chas. W. Turner, c/o Booth Fisheries; dot on flap

Aug 5th/14.

My Dear little Wifie, -

Glad to hear you are able to be around again, because if anything happens to my little sweetheart I surely don't know what I would do. I really feel leary [sic] about thinking of you going in bathing again lest something happen of course if I were with you then I would be able to see that you did not get drown [sic] or something like that, It certainly pleased me when you say you are not going bathing at any particular time.

Don't forget to let me know what Claribel said about that hug.

I received your two inclosures [sic], I think the little motto you sent will worth a place in anybody's hat, of course I knew about the reduction on Ford cars but could not have waited so long. The engine in my car is working better than ever have done a lot of driving lately. Mrs. Turner usually spends the day driving around with me. And I know my little wifie will enjoy auto riding. See what you are missing by waiting so long. Next month I will be saying next month. Just think of it.

Business is running along about the same, made $16.00 yesterday. Got 3 new patients last night. A Dr. that I turned a patient over to with an operative condition of his eye, just was going to send in his statement and would see later, that means he is going to split a certain amount of his fee with me. He is going to charge $125.00 for the operation.

We certainly are having very nice weather not too hot or cold just right all the time.

Tell Uncle Chas. I am going to write him in a few days and that it would be a good idea for him to come this way to be with Aunt Lizzie when she goes to the Toronto Fair. I think the fair in Toronto takes place this month does it not.

Well Hildred I must get busy and do some posting in my Ledger. I am getting away back along book keeping time.

Wishing you all kinds of happiness, along with Loads of OOO, XXX & ⑥⑥⑥,

From Your Hubby,

Chas.

———————◆———————

Postmark: 8:30 p.m. August 6, 1914, Detroit, Mich.

Addressed to Miss H.L. Cress, c/o Booth Fisheries

Aug. 6th/14.

My Dear Little Wifie, -

Read – your letter, I sure will give you a good speedy drive, one every time we go out if you wish, how fast do you want to go, you know 50 miles an hour is our speed limit.

I am surely pleased to hear that your hand is all O.K. Again, glad you kept me posted.

The weather is a little warmer today and your hubby feels just a little lazy. I suppose you won't like me when you find out how lazy I am but honestly I get tired once in awhile after I get through my own evening office hours I go over and keep Dr. Howard's office open, until about 10 o'clock at night, when my little wifie comes she will have to go along with me to keep me company when such things turn up. I never go out any place for pleasure, even stick to business on Sunday, so I suppose I have a right to feel tired once in a while.

Just got a call over on 29th St. Am going to take My Mother, Hildred's Mother-in-Law, along with me, took Aunt Lena around with me this AM. Now in regard to the insurance on my self Hildred, just wait until we are married, then I will take out a policy and I can make it out to you otherwise I would have to have it changed later on.

In your last letter you had P.S. then what Hildred said about the hugs, and Mr. Turner's initials on the bottom. You must have been thinking of him. All kinds of OOO, XXX, & ⓛⓛⓛ, and a big Hug.

Chas.

———————◆———————

Postmark: 9:30 a.m. August 7, 1914, St. Paul, Minn.

Thursday evening.

My dear Sweetheart,

Don't think I will write very much tonight as I am pretty tired. This morning mamma and I put up twenty four quarts of blueberries and this afternoon spent down town shopping. That is what I call a tiresome job. Claribel had a harder job than we did though this morning, she picked all the black currants that grow on our small farm.

As to leaving the house, your plan is all right too, but if they should happen to see us leave they would sure follow us and if they saw where we went, stuff would all be off because they would camp outside and wait for us at least I know I would if I were in their place whereas if we had the machine a block away we could make that far and there they could not follow us. I would say have the machine stop in the alley but if it did and they should see the lights they would be suspicious right away. What do you think we better do?

As to where we should take our train, really it is immaterial to me but if we take it in Mpls. we would have to stay there over night. As to finding our way to the depot, I am sure I don't know how to get there but of course I can easy [sic] find out. I presume we would leave here on the Northwestern Live and I can find out what that depot is but then I should know what hotel we will stop at so we could find our way from there. What do you say?

Regarding stopping over in Chgo., if we do not stop, what kind of connections can we make. We leave here in the morning, get to Chgo. at night and then can we make connections that same night, and what time do we get to Detroit? This will give you a little side line to work on although I know you have plenty to do as it is.

Glad you are doing so well and I predict August will be a banner month considering the hard times all over. Let's see now!

Elizabeth Gregory from Milwaukee is visiting her grandparents here and of course she knows I am going to be married this fall and made me a lovely dresser scarf. Things sure seem to be coming my way. Must get to bed now because Mr. Turner will be back in the morning, that means a big day.

Lots of love, kisses and squeezes from

"Wifie"

———————◆———————

Postmark: 6:30 p.m. August 7, 1914, St. Paul, Minn.

Booth's Cold Storage envelope; letter typed

August 7, 1914

My dear Charles: –

Just time for a little today, pretty busy again. Mr. Turner is gone so much lately that I have to keep right at it when he is here to catch up. I asked him about going to Detroit when Mrs. Turner goes to the Fair in Toronto and he says he believes all you want is to give him a fast ride in your automobile and blow out a few more tires. He seems to be kind of suspicious of you as a chauffeur but wait until I get there, you can go as fast as you like.

Glad business is so good and hope that Doctor divides up liberally with you on that operation you turned over to him.

Sunday Elizabeth, Margrat [sic], (the two girls from Milwaukee), Claribel, Gladys and myself are expecting to go to some park, take our lunches with us and then stay for the band concert in the evening. We were kind of planning on going in bathing in the afternoon but they wont [sic] go in unless I do and my hand isn't well enough yet, the folks wont [sic] of letting me go in so that ends it again. I am losing out all around.

Must get busy again will try and write you more tomorrow. I have sort of got the "blue willies" as you call them today, wish I could see you. Lots of love from

H i l d r e d.

———————◆———————

Postmark: 11:30 p.m. August 7, 1914, Detroit, Mich.

Addressed to: Miss H.L. Cress, c/o Booth Fisheries

Aug 7th/14.

My Dear Hildred, -

Pleased to hear from you.

In regard to the wedding I thought we had already settled on Oct. 26th. My reason for suggesting a Monday wedding is because it is so much easier for me to get away on Monday than on a week day and another thing it would cost me $25.00 more to have the wedding on Tuesday than on Monday as I would lose that much by being away a week day longer at that season of the year, however if you have a better reason we will make it Oct. 27th. But as I mentioned before I thought we had decided on Oct. 26th.

Made $20.00 this AM. and hope to make quite a little more before the day is over with. (heres [sic] hoping.)

This is the warmest day we have had in some time. You must be sending some St. Paul weather along for us to enjoy.

By the way I was driving along the boulevard going over to Dr. Howard's office at 8:30 last night when I run over a nail in a little casing that they use for taking tar paper on houses [a sketch of a tack] had a nasty puncture. The nail went inside my casing and gave me a puncture like the following <3/4" a bad one to patch up. I suppose I will be getting all kinds of punctures since I have got started in. By the way I had to change tires in the middle of the road. Got my hands all dirty.

Will write more tomorrow as I am in a hurry to-day, all kinds of love and kisses to my sweetheart and a great Big Hug.

Lovingly,
Chas.

———————◆———————

Postmark: 5:30 p.m. August 8, 1914, St. Paul, Minn.

Typed with hand-written envelope

Aug. 8, 1914.

My dear Charles:

Was surely pleased to get your letter today and wish I could have that fast automobile ride with you today because it is so hot it is almost roasting people. I tell you, I will be willing to go as fast as you can open the machine up, that is providing you will guarantee we will not land in a ditch some place.

Note you say you feel lazy, I don't think you should call it that, simply own up and say you have worked so hard that you feel a little weary because you know you are not lazy. Just think to work all day for yourself and then spend your evenings at Dr. Howard's office, that sure isn't laziness.

Last night Elizabeth and Margaret came out and we surely had a good time. They wanted to see the things I have made so far and then they insisted that I give them something to do because they have nothing to do in the morning, although they do go some place every afternoon and evening so I gave them some towels to hem. Isn't that dandy of them to help me, I surely appreciate it because every little turn like that helps. Margaret's father is a doctor and she says she can sympathize with me in one thing and that is answering telephone she says it simply keeps them busy at that all day, one or the other has to keep at it all the time. Of course I wont [sic] mind that, the more it rings the better it will suit me because it will mean more money in all probability.

Tomorrow we are going to take our lunch and go to some park, think over at Lake Harriet, in Minneapolis but will sure write to you tomorrow evening. I suppose you think I am a great one writing to you on the machine so much but I don't know, it seems I am busy every minute lately with something. Do you mind if I write on the machine sometimes?

As to that postscript, don't know how I ever signed C.W.T. unless it is because I sign all Mr. Turner's letters that way when I write a postscript on then but then guess I am absent minded lately anyway so forgive me.

Am going to write you a nice long letter tomorrow so goodbye for this time. Just loads of love to you and the biggest kiss you ever had.

Yours lovingly,

H i l d r e d.

Postmark: 9 p.m. August 8, 1914, Detroit, Mich.

Addressed to: Chas. W. Turner, c/o Booth Fisheries; dot on flap

Aug. 8th/14

My Dear Hildred, -

Did not hear from you this morning, think possibly I will get a letter this afternoon. But I am going to write you anyway.

Your Hubby is getting next to himself the last few days made $28.00 yesterday, and made about $16.00 this A.M. Of course, I am working for all I am worth even though it is hot. Going to try and fix my punctured tire in a few minutes, then I have to make a call about nine miles away from here. It takes me about 13 minutes to get there around the boulevard don't you squeel [sic] on me now will you, because you like to go fast.

Will write you more tomorrow. Loads of hugs, kisses and a great big Hug.

Chas.

Postmark: 9:30 a.m. August 10, 1914, St. Paul, Minn.

Sunday evening.

My dear Sweetheart: -

Was surely glad to get my Sunday letter as that is always my "blue" day. I don't know, I like to get the kisses and hugs you send, but they don't seem to satisfy any more, I want something real, something that I know I have got it and can hardly wait now until I see you again. Just think, eleven long weeks yet but still I guess they will fly by before we know it and then I can have a really, truly, hug and kiss, but best of all see you again.

As to the 26th of October, guess we will leave it at that. My reason for suggesting the 27th is because mamma thought it would be inconvenient to do the cleaning and everything in one day and we would have to do that account of Sunday being the day before. However if it is going to be more convenient to you, Monday it shall be. I might have known Monday would be better for you if I had given it a second thought, in fact believe you told me once before however we have it all settled now, 26th of October, remember.

You sure seem to be having lots of fun getting punctures lately, rather expensive though but guess you must expect those things. How long are you going to help Dr. Howard out? That sure must keep you busy also kind of hard on you to spend every evening in his office, wish I were there to keep you company.

Just as we started out this afternoon with our lunch, it started to rain but the girls didn't want to let that hinder us, so off we went. It didn't rain very hard until we got to Lake Phalen and then how it did pour, thunder and lightning. Luckily we just had a block to the pavilion which is right on the lake and there we stayed until we came home. My goodness, you never saw it rain so hard in your life and keep up so long. There was one fellow out in a canoe with two girls in it and he paddled until he couldn't any more, the wind was so strong and finally they sent another canoe with two men in it out to bring them to shore. The canoe pretty near went over several times and when they got in they had to help the fellow to the pavilion, he was so exhausted. I sure was thankful that I was not one of those girls. We got pretty well soaked before we got home but changed our clothes right away so guess there will be no colds, hope not anyway.

I surely am going to write to your mother tomorrow, know I should have done so before but I have been doing such terrible scratching, account of my hand, thought I better wait.

All kinds of love and kisses to the best lover ever, from,

Hildred

Postmark: 5:30 p.m. August 10, 1914, St. Paul, Minn.

August 10, 1914

My dear Charles:

Was pleased to receive your letter this morning, short but sweet. My goodness but business sure is picking up and it pleases me very much but suppose not any more than it does you when you work so hard to make it come up.

You haven't had any more punctures have you? That is hard luck but still you must expect it when you run an automobile. Cheer up, pretty soon a time will come when we won't mind a little thing like that and you will be having a colored man as chauffeur and he can change the tires for you "Air Castles".

Mr. Turner leaves the city again tonight, going to Chicago and will return Wednesday or Thursday. I think he is planning on spending a couple of hours in Detroit, possibly Sunday or Monday, on his way to Toronto but it all depends on what transpires in Chicago this trip. I think I will have to jump in his traveling bag and go too. I know nothing would please me more. Don't give him a fast ride in the machine now, because if you do, you will never hear the last of it, go slow.

Say I had an awful dream Saturday night, thought I lost the stone out of my ring. I found it again but lost it two or three times before the night was over with. When I woke up I started hunting for my ring in the dark.

Must make this short, quite busy but will try and do better next time. "Oodles" of love from

Your "K.W"

Hildred

———————◆———————

Postmark: 8 p.m. August 10, 1914, Detroit, Mich.

Addressed to: Miss H.L. Cress, Booth Fisheries

Aug 10th/14

Hildred My Dear little Wife To Be, -

Have been so busy the last few days have not even had time to reckon up how much my business amounts to each day. Have got to hurry up and get out and make 5 more calls intend to leave the office at 3:30 pm, run my machine as fast as I could go trying to get around this morning but did not succeed. Had Mrs. Turner along with me, everybody asks me if she is my wife what do you know about that. I am starting to tell everybody that I am going to be married in Oct., month after next.

Tried to write you yesterday awfully sorry I didn't. I drove as near as I can figure 100 miles Sunday, we had company then again business was pretty brisk but I have been pretty regular about writing so do not think you will be put with me over it. I even got up at 5 o'clock Sunday morning, so you know I put in a full day. Don't think I will want to get up before 6:30 Am when we get married will want to stay in bed a little while and talk with my wifie.

In regard to leaving St. Paul I don't think we had better worry about that part of it until Oct. comes then we will get busy and figure out these things.

Note your friends are awfully good to you which I am glad to hear.

We are getting a little rain today for the first time in two or three weeks. It will be so slippery driving that I will have to go slow this afternoon.

Am going to try to write you a big long letter tomorrow Hildred.

All kinds of love & kisses and a great big Hug.

Lovingly

Chas.

———————◆———————

Postmark: 7 p.m. August 11, 1914, St. Paul, Minn.

Tuesday afternoon

My dear Charles:

What have I done that I didn't hear from you today? I [am] sure lost without your letter. This is the first time for over a month that I have not heard from you. I suppose you were real busy Sunday and of course when you are, I don't expect you to leave your work to write to me but I hope I get a nice fat letter tomorrow.

Mrs. Turner and Myrtle (Goodjohn) were downtown this morning to have their hair shampooed and then they stayed down for lunch and took me with them. I sure enjoyed it, feel as though I ate enough to last me all week but suppose when I get home tonight I will be ready for some more. Tomorrow noon Margaret and Elizabeth are coming down to lunch, also think Claribel and Myrtle are coming, that will make five of us. Gladys says she thinks she will have to go home tomorrow noon but she is going to try and fix it so she can stay downtown.

As to our wedding, I better ask the minister pretty soon so he won't have any other dates for October 26th (Monday). What do you think about being married in the evening about eight o'clock? Also, have you any particular choice as to what minister we have? Of course I won't have to ask just yet but there will be enough to do the very last thing. Just think how easy you are getting out of it. I even have to ask the minister. I bet my face will change fifty different colors when I do. I am anxiously waiting for tomorrow as I am pretty sure I will get a letter from my sweetheart.

Billions of OOO XXX and ☺☺☺

Lovingly,

Hildred

◆

Postmark: 8:30 p.m. August 11, 1914, Detroit, Mich.

Addressed to: C.W. Turner, Booth Fisheries; dot on envelope

Aug 11th/14.

My Dear Little Hildred, -

Have not heard from you so far today but think possible [sic] I will get a letter on this afternoon's mail. At least here's hoping.

Business still keeps pretty good, I have averaged $19.25 a day so far this month how does that suit my wife. But I have quite a lot of posting in my Ledger to do seems as though I am unable to find the time to do it.

About 5 pm last night I was out in one of the most severe storms we have had with my machine it sure did come down in torrents, once I took quite a side slew the road was so slippery and of course I could not make very good time this Am. I was away out in the country after all that rain and you just ought to have seen my car go through the mud hub deep in some places, I have more confidence in my car than ever now, I suppose I will have to get a self starter put on when my wife comes to live here, or she will break her back and have a sore shoulder working the Crank.

Last Sunday I had planned on getting my list made out, but was surely disappointed when I did not get at it, intend to get it fixed up next Sunday.

Have got to make a call 8 miles away from here this afternoon, if my little wifie were here than [sic] I could have company.

Write me a big long letter Hildred.

All kinds of love and kisses and a great big hug.

Lovingly

Chas.

(ps) Am going to write Mrs. Turner in a day or so. C.W.H.

———————◆———————

Postmark: 8:30 p.m. August 12, 1914, Detroit, Mich.

Addressed to Miss H.L. Cress, c/o Booth Fisheries

Aug 12/14

Hildred My Dear, -

I don't know as there is anybody who can appreciate concerning what you have to say in regard to those kisses & hugs more than I can. I think in regard to it to you before by saying I would love you to death when I see you and it seems as though you feel about the same as I do in that respect which is a good way to have it. And I surely trust when I see you there won't be too many around;

Pleased that you have decided on Oct. 26th. I wish it were Aug. 26th instead. You want to look St. Paul over good, because Detroit will soon be your home.

Hildred I feel nervous about you going to those different parks on Sunday that is if you go in bathing and go out canoeing, if I were there to get drown[sic] too I would not mind it so much, but if you should get drown, you know what it would mean to me, hence I wish you would make me a couple of promises but I leave it to you. I also think for some reason or other you would be more on the speedy automobile driving than I am, what do you think.

Business is going right along, can't complain in the least, I am afraid my automobile will be worn out before you get here, have not had any more punctures.

Will write to you more tomorrow Hildred, and I surely send all the love and kisses in me and a great big Hug.

Lovingly,

Chas.

———————◆———————

Postmark: 10 a.m. August 13, 1914, St. Paul, Minn.

August 12, 1914

My dear Charles:

I would love to write you a long letter tonight but I am pretty tired. Could not find time to write you a letter at the office so thought I would write tonight but if you will excuse me, I will write a good sized letter in the morning. Mr. Turner will be in Mpls.

All kinds of love to my dear sweetheart,
Hildred

Postmark: 7 p.m. August 13, 1914, St. Paul, Minn.

Thursday morning

My dear Charles:

Was surely pleased to hear from you again yesterday and today, in fact love to hear from you always but if you are busy I will take the will for the deed. You sure are doing splendid, $19.50 a day, my goodness don't I wish I were making that much but I guess a person must have an extra supply of brains to do such things.

You must have got in the storm Monday night that we were in Sunday and if it was as hard as the one we had here, it was certainly a dandy. I bet somebody was busy cleaning the machine when you got home. As to taking Mrs. Turner for your wife, I wonder who they will think I am! That is pretty good though, why don't you let them keep thinking that they wouldn't know the difference anyway.

You should have been with us yesterday. My we had a good lunch! (Mr. Turner came back from Mpls. when I got this far and it is now 4:30 P.M.) The girls wanted to be a Dutch treat so we went to Fields, Elizabeth, Margaret, Claribel and myself. When it came to footing the bill Elizabeth insisted on paying for it all herself because I took her out one noon and last fall when she was here I had her to lunch twice with me. I sure thought it great of her to take a lunch like that to Fields, I think I would have had the shivers if I had to foot the bill. Goodness! I must be stingy. Tonight the girls are coming out to the house and we are going to make some chocolate creams. Elizabeth makes them simply great. At Xmas she always makes a bunch of candy to sell. Does that make your mouth water? Tomorrow night Elizabeth's aunt is going to give a dinner party for the girls and Claribel and I are invited. I don't know where this week has gone. I don't seem to have accomplished anything. Monday night Claribel and I went to see a dressmaker but she only wants $18.00 to make a dress but that doesn't say she will get it, it is too much like throwing money away. Tuesday night Sibyl Burton was over, she is the girl I would like to have play the wedding march at our big event and of course I had to let her know in plenty of time so she could practice on it. Last night I had my ironing and mending to do, got through about 9:30 and was so "inski" [sic] that I hustled right to bed. That is the way it seems things go all the time and it is hard to do any sewing. Claribel sure has helped me dandy though and I appreciate it too.

The "honorable" Mr. Smithers from Chicago will arrive tomorrow, sooner than he expected, so probably they can have the meeting Sunday and then Mr. Turner would be able to leave all the sooner for Detroit and Toronto.

Guess I will have to hurry and finish my work now, think this is a pretty long letter though, see if my sweetheart can do as well of course if you are busy, business first.

Lots of OOO XXX and ☺☺☺ *and an extra big smacking kiss from*

Yours lovingly,

Hildred

P.S. Just found out Mr. and Mrs. Turner and Myrtle are coming over tonight so we sure will have a house full.

S.W.A.K.

———————◆———————

Postmark: 8:30 p.m. August 13, 1914, Detroit, Mich.

Addressed to Chas. W. Turner, c/o Booth Fisheries; dot on flap

Aug 13/14.

Hildred My Dear, -

What do you think it was 4:30 p.m. and your Hubby just had his lunch, sometimes when I get busy I forget all about the eat business, don't know how much I have made today but business is keeping up pretty good.

Now in regard to the wedding I believe Mother is going to be among those present, as far as the minister is concerned, we all go to the same church, and the who does not make much difference to me as long as he has a license to do that work. If you do not care to ask him let me know and I will write him a letter. Of course you would have to send me the name and his address. If my mother goes to St. Paul for the big event, in all probability she will stay there for a couple of weeks and then go on to Duluth for a couple of weeks more.

We sure have just had a very hard electrical storm, it did not rain, it just poured. My car is having a bath, but I suppose it will get all dirty again tomorrow as I have got to make a trip out in the country.

Your Hubby has made suggestions to you that he would like you to wear how about you making a suggestion to me. Do you want me to wear a dress suit or dark blue suit, I had thought of just wearing a dark blue suit what do you think.

If business will just give me a chance Hildred will write you more tomorrow.

Just Loads and Loads of love, and a great big Hug.

Lovingly,

Chas.

Postmark: 1:21 p.m. August 14, 1914, Detroit, Mich.

Addressed to Miss H.L. Cress, c/o Booth Fisheries

Aug 14/14

My Dear Hildred, -

Awfully busy today have made $56.00 so far today and it is just 6 p.m. How do you like that.

Sorry I did not hear from you to-day, I trust & feel sure I will hear from you tomorrow because I will surely have the blue willies if I don't.

This is my evening office hours kindly excuse scribbling & spelling.

I send all kinds of OOO, XXX, & ⓖ ⓖ ⓖ and the biggest hug ever. And the same sized kiss.

Lovingly,

Chas.

Postmark: 1:30 p.m. August 14, 1914, St. Paul, Minn.

Friday, Aug. 14th.

My own dear Lover:

As usual, I was happy as could be to hear from you again and I should say, I like yourself hope there are not many around when you come this fall but I suppose no such luck.

Now as to bathing, canoeing etc. I don't want you to worry about me at all, because really nothing is going to happen and besides I haven't been in bathing or in a boat either since that Sunday I caught my cold. Last Sunday when we girls got to the park it had started to rain so we couldn't do any of those stunts. Now next Sunday papa is going to take us to Sunfish Lake, out in the country about six miles and Margaret and Elizabeth are going along. The people that we are going to see have a little gasoline launch on the lake and if dad is along I should think it would be all right to go out don't you. If it is raining though we won't go out there so there is nothing positive about it at all. Don't you think I have regarded your wishes pretty well this summer by not going bathing? Nobody else could influence me that way.

Oh say! Elizabeth made some chocolate creams last night to show me how and they were simply delicious. Mrs. Turner said I should make some and she would take them with her when she goes to Detroit but I don't think I will have mastered the art by that time so Elizabeth said she would make them for me to see, you have something coming providing they turn out all right. My I ate so many last night, all I see is chocolate jumping before my eyes. I sure like candy.

Expect Mr. Turner and the Chgo. People here any minute, they left Minneapolis some time ago and I don't want them to catch me writing a love letter, they may think I haven't anything else to do.

So long until tomorrow Charles and just loads of kisses and hugs from

Hildred

◆

Postmark: 3 p.m. August 15, 1914, St. Paul, Minn.

Aug. 15, 1914

My dear Charles:

Just a little note today, it is now 1:15 and have not had any lunch but that is not near as bad as you going until 4 o'clock without anything to eat you mustn't do that again.

Another thing, you shouldn't go and tell Mr. Turner I like to speed, that is all I have heard all morning, he did not open your letter until today, busy with Chgo. Company yesterday. I sure got a dandy lecture and guess I don't dare to do any speeding.

As to your suit, to tell the truth I don't know much about that but I asked Mr. Turner and he said he would talk that over with you when he saw you Tuesday. I am surely pleased to hear your mother is thinking of coming to the wedding and hope you will not change your mind.

I am afraid I will have to disappoint you as to that candy but the folks are going to leave sooner than expected and the girls are busy with previous engagements up to Monday and I wouldn't want to put them out any so told them to let it go this time.

Mr. Turner can give you the news when he sees you, wish I were going too.

Loads and loads of love to my sweetheart,
Hildred

Postmark: 7:30 p.m. August 15, 1914, Detroit, Mich. – Grand River Station

Addressed to: Chas. W. Turner, c/o Booth Fisheries; dot on envelope

Aug 15th/14

Hildred My Dear, -

Received two letters from you this morning did not hear from you yesterday if you get your letter in for the 9:30 a.m. collection I get it the following afternoon.

Feel rather tired after my big day yesterday. How did you like the looks of it anyway. In the 14 days of this month I have made $312.00 and taken in $227.50. Got up early this a.m. and gave my machine a little bath and greased up.

Note you are a pretty busy woman, better not over do yourself, leave that for your Hubby to do. I bet when I get to sleep tonight, all Jerusalem will not be able to wake me.

Received Uncle Chas' Telegram this am. to the effect that he would be in the city at 3:30 Tuesday. My if my little wifie were only coming too, I believe I would get awfully excited.

What do you say about having a little rehearsal on the afternoon of Oct. 26th. Don't tell anybody if I tell you that I have never attended a wedding. By having a rehearsal things will go along a little smoother, also let me know in regard to a dress suit.

Now in regard to all those good things to eat that you are getting, be careful now don't get any boils.

Mr. Turner left for Cincin – this a.m. So I have lost my side partner who will I get now.

Will write you again tomorrow Hildred I want to go over the way and get my shoes shined as I have to leave at four o'clock on a call.

All kinds of OOO, XXX, and ⓖ ⓖ ⓖ, and a great big Hug and Kiss.
Chas.

———————◆———————

Postmark: 10 p.m. August 16, 1914, Detroit, Mich.

Addressed to: Miss H.L. Cress, c/o Booth Fisheries Cop., St. Paul Minn.
(envelope flap unavailable)

August 16th/14.

Hildred My Dear Sweetheart, -

These Sunday mornings seem to roll around pretty fast, but the weeks roll by none to fast for yours truly. Just about two months more, Hunny Bub and Detroit for you.

Business will be quite slow today that is in comparison to other days. I believe, when things really quiet down a little I really feel lost, I like to be on the jump every minute. A man just called up and said he was coming over to see me, that makes another new one.

Dr. Moon just called up and wants me to take a boat ride with him this afternoon, don't know whether I will go or not, I surely would hate to lose any business by being away and at the same time I know it would be quite a change for me, and that I would enjoy myself.

I will be almost tempted to give the Turner's a good fast automobile ride on Tuesday, and I feel it in my bones that Uncle Chas. is going to hope he doesn't. I hate the thoughts of spending about $50.00 a year on automobile insurance.

You have not said anything about your hand the last few days, let me know if you went in boating today. Something seems to tell me that your ought not go in.

Just Loads & Loads of OOO, XXX, & 6 6 6 s to my little wifie to be and a great big hug & kiss.

Lovingly,

Chas.

———————◆———————

Postmark: 9 a.m. August 17, 1914, St. Paul, Minn.

Aug. 16, 1914

My dear Sweetheart:

Glad you did not forget me Friday with all the rush of business, $56.00!! My but that looks good and you certainly are to be congratulated. If you keep on doing so splendidly you will break all records this month.

Am just going to make this a little note tonight, had a pretty strenuous day and will tell you about it tomorrow. We did not get home until five minutes of eleven and we left in such a rush this noon that we left the dishes so Claribel and I done them when we got home. It is after 11:30 now but don't scold me and please don't say anything to Mr. Turner because I know what is coming tomorrow.

Just millions of kisses and hugs and here is hoping you have some more of those $56.00 days.

Lovingly,

Hildred

Postmark: 8:30 p.m. August 17, 1914, Detroit, Mich.

Addressed c/o Booth Fisheries; no dot on envelope flap

August 17th/14.

Hildred My Dear Little Sweetheart, -

Just received your Friday letter, It surely seemed good to hear from you to-day. I don't know but I do not feel very good to-day, I think I took a little cold in my back last night, because when I woke up I was nearly parlized [sic] and after I got to sleep it turned real cool, but it is surely warm enough today. I just feel real dopy and my head rumbles a little but I am going to take a tablet and fight it off.

Now in regard to your canoeing and bathing note you have kept away from these things on my account which I certainly appreciate very much. You no doubt realize what it would mean if anything would happen, of course if I were there it would be different, just as you say in regard to auto riding we would be together.

I surely will be on the look out for those chocolate creams, my mouth is already waiting even if I do feel punk, I trust you will eat part of one and send the rest of it on.

By the way I made out part of my list yesterday and you will have it by Sept. 1st or sooner if you wish. I am just aching for the time to come when I can cuddle right up to my little sweetheart. I wish the days would go by like minutes, I believe if I had just kept after my little honey bub we could have made it in Sept.

I met Sister Lucina this AM, I told her I was going to be married in Oct. and I really thought she was going to put her arms around me, what do you know about that, she says she would be delighted to meet you. I will be taking you to see her before so very long. She is quite stout and wears one of those big white winged hats and dresses in blue, her hair is all cut off.

Mother went to the city this afternoon and I am all alone. I must give my machine a little rub up after office hours, else Uncle Chas will think I keep a dirty house.

Business was quite slow on Sunday only made $5.50 quite a difference between Friday & Sunday. Friday I made $58.00, Saturday only $8.25, however so far this month I have run at the rate of over $600.00 a month. Of course this is our dull season.

The Dr. across the street is rushing his house right along, but I do not think his location there will make very much difference with me.

Just imagine the most kisses hugs & squeezes ever enclosed and a great big hug and kisses.

Lovingly,

Chas.

———————◆———————

Postmark: 6 p.m. August 18, 1914, St. Paul, Minn.

- Monday –

My dear Sweetheart: -

Got your letter first thing this morning and it gave me a dandy start for the day. After this when I write a letter at home I will mail it first thing in the morning so you will not be getting two letters in one day.

How did I like the looks of your big day? Well really I couldn't begin to tell you but if you were here I would just hug you so hard that maybe you would know how it pleased me. You certainly do fine and by the way, that is your biggest day yet, isn't it? I can just see dandy bright results before you for August so go to it.

As to a rehearsal Monday afternoon, yes surely we would have to have one whether you had been to a wedding or not. Cheer up though you will get through it as well as I will, when I think of it now I even begin to shake. Last fall at Vera's wedding when the choir had to sing of course we had processional and even then I was weak-kneed. By the way, Alice Hillman, one of the girls from the Park is going to be married Sept. 2 and she wants the choir to sing and has invited us all over to her house for tomorrow evening. Do not know as yet whether I will go or not although I would like to very much. There is another girl, Marion Freedy, who is going to be married in Sept. to some young man from Detroit. She like myself does not know anyone there. I have never met the girl but Vera is going to have us both over to her house some evening so we can "get acquainted." I think that will be pretty fine.

One more thing along this line, Ethel Crosby is planning on giving a "Handy Shower" for me, that is things useful around the house. I think it is pretty nice of her. Gladys also wants to have some of the girls at her house before I go. I think after all this excitement I will want to take some of your sugar coated pills for my nerves but not yet.

Mr. Turner said he would tell you what kind of a suit he thought you should wear, let me know what he says and how it appeals to you.

This letter is nothing but weddings all the way through, will find something different for tomorrow, for instance bathing, – never again for me this summer.

Goodnight for tonight dear. Oh! if I could only see you for about five minutes, your picture is pretty well worn.

Loads of love from

Hildred.

———————◆———————

Postmark: 8 p.m. August 18, 1914, Detroit, Mich.

Addressed to: Charles W. Turner, c/o Booth Fisheries - Dot on envelope flap

Aug. 18th/14

Hildred, My Dear, -

Just received your Saturday letter it was stamped as being in the city Monday morning at 7:30 AM and I don't see why I did not get it yesterday. Just imagine it was in Detroit 24 hrs. before being delivered and the same thing holds true with Mr. Turner's letter, the result is that I had to call up and make reservations for Toronto and think I was pretty lucky in getting them.

I awfully hated to tell Mr. Turner about your desire for speeding, but I just thought this way about it, when you would come to Detroit in all probability you might meet with an accident by driving fast, and I thought a few words from Mr. Turner might be of benefit to you, although as I say I hated to tell on you, but in all probability if you think seriously over it you will think I am right, or done right by telling. Of course I know you would get a lecture.

Expect to leave in a few minutes to meet the 3:20 train, I suppose Mrs. Turner will be nervous about riding with me but if she's going along even if I do have to pick her up and put her in the machine, gee winnigers but I wish my wifie were coming, I would forget all about the bum feeling I have to-day. The trouble is that Mother always closes down one window in my room, that is where the breeze blows across my bed, I opened it up once to often and caught cold in my liver [sic].

Just loads & Loads of hugs & kisses and a great big hug & kiss.

Lovingly
Chas.

———————◆———————

Postmark: 10 a.m. August 19, 1914, St. Paul, Minn.

Aug. 18, 1914.

My dear Honey Bub:

See what lessons you are giving me. Where did you learn that, it is a new one to me.

It is kind of late tonight, just got back from Alice Heilman's. We had a pretty good time and by the way I met Marion Freedy. She seems to be quite a nice girl, was glad to meet her. She is going to marry a Mr. Morgan from Detroit.

I do hope you took that little trip with Dr. Moon Sunday. You know all work and no play makes Charlie (in this case) a dull boy. I think a little pleasure once in a while is a good thing but not too much. Let me know if you went Sunday and how you enjoyed yourself. Hope you had a real good time.

I obeyed the instructions of my dear Hubby Sunday and did not go in bathing and am not going in again this summer. Monday papa came home and told us Ernest (my cousin) had been poisoned while in swimming at Lake Calhoun and is in the hospital. The doctors don't know just what it is, it came on him real suddenly and this is the second case they have had this summer. He seems a little better today but he is too weak to move at all. Papa has given positive orders that nobody in our house goes swimming so home we stay. I think I know somebody that is glad.

That dad of mine sure is the limit. You know Mr. Turner gave me two days to stay at home this week so last night I wrote to you at home and gave papa the letter this morning to mail for me and if he didn't walk off without it. This explains your getting two letters in one day again.

I have finally located a dress maker and you don't know what a load it is off my mind. I hunted high and low for one. Guess I am on the right track now.

I am off for bed now, wish I could have a real good night kiss but guess I must imagine it a while longer.

All kinds of love and XXX's

From

Hildred

———◆———

Postmark: 12 p.m. August 19, 1914, Detroit, Mich.

Addressed to Miss H.L. Cress, c/o Booth Fisheries

No dot on envelope flap

Aug. 19th/6 p.m.

My Dear Hildred, -

Am just wondering whether or not my little wifie forgot to write that long letter on Monday that you promised me in your Sunday letter. Something surely must be wrong because I did not hear from you to-day and especially when Mr. Turner left St. Paul Monday.

Well both Aunt Lizzie and Uncle Chas. have had auto rides with me and they left Detroit last night at 11 p.m. all safe and sound. Uncle Chas. tells me I drive too fast, I always drive from 20 – 30 miles an hour, so you no doubt know what he said to me.

Aunt Lizzie gave me the kiss you sent thank you Very Very Much it was pretty good but I hope to have a real one before very long, not one but millions in time how about it.

It is awfully warm to-day, have not made very much money to-day but have taken in about $40.00, which helps out.

Next week I am going to send you my list of names, so you will be able to get that part of it fixed up.

Now Hildred I trust you will write me a big long letter to make up for the one I missed to-day and put lots of XX in it too.

All kinds of love and kisses to my sweetheart and a great big hug & kisses.

Lovingly

Chas.

(ps) Am going to have my machine changed so that I will have electric headlights. CH

———————◆———————

Postmark: 9:30 a.m. August 20, 1914, St. Paul, Minn.

Thursday evening

My own dear Sweetheart:

The only part I dislike in staying home is that I do not get your letter until the evening whereas at the office I get it in the morning.

Am sorry you have caught cold, you should keep the covers on at night. Claribel must be something like you in that respect, and in the winter if I didn't cover her about twenty-five times more or less during the night we would find her frozen in the morning. She surely does jump around during the night. I hope you feel better now and don't get to feeling like that when October comes. Pretty near the last of August and then we can say "next month."

As to Sister Lucina pretty near putting her arms around you, better tell her to be careful or she might get herself disliked. You know I am kind of a jealous person in some things. I like to do the hugging myself. I would surely like to meet her but maybe I will forget myself and stand and stare at her because I have never seen a sister dressed as they dress.

I am awfully sorry that I disappointed you on the candy but really couldn't help it. Mr. and Mrs. Turner left so much sooner than I expected and the girls could not make it any more. If I can though I am going to surprise you some day with a box.

Poor Claribel has to go through another operation tomorrow. At first they thought they would just have to use cocaine but now they think it will be as big an operation as the first was. You ought to hear her run the doctor's down, she hasn't much love for them. I told her she could say that about any of them but one and she is willing to make an allowance there until she knows you better. I certainly feel sorry for her, it is something all the time, if it isn't one thing it is another.

As to your list, if you have it here by Sept. 1st that will be dandy. I am beginning to feel quite bridey now, have my slippers, gloves and veil and my dress planned and dressmaker found. She is not going to make my dress until the latter part of September in case I should change my mind in the meantime. She is going to make mamma's dress too. What did Mr. Turner advise you as to your suit? That is something I have to get too, and a hat. My I wish it would rain $5.00 bills for a change, think I could make use of all I could gather in.

Claribel wants me to hurry and turn the light out. Sorry dear lover, good night. Kisses and hugs by the millions to you.

Lovingly,

Hildred.

———————◆———————

Postmark: 8:30 p.m. August 20, 1914, Detroit, Mich.

Addressed to: Mr. Chas. W. Turner, c/o Booth Fisheries - Dot on envelope flap

Thursday Afternoon,

Hildred My Dear, -

Anybody would think I am nervous by the looks of my writing this afternoon, but honestly I am not. I was interrupted two or three times in the beginning that accounts for it.

Now in regard to the suit I am going to wear Mr. Turner suggests a three piece button cutaway a cut of which he has promised to send me so do not let him forget it will you. I think I will have it made up in two or three weeks so your hubby will soon be already. I wish we could make it Sept. 26th if you would just say yes I would say great business go ahead however I suppose patience is a virtue and I must wait.

Business is slow as slow can be today will not tell you how much I have made so far today because I know you would laugh at me. Only made $8.50 yesterday, but I took in $38.50. I do like to take in but here is hoping tomorrow will be better. Along business lines, I have some work lined up for tomorrow.

I just wonder who next is going to be married in St. Paul. By the way are you going to send your friend Theresa Lucius an invitation.

At 4 P.M. I have to attend a meeting of the executive committee of the Detroit College of Medicine. My speller is out of kilter this afternoon, or else I am loose in my upper stories.

Just Myriads of hugs and kisses and a great big hug & kiss.

Lovingly

Chas.

———————◆———————

Postmark: 10 a.m. August 21, 1914, St. Paul, Minn.

Thursday

My dear Charles:

Just a little note tonight, am awfully tired.

Claribel was operated on this noon and is getting along fine. The operation was not as long this time but the doctor's said it would be more painful. I surely pity the girl and hope to goodness she doesn't have to go through it again.

This morning we cleaned the whole house and had everything to get ready for the operation so it kept us busy until noon. This afternoon I done the washing, that is all the sheets etc. that the doctors used. Mamma couldn't help, guess the smell of the chloroform made her sick.

Thought I was sewing until 10 o'clock so maybe I am not ready for bed.

Mamma and dad are down town tonight, they gave me instructions to go to bed early but I forgot the time until I heard the clock strike.

How is your cold hope you are all well now. After this when your mother closes the window, you better keep it closed.

All my love and kisses to you and will write you more tomorrow.

Lovingly,

Hildred

Postmark: 6:30 p.m. August 21, 1914, St. Paul, Minn.

Aug. 21st, 1914

My dear Sweetheart:

So you think I am forgetting you, or rather to write to you, well I should say not. I know I have been a little irregular lately but that is account of being home for several days and your Monday letter I wrote in the evening and in the morning papa forgot to take it with him so it was delayed.

I did not plan on being home yesterday but we did not know Claribel was going to be operated on until the day before and papa wanted me to stay home and help this time, there is almost too much for one to do but my dear, I am going to be more prompt hereafter.

Goodness, I never thought an operation was as bad as it really is and the way Claribel was crying when she took the chloroform. My but she hollered. I guess I done pretty near as much crying as she did but nobody heard or saw me, I looked out for that. I think I will make rather a poor helper for you along that line because I can't stand to see anybody suffer. Claribel is getting along just fine and I never saw a more patient girl in my life, she doesn't ask for one thing because she is afraid she is bothering us. I wish she would, though, then we would know what she wanted.

I am glad Mr. Turner gave you a lecture on Tuesday because I think you like to speed as well as I do. Must blame it all on wifie you know.

Glad you got the kiss, did she give you an extra big one because I told her to. I hope you sent one back because I have my mouth all shaped – waiting and when that train comes in October 26th, maybe I won't have a bunch stored up for you, be prepared for a whole shower of them. The only trouble, I am afraid I will be all out of practice by that time, maybe I better practice on somebody in the meantime, what do you say? You wouldn't care, would you?

We have been having simply dandy weather here, not too hot or cold, don't send any of your warm weather here though. As to business, how do you think you will come out this month, that is what do you think you will charge up? I think from reports that are coming it, that you will have a dandy month.

I do not think I understood your P.S. are you just going to change the lights or the machine?

Imagine some of those millions of kisses that are in store for you, enclosed in this letter and some of the OO's and ☺s too. Take as many as you like, but send as many of yours back.

Lovingly,

Hildred

Here is one extra big hug and kiss.

———————◆———————

Postmark: 8:30 p.m. August 21st, 1914, Detroit, Mich.

Addressed to Miss H.L. Cress c/o Booth Fisheries - No dot on envelope flap

Friday 1 p.m.

My Dear Wifie, -

I am just wondering what you are doing today. You must have your little storehouse full of letters by this time or else you have quite a large place to keep them.

In regard to your inquiry as to whether I went to Bob-lo last Sunday with Dr. Moon, may say that just before the time came to go we had company come to the house so I stayed home and took them all out for a ride in my machine, but I sure feel the need of a day off, this business gets strenuous in time.

I am going to tell you something, that is when I came home last June I figured where I took in $500.00 that is over and above certain amounts that I would have to pay out to keep up running expenses etc. I would have enough money to get married on, now I have taken in this amount with the exception of $40.00. May say that I expect to take in $30.00 tonight on an account, so you see I am just about ready as far as money is concerned.

Now in regard to the minister we are going to have I think you better have your own minister that is from your church, I know that if he knew you were going to have somebody else and another thing you are your own boss, so do not let anybody else dictate to you without making your self known, if you wish you can send me his address and I will fix matters up for you.

Glad you have given up the idea of bathing for this summer and I firmly believe that had I not written to you along these lines the way I have you would have been poisoned instead of your cousin. I just felt in my bones that you ought not to go, and I may add that I am not at all superstitious.

I am going to ask you to write me a big long letter Sunday, because I surely like to hear all the news.

Glad you met with that girl Marion Freedy. I suppose all these things turning up make you feel better.

All kinds of love and kisses to my sweetheart. Just wish that I could hug you for about 2 hrs. with out stopping. Just imagine a great big Hug & Kiss.

Lovingly,

Chas.

———————◆———————

Postmark: 6:30 p.m. August 22, 1914, St. Paul, Minn.

Aug. 22, 4 p.m.

My dear Lover:

Glad to hear from you again, and also glad to get that dandy package Mr. Turner brought with him. Thank you ever ever so much it is simply great. I am overly sorry I had to disappoint you as to the candy because I know you have the same failings as I have when it comes to candy. That box is half empty allready [sic] and Mr. Turner and dad only ate a couple of pieces. Why didn't you eat part of one as you said in your letter?

Mr. Turner came back all worked up over the way you drive and how nervous you are getting. No doubt his letter to you today will partly express his feelings but that is not near as strong as he put it up to me. Really I am worried about you, can't help it because while I thought you drove quite fast, thought you were more careful and did not think you went as fast as you really do. Mr. Turner partly blames me for your inclination to drive fast and if anything should happen to you Charlie I could never forgive myself, would always feel partly to blame. I always thought you liked to drive fast before I spoke of it. Now I want you to promise me something and hope for my sake you will do it. If you have not bought a speedometer as yet go out right away, Monday, and have one put on your machine and then keep with the twenty mile limit and every time you go over that you should report to me. I have promised to stay out of the water, namely on your account and hope you will do this

*favor I am asking for me. Really I wouldn't rest easy until I hear from you because I feel I
am partly to blame for this and you should know that I wouldn't have anything happen to
you for the world if I could help it.*

*Mr. Turner seems to think you do not just like the idea of a house wedding. Now when I
suggested it, I thought you agreed to it right away and if I had known you did not want
it that way we could have dropped it right away. Of course I know at first we had just
planned on the family but I don't know, it seemed so small to me, hardly anything to it. Let
me know what you think.*

*If I had the mazuna [sic] I would say yes to Sept. 26th right away but you see four more
pay days come in between that and I need the money almost to badly but cheer up, in a few
days we can say next month and maybe I won't be glad. Again, I can then see that you keep
within the speed limit so be good.*

*Just to satisfy my curiosity, tell me what you made Thursday and I won't laugh, really.
Come on now and tell me.*

*As to inviting my friend Theresa, you surely put that nicely but you know that ought to be
turned around. Mr. Turner I guess thinks if we have a wedding we should invite them,
what do you say? Hope you write a dandy long letter Sunday.*

All my love and kisses to my sweetheart, from

Hildred

*P.S. Hope that machine of yours don't turn over before I hear from you again. Mr. Turner
has suggested everything imaginable that might happen.*

H.

◆

Postmark: 7:30 p.m. August 22, 1914, Detroit, Mich. – Grand River Station

Addressed to Mr. Chas W. Turner, c/o Booth Fisheries - Envelope flap did not survive

Saturday Afternoon,

Hildred My Dear, -

Thanks for your sympathy in regard to my little spell was just on the outs with myself
for one day that is all, but don't worry about anything turning up with me in Oct. Just
be feeling good your self, and your hubby will be on time.

Glad you are getting your wearing apparel to-gether it sure looks like business when
you are getting your things together, have you purchased a trunk as yet, I wish I could
send my trunk to you and save you some money, but I guess it is just as well for you to
have one anyway.

Surely sorry to hear concerning Claribel, tell her I wish her a speedy recovery. She certainly has had her share of trouble, but one may be alright from this out.

Business is running along slowly made $12.25 and took in $38.00 yesterday, drugs and all going up in price on account the war, I suppose this war will put a damper on money before long. Supposing we starve next winter my Dear Honey-Bub what will you think of me then. By the way you are a little German too aren't you. Somebody's country is coming to an end before long what do you think.

Send me a sample of your dress when you get it will you Hildred, see how interested I am.

Great Loads and Loads of hugs & kisses and a great big, big hug and kiss with a good squeeze.

Lovingly,

Chas.

———————◆———————

Postmark: 8 p.m. August 23, 1914, Detroit, Mich.

Addressed to Miss H.L. Cress c/o Booth Fisheries - Dot on envelope flap

August 23rd/14

Hildred My Dear, -

Sunday again always glad to see Sunday come as I know another week has passed, but I do not care very much for Sunday in itself it is a lonesome day for Yours Truly.

Let me know how Claribel is getting along hope she is feeling better by this time.

Another thing I will be glad when you get back to the office they make you work too hard at home. I also get my letter in the morning when you are at the office.

Got up early this morning met the 7:10 train from Cincinnati, Horace Turner is here to spend a few days with us. So I suppose he will be doing some auto riding with your Hubby today, intend to do quite a lot of driving today.

Hildred if you do not make somebody else share in that house work I will arrive in St. Paul at once and make you marry me and come right here. You know I am just about ready.

This is a grand day, do not use it part to do much business today. Going to leave in a few minutes for St. Mary's Hospital have a patient there. Have another call to make on Whitney Ave. and another on Williams St. had two office patients so far this morning.

All kinds of OOOO, XXX's and (6) (6) (6) to my sweetheart and a great big hug and kiss the biggest Ever.

Lots of Love,

Chas.

◆

Postmark: 9:30 a.m., August 24, 1914, St. Paul, Minn.

Sunday 3 P.M.

My dear "Hubbykins":

Today sure is blue Sunday, even the sun refuses to shine. Mamma and papa have gone to Minnetonka. Claribel is reading and I hardly know what to do with myself. Claribel is getting along just dandy, she came down for dinner this noon and is still down stairs. The doctors say her cut healed too quickly last time and now they have two drainages in. They took them out this morning but put others in and expect to do that for several days so it will be a while before she can get around very spryly. She cannot eat any candy as yet so I saved a couple of pieces for her. She is pretty nearly as good at eating candy as I am.

I am sorry you could not go with Dr. Moon last Sunday. Now I tell you what you do, next Sunday simply pack up and leave for the whole afternoon, try and get somebody to go with you and have a real good time and simply forget there is such a thing as the practice of medicine. But when you are out, don't get to thinking that you might be losing a call, what of it, I bet you will feel 50% better when you get back and have had a little rest from the same daily routine of business. Now you do this, won't you?

As to the minister, nobody has really been influencing me one way or the other. The folks now say to have who I want although I know by the way they talk they would like me to have the one they had but I think I would rather have Dr. Stevens so if you like you can write to him and ask him about the evening of the 26th. His address is Laurel Ave, St. Paul. Maybe you better do this pretty soon so we are sure of getting him as he is a pretty busy man. I forgot to give you his initials so his whole name is Dr. A. C. Stevens. I kind of think Mr. Turner talked to you regarding this because that is the way he spoke to me. He intends to get that cut for you tomorrow that is of your suit. I asked dad what his suit was and he says a three button cutaway. I imagine it would look good on you because you are so tall.

I am sure glad you have taken in the amount of money you wanted to before getting married. Wouldn't it have been a great note if you hadn't made it?

Mr. Turner took Harriet and some of her friends out for a ride today. Guess they have promised it to her for some time. Just before they left he called up and I wished him a good time and he said, "Yes, hot chance with a bunch of old hens." If Harriet could only have heard him then. La La!! She never would have cooked another meal for him I bet.

I surely was glad to meet Miss Freedy, expect to see her again Tuesday night, we have to go to church to practice again for Alice's wedding and she is going to be in the choir. She used to sing in the choir about three years ago but her folks moved down nearer to town and it was almost too far to come.

My imagination is getting pretty well stretched because I have to use it so much imagining hugs and kisses from you and I sure will be glad to get some real ones.

This is a pretty long letter, now let me have a good long one from you that is providing you have time. Claribel wants me to come down and keep her company, guess she is tired reading. So long dear until tomorrow!

Yours

"Wifikins"

P.S. R E M E M B E R --- Go Slow and Speedometer
Were you asked about insurance?

◆

Postmark lost – Booth Fisheries envelope heavily deteriorated

Envelope typed; letter hand-written

Monday evening, August 24, 1914

My dear Charles:

I am surely glad to hear that cold of yours is O.K. again, don't catch any more of them. I wish I could get rid of mine as quick as you do, mine usually last a month or more.

I did not have time to write to you at the office today, had some shopping to do this noon and we left the office at 4:30 tonight so I was busy all the time. The reason we left so early, Mr. Turner took Mamma, dad and myself out to Ford Snelling before dinner. I forgot to mention we had an awful storm here Saturday night and it was a regular cyclone at the Fort. You never saw such an awful looking sight in your life, hardly a building whole. New brick buildings, whole sides would be blown out and slate roofs all blown to pieces, wooden porches and roofs carried for over a block. It is the first time I have seen the results of a real wind storm and it surely did damage there.

I am enclosing a cut that Mr. Turner got for you today of a three button cutaway I think I will have to watch you that night or some of the girls may try to make eyes at you. What do you think of the looks of it?

No I did not get my trunk as yet but think I ought to pretty soon. It sure is dandy of you to offer me yours but it would be such a bother sending it and anyway it is something that will always be a handy thing.

Don't you talk war to me or you will get me all riled up. Of course naturally I talk for Germany and if they don't win I tell you it will not be their fault, they are a bunch of stickers and will fight to the last. That is where they show some of their stubbornness for which I guess they are noted. Grandma won't have it that way, she says they are firm not stubborn. If they need any extra help maybe I will join the suffragettes and go to, will you go along. The folks laid in an extra supply of sugar, flour, etc so they are partly prepared for the advance that is keeping right up.

As to sending you samples of my dress, I would love to do it but don't you know that is bad luck? A bride should never show her dress to anyone until the eventful day and you will be the first one to see it. Of course, mamma will see it but she is positively the only one but I want her to go along when I have it fitted. What do you think of my superstition? Foolish child don't you think? Goodnight "hubbykins" will talk to you again tomorrow. Lots of goodnight kisses and hugs, from

Hildred

Enclosure: Colored cardboard of a man wearing a cutaway suit, top hat and carrying gloves and cane. Face resembles Woodrow Wilson. The number "71" is at the feet and is copyrighted 1911 by Fred'k T. Croonborg Both front and back are stamped: A.F. McBride, Merchant Tailor 112 East 4th St. St. Paul, Minn.

———————◆———————

Postmark: 5:30 p.m. August 24, 1914, Detroit, Mich. – North End Station

Addressed to Miss H.L. Cress c/o Booth Fisheries - Envelope flap does not survive

Aug. 24th/14

Hildred my Dear Sweetheart, -

If you were only here so that I could love you, I am getting so awfully lonesome to see you, I think Oct. 26th will be the biggest day of my life so far. Just think I will not only see you, but take you with me. My Wifie.

Glad Claribel is getting along so nicely, give her a little wee smack and tell her it is from her Brother in law and see what she says. In regard to standing chloroform you will never have to be around with me at any operation.

I surely got the kiss, Aunt Lizzie I expect will be staying with us next week, and then I will send one back with her. But when it comes to you practicing on anybody else, I say nix of course. You can kiss your Daddy and your people, but when it comes to practicing you will have an opportunity to practice on me, before long. I want you as you are.

Really Hildred you don't know how much surprised I was when I read Uncle Chas. letter. Honestly I am not nervous, or doing any harm to myself in regard to driving my machine, may say that I never felt better, why Hildred I have a nervous system on me like a horse, and another thing when I was working my way through college and going to college I worked twice as hard and worked almost night & day & I did not play out, and why should I play out now, as far as working is concerned I am twice as healthy when I have lots to do, I can stand anything, so please do not worry about me, as far as driving fast is concerned why Hildred I think I am a very careful driver, I never go fast unless the way is clean, and another thing I have not had an accident so far. Don't say anything about what I have written to you Hildred to Mr. Turner. Just let me think over it just one more day until tomorrow. Then if there are any promises that I can really truly make and keep them I will do it tomorrow.

Now in regard to the wedding I understand that you had decided to have it at the house, and as I told you before you are doing all O.K. so go ahead, anything that suits you, suits me.

Made $5.25 that Thursday, took in $1.75.

Now don't worry about me at all because I will be all O.K.

By the way if Mother writes to you about me as she said she was going to do, I don't know what you will think of me I am sure. Yesterday mother had my bed all fixed up fine clean sheets etc. This morning the sheets were nothing else but wrinkles and the mattress exposed head & foot, mother said she would awfully hate to be my bed partner and was going to write to tell you what a rouster I was and what a time you would have sleeping with me. I know I am a rouster but thought I would rather tell you my self, but when we are married I am going to sleep with my arms around you then I will be quiet.

I send more love than ever, OOO, XXX, (6) (6) (6), by the millions and all my love
to my sweetheart and a real big hug.

Si – [**Editor's Note:** the beginning of sincerely? crossed out] Lovingly,

Chas.

———————◆———————

Postmark: 7:30 p.m. August 25, 1914, St. Paul, Minn.

Tuesday 3 P.M.

My dear Charles:

*Note Sunday is always your blue day. Last Sunday sure was mine and I am glad it is over
with. Just think only nine more Sundays! Really I can't imagine where all the time
is flying to, never saw it go so fast in my life and then again it goes too slow.*

*Suppose you will be giving Horace some of those fast automobile rides, now please don't go
so fast. I tell you what you do, you go and buy a speedometer, have it put on your machine
and send me the bill and I will pay half of it. Money isn't so terribly flush at this end but no
doubt if I ever drive the car I will have to keep my eye on the speedometer or I will be going
too fast and again I would rather help pay for that than for a bunch of sticking plaster,
bandages, splints etc. for my precious Hubby. Did you buy that Omega speedometer yet?
I forgot to tell you yesterday, maybe I shouldn't though, that when we came home from
the Fort we got too near to a street car and you know the motorman's looking glass that
stands out on the side, well we hit that and bent it flat against the car. Don't know whether
we will ever hear about it again, Mr. Turner simply put on more power and we turned
the first corner and hustled away.*

*Now don't you go worrying about the little housework I do, I am getting fat over it
anyway, weight 125 again. Anyway, if I wasn't willing to help a little extra account
of Claribel's sickness you couldn't expect mamma to because Claribel is nearer to me than
to mamma, therefore I ought to be willing to do a little more. Don't you agree with me?
Claribel is getting along dandy, parades all over the house, the doctor wants her to keep
moving so it won't heal up, says it healed too fast last time. He says he wants to keep it
open four or five weeks so it will be quite a while before she can really do any thing.*

*I must get busy now and finish my letters. Mr. Turner left about 2 o'clock for Duluth,
Bayfield and Ashland. By the way Mr. M.B. Johnson was in town today and it is good
you didn't hear the good things he said about you, if you had, don't think your hat would be
large enough.*

*By the way you did a dandy job to Mr. Turner's hat. I didn't notice it until yesterday when
I asked a few questions and found out. Think I will look out for mine now.*

Expect a letter from you tomorrow as to your speeding.

I must get busy now so tra la. I kissed your name at the beginning of this letter, you do likewise and then you will be getting one of the "oodles" of kisses I am sending.

Lovingly,

Hildred

———————◆———————

Postmark: 8:30 p.m. August 25, 1914, Detroit, Mich.

Addressed to Miss H.L. Cress c/o Booth Fisheries - Envelope flap did not survive

Aug 25th/14

My Dear Sweetheart, -

Just think two months from today, and what, I leave for St. Paul, and what, to marry my little lover, I wish I were leaving to-day, how can I wait all that time.

Hildred to show you how much I appreciate your promise concerning your going in bathing, I am going to make you a promise that is to buy a speedometer as soon as the Ford people get their new one on the market and keep within the speed limit, you no doubt realize that Uncle Chas. over estimates things just a little, for instance he will give you a pill to take and will tell you in five minutes time how much better you look. You do not need to worry about me. I am alright. I can stand anything as far as that part of it is concerned.

Business is a little dull today, things were fairly good yesterday. I hope it will pick up again one of these days. In the 24 days of this month I have charged up $419.25 and taken in $357.00. I trust you will say a little prayer for me so that I can beat the month of May which I would surely like to do.

The weather is pretty cool to-day, quite a change from last week.

I never get your Sunday letter until Tuesday afternoon, but I am living in high hopes of getting a nice long letter this afternoon.

Just loads and loads of love and millions of hugs and kisses and a great big hug & kiss.

Lovingly,

Chas.

Postmark: 7:30 p.m. August 26, 1914, Detroit, Mich. – Grand River Station

Addressed to: Mr. Chas. W. Turner, c/o Booth Fisheries - Dot on envelope flap

August 26th/14.

My Dear Hildred, -

Received your Sunday letter last evening. I ought to have received your Monday letter this morning but it has not arrived so far. I surely hope I will get it this afternoon.

Glad to hear that Claribel is getting along so nicely. I do not think it would hurt her to eat a little candy now.

In regard to Mr. Stevens will write him tomorrow, if it will save my little wifie any along the face blushing line.

Business is quite slow today, I will be glad when another rush comes it can't come any too soon to suit me.

Our city is all being decorated for the G.A.R. encampment, you better come and see us while we look good.

Two months from today and we are married, there was a piece in the paper just recently concerning a bride who had never had a kiss from her husband since their marriage. I know if my wifie suffered along this line it will be from too many, other than not enough.

Mother took my cousin over to the Island this afternoon, it is certainly some dandy place to go. I just know you won't want to leave Detroit after you are here for a little time.

Just a whole world of hugs and kisses and a great big hug and kiss from your Hubby.

Chas.

Postmark: 9 a.m. August 27, 1914, St. Paul, Minn.

August 27th 1914

Dearest Hubbykins:

I was so glad to hear from you this morning, really I look for it every morning and if I fail to hear from you like one morning several weeks ago, things seem to go wrong all day.

I am awfully glad you are going to get a speedometer but when will they be on the market?

You know you could do an awful lot of damage in a months time so be careful until you do get it.

As I wrote you yesterday, I too think Mr. Turner over estimates some things. I suppose when he was riding with you he thought you were going pretty fast and no doubt said something to you at the time and after leaving Detroit he imagined he was faster than it really was. I know the morning he came here that is about all he talked about and he actually had me awfully worried and he partly blamed me so for goodness sake be careful and I am never going to ask to go fast when we are out riding.

Mr. Turner is coming in on the same train that Flora Marcella and Addison are coming on. They will get here about 10:30 tonight. I didn't know how long mamma's sister is going to stay. I know she will stay until after the Fair though. Addison sure has had a dandy vacation, he has been gone over a month now.

Wouldn't it be simply great if you could make more this month than in May. I offered up a little silent prayer for you right away and I do hope so much you can make it $450.00 If you made $419.25 in 24 days you have seven more days to make the rest of the way and I bet you do. Here's hoping with all my heart that you can make it anyway.

Note you are getting a little cold weather, we sure are it is just like fall and I have an extra cover on my bed too. I wanted to stay home tonight and do some sewing but one of the girls in the office is going to have a few girls over to her house this evening and she wants me to surely come. She asked Claribel too but of course she couldn't think of it. I would like to stay home but I know she will be good and angry at me if I don't go. Her name is Anna Deyen, do you know which one that is?

I must get busy now and try to make up for the days' vacation I had yesterday.

All my love and kisses to you Charles and the biggest hug ever.

Yours lovingly,

Hildred

———◆———

Postmark: 5 p.m. August 27, 1914, St. Paul, Minn.

Wednesday 8 P.M.

Dearest Sweetheart:

Just think two months from today and I will be down to the depot bright and early to meet my sweetheart. Like yourself, the time hardly goes fast enough. I gave Claribel the wee smack you sent and she said it tasted just like mine, she didn't know the real color of yours as yet. As to my practicing along that line, I just wanted to tease you a little. The only one I practice on is Claribel, don't get much chance to practice on dad, his time is pretty well occupied along that line.

As to your speeding, nervous condition etc. I think after Mr. Turner got thinking he imagined a lot of things happening and that is the reason he wrote you so strongly but at the same time, think you must admit he is partly right. You know when you get a new patient you are so anxious to make good, get here in a hurry etc. that you forget how fast you are going or how many other autos you pass on the way, you simply put on more steam and away you go. As to your being nervous, no doubt you did work harder when you went to College but probably you have been at it so long, on the goal all the time, that it is beginning to tell on you so be real careful. I hope you get that speedometer, how much are they?

From your letter, guess you will be a restless bed partner allright [sic] but goodness if you are worse than Claribel, don't know what I will do with you. I will either have to strap you in or hug you real tight so you will be still. Do you kick so hard that I might wake up some morning to find myself on the floor? Guess you go so hard all day it is even hard for you to lie still at night.

I had a funny dream last night, thought we lived in Chgo. [Chicago] and I was down town having my hair shampooed. I had to be home at a certain time and my hair didn't get dry so I had them make it in one braid down my back and went home that way. When I got home I took hold of my braid to show it to you and all my hair came off. Was I scared, oh my! I started to cry and hustled back to the hair dressers to see what they would charge to put it back on and they said $5.00 a hair. Don't know how it all turned out but anyway when I was called this morning the first thing I grabbed for was my wig to see if it was all there.

Today was a busy day for yours truly, mamma and I made one of the wedding cakes this morning, a dark fruit cake. We made a double recipe and maybe it wasn't a long job to prepare all the fruit and crack the nuts. It took us a whole two hours to mix it and get things ready and then it had to bake a good two hours.

By the way, mamma has been bothered with that neuralgia again and papa said when you were here you were talking about some good medicine and would like to know if you could send the prescription so he can have it filled for her. She usually gets it in her left eye if that is any information for you. Maybe you remember talking to dad about this.

When you get your suit are you going to get an all dark suit or a dark coat and then a real dark pair of trousers? Why don't you ask the tailor what they are wearing now, tell him what it is for and he surely ought to be able to give you some good pointers. I know dad's trousers were different than his coat but possibly they have some new stunt now. I guess I am about as interested in your suit as I am in my dress.

I hope I understand you now as to the wedding. The way Mr. Turner talked I thought you were rather displeased with the plans, but as long as you say "no" I am going to take your word for it. What made him think you did not like it?

Wish I had a bed partner tonight, it is awfully cold and I can't sleep with Claribel until she feels better. I must get busy and sew now, have not done any sewing this evening and I must make good use of my time the next two months.

Goodnight honey bub. I send all the hugs and kisses are – aguiable [sic]. Send me another long letter like the one I got today, that was peachy.

Here is for a couple of good smacks.
Lovingly,
"Wifie"

———————◆———————

Postmark: 8:30 p.m. August 27, 1914, Detroit, Mich.

Addressed to: Chas. W. Turner, c/o Booth Fisheries - Envelope does not survive

Aug 27/14.

My Dear Sweetheart,

Received your letter with the two enclosures. Kindly accept thanks, now I must get busy and get into shape for the big event. It seems awfully lonesome to have to wait so long. But you will let me hug you all I want to when we are married so as to make up for lost time, won't you Hildred?

Now Hildred I surely appreciate your offer in regard to the speedometer, but no doubt you have received my Monday letter by this time with an explanation from me. I don't see how my little wifie can spare any money at this time, but just wait a little while longer Hildred and I will have things all fixed up.

By the way I believe that Mr. Turner is a more reckless driver than what I am, in as much as he ran into a dirt wagon a short time ago, and this time a street car.

Note you were talking to Mr. Johnson from Bayfield about me, I remember Mr. Johnson from the time I was about 6 yrs. old, he took me home with him once and I surely did enjoy myself.

Mr. Turner the night he was leaving our place got into a little too much of a hurray [sic] when he crushed his straw hat.

I kissed my name at the head of your letter now you kiss sweetheart at the beginning of my letter and imagine yourself kissing me because I have kissed it.

Business is pretty slow today, missed a call this morning was out, they would not wait however I have made out pretty well this month anyway.

Just all kinds of hugs & kisses and a great big hug & kiss.

Lovingly

Chas.

———————◆———————

Postmark: 5:30 p.m. August 29, 1914, Detroit, Mich.

Addressed to: Miss H.L. Cress, c/o Booth Fisheries - No dot on envelope flap

Friday Afternoon,

My Dear Honey-Bub, -

Have not heard from you so far today but surely hope I will get a letter on this afternoon's mail. I presume you stayed home on Wednesday.

My Dear little sweetheart what do you think my charge column is now, $10.00 ahead of all previous records for any one month, business was good yesterday and have or did make $23.00 this am. If you were only here now Hildred wouldn't we have some jig. I believe I would get so excited that I would before I got through stand you on your little heady in a corner, now Hildred write me right back and let me know how much you love me and how hard you love me for breaking previous records. Of course I have only taken in $37.00 so far which is $9.00 I believe less than what I took in last May.

By the way Hildred I am enclosing to you a check for $60.00 in payment of my interest on that $3,000 note, think possibly you can make use of the money then at the end of Sept. you can make it up to Mr. Turner, of course this is entirely up to your consideration and you can ask Mr. Turner about it, I will also have to have my note received.

Am in a hurry, write a big long letter Sunday Hildred, just all kinds of love hugs & kisses from your Hubby and a great big hug & kiss.

Lovingly,

Chas.

———————◆———————

Postmark: 7:30 p.m. August 28, 1914, St. Paul, Minn.

Friday August 28, 1914

My dear Charles:

Just a little note today but guess you will excuse me because I have been writing pretty lengthy letters lately. Maybe you are getting tired of them.

As to Claribel, she has had her candy, she can eat everything and anything now.

If you write to Mr. Stevens I sure will thank you with all my heart because I know if I had

to, I would turn all colors of the rainbow and possibly get all mixed up in the bargain.

I am enclosing you a place card, one that was used last night. No wonder the girl wanted me to come so bad, she gave the little stunt or rather party for me. The rest of the girls knew it was for me but they didn't tell me a thing about it until I got there, it sure was some surprise.

We had a dandy time and I was home early too, considering, about 11:30. It is not as far from the house as I thought. Guess what I did I was just coffee hungry last night drank one cup at the party and when I got home I drank two more and it didn't affect me at all, slept great. Mamma got lunch for Flora and the youngsters. You know I very very seldom drink coffee and here I drank three whole cups.

I must get busy again will do better tomorrow. Just heaps and heaps of love and kisses,

Ever lovingly,

Hildred

Postmark: 8 p.m. August 29, 1914, Detroit, Mich.

Addressed to Chas. W. Turner, c/o Booth Fisheries - Dot on envelope flap

[**Editor's Note:** A double pin hole is in the pages of the letter.]

August 29th/14

My Dear Little Wifie, -

Do you realize that when you receive this letter, that the next day we can say next month and you will be my truly wife to live with me for ever more.

Thanks for your longer letter of Wednesday. Those are the kind your hubby likes to receive.

A Ford speedometer only costs $6.00 and I am sure going to get one as soon as they are on the market.

You are some dreamer Hildred. I guess your mind will be a whole lot easier after in regard to this big event. Mr. Turner surely misunderstood me, I am certainly pleased with the way you are having things to go ahead. Don't eat that cake now before the time comes just put it away in some secret place.

Inclosed [sic] you will find a ppt. for Mrs. Cress. Let me know how it acts on her neuralgia.

In regard to my suit I think possibly I will see about it next week then I will let you know all about, suppose it will be unlucky too if I send you a sample. Let me know.

Your little prayer has worked wonders in as much as up to the present time I have charged up $477.25 and taken in $387.00. Now Hildred you know I would just like to know how much and how many times you love me for breaking all previous records. Now I will have to break that if the war does not kill this country. Honestly Hildred, I do not think the Emperor has any right to kick up such a racket and keep us from making as much money as we otherwise would then again look how many will be killed, I think he ought to consider these things, don't you.

Did I tell you that yesterday morning I got up at 5:30 AM and went to market with a neighbor lady across the street, we bought a whole auto load of stuff. While I was there I got another early morning call but I rushed home and did not lose it.

Just Millions and millions of kisses & hugs and a great big Hug and kiss from your Hubby who loves you.

Chas.

———————◆———————

Postmark: 9:30 p.m. August 30, 1914, Detroit, Mich.

Addressed to Miss H.L. Cress, c/o Booth Fisheries - No dot on envelope flap

Sunday 2 p.m.

My Dear Sweetheart, -

The weeks roll around, goody, we will soon be hubby & wifie and I will be happy, here's to Oct. 26th. I'll just have to love somebody if that time does not hurry by.

By the way Hildred I made $8.00 so far today and have taken in $21.50 which is better than what I expected to do today. I am going to make $500.00 this month or know the reason why. If I see that I am not going to do it I will surely do something desperate like pulling people into my office and trying to make them believe they are sick what do you say.

In a few minutes I am going to take Mother over to Woodmere Cemetery that is where my Brother is buried.

It tried real hard this AM to be a bad day for business but the weather has cleared up fine.

I am going to hurry home and get my list of names completed for you, have been quite busy with the alumni association lately which has taken up considerable of my time and I have to finish my posting and get out my monthly accounts.

All the love in me I send to my sweetheart with the biggest kiss and hug ever with another great big kiss & hug.

Lovingly

Chas.

------------◆------------

Postmark: 9:30 a.m. August 31,1914, St. Paul, Minn.

Aug. 30, 1914

My dearest Sweetheart:

Will you excuse me for writing to you with pencil but about 10:30 this morning the folks decided to take our dinner to Como and I knew if we ever got here it would be late tonight before we got home and I would be almost too tired to write to my sweetheart and I surely wouldn't miss that one Sunday.

I received the check this A.M. in your letter and surely thank you for thinking of me in my tight straights but really it took me so by surprise I don't know what to say. Mr. Turner offered to give me enough to make $100.00 so I could start a checking account, but I couldn't just make up my mind to it. You see I have $55.00 now besides the $15.00 dad has of mine and the 25.00 I saved 10-cents a day. Papa said if I wanted he would keep the $55.00 for me and I could take it out just as I wanted. If I gave it to him I know I could get it as I wanted and I wouldn't have to be thinking of what I owed Mr. Turner. It sure is dandy of both of you though and as soon as Mr. Turner gets back from Port Arther (Wednesday) I will take this up with him. In the meantime, just imagine me guarding that check. I am not going to say anything to the folks about this at all.

My dear I can't begin to tell you how much or how hard I love you even if you didn't make any money but when you break all previous records by $10.00 -- $509.00 in all with still a few days ahead of you why it is simply great and you just be prepared for the most hugs, kisses and loves imaginable when I see you, Oct. 29th and will do all the jigging you want. Maybe my prayer helped just a little along this line but if anybody deserves to get ahead I think it should be you because just think how hard you work for it. I think you will make that doctor across the street wish he had never built there. When does he move in?

I got a letter from your sister [note: sister-in-law Catherine, married to Leonard, Charles' brother] in Duluth yesterday and I am going to quote a bit to you:

"Of course Leonard and I are planning to be there with both hands and feet and I give you fair warning to have us searched before we enter for if there is any fun to be had we are going to have it and we may have a trick or two up our sleeves."

This sure looks as though we are up against it and you just bet we will keep all of the suit cases away from their reach if there is any way of doing so.

Now she says she had a letter from your mother stating she did not think she could attend the wedding account of your father not being able to come. I will be terribly disappointed if it turns out this way because I thought you said she was coming, and was planning on seeing her here. Of course I don't pretend to be a good cook but if you and your father can stand the board for a week or two I will be willing to make a try at it anyway so it is up to you people. I think though that being your mother could not be at your brother's wedding, she should at least try and come to yours, this is her last chance to see one of her sons married at least we hope so. Try and persuade her now, won't you?

Just before we left this noon Alice Hillman called up and wants me to help serve at her wedding Wednesday night. I told her I would but I don't know what under the sun to wear. She is going to have a big church wedding and then a reception afterwards. The choir has to go and practice at church both Monday and Tuesday night then the wedding Wednesday, that is three nights of this week gone again.

Well my dear, I should like to write more but I have run out of paper and besides I have been interrupted three different times, excuse scribbling too, won't you but I will do better tomorrow. It is hard to write at a picnic.

Just the mostest love ever and I hope you can beat last May on your "Take In" Column. I just wish I could have you here to love and kiss so you could realize how much I love you but there will come a time some day.

Lovingly

Hildred

XXXXXXXXXXX

OOOOOOOOOOO

ⓒⓒⓒⓒⓒⓒⓒⓒⓒⓒⓒ

How's that?

———————◆———————

Postmark: 7 p.m. August 31, 1914, St. Paul, Minn.

Monday, August 31st 1914

My dear Charles:

Always so glad to hear from you, especially when you have such cheering news as in your last few letters. Yesterday I thought it was $499.00 you made in May but it was $449.00, I got mixed. You sure are doing perfectly great and I bet in September you reach the $500.00 mark. Maybe I don't wish you were here right now so I could give you the biggest hug ever and as little Marcella says, I love you with all my soul and heart and more too.

Thank you ever so much for sending the ppt. for mamma. I gave it to papa this morning and he is going to have it filled. Will let you know how it acts after she has taken some of it.

I guess you are quite displeased with the Kaiser all right and maybe you are right. I really don't know enough about it but if the other fellows would give in they could quit all this. If England and the rest won't give in you can't blame Germany for showing what they can do. As to him keeping us from making money, papa thinks it will help because rich people who otherwise go abroad a year and more at a time will spend their money at home instead. Of course in other ways again I guess it is a drawback for this country but let us not worry about this, as long as the U.S. keeps out of it I will be happy because I don't want my hubby going to war, if you go I follow.

I copied some recipes on the machine today, some I will be trying on you some day so get your medicine prepared in case of indigestion which will come as sure as fate. Maybe you better make out your "Will."

I was out looking at suits this noon, and what color should I get? I want to get my suit first and then my hat afterwards so I can get something that will go good together. What do you think of a real dark green? I saw a couple of beauties this noon and they say that is going to be worn quite a bit this fall or are you like Mr. Turner, that you prefer blue? Of course I would like to get something that I think would suit you.

Well my dear pretty near time to go home so will say "goodnight." Hope I get a nice long Sunday letter.

Just the most kisses ever, also hugs and squeezes but oh! for some real ones.

Ever lovingly

Hildred

Postmark: 9 p.m. August 31, 1914, Detroit, Mich.

Addressed to: Mr. Chas. W. Turner, c/o Booth Fisheries - Dot on envelope flap

Aug 31st/14

My Dear Hildred –

Don't you worry about me getting tired of hearing from you, am just anxious for the days to go so that I get another letter.

Glad to hear that Claribel is getting along so nicely, remember me to her.

Now in regard to Mr. Stevens I wrote to him this morning so the letter is in la route, and I did not blush but was tickled to Death to do it. Oh for the time when I can just hug & love my little wife all I want to, I could not want longer than to Oct. 26th Hildred

That was real nice of the office girls to entertain you, aren't you glad you did not refuse to go, I am going to try to get my wifie out of the habit of drinking tea & coffee, all I drink is water & cocoa for breakfast in the winter.

I am going to save that card for you when you come to Detroit.

Yesterday I was busy all day. I got up early in the morning 5:45 AM, worked on my machine until 7:30 AM, had breakfast, was then called out in the country, a man out there got drunk and his horse kicked him in the head and he sure did bleed, worked all day, then at night I wrote some letters in connection with the alumni assoc. made out my list of names and did all my posting for last week. I was surely tired at night.

Am not going to say any more about business until tomorrow then I will give you my results for Aug.

Just myriads of kisses hugs and a great big Kiss & hug. From Your Hubby

Chas.

SEPTEMBER 1914

❖

𝕹𝖊𝖜𝖘𝖕𝖆𝖕𝖊𝖗 𝕳𝖊𝖆𝖉𝖑𝖎𝖓𝖊𝖘

𝕯𝖊𝖙𝖗𝖔𝖎𝖙 𝖋𝖗𝖊𝖊 𝕻𝖗𝖊𝖘𝖘

- Germany declares war on Russia; first shots fired; France to enter fight today
- Emperor of Austria is reported slain – London, Aug 3
  - The Daily Chronicle has received an unconfirmed dispatch that the Emperor, Francis Joseph of Austria-Hungary, has been assassinated
- Veterans, vast Army of Peace Camp in Detroit
- Fifty-seven Cardinals closeted to choose Pope
- Wilson said to be candidate for new term
- Czar crushes Austria in Galicia, says reports
- New defenses make Paris one of greatest strongholds of war
- Crowning of Pope Benedict XV is set for Sunday, Sept. 6
- Germans closing on Paris by three ways; first guns expected hourly, Russia begins new attack on Galicia
- Five conventions secured by city by local bureau – Four national, one state organization to visit set in 1915
- Band concerts of 1914 are biggest success of year; new records are established at Belle Isle and city parks

- State Fair all ready for big opening Monday
- First decisive battle of War now on with advantage on side of Allies; Germans reported to be in retreat
- Labor's Army, 16,000 strong, parades here
- Horse show held at fair grounds decided success
- Wilson's veto to increased income tax changes plan – Democrat leaders revise proposed war revenue measure
- Flag made of apples an attractive exhibit
- Rescue cutter finds eight of Karluk's crew (ship stuck in the ice in the Arctic)
- Many wagon makers find demand good for their vehicles
- Million Russian troops to march against Berlin
- Alaska wolverine on way to Belle Isle Zoo
- Czar's four daughters officers in Russian Army
- Peace dove can't find any place to light, and Wilson only watches
- Calls art museum city institution
- Great Cathedral of Rheims only blackened shell
- Marconi to test right of Daniels to stop wireless; company defends neutrality of station at Siasconset
- Martial hats few in Himelhoch Bros.; war's effect not apparent in display of new fall millinery; black and white touch of color is ruling scheme
  - Both extremes in size in fashion, plumes of all kinds popular
- Dublin to give support to war without discord
- Kaiser's aviators drop bombs into 12 cities

St. Paul Pioneer Press

- Another retirement for Allies recorded in official statement issued at Paris; Davis says countryside is a graveyard
- Say Wilson will ask second term – Moreover, President and Bryan are found to have no agreement on question
- Bear fails to get Karluk castaways
- Doors close on Cardinals – they will not be reopened until successor to late Pope Pius X is chosen
- New Pension Law urged – Spanish-American veterans would favor widows and

orphans of their comrades

- Reaches Frisco via Canal – Admiral Dewey, first passenger boat through Panama, makes trip in 23 days (from New York City)

- "Boys of 61" see war preparations – Delegates to Detroit encampment thrills of Canadian mobilization (Civil War veterans sail to Detroit and around Belle Isle to view war preparations)

- Wilson to read message tomorrow asking legislation to raise $100 million – message on Friday to urge war funds

- Third ballot for Pope is fruitless

- Social Club Events: Alice Hillman becomes bride ("Mildred" Cress is mentioned as a participant in Hillman's reception. This wedding is referenced in the letters)

- New Pope assures safety of Church (Pope Benefice XV); American Cardinals too late for election

- Committee decides that beer, wine and soft drinks will produce war fund

- Motor trucks have become necessary

- The terrible fate of Mamah Borthwick in her Bungalow of Love
  - Woman, who with Frank Lloyd Wright, dared to live contrary to accepted rules of conduct, meets disaster in a few short years (feature)

- Take those stockings off!!!!
  - Fashion experts will argue through the winter the propriety of barefoot swimming as ordered recently by recreation official [women]

- Move to protect Paris' artworks

- War brings all factions of Russian citizens solidly behind the Czar

- Germany considering peace proposal; America inquiries concerning report of desire to talk terms with foes

- President labors while on vacation

- Many German Societies boost Red Cross fund

- Wake Up Americans and take a look at yourself ! There are things to be seen in America, more strange and wonderful than anything in Europe, on which to spend our dollars (feature)

- U.S. cannot pass on war, Wilson reply

- Czar should worry – national coffers are running over

- Minimum wage for women to be close to $9.00

- Historic Cathedral at Rheims is destroyed; famous structure set afire by bombardment; artillery duel fiercest in history of the world

- Stores boost for Peace in windows

- Kaiser's third son reported to have died

SEPTEMBER 1914

◆

LETTERS

Postmark: 4:30 p.m. September 1, 1914, St. Paul, Minn.

Sept. 1st, 1914.

My dear Lover:

Just think, now we can say next month and we will be married, isn't it great? I wish it was our wedding tomorrow instead of Alice's. Don't you go and get so excited that you hug somebody else before the time comes though, you told me not to so it wouldn't be fair, of course I don't want to anyway.

Maybe I don't hope you make $500.00 this month. I sure would dance a jig if you did. I didn't expect it this month but thought possibly you would next. For goodness sake write right away and let me know how much you made.

We were at church last night practicing for the wedding. Saw Miss Freedy again. She had written Mr. Morgan and told him where you lived and he and some friends were looking at some property out in that direction one day, so passed right by the house and he wrote back and told her all about it, thought it was a nice place too. She is going to be my side partner in processional Wed. night.

I have solved the problem as to what I will wear. I haven't a thing in a white dress and my pink dress that I wore to the parties last winter they have seen that so often so yesterday I ransacked the town for something pretty and still reasonable but the two didn't work very well together and I didn't know what on earth to do. This morning I was fretting over the fact and mamma said she never gave it a thought but I might as well wear her white dress. Maybe I am not happy! Nobody in that crowd has ever seen it and it saves me investing any money. I tried it on this morning and it couldn't fit better. Now just so nobody comes up and says "How do Mrs. Cress."

Mamma is going to wash my hair for me tonight, that will save me another 7.50. I can't manage it myself and when I have it done downtown that is what it costs me.

Today I was out getting prices on wedding invitations and announcements so as soon as we get your list we can get busy. I got prices at several different places. Also got prices on palms, that is to rent, and then the flowers. They charge $4.00 a doz. for the palms and then of course, the ferns, surlax [sic] etc. is all extra. Of course it is too early to order all these things but it is a good thing to get an idea of the prices anyway.

Have you written to Dr. Stevens as yet? Of course there is plent of time to do that yet but let me know when you write, won't you?

I meant to tell you yesterday that it is not bad luck for the groom to send a sample of his suit to his sweetheart, that only applies to the bride so don't forget me as I am awfully anxious to know what you decide on. Ask the tailor what he thinks about it because they are supposed to know, that is the goods, not about sending me a sample.

The most love ever to my own dear sweetheart.

Hildred

Xxxx Oooo

———————◆———————

Postmark: 8:30 p.m. Sept. 1, 1914, Detroit, Mich.

Addressed to Miss H.L. Cress, c/o Booth Fisheries - No dot on envelope flap

Tuesday Afternoon

My Dear Hildred, -

Feel quite down hearted this afternoon because I have not received a letter later from you than your Friday letter. You surely have not forgotten me have you?

Last month was my best month all around

August { Charged up $513.25
        Took in $423.75

How do those figures look to you. Sept. I think will be a little on the quiet side, however it is pretty hard to prophesy the end.

I wish you would add to my announcement list Dr. and Mrs. J.J. Howard Junction Ave, Detroit. I forgot my old pal.

Now Hildred write me a nice long letter.

Just Loads & Loads of love & Kisses, and a great big hug & kiss.

Lovingly,

Chas.

———————◆———————

Postmark: 12 p.m. Sept. 2, 1914, Detroit, Mich.

Addressed to: Mr. Chas. W. Turner, c/o Booth Fisheries - Dot on envelope flap

Sept. 2nd/14.

My Dear Hildred, -

Thought you surely had gone back on me when you did not write on Saturday and your Sunday letter did not get here until this morning. I sure had the blues.

Note that you will jig with me next month if business keeps up, which looks good to me.

I really don't know what to think about the Duluth people, if they can they will make you blush somehow or other. In regard to mother going she thinks it would not look right her going, whereas my dad will go so I would not say just whether she will be present or not. Of course I am trying to persuade her to go.

Now in regard to the color of your dress or suit green is the first that comes into my head, of course I like blue & purple awfully well, I suppose what made me think of green I was looking at the outside cover of the Ladies Home Journal for Sept. I also like one suit there shown to the right on the cover it is made of white, brown, and green stripes and a brown hat if I remember it correctly.

Tell Uncle Chas. that Aunt Lizzie called up by long distance this a.m. and that I am going to meet her Thursday.

By the way I never want to have such an experience has [sic] what I had about 5 O'clock yesterday afternoon. Was going out in the country to make a call and needless to say this is the first time in 24 hrs. that we have been without rain in a week. On one road I drove along to where two teams were stuck with a heavy load. So I had to turn onto the side of the road to get by. I got by them but just ten yards farther on I sunk in and got stuck, I could back about 3 feet and then I would stall again so there I was alone in the country, could not go either way and I had one of the strangest feelings come over me, I could not describe it to you, even yet it makes me feel funny to think of it. Finally by backing in the throttle wide open my wheels spinning like the wind I got through it. The water in my radiator boiled like everything, my muffler under the car got heated up and smoked so I stuffed a piece of rag in my exhaust pipe so that if it caught fire it would not get any air. I let my engine cool down some time and come back another way. Home never seemed so good before.

Just millions of kisses & hugs and a great big hug & kiss.

Lovingly,

Chas.

———————◆———————

Postmark: 7:30 p.m. Sept. 2, 1914, St. Paul, Minn.

Typed

Sept. 2, 1914

My dear Charles: –

It is just about 5:30 and have been busy every minute today but if you will excuse me for today I will surely write you a big letter tomorrow, will have lots of news stored up by that time.

I am glad you have written to Mr. Stevens and saved me all that. I wonder what he will say to me. He is the biggest tease that ever happened and when he heard I was engaged he said remember he always had the privilege of kissing the brides, guess he expected then to do the honors at the great event.

Also glad to get your list, we will get busy at that right away, I have just glanced at it, have not had time to even read the names but I surely will tonight.

Just loads of love until tomorrow,

Lovingly,

H i l d r e d

———————◆———————

Postmark: 12 p.m. Sept. 3, 1914, Detroit, Mich.

Addressed to Chas. W. Turner, c/o Booth Fisheries - Dot on envelope flap

Thursday 6:30 p.m.

My Dear Hildred, -

Just a short letter today as it is nearly mail time.

Don't you worry about me hugging anybody else, I think possibly you will not like as much loving as I will want to give you after we are married. We just got to make up for lost time.

I would like to meet that Mr. Morgan some time.

Will send you a sample of what I am going to have my suit made of. I intend to see the Taylor [sic] in a few days.

You are apparently a pretty busy woman, never mind though you can almost count the remaining weeks on your one hand.

Aunt Lizzie came today. I am going to send a great big kiss with her to you when she leaves.

There is going to be fireworks over to the Island tonight, if the people will go I am going to drive them over there wish my wifie were here to go with me.

Business has been fairly good so far today. Dr. Howard just called me up to give an anesthetic for him tomorrow morning.

Must hurry. All kinds of love and kisses and a great big hug and kiss to my sweetheart.

Lovingly,

Chas.

Postmark: 10 a.m. Sept. 4, 1914, St. Paul, Minn.

Sept. 3, 1914

My dear Sweetheart:

I should say I have not forgotten you, never will. I admit I did not write Saturday but did Sunday and mailed it first thing Monday morning so you should have had it Tuesday afternoon.

My goodness, $513.25 for August, that is simply grand! I didn't think you would reach the $500.00 mark this month but then you deserve the best of anything and everything anyway and I certainly am more than glad you made out so well. It doesn't look as though the war is hurting your business so far.

When I got this far Mr. Turner came back from Mpls. and could not finish until tonight. I won't tell you what time it is because you might scold but there I am spending my time to good advantage anyway.

Mr. Turner got back about 10:00 A.M. we worked until 12:00 then went to lunch and it only took me 25 minutes but I hustled. I worked until 1:30 and then what do you think, Mr. Turner took all the folks, including Flora and Marcella out to the White Bear Club, that is the Automobile Club. My! Talk about grand it is simply beautiful. I am not used to seeing such luxury and have not quite gotten down to normal yet, every once in a while I see those beautiful rooms before me. I am awfully sorry you did not get to see that this summer because it certainly is worthwhile and I know you would have to say St. Paul has something worthwhile anyway. We did not get back until quite late so I did not have to go back to the office.

Well, Alice is married and off somewhere for a trip, nobody knows. She certainly had a dandy wedding and such a crowd goodness! The church was filled to the limit. She had an awfully large reception too and what do you think, I had the honor of eating with the bridal party. Two of the bridal ushers were from out of town and Allen (the groom) introduced them to two of we girls and wanted us to go to supper with them. After all my fineness I had to change to a K.M. and help wait on second table and I didn't spill any coffee over anyone either. They didn't do very much to them when they left, just showered them with rice and some tin cans on the machine but that is about all so guess we will get through alright too. I did something else too, not that I wanted to but everybody else did so I had to follow suit. I kissed both the bride and groom. If I had only been kissing you then there would have been something to it but this only made me homesick for a real true kiss from somebody I love with all my heart. I think you know him too, I am going to store all kinds away for you and I am pretty near filled to bursting point by now.

I nearly forgot to tell you something that Mr. Turner told me to be sure and write you about. He says to tell you that he believes in just having the phone downstairs it causes a lot of extra steps for your mother especially now that you are getting business and he believes you should have a connection upstairs. In St. Paul there are three different connections you can have, or three different prices. The cheapest is to have it on the wall and just ring downstairs but you can talk from either up or down stairs. That is the kind we have. The other one is the phone on the wall but one that will ring up and down stairs at once and the last is the desk phone that rings both places at once. I think I have this straight now but maybe it is not the same in Detroit. Mr. Turner would like you to think this over and then let him hear from you. I think the most expensive of the three is $1.00 extra a month but not positive. Of course when I am there, there will be two of us to answer and it will not be quite so bad but let Mr. Turner hear from you as to what you think.

I have added Dr. and Mrs. Howards' name to your list, if you think of any more, send them along.

I simply must get to bed now, hope I get a real long letter from you at your first spare time but if you have not much time, I like the short ones too.

All the hugs, kisses, squeezes and loves to my dear from our dear,

Hildred

XXX OOO ⓞⓞⓞ

The size is supposed to indicate extra good measure. H.C.

———————◆———————

Postmark: 5:30 p.m. Sept. 4, 1914, St. Paul, Minn.

Friday, Sept. 4, 1914

My dear Charles:

I am sorry I gave you the blues by not writing Saturday but just remember I never forget you even if I do miss writing once in while and I always write when I possibly can.

I am disappointed to hear your mother has not decided definitely as to coming to our wedding. Couldn't your father come or will it be too hard to get away? Anyway do try and persuade your mother to come. What do you think about it anyway? Of course you people know conditions there best, and possibly it would be better not to persuade her although I know no one could be more pleased to see her here than I would be. I sure would like to know what your people from Duluth have up their sleeve they are the only ones I am really afraid of.

I tried my best to get hold of a Sept. Ladies' Home Journal today to see what that suit looked like that you took a fancy to but I did not succeed. The Golden Rule carries that book and they were all sold out but I will find one somewhere.

I was trying on suits today, green and brown, those were the only colors and certainly saw some beauties but I don't think I will get it until the last of September, you can see more what they are wearing then. I will get my hat at the same time so I can get something to match.

You surely had an experience in the country, hope you don't have any more of them. You people are not the only ones blest [sic] with all kinds of rain, it rains here pretty near all the time although today has been dandy.

I asked Mr. Turner about the check Charlie and he says while I don't need it just now, to keep it that it may come in handy. I have enough money for my suit and dress of course. I have my shoes, hat, gloves, trunk and lots of other things like that to get but I get something every week, figure on $10.00 to spend, $4.00 board and it just takes $1.00 a week carfare and lunches because I bring my lunch most of the time now and go over to the Y.W. and get a cup of hot chocolate or something on that order, anything to get out of it cheap. Of course, when Mr. Turner is here I don't have the car fare to spend. Now if I need any money I am going to call on your check, sure thing, and thanks ever so much for sending it.

You should see the pretty things I got from Mrs. Schmitt (mamma's mother). I got a set of crocheted collars and cuffs, some crocheted inserting for in a towel and lace for center piece. They are all beauties, will be glad when hubby can see them. I am going to do some serving tonight, the folks are going to the Orpheum. I had the dandiest dream last night, I was getting some really truly kisses again, my they were good and I was provoked that I had to waken so soon.

Just loads of love and kisses,

Hildred

◆

Postmark: 8:30 p.m. September 4, 1914, Detroit, Mich.

Addressed to Miss. H.L. Cress, c/o Booth Fisheries - Envelope flap missing

Sept. 4/14.

My Dear Sweetheart, -

Glad you wrote me Wednesday even if you did not write much. You know that nothing makes me feel worse than not to hear from you every day. So don't miss writing to me every single day will you?

Aunt Lizzie and your future mother are in to the city this afternoon, I have been quite busy today did not get my dinner until after two o'clock, and have been busy in the office all afternoon.

I just wonder if I can add two more names to my list of announ – 1) Dr. & Mrs. B. Nubbelink, Oakland Drive, Kalamazoo, Mich. 2) Dr. & Mrs. S.B. Smith, Westminster Detroit Mich. Another thing Hildred if your people do not give you enough money to get along on you just let your Hubby know and he will fix matters up for you, why I did not mention this before is that I have always felt that it is the duty of the parents to take care of their children along these lines, they ought to expect to help you out.

Let me know what Mr. Stevens has to say to you when he sees you. I suppose you will all flush up when you see him.

Had Aunt Lizzie all through the busy streets in my machine yesterday don't think she was nervous I do not know though.

Next week there will be six weeks left my dear. I hope it goes fast.

Just loads & loads of love and a great big hug & kisses from your Hubby.

Chas.

———◆———

Postmark: 1:30 p.m. Sept. 14, 1914, St. Paul, Minn.

[Editor's Note: *This letter may be out of order.]*

Saturday, 10:30 A.M.

My dear Charles:

Glad as ever to hear from you today. It is sort of a lazy day for me, I am helping with some circular work, Mr. Turner has gone to Denver and Salt Lake City, will not be back for a week.

I am glad you are going to send me a sample of your suit. I am anxious to see it.

How is business coming this month? Do you think you will equal last month?

Seeing it is Saturday, guess I will do a little shopping this afternoon and then go home and do some sewing. Tomorrow I am planning on staying home all day. A week from Saturday I am going to meet the much-talked-of Mr. Morgan. He is coming on Sunday the 13th and they are to be married the following Wednesday. My, I wish it were you coming but only seven more weeks and you will be coming.

Not you think I will not like as much loving as you will. All I can say, is that remains to be seen but I know I can stand a good bit anyway.

I am going to make this letter short, will write a long one tomorrow. I am waiting for that big kiss you are going to send, hope it is immense.

All kinds of love and kisses,

Lovingly,

Hildred

———◆———

Postmark: 2 p.m. Sept. 5, 1914, Payne Minn.

Hand-written, addressed to Miss Hildred Cress

Friday evening

Sept. 4th, 1914

Dear Hildred:

It was real dear of you to remember our little girlie. She likes her spoon to play with and I shall some day teach her who it was she received it from.

Thank you very much. We had her baptized last Sunday at church she behaved beautifully, and looked so dear. We are all so fond of her, and make a great deal of her. She is a little fatty. I will send you a Kodak picture of her some time.

I have heard that you are to be married next month. I am sure I wish you well and that God's richest blessing may rest on you and your home. Claribel and Addison will miss you, I am sure, but they too will be happy to see you happy.

We are well but badly rushed with work – don't know what to take up first.

Mr. Manz and Margaret are going to the Fair for two days – Thursday and Friday. She is real excited over the prospect of going.

Sincerest love to you and many good wishes.

Yours sincerely –

Annie S. Manz

———————◆———————

Postmark: 11:30 p.m. Sept. 5, 1914, Detroit, Mich.

Addressed to: Mr. Chas. W. Turner, c/o Booth Fisheries - Envelope flap did not survive

Enc: A medication envelope containing a bent and rusted nail

Sept. 5th/14.

My Dear Hildred, -

I have not heard from you so far today so can not write you but a few lines. I guess my little wifie is so busy that occasionally she forgets all about me, that is as far as writing is concerned.

Had another puncture this AM. A nail run into one of my back tires. I am inclosing [sic] the little [illegible] to you.

I suppose you will be having some more holidays if Uncle Chas. is away.

Loads of love and kisses from your Hubby and a great big hug & kiss.

Chas.

Try not to forget writing to me will you Hildred, I did not get a letter last Monday, Tuesday. C.W.H.

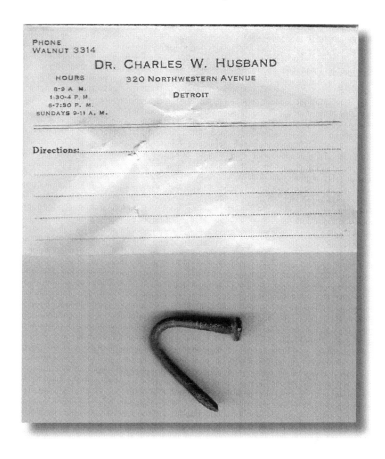

Postmark: 11:30 p.m. Sept. 6, 1914, Detroit, Mich.

Addressed to: Miss H.L. Cress, c/o Booth Fisheries - No dot on envelope flap

Sept. 6/14.

My Dear Hildred, -

Just a few lines today, will write you more tomorrow, that is Tuesday and I never get your letter (Sunday) until Tuesday afternoon. I am going to be busy this afternoon and thought I would write a few lines while I had the chance.

Business was a little better yesterday, made $20.00 & took in $28.00. Next month I hope it will spruce up, and be good all the time.

Don't tell Mr. Turner, but I surely did something this AM. The pavement was wet and I [illegible] into the curve and strained my back axle a little, guess I was lucky

I did not break my wheel, when I was returning home I passed another fellow who had [illegible] into the curb almost in the same place and broke his back wheel all to pieces. Don't know whether I had better get my axle straightened or not as my back wheel now wobbles considerable, be sure not to tell Mr. Turner.

Mother is getting ready to go into the city so I think I will let her take this letter along with her.

Millions and Millions of hugs & kisses to my sweetheart and a great big hug & kiss and another one.

Lovingly,

Chas.

◆

Postmark: 9 a.m. Sept. 7, 1914, St. Paul, Minn.

Sunday evening

Dearest Sweetheart: -

I intended to write a big long letter this afternoon but did not get to it until tonight. Yesterday afternoon I intended coming right home and sew but mamma called up and said all the folks were going to the "movies" and wanted me to go so off I hiked. In the evening I was sewing until 11:30 but that was an exception. I never sew that late. This morning Claribel and I went to church and stayed for Sunday School. Dr. Stevens spoke to us this morning, not a regular S.S. lesson but more on the work it was necessary for the church to accomplish this coming year. Anyway, he got to talking about all the young people getting married and said, "I don't know but it seems to be the fad for people of Trinity Church to get married, they all seem to be getting married, don't you think so?" and he looked right at me and nodded his head. Well it was so unexpected from him, and everybody laughed so that I didn't know where I was. If the earth would have swallowed me up for about three minutes I would have felt better, because of course I foolishly had to change about twenty-five different colors.

This afternoon Celia Brown and I went out taking pictures and if they are good I will send you some but if they look the way I felt about that time, don't think they are worth the postage to send them to you, here is hoping they are good though.

Tonight we have all been home, talking over what we did this afternoon. The folks were all down to South St. Paul this afternoon. Now you know just what I have been doing since yesterday noon.

As to money matters, thanks dear ever ever so much for your offer and if I am needy of some cash I will surely know where I can go but I think I can about see my way clear now, in fact almost positive I can.

I had an awful mean dream last night. I thought my sweetheart had hurt himself, nothing so terribly serious but you had a big long, deep cut on the fore part of each arm. I woke up before it was finished but you were bound to get well because I was playing the part of Red Cross nurse and was bandaging your arms. Now you be careful so you don't get hurt won't you?

I have put the two extra names on your list. Papa is going to take the form of invitations and announcement to the printer's tomorrow so they can make the plates. Just think, only a few more short weeks.

Write me a long letter some day, will you? I like to get those once in a while. All my love and kisses to my dear and an extra big hug and kiss from

Hildred.

Postmark: 10 p.m. Sept. 7, 1914, Detroit, Mich.

Addressed to Chas. W. Turner, c/o Booth Fisheries - Dot on envelope flap

Sept. 7th/14.

My Dear Sweetheart, -

Now in regard to my Mother attending the wedding, I have tried my best to persuade her, but I guess she has decided not to go, the trouble is my Dad cannot get away and my mother thinks it would look awfully selfish of her to go alone. She also thinks that if would be asking too much to have you come here and she be away.

It is the Woman's Home Companion that I saw those fashion plates on on the outside cover.

You have told me considerable about Mr. Morgan, what does he do in Detroit or work at and where are they going to live, if I may ask.

Business is moving along slowly this month have averaged about $11.00 a day so far.

Now Hildred I am going to ask a few questions in regard to the wedding if I may. I received my information from Aunt Lizzie but don't say anything to anybody that I told you. She seemed to think that Mrs. Cress was going to get you into spending a whole lot of money on just making a great big showing at the wedding and that you would not have any money left to buy what clothes you needed, if this is so why you let Mrs. Cress pay for the showing and spend your own money on yourself. It is the duty of the parents to take care of you along these lines anyway, they surely are not planning on making you supply eatables and do all the work for the wedding are they. If Mrs. Cress does not help you do the work why I would suggest that you have a quiet wedding, otherwise you would be worked to death and get sick in the bargain.

Sometime this week I am going to see about my suit etc. may be tomorrow.

May be I won't be glad when the time comes I surely put in some lonesome hours. I even get lonesome in my sleep.

By the way I sent a great big kiss to you with Aunt Lizzie.

Just Loads & Loads of hugs & kisses and a great big hug & kiss!

Lovingly

Chas.

P.S. Write some nice long letters while Mr. Turner is away and I will be delighted.

C.W.H.

———————◆———————

Postmark: 9 a.m. Sept. 8, 1914, St. Paul, Minn.

Monday 10 P.M.

My dear Charles:

Don't you ever think I forget my sweetheart for one minute and I have written you every day for a long time with the exception of a week ago Saturday. When I stay home I have to wait until the next morning to mail your letter but I always mail it the first thing and you should get it the following afternoon and I can't see why you don't. Today being Labor Day I did not have to go down. Only two of the girls were there, one stenographer and the telephone operator. I will mail this first thing in the morning and you should get it Wednesday afternoon. Will you let me know if you do because I wouldn't want you to think I was forgetting you when I am so anxiously waiting for October 26th when I will see you again.

I bet somebody was angry to get that puncture again. Now what would I do if anything like that would happen when I was driving? I think I will only attempt it when my hubby is right with me and then I won't be running any chances.

Addison had the time of his life today, he and three of his boy friends took their lunch and went to the Fair this morning a quarter to eight and did not get home until 7:30 tonight. On Labor Day they always let the children in free so of course he made use of that and had a quarter extra to spend after he was in by going today.

The rest of us were home all day but mamma and dad are down town tonight. I helped mamma some today and also done some sewing.

Now my dear Charles, don't think I am forgetting you and just imagine the most hugs and kisses and loves ever, just millions of them, from

"Wifey"

xxxxxx

oooooo

⑥⑥⑥⑥⑥⑥

———————◆———————

Postmark: 4:40 p.m. Sept. 8, 1914, St. Paul, Minn.

Tuesday, Sept. 8, 1914

My dear Charles:

Was glad to get a longer letter today. I surely like that kind. You are not the only one that gets so lonesome, so do I and I would like nothing better then to have you come to St. Paul again if it was just a few hours so I could see you again and have a few good hugs and kisses. Don't suggest it again or I will be coaxing you to come and then what would you do? I won't be kissing any more grooms until you are the one and then I will be kissing one worth while. Claribel says she is going to be the first one to kiss you after I do so you see you will be getting a mixture that night.

I take from your letter that Mrs. Turner bought some of the fixtures for your bathroom, am I right? I don't know whether I read it correctly but if she did it surely it is great and I will most certainly thank her when she gets back.

I guess you are going to clean up the country near by! Here it is just a year and two doctors have left the neighborhood already. I wonder how long it will take to get the one across the street out!

As to the outing at Pine Lake, I am sorry you were not one of the party becase I suppose they had a jolly good time. However, if conditions had been turned about, and I wuld have had to go with a gentleman, I think I would prefer staying home, in fact know I would but if you had gone I would not say a word but wish you had a good time but I think away down in the bottom of my heart some place there would be a funny little stirring, not jealousy, I don't know what you would call it but it would be there just the same. If it is just a crowd of young people out for a good time, then I think it is all right but when they go in couples I think I would only want one partner, what do you think of my ideas. I appreciate this little sacrifice on your part and hope I am worthy of it all.

I don't know when Mr. Turner will be back, he has been gone since last Thursday night. Got a little note from him this morning to stay home tomorrow as I may have to work Sunday, suppose he will not get here until then.

Countless numbers of kisses and hugs to you but oh! for a real one.

Lovingly,

Hildred

P.S. I forgot Dr. Stevens called me up this morning, wanted your address. He was at his study in church and had left your letter in another coat at home and he wanted to write today.

H.L.C.

———————◆———————

Trinity Methodist Episcopal Church
Incorporated
Alexander C. Stevens. D. D., Pastor
Merriam Park, Minn.
No envelope; typed with green ribbon

My dear Dr. Husband: I have your letter. You may count on me for the very important business of Monday October 26th. I do not need to tell you how fortunate I am sure you are in the partnership contemplated. The only objection that I would make is the taking this particular young lady away from St. Paul. However that soon comes to be your own right. I congratulate you. I remember meeting you some months ago on the occasion of your attending church services.

with best wishes, I am sincerely,

A. C. Stevens (signature)

St. Paul, Minn Sept 8th, 14.

1020 Laurel Avenue.

———————◆———————

Postmark: 8:30 p.m. Sept. 8, 1914, Detroit, Mich.

Addressed to: Mr. Chas. W. Turner, c/o Booth Fisheries - Envelope flap missing

Sept. 8/14.

My Dear Hildred, -

This is Tuesday so I have not received your Sunday letter as yet usually get it on the afternoon mail. I trust I will receive a big long one this time.

I am inclosing [sic] an announcement sent me some time since, I sure like the style of it immensely, how do you like it.

In all probability I will take time to see about my suit in the AM, bought a hat this AM, I suppose the groom wears white gloves up in your part of the country does he not.

Have only made $5.75 so far today, have had two new patients so far, one when Hildred comes do you know her.

Do you know what Dutch love is. [Ed. Note: This appears to be a colloquial expression referring to passionate love and is traced to the Pennsylvania Dutch, who were of German heritage] I will surely get some next winter won't I, just think six more weeks, and one year ago I was with my sweetheart, I want to or would like to know if my wifie ever gets cold feet in the winter time and what she does if you does [sic] get them.

Will write you more tomorrow after I hear from you.

I surely send all my love and kisses to my sweetheart and a great big hug & kisses.

Lovingly,

Chas.

———————◆———————

Postmark: 9 p.m. Sept. 9, 1914, Detroit, Mich.

Addressed to Miss H.L. Cress, c/o Booth Fisheries - No dot on envelope flap

My Dear Little Sweetheart, -

Received your Sunday letter Tuesday afternoon. Glad to hear from you. Have been looking for a letter from Dr. Stevens, I presume he received my letter, according to his attitude toward you Sunday.

I surely trust you will send me some of those pictures whether they are good or bad, where [sic] you sick last Sunday afternoon, tell me if you were and what was the trouble.

Note you have been dreaming about me lately, glad somebody dreams about me. By the way since we have been having colder weather I have not been raising so much of a rumpus at night so you do not need to worry about landing our on the floor some night. Just think six more weeks and Claribel loses her little bed partner. I bet she will ball [sic] her head off, don't you.

Business is awful slow today, punk in other words, made $9.75 yesterday, only have one outside call to make so far today. This morning I called on two parties who owed me money, and took my car over to the Ford plant to have the upper hose connection of the radiator tightened up. Just interrupted had two office patients in.

I have been thinking over your suggestion as to skipping away the mgmt. of the wedding, Hildred don't you think it would look a whole lot better if we had a taxi come right up to the house for us. It looks bad to run away and what do we care about a little rice or a tin can or two we will stop on the road and get squared away, if you only knew some place where we could go and get fixed up the rice if any out of our clothes and then go to the Hotel, another thing you might fall and tear your suit and get muddy running down some dark alley at night. Let's be brave and take our medicine and then there won't be anything for the people to talk about afterwards, write me and let me know what you think.

Was to one Tailor and got some samples this A.M. have not decided on anything as yet.

I think possibly it would be a good idea to go to the St. Paul Hotel and register under some strange name as Mr. & Mrs. S. P. L'Esperance or something like that what do you think. Don't worry about those Duluth people if they do not act right we will kill their kid and punch them in the eye.

Mother has been intending to write you for some time. I think you will hear from her in a day or so.

Going to get up early tomorrow morning and go to market with a neighbor lady, I suppose you will best the neighbor woman out of this market business next summer.

Now Hildred one long letter deserves another and if you write me early Friday morning I will get it Saturday afternoon.

Now I must tell you how much I love you and close, with all my heart & ten times more. Just Loads and loads of love and a Great big hug and kiss. ooo, xxx, ⓛ ⓛ ⓛ

Lovingly,

Chas.

Postmark: 6:30 p.m. Sept. 10, 1914, St. Paul, Minn.

Hand-written, Mailed in Booth Fisheries envelope

Sept. 10, 1014

My dear Charles:

I am glad you sent that announcement, it just came in right. I was going to ask you before, which way to you want your name in,

Charles William Husband, M.D.

or

Dr. C' W' H'

I have seen it both ways and wondered which you would like so let me know real soon won't you? As to the "At Home" cards, don't you think we should put it at about December 1st? Even if a person is at home before that time, I think they usually figure about a month's time. I like yourself like the Script so guess we will have it done in the Script, what do you say? I figure you will get this Saturday and will you write to me then so we will know by Monday and then we can give it to the printer.

I got my shoes today, they are patent leather and cloth tops. I paid the enormous sum of five dollars for them, that is more than I have ever paid before, four dollars has been my limit but I figured this was for a special occasion. Do you think I was extravagant? I think the next thing I get will be my trunk, my I am getting anxious now!

You surely will get some Dutch love this winter, all you want and maybe more you know the Dutch are great on that.

As to the cold feet, that is something I don't very often have but when I do, you will let me snuggle up and get warm, won't you? Claribel says she does not know what she will do without me this winter, she says she is afraid she will freeze sleeping all alone.

I am going to offer up a little prayer again tonight so hope business will take a jump again. I guess you will have a new patient when Hildred comes, a steady one too especially if she keeps getting so many colds. I still have it but for all that, feel fine.

I am looking for a big letter tomorrow, hope it comes. Just loads and loads and loads of love, kisses, hugs and everything good for my dear sweetheart.

Hildred

--------◆--------

Postmark: 11 a.m. Sept. 10, 1914, St. Paul, Minn.

Wednesday evening

Dearest Sweetheart: –

My, I am so disappointed that your mother is not coming for the wedding. I surely thought she would be here. There is pretty near seven weeks to elapse before that time and I surely hope in that time she will decide to come anyway.

As to Mr. Morgan, I really don't know what he does, all I know is that he works in the Michigan Central Offices and they are going to live in an apartments, are going to try and get something suitable in walking distance from the office.

I have not seen Miss Friedy since Alice's wedding. She has been visiting with relatives in the country, that is some small town near here. If they go to church Sunday evening she is going to call me up so I can meet her "Prince Charming."

As to the wedding, you know of course at first I preferred just having a quiet wedding but both of the folks said they thought it would be nice to have a little house wedding anyway, so finally I got to their way of thinking and wrote you. When you thought it was all right, I talked it over again with the folks and they said they would pay for invitations, announcements and the refreshments. Papa has told me since that he will pay for the decorations of which of course there will have to be some but mamma has not said anything as to that and what she says goes, usually. Of course there are always a lot of extra things that a person doesn't figure on at first and I will be expected to help some. Now that we have decided on having a house wedding (don't think we will have over forty) sometimes she is real enthusiastic and again she talks so much of the expense, that I don't know what to think. I guess I never will understand her though.

I am enclosing a couple of pictures that Elizabeth Goodjohn took while she was here. I had to keep my one arm out of sight, that was where I had my sleeve rolled up and my arm all bandaged. Elizabeth said I might use the one as my announcement card, I have my hand placed so prominently in the front and that I must be mighty proud of my ring which of course you know I am. Do you know Myrtle Goodjohn? She is the girl on the one picture with us.

What are you going to say when I tell you, but I have another cold in my head again. I thought I was getting one yesterday and took a couple of pills but today I have it in all its glory. Mr. Turner said if we wanted to, Claribel and I should go to the Orpheum today on his treat. The folks were all going to the Fair, Dad too and wanted us to go with them so we did. I surely enjoyed it all but it was so cold and if you see it once there is really nothing new but you have a good time anyway.

I am getting so lonesome for you lately, don't know what I will do. Today with all the excitement, I don't know when I thought of you so much, every little while I would wonder what you were doing or wish you were with me. I have also dreamed of you, three nights in succession, last night I thought you came to St. Paul and surprised me, came out to the house one Sunday noon in the machine with dad and Mr. Turner. I suppose this is because you wrote that you felt like taking three days off and coming to St. Paul. I tell you what you can do and what would surely please me, come to St. Paul the day before the wedding – Sunday – and surprise me. That surely would be great.

Goodnight dear. I hope I dream something real nice about you, hope I get some kisses, they seem good at the time even if they are only dream kisses. Loads and loads of love from

Hildred

———◆———

Postmark: 12:30 a.m. Sept. 11, 1914, Detroit, Mich.

Addressed to: Mr. Chas. W. Turner, c/o Booth Fisheries - Envelope flap did not survive

Sept. 10th/14.

My Dear Little Sweetheart, -

I received your Sunday letter Tuesday afternoon, your Monday letter Wednesday afternoon, your Tuesday letter this AM. This morning a letter came from Dr. Stevens, he says "You can count on me for the very important business of Monday Oct. 26th. Sometime when you get talking to him ask him about a rehearsal for Monday afternoon, I would suggest it be late Monday afternoon. What do you say.

I don't know but it seems to me that I will be wanting to hurry the wedding on Oct. 26 so I can get a good chance to hug & kiss my wifie, especially after not seeing her for so long.

Mrs. Turner bought some fixtures for our bathroom. Don't forget to speak to her about it.

In regard to what your said about Pine Lake your sentiments were mine at the time, I know I would not have enjoyed myself anyway. But if you were there it sure would have been great sport.

Gulleys I am glad we won't have to get married again next year, my suit will cost me about $60.00, I believe. Bought a few little [illegible] this AM. Now do the grooms in your part of the country wear white gloves. I just wish you had time to describe or tell me all you know about this wedding business as for instance describe one of the St. Paul weddings as to how they dress, act position and etc. I imagine the St. Paul style will be a little different than Detroit style.

Just Millions and Millions of hugs and kisses and a great big hug & kiss.

Lovingly,

Chas.

◆

Postmark: 9 a.m. Sept. 12, 1914, St. Paul, Minn.

Friday

My own dear Sweetheart:

Maybe I wasn't pleased to get that dandy long letter today those ar the kind I love to get.

Papa made me stay home on account of my cold and I have had the blues more or less all day, so your letter sure cheered me up. It doesn't do me any good to doctor though because I will have it a couple of weeks no matter what I do and then it leaves all of a sudden.

I meant to tell you that at Alice's reception Dr. Stevens said he had received your letter that day but did not get a chance to say any more. I presume you have heard from him by this time.

I am glad you do not do so much kicking any more because I was trying to think of some plan whereby I could stay in bed with safety, was afraid I would wake up some morning and find myself under the bed instead of on top. Claribel sure hates to think of my going but I have given her strict instructions that she dare not cry at the wedding because I do not like to see anybody cry. She is already planning on buying some bed slippers before I go, she says she knows she will freeze if she doesn't.

As to our getting away after the wedding, why your plan is all right if you are not afraid of the rice. I only hope they don't follow us in another machine. They did that at one of the girl's weddings and at Vera's, one of the girls and one of the ushers made believe they were the bride and groom and got away in their machine and when they came to go, no machine. I don't imagine they will do any very terrible stunts to us except it be your brother because the crowd won't know you so well and again their [sic] won't be so many. You see both Vera and Alice had over 150 at the house and in a crowd like that, what they don't think of is hardly worth thinking of. If our clothes are full of rice we can go to Mrs. Otis'. She lives on Grand Avenue and has already told me we could leave our suit cases there and get them on our way to the train as she supposes we can then start out without advertising the fact that we are bride and groom. The only thing about staying in St. Paul over night, we would have to start from St. Paul depot and grandpa, Uncle Louie and Flora I know are going to leave the next morning about the same time our train would leave and I wouldn't want to meet them for anything. This would be my only reason for wanting to go to Mpls. though. Now what do you think?

As to the white gloves, for a small house wedding I don't think it is necessary. I know dad did not wear any but I can find out and I will let you know.

Wish I could take a trip to market with you but that is all coming isn't it?

I am going to save my big long letter until Sunday when I hope my head will be a little clearer. The best and most love ever to my sweet "hubby to be" from Hildred

Postmark: 12:30 a.m. Sept. 12, 1914, Detroit, Mich.

Addressed to Miss H.L. Cress, c/o Booth Fisheries - Envelope flap missing

Friday 2 p.m.

My Dear Sweetheart, -

Thought I would not wait for your letter, which I expect on this afternoon's mail, but would write you, then I am sure I will not miss a day.

We surely are having some bad weather, it is not satisfied with being cold but it has to rain and make it wet and nasty for your Uncle Doodly.

Business just keeps going along slowly Wednesday made $5.75 Thursday $9.75. Dr. Howard tells me business is quiet with him at this present time.

Five Sundays from the time you receive this letter just think I will be on my way for my Sweetheart. You won't get cold feet when it comes to leaving St. Paul. Just think you are going to give up your position too, who do you think will take your place? Have you any idea.

Let me know what you do Sunday and all you know or part of what you know about Mr. Morgan.

Don't forget that I sent a great big smack with Aunt Lizzie for you, I surely hope you will get it Sunday.

Made my shoulder sore this AM, trying to crank my machine, there is a little water I believe in the last gasoline I bought.

Write me a big long letter Sunday Hildred and send lots of hugs kisses etc. for your Hubby.

Just Millions and Millions of hugs and kisses and a great big hug and kiss, from your Hubby,

Chas.

Postmark: 10 p.m. Sept. 12, 1914, Detroit, Mich.

Addressed to: Miss H.L. Cress, c/o Booth Fisheries - No dot on envelope flap

Sept. 12th/14

My Dear Sweetheart, -

Kindly accept thanks for the pictures. It took me about one minute to figure out first whether or not that was my sweetheart standing up with Claribel, of course Claribel looking very natural I recognized her right away. The other picture is quite natural of you. Pictures help out some when you are so far away.

Now in regard to the wedding everything is O.K. as far as I am concerned, the only thing that struck me as not being right, was the idea of you paying for something that was part of somebody else's duty. You know I like to see you used in proper manner.

Sorry to hear concerning your cold, if you wish some more of those tablets let me know and I will send them to you. Let me know how it gets along anyway.

May say that nothing would please me better than to arrive in St. Paul a day before time, why I am waiting so near the time is all on account of business, and trying to make lots of what my wifie likes, but I will do the best I can.

Now in regard to the announcements, think I would prefer having my name with the M.D. following as Charles William Husband M.D. what do you think. The script is O.K.

Now Young Lady I take it that you have made me a promise that you will give me lots of good Dutch Love next winter, may say that I had a sample of it last June and nothing suits me better and just like it immensely and am going to hold you to your promise, Just Loads & Loads of it for mine, as far as the snuggling up is concerned I guess your Hubby will want you to do that all the time whether you have cold feet or not, and remember your Hubby has long arms I may be able to stretch them around twice. Don't get to stout now else I may fail.

Your little prayer helped out some because I was a little busier this AM. How would it be to say another little prayer.

The whole world of love & kisses to my sweetheart. And a great big hug & kiss.

Lovingly,

Chas.

———————◆———————

Postmark: 7 p.m. Sept. 12, 1914, St. Paul, Minn.

Typed, Booth Fisheries envelope

Sept. 12, 1914.

My dear Charles: –

Today is my busy day again but I know I must just drop my sweetheart a line or you will think I have forgotten you again or else say I have not written for a week. Tomorrow I will write you a great big letter to make up for the short one of today.

Mr. Turner told me to put down the following just as he said it so here goes: "Have you got the telephone extension in, if not, why?" I guess he would like to hear from you on this so write to him real soon wont [sic] you. I have something to tell you tomorrow that Mr. Turner has given me my choice on, something pretty nice.

Lots of love and kisses from wifie until tomorrow.

Lovingly,

H i l d r e d.

———————◆———————

Postmark: 10 p.m. Sept. 13, 1914, Detroit, Mich.

Addressed to: Mr. Chas. W. Turner, c/o Booth Fisheries - Dot on envelope flap

Sept. 13th/14

My Dear Sweetheart –

Six weeks from today and the time will surely be short, won't that be great wish we were already that near to it, what do you say. Will probably go to see about my suit tomorrow A.M. Now in regard to your patent leather shoes, they are alright for travelling, but with a white dress won't you have to wear some white foot wear, of course you know more about these things than I do. How are you going to do your hair, I don't know whether I am supposed to ask that or not, but if I was not interested in you I would not ask, because I am always going to be interested in how my wifie dresses & looks. I believe I like your hair the way you had it done in the picture you sent me last winter than in the little pictures you sent a few days ago. What do you think. Have you decided what color you are going to wear as a traveling dress, I suppose it will be dark green or blue, what do you want me to wear dark blue or black. Soft or hard finish (suit)

Made $11.25 and took in $11.75 yesterday, made $4.00 this a.m. Have an operation (minor) lined up for Wednesday AM. Keep right on praying Hildred we need the money.

Mother got $12.00 out of me for fruit last night therefore I am enclosing an account to you with the privilege of paying it when you get ready. Expenses are right after you how about it. Don't forget that you owe me $12.00 will you, 20% off for cash.

Summer has returned this is one peach of a day not to [sic] hot or cold just right.

This afternoon I am going to give Dad a lesson on driving my machine and take mother out for a ride, seven weeks from today you can go how about it.

Did you get the kiss I sent with Aunt Lizzie it was a great big one too.

Don't forget to write me some nice long letters Hildred you know I like them.

All kinds of Love & Kisses to my sweetheart and a great big hug and Kiss, and another great big hug & kisses.

Lovingly,

Chas.

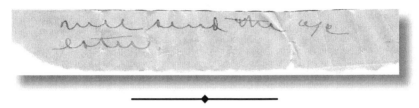

———————◆———————

Postmark: 9 a.m. Sept. 14, 1914, St. Paul, Minn.

Hand-written, sent in Booth Fisheries envelope; address typed

Sunday afternoon.

My dear Sweetheart:

Today is the meanest kind of a day, raining and cold and I just wish you were here to keep me company. Mamma and dad are asleep. Claribel and Addison are reading. Mr. Turner said there was a box waiting for me at the house from Detroit, wonder what it is but think I can guess, will let you know before I close this letter. I am anxious to get that kiss too couldn't get it this morning as I didn't go to church but if it quits raining will go tonight.

Mr. Stevens surely wrote a nice little letter and some time when I see him, will ask about a rehearsal for Monday afternoon. By the way, your brother is going to be best man isn't he? Monday sure will be a busy day, there will be so many things to do the last thing. Mr. Turner says he would like about half an hour to talk with us together on that date to give us a little advice etc. I suppose you will arrive about the same time as you did this summer and I will surely be on hand to meet you. I will have to go down early that morning to have my hair washed, can't have it done the day before account of it being Sunday. How are you going to manage about changing your clothes? You know if you change to your wedding suit at Mr. Turner's you will have the other on hand and we don't want any suitcases around the premises because they will sure find them if we do. I am going to take my bag over to Mrs. Otis' the day before and when I change to my suit afterwards, I will not take my dress along, the folks will send my dress, slippers etc. along with some of my things later. Now if you dress up at Mr. Turner's what will you do with your suit because we don't want to have any suitcases when we leave the house. Can you think of some stunt? We could hardly want to go back to their house after we are married. It might be all right to bring it with you when you come to the house that evening and then change again before we leave and have your wedding suit sent with my dress. How would that be?

I don't know just how or where we will stand, we can plan on that definitely a little later and will let you know. You and your brother are the first to come in, then Claribel, then dad and I. Dr. Stevens will ask you some questions first, I forget what they are, then he asks me, next you have to repeat something after him, then I do, then I think you put the wedding ring on my hand and he says a prayer and pronounces us man and wife and you give me a big kiss and it is all over with. Doesn't it go quick though the way I describe it? All we do then is turn around and receive the people and then they usually have the refreshments right after that. Of course they are not all served at once and after we are through we can wait a while or go right up stairs and dress. I think we will want to go right up and get away don't you?

I suppose your brother will want to leave first thing next morning for Duluth as will my grandpa and uncle. I am going to call up and find out what time their trains leave, what time ours does and if it is very near the same time, think maybe we better go to Mpls. because I wouldn't want to run into any of them. Should I say anything to Mr. Turner about this because he knows of course that we intend to stay here over night.

Guess what Mr. Turner told me yesterday. He said he and Mrs. Turner intended giving us something as a wedding present and wondered whether I would rather they buy something or give us a check and let us make the purchase when we get to Detroit. I told him I would ask you first. In a way I think it would almost be best to get something when we get to Detroit, we can then see what we would like best however it doesn't make any difference to me. Wasn't that great of him and what do you think would be best? I will finish this letter tonight dear.

10 p.m.

Well, Claribel and I have been to church, there were not very many there account of the weather. Marion was not there, guess she found enough to talk about after not seeing Mr. Morgan for a month. Just think of all we will have to say and all the kissing to make up after not seeing each other for four months and over. Since we are home tonight the folks were just remarking that six weeks from Sundays and I will be gone to Detroit. Dad pulled out his handkerchief and started to sniffle and Claribel found something to do in the other room. It made me laugh because they seem to think I will be gone forever when I get married.

Say dear, I thank you ever ever so much for the dandy box of candy. Also the big swack you sent. I am just eating a piece of candy with a big walnut in it and a lot of cream candy in it, with thick chocolate all around. Does that make you hungry? I did not get a chance to say very much to Mrs. Turner tonight but I want to ask some questions, if you still seem to be so nervous how she liked automobiling with you and lots of other things. We were just there a few minutes before and after church tonight

I am sending you have a piece of candy, wifie ate the rest. The reason I am sending this hard piece, it is easier to send in a letter – hope it tastes good.

By the way, Mrs. Turner says I will have to take lots of pills when I get to Detroit. Let me say I am practicing a bit of Christian Science with this cold, have not taken one pill since the day before it really broke out and it is already getting better so maybe I won't want to take any pills, what then?

This is a pretty lengthy epistle again, hope you won't tire before you finished reading it. I send all of the kisses, hugs, loves and squeezes ever to my dear hubby and hope you have good luck, that business picks up again but cheer up if you always make as much as you are now, don't think we will go hungry anyway. Here is for another big hug and kiss for the best and dearest hubby ever.

Lovingly,

Hildred

———————◆———————

Postmark: 12:30 a.m. Sept. 15, 1914, Detroit Mich.

Addressed to: Miss H.L. Cress, c/o Booth Fisheries - No dot on envelope

Sept. 14/14.

My Dear Sweetheart,

Now in regard to the cold in your head, I want you to promise me that you will keep right after it, I know medicine will help you out, another thing you don't want to get hay-fever or some [illegible] condition of your nose or throat do you, write right back to me about this.

Now in regard to the wedding, I think possibly we better as you say stay in Minneapolis over night, of course the train leaves Mpls. about one hour earlier in the morning than it does in St. Paul. I would also like for you to look over matters in regard to getting a place to stay over night, find the best possible place two or within three blocks of the Depot, of course we will take the Northwestern to Chicago. I even would not if I were you let Uncle Chas. know our plans let him think as he now thinks that we will stay at the St. Paul hotel in St. Paul. And do not confide these things to Mrs. Cress or anybody. Something between we/us & co. Another thing I think you better make arrangements with Mrs. Otis and we will leave our suit cases there and get prepared a little before we go to the Hotel but let her believe if she does that we are going to leave St. Paul that night. These things must also be kept away from Mrs. Cress, Claribel etc. because just for the fun of it I'll bet they would squeel. [sic] Also let me know about gloves, did the groom wear them at Alice's wedding? Did you meet Mr. Morgan?

If it isn't too late would like you to send announcements to Mrs. W. McMillen S. Second St. Leavenworth Kas, as she sent me an announcement of her wedding. Also Dr. Leon E. Grajewski Fifth Ave. New Kensington PA.

Just called down street in a hurry a man fell off a dirt wagon on his head, he was dead when I go [sic] there so I did not need to stay very long.

Tell me about the choice of things Mr. Turner has offered you. Don't keep me waiting too long will you.

Dr. Moon came over last night he got a puncture just a little distance from the house so I got out my Bus and we went to church like good little boys. When we got back we pulled off his tire and he drove on the rim over to the nearest garage, his first puncture in two months.

Just Loads & Loads of love, hugs & kisses and a great big hug & kiss to my Dearest sweetheart.

Lovingly,

Chas.

———————◆———————

Postmark: 9 a.m. Sept. 15, 1914, St. Paul, Minn.

Monday evening.

Dearest Sweetheart:

I did not have time to write to you today, was busy every minute. You should have followed me, this noon, I sure would have led you a merry chase. I was in five different stores shopping and they were scattered between Wabasha and Robert street and I was only five minutes late in getting back to the office but maybe I didn't hustle, had to eat lunch too but it wasn't served in courses and there were no finger bowls.

You know at the wedding each person is given a piece of the groom's cake or fruit cake to take home to dream on. To buy the little individual boxes, the cheapest you can get is 5-cents a piece and fifty of those or $2.50 looks pretty big to me to spend for anything like that so I am going to see if I can get some fancy stiff paper, some gold initials etc. and figure up what it will cost to make them ourselves. Of course it will mean more work but the folks said they would all get busy and in one evening we should be able to make them all.

We have changed the announcements to C.W.H., M.D., and papa sent them to the printers today so we should get the proof in a day or two. It sure is getting to look like business today (stricken) now.

Mrs. Turner was in the office this afternoon and going home I spoke of the fixtures she got for the bathroom. She laughed and said she guessed you did, not like where she had your dad put the hooks. It surely was nice of her to get them though.

Just think, six weeks from tonight and I will be your truly wife and you my truly hubby.

My goodness I hope you don't think I will get so stout that you can't put your arms around me, that would be terrible, if I do you surely must give me something to make me thin quick because I have always had a horror of being stout. I hope you can make it and get here a day or two before the wedding, that sure would please me immensely. What do you think you will do?

Love and love and some more love and kisses, from

"Your Bestest"

Hildred

———————◆———————

Postmark: 5:30 p.m. Sept. 15, 1914, St. Paul, Minn.

Typed, return mailing to Booth Fisheries

Sept. 15, 1914.

Hubbykins Dear: –

Busier than the dickens today so will you will excuse me until tomorrow and I will surely write you a good long letter to make up. Mr. Turner is going to Minneapolis in the morning so I will take part of that time to write to you.

The $12.00 sure comes like a blow to me, how long do you let your accounts run and how many days do you consider it cash. I think we will have to postpone the wedding if I must pay it right away because I have my money figured out just about to the last but if you are willing, I will work a week longer and pay you right away. What do you say? I guess the jelly, jam and labor connected with it is easy worth $12.00 and it will taste mighty good this winter.

Lots of love until tomorrow,

H i l d r e d.

———————◆———————

Postmark: 8:30 p.m. Sept. 15, 1914, Detroit, Mich.

Addressed to: Mr. Chas. W. Turner, c/o Booth Fisheries - Dot on envelope flap

Sept. 15th/14

My Dear Sweetheart, -

You surely are a dandy little girl to write me that big long letter Sunday, just wish I could give you a great big hug & kiss for it.

We had an ideal day Sunday could not have been nicer.

Now in regard to getting your hair washed if I were you I would get it washed about 4 or 5 days before time and another thing it would be awfully hard for you to get it fixed up to stay in place washing it the day of the wedding.

Now in regard to my suit possible I will get dressed up Monday afternoon and bring my plain suit over to your house then change and leave my wedding suit to be sent later on. I could take my suit case over to Mr. Otis' place in the afternoon.

Now in regard to Mr. Turner I would suggest your acceptance of the check then you could buy what you felt would be most needful to you.

Surely pleased to receive the candy you are surely generous but I certainly am delighted you took a little bite anyway, almost felt like saving it there again knowing that you had tasted it I just had to eat it. Thanks to my Hildred.

Glad to hear that your cold is improving, I think I can coax you to take some tablets when I think it is necessary. I think I'll be able to get around to most of these things.

By the way, while I was over to see the Taylor this a.m. my car was stoped [sic] on the side of Woodward Ave. another man was parked behind me, he was leaving before I was ready when he pulled out another man ran into him and threw his car into the back of my machine took a little paint off and put a little dent into the end of my car, I am going to turn a letter in for damages tonight, if they will hand over ten dollars I will call it square.

 Business was a little better yesterday made $12.00, I'll be getting busy and doing something this winter. Hurried and wrote my letter in 12 minutes, hope you can read it.

The most love ever to my sweetheart and a great big hug & kiss.

Lovingly

Chas.

◆

Postmark: 5 p.m. Sept. 16, 1914, St. Paul, Minn.

Wednesday, Sept. 16, 1914

Dearest Sweetheart:

It is 10 o'clock, supposed Mr. Turner will be here in a few minutes, said he would be here about 10 or 10:30 so I must hurry.

Again speaking of that most important event, I got those shoes to wear with my suit, got my white slippers some time since. Didn't I mention it some time since? Sure you can ask all the questions you want, that is what I like because lots of times I mean to say something about these things and forget to do it so ask all you think of. I don't know as yet whether I will wear my hair the way I did early this summer or the way I am wearing it now. When you come I will let you be the judge. I started wearing it a new way the other day and like it quite well, it is done up kind of high on my head.

As to my suit, I have never worn anything green but I like the color awfully well and that will be my first choice providing the color looks well on me, of course I have to go by that too.

Regarding your suit, do you mean your wedding suit or the one you will wear on the train? For your wedding suit I think it should be a soft finish but for on the train I should think a hard finish and for general wear afterwards I should think it would last longer. I think I prefer dark blue for traveling to black but again if you get a black I think it looks better in a soft finish. Have you ever worn anything more in a mixed goods? I don't know but isn't there a tweed cloth or something like that they use, that they call salt and pepper mixture? It is black and white mixed, mostly black and it looks quite dark. Do you like anything on this order or not?

Of course I always like dark blue, think it is always good. Let me know what you decide on won't you?

I sure am in a delicate position here, always afraid I will say something I shouldn't and just wish you were here so I could talk things over with you. I have led them to believe that we are going to leave town the same night and dad on one hand insists we should not do this, he can't hear to it all and he doesn't believe we are going either. Again, Mr. Turner doesn't want me to say anything but at the same time he wants to know himself. He suggests your getting a room at the St. Paul in the afternoon and taking our suitcases there, then we could go right to the hotel after the wedding and in the morning if we wanted he would call for us and take us to the depot, says we should have our tickets ahead and we would not have to go through the depot, we could go the same way you did when you left this summer. I have to tell a different story to all of them and if they ever get together they will think I am an expert prevaricator, I am afraid. Mr. Turner also says he will get the room or engage it because he knows Mr. Roth the manager and that way can get a good one. So far I have had to agree with him that it would all be satisfactory. Now if you could only get the room without him going along, you could tell him you were going out to the house first to get the suitcases and instead of coming back, go to Mpls. and engage the room and take our suitcases right over there. We could go to Mrs. Otis' anyway to get rid of the rice etc. and say we had our suitcases checked. How would that be? We would have to manufacture some story to tell Mr. Turner though and what would we do about the next morning, he would want to call for us. Really I don't know how we are going to get out of all this but when you come and we can talk it over together then I think we can come to some arrangement but I really think I would prefer to leave from Minneapolis because there will be so many leaving in the morning – not many but to many to run into.

You surely are good going to church on Sunday. By the way when does Dr. Moon get married? He was to be married some time in September was he not?

I sure offer up a little prayer in your behalf every night but not only for the money part of it.

As to my cold, it is getting along dandy, of course not all well yet but it is not bad at all this time and think it will be all well in a short while.

I had to finish this letter this afternoon, Mr. Turner came in a few minutes after I had started.

Between you and me I will be glad when this is all over with, mean the wedding because it sure means hustle and plan. I don't know what a girl ever does when she has a big wedding a small one is enough for me.

I meant to mention as to the gloves. Allen wore white kid gloves but theirs was a big church wedding and they were in full dress suits but I don't hardly think it is necessary for the house but I will find out and let you know.

This sure is another lengthy letter, send one likewise when you are not busy. Love and kisses by the bushels to my dear sweetheart.

Hildred

Postmark: 8:30 p.m. Sept. 16, 1914, Detroit, Mich.

Addressed to Chas. W. Turner, c/o Booth Fisheries - Dot on envelope flap

Sept. 16,/14.

My Dear Sweetheart, -

Did not receive a letter from you this am. but I am going to drop you a few lines just the same isn't that good of me?

Forgot to tell you yesterday that I am planning to have my big Brother along with me at the big event. What do you think I ought to buy him, I believe I will get a little necklace about the same as yours for Claribel what do you say about it.

Decided on my suit and overcoat this am (Just interrupted had another new patient $1.00 more). I don't know but your hubby will be nearly broke after the big event, I would surely scare you if I told you how much my suit and light coat were going to cost. Don't think I had better send you any samples then their [sic] will be a little more newiness to my coming, another thing I am afraid it is bad luck how about it.

Business is slow today have had a number of new ones lately but they are not very sick, hence do not need much attention.

I sure hope the next five weeks will soon go by. I wish we were going to be married this month instead of next.

Trust I will hear from you this afternoon or I will be disappointed.

Just Loads of Love, hugs & kisses to my sweetheart and a great big hug & Kiss.

Lovingly

Chas.

———————◆———————

Postmark: 6:30 p.m. Sept. 17, 1914, St. Paul, Minn.

Thursday afternoon

My dear Charles: -

I must hurry and write today, have just loads of work to do. For a few seconds this morning I thought I wouldn't be able to write to my sweetheart any more, pretty near got dad, Mr. Turner and myself in a bad smash up. It is the first time I have tried to run the car since you were here and Mr. Turner insisted I run it all the way down, he was going to market. I didn't want to, said I just felt something would happen. Well, we wee away down at the East end of Summit Avenue where you go down quite a steep incline and crossing the street there are the car tracks and I was supposed to turn to the tracks and I saw a car coming likety-split and a big truck coming the other way. I guess I lost my head and didn't hear a word Mr. Turner said anyway he grabbed the wheel and stood up and used the brake and we turned the corner but just missed the car about an inch. I think I will hesitate before I try to do anything like that again and think when I get to Detroit and see all the other cars and people that I will be satisfied to be a passenger only. I sure got the scare of my life this morning.

Now sweetheart as to our wedding present from Mr. Turner I think the check would be best too and it surely is dandy of him to give us our choice but why do you say you suggest my acceptance of the check then I could buy what I felt would be most needful to me. I would rather you would have put it we would etc. because it surely is for you as much as for me if not more as you are his very own nephew and when it comes to buying something, you are going to have every bit as much to say about it as I will.

You can't imagine the dandy surprise I had when I got home last night, mamma was shopping in the afternoon and bought me enough goods for six sheets and enough tubing for six pair of pillow cases and a beauty breakfast cloth and half a dozen napkins. She also got a pair of dandy pillows for our bed. Was I surprised, well I should say so. She told Claribel she wasn't going to get me anything and meant it at the time. Of course Claribel told me and maybe it didn't surprise me when I saw all those things, a mighty pleasant one too.

Gladys just got back from her vacation yesterday, I haven't seen her for pretty near three weeks. She doesn't come to work until next Monday. She called me up last night and wants me to come over tonight. I haven't been to her house for about two months so guess I will go and take some fancy work along.

Just ever so much love and kisses from your lonesome sweetheart,

Hildred

P.S. I forgot to say, hope you get your $10.00 for damages. Don't smash the machine before I have a ride.

Postmark: 6:30 p.m. Sept. 17, 1914, Detroit, Mich.

Addressed to Chas. W. Turner, c/o Booth Fisheries - Dot on envelope flap

Sept. 17th/14

My Dear Hildred, -

Received your short letter this am. Your better tell Mr. Turner that he is working you too hard if anybody else made your work so that you hardly had time to write me a letter he would have something to say about it. Don't you think so. Another thing you will get indigestion by eating so fast, better take a little more time in that respect.

Mrs. Turner is rather notional at times that is the first time I knew I was not pleased with the way the hooks were put up in the bathroom, in fact I had just as much to do with having them put where they are as anybody.

Now in regard to paying for the fruit, you are in debt to be sure, but you don't want to delay the wedding another week on account of that, do you. I think we better make it one week sooner, it will cost you $25.00 a day to postpone it, and may be your life, I am very serious today don't you think so.

Missed a call today had an operation at Grace Hospital and while there a hurry up call came in and I lost out.

Now in regard to getting to St. Paul a day or so ahead of time all I can faithfully promise is that I will do my best, you know I would like nothing better, but I have to see after business pretty close else I am idle and somebody else is busy.

Five weeks more I can love my little wifey all I want to won't that be great.

Just Loads and Loads of love hugs and kisses From your Hubby

Lovingly

Chas.

Postmark: 6:30 p.m. Sept. 18, 1914, St. Paul, Minn.

Friday noon.

Dearest Sweetheart:

Honestly, I am getting so anxious to see you I just wish I could sleep for a few weeks so the time would seem to go quicker. If this next five weeks don't go faster than the past five, I am afraid you will get a wire to come at once. Would you do it?

As to what you should get your brother, what do you think of a set of cuff links with his monogram on or has he a pair. Again are you superstitious about anything sharp? If not I think a real pretty tie pin would be nice. Of course if you are real flush with money I think the nicest thing to get for a gentleman is a set of military brushes but they are pretty steep, that is a good pair. As to getting Claribel something, it surely is dandy of you to think of it but I don't hardly think it is necessary. If you get your brother something and I get Claribel something, I think that is all they usually do, the groom gets something for the best man and the bride something for the bridesmaid.

It is costing so much anyway I think it would almost be best not to she doesn't expect it of you I know. Mr. Jones but the money sure does go fast. I don't know where it slips to but it slips some place. Mr. Turner said this morning that it was my pride that would not let me use the check you sent, now dear if I do need it I am going to use it and when I come to getting my suit and hat (next week I think) I may have to borrow part of that sixty. Mr. Turner just imagines what he said.

Now as to the white gloves, I can't see how that would be necessary, never thought of it until you mentioned it. It isn't going to be a real formal full dress affair, just a home wedding, less than fifty people. If the other people were coming full dress like at a church wedding, then it would be in order but not for ours because ours will be an informal affair. If I were to tell my grandmother we were going to have a formal wedding, you couldn't see her for dust she would run so fast but now she is planning on coming and says she imagines she is as anxious as I am for the time to come. She is pretty anxious if she is.

Come on, it won't be bad luck to send those samples and I want to see them real bad and the suit will look just as new when I see it. Please, won't you?

I forgot to say, Gladys wants to give a shower for me a week from Saturday, ten of the girls I know. Pretty nice don't you think? We sure had a lot to gossip about last night, pretty near three weeks to make up. All the love imaginable and kisses galore from

Hildred.

———————◆———————

Postmark: 8:30 p.m. Sept. 18, 1914, Detroit, Mich.

Addressed to Miss H.L. Cress, c/o Booth Fisheries - Dot on envelope flap

Sept. 18th/14

My Dear Hildred, -

Pleased to receive a longer letter from you this am. Those are the kind I like.

As I told you before my suit and light overcoat are being made. I would like to send you a sample in one way than in another way I would rather not then you will be more interested than ever when the time comes don't you think so, then again it may be as you say bad luck. I think I will wear my blue suit to travel in and take my wedding suit along in my suit case and have it pressed when I get to St. Paul. What do you say, or do you think I better wear it. Of course I will feel pretty dirty when I get to St. Paul and will want a little time to shine up. Then I could put on my wedding suit and pack my suit case and leave it someplace.

Now in regard to staying at the St. Paul overnight why that would be alright providing that we could get up early enough in the am to make our train over to Mpls. I think we better decide on leaving from Mpls. I don't think Mr. Turner would squeel [sic] if you made him promise before you told him that you wanted to leave from Mpls. and your reason for so doing. Of course if we leave from Mpls. staying at a Hotel there would be more convenient ask Mr. Turner what he thinks about me engaging a room Monday afternoon at a hotel over in Mpls. near the depot and leaving from there instead of St. Paul, and tell him those are your plans and registering under another name, then we sure will be alright. If you do not tell Mr. Turner he may feel sore then again he will keep after you until you do tell no doubt, but make him promise you faithfully first of all not to tell a single sole [sic]. Of course it would be a good plan to go to Mrs. Otis' and get the office if any cleared away. If we checked our suit cases they would not only break them to pieces but they might go on another train then we would be up against it getting into Chicago late at night, then again you would want your suit case at the Hotel in Mpls. or St. Paul on the Monday night.

Now in regard to Dr. Moon he is a funny fellow he is on the outs with his Lady Friend just at present, he says he will not believe he is going to be married until he gets up before the preacher.

Glad to hear that your cold is getting better but keep me posted. Also let me know in regard to the gloves.

Now Hildred I have written you a big long letter, let me see what you can do Sunday, let me know how you spend the day.

Will be glad when I can get you all by my lonesome believe me you will get some great hugging and squeezing and a few big smacks, etc. don't you wish were were there now?

Just Loads and loads of hugs & kisses and a great big hug and kisses.

Lovingly,

Chas.

———————◆———————

Postmark: 5:30 p.m. Sept. 19, 1914, St. Paul, Minn.

Typed; Booth Fisheries envelope

My dear Sweetheart:

Mr. Turner wants to leave at 4:30 today (Saturday) so it has kept me busy to get the mail out by that time but I will write you a big long letter tomorrow to make up for it and tell you of all the happenings. You will be getting two letters on Monday anyway, so guess you wont [sic] mind this short one.

While it is short, it is just as full of love and kisses to my sweetheart as ever and wont [sic] I be happy when October 26th comes, just about five weeks.

Loads of kisses and hugs,

Lovingly,

H i l d r e d.

———————◆———————

Postmark: 11:30 p.m. Sept. 19, 1914, Detroit, Mich.

Stamped: Private Office Sept. 21, 1914 Dist. Mngr.

Addressed to Chas. W. Turner, c/o Booth Fisheries - Dot on Envelope flap

Sept. 19th/14.

My Dear Sweetheart,

I just don't know what I did think when I read your letter and I don't know just whether I had better give you any lessons on driving my machine or not, honestly I think Mr. Turner is not nearly as careful a driver as what I am and you can tell him so if you wish, seems to me that machine is always in trouble either burning up or some how banged around, some way or other. Please don't drive that car anymore. In Detroit there are greater excuses for accidents, Detroit has 25 automobiles to 1 in St. Paul, nearly 3 times as many people wider streets and more cars. The crossings are harder to make on account of the width of the streets.

You surely have a big heart I forgot that Mr. Turner's check had anything to do with me.

Mrs. Cress surely was good to give you all those things honestly I don't believe she is half as bad as some people make her out to be, then again she always has been nice to me, hope she uses you alright for the 5 remaining weeks anyway.

Just imagine only a few more days and we will be saying, not next month but this month, how will you like that.

Business is just slowly making a go of it only made $5.00 yesterday, but I think I will do quite a little better than that today.

We are having some dandy summery weather, hope it doesn't get too cold before you come.

Just Loads and Loads of love and kisses to my sweetheart & a great big hug & kiss.

Lovingly

Chas.

P.S. dreampt [sic] somebody swiped my machine last night and burned our house maybe I didn't worry all night nearly crazy.

———◆———

Postmark: 10 a.m. Sept. 21, 1914, St. Paul, Minn.

Typed; Booth Fisheries envelope

Sept. 21st, 1914.

My dear Sweetheart:-

Do you know what I done? I wrote a letter to you yesterday and forgot to bring it down this morning, just called Claribel up and told her to mail it to you so guess it will be a day late. The way it happened, I was busy at something when the machine come and I had to make a grand rush to get into my coat and hat and gather my things together, can't see how I forgot that though. Hope you get this Tuesday as an explanation.

Loads of love from

Hildred.

Postmark: 7 p.m. Sept. 21, 1914, St. Paul, Minn.

Sunday evening

My dear Sweetheart: -

I surely was pleased to get your dandy long letter today, just five more weeks. I think what I better do is not write to you for a week now because you know pretty soon you will not be getting letters every day so you better get used to it, so don't expect a letter for a week.

I surely would like to see a sample of your suit and overcoat but if you have not sent them as yet, never mind because as you say, I will be so much more interested but I can hardly wait to see it. What kind of a hat did you get, a derby or a soft hat? You know I am as interested in your things as you are in mine so tell me will you?

Now as to our wedding, I think I have misunderstood you and you me. In the first place I took your letter to read that you would have another suit besides your wedding suit to travel in. That at the time seemed strange to me, thought your blue suit to be practically new and you would wear that. Now do I understand you, you are getting your wedding suit and light overcoat made and wear your blue suit to travel in. Am I right? Imagine that would be a pretty good way.

I think you misunderstood me as to what city we should leave from, also having our suitcases checked. I suppose I had so much on my mind to say that I got it down too fast and got mixed. If we leave from Mpls. in the morning of course I think we should stay at some hotel in Mpls. but if we leave from St. Paul we can stay at the St. Paul Hotel. As to our suitcases, I meant you could take them to the hotel in the afternoon and tell Mrs. Otis we had them checked if she should ask, then we would not have any suitcases to bother with that night and they would be safe at the hotel. I hope you can arrange to get here Sunday because then we can do all our planning and first thing Monday you could go down and attend to the necessaries, engage the room etc., the rehearsal, you will have to get dressed and there will be almost enough to keep you busy all day but as you say when you are idle somebody else is busy so do the best you can, if you think you better not come until Monday, all O.K. but I sure would be tickled to see you Sunday. I hope your mother changes her mind and will come, I am still planning on seeing her here am going to write to her in a day or two.

As to the gloves, I wrote you the other day as to that and I find it is not necessary for an informal wedding so don't spend your money. You have written Leonard I suppose as to the wedding. He won't need a suit like yours, all he wants is a dark business suit, what do you say?

My cold is just about all gone, in fact all is well again.

Dr. Moon sure must be a funny fellow, he better get married before he is on the outs altogether. Remember we are never going to do anything like that.

Tomorrow evening mamma and I are going to the dress makers to make definite plans as to our dresses. Claribel's is all done.

Claribel and I sure had a busy day of it today, will write you all about it tomorrow. I enjoyed myself but couldn't help wishing you were along, it would have been so much nicer. I never enjoy myself the way I used too [sic], hope I will when we can go together.

Oceans of love and kisses and hugs to my Hubby from yours,

Ever lovingly
Hildred

Addressed to Mr. Chas. W. Turner, c/o Booth Fisheries - Dot on envelope flap

Sunday A.M.

My Dear Sweetheart, -

Well Hildred five weeks from today things will be early did [sic] won't they and somebody will be pretty anxious won't they.

Hildred I don't know what is wrong with me, it has been quite warm at nights lately and I have started to roll around again, not only roll around but have some of the worst dreams anybody could imagine, see it was night before last that I dreamed someone had stolen my car and burnt our house and I was so worried, I never worried so before, then last night after getting your letter I dreampt [sic] that you were killed driving Mr. Turner's machine, and just as worried as could be, I am just going to stay up all night if I have to dream about such awful things, these are the only dreams I have had in months, would not mind at all if I would dream about nice things the way you do. Just can't wait until five more weeks passes then I can have my little sweetheart hugged right up to my lonesome, then simply I won't dream.

This is one dandy day could not be nicer just great.

Had a new patient from Dexter Blvd. this AM. they are a dandy family. Yesterday I made $12.75 and took in $16.25 have a little operation lined up for Monday morning so I will do better Monday.

Mother asked me if you got her letter, I told her you had not said anything about it.

The most love ever to my sweetheart and all the hugs and kisses in the world and a great big hug & kiss from your Hubby.

Lovingly,
Chas.

P.S. What do you think I am getting stouter. - C.W.H.

Postmark: 8 p.m. Sept. 21, 1914, Detroit, Mich.

Addressed to Miss H.L. Cress, c/o Booth Fisheries - Dot on envelope flap

Sept. 21st/14

My Dear Sweetheart, -

Now in regard to me going to St. Paul if you wire me to come at once I will make this bargain with you. I will go at once if you will marry me as soon as I get there, isn't that not fair.

Think your suggestions are good in regard to the presents, think possibly I will get Leonard a tie pin and kindly let me take care of Claribel, I rather feel it is up to me to look after her, we will say that anyway.

Pretty good of your friends to give you a shower do you know what kind of a shower they are going to give you.

I am inclosing [sic] to you a couple of samples and would like to have them back after you look over them. My light overcoat will be made of the same material as my two button cutaway.

By the way had another one of those dreams last night, may say that I wore a new pair of shoes Sunday, last night I drempt [sic] that when I was taking them off I found a whole [sic] clean through the sole of one. I surely hope this ends the dreaming business.

I think why mother is hesitating to a great extent on going to the wedding is because she thinks it is not right or is asking to much of you to come here in a strange place and she be absent.

Don't say anything to Uncle Chas. but I am going to write him. Don't you think he is too persistent in regard to this telephone business if there was any great need of an extension right away I would not hesitate a minute, he surely throws away a lot of money foolishly I think if anybody offered me $1.00 for coming down stairs two or three times a month to answer a telephone call I would surely do it, wouldn't you. I think his statement to get it or else close up shop is pretty radical don't you. Then again I answer nearly all the calls.

I am inclosing [sic] a post card that I received from a little kid friend of mine today, see how a bluffed him, he always wanted to know if I had a girl [ed. note: the postcard did not survive].

Made $16.50 so far today and $7.00 Sunday.

Loads & Loads of love to my sweetheart and all the love in the world. And a great big hug & kiss.

Lovingly

Chas.

Postmark: 10 a.m. Sept. 22, 1914, St. Paul, Minn.

My dear Charles: –

No sir, I couldn't wait a whole long week without writing, I was just fooling anyway and I have got to spend a few minutes every day talking to my sweetheart.

Don't worry about me driving the machine again. I have that desire scared right out of me. Mr. Turner wanted me to drive it this morning but I was just glued to the back seat. We pretty near had a collision this morning, Mr. Turner passed on the wrong side of the car but nothing near as close as mine.

Mamma sure has been dandy to me lately, couldn't ask any more. We expected to go to the dressmakers tonight but she asked us to postpone it until tomorrow night.

Mr. Turner intended to go to Mpls. in the morning and leave tomorrow night for Sioux City. He got a wire at 5:05 tonight from Mr. Smithers asking him to go to Omaha tonight to meet some gentlemen so he hustled away and left a little after eight tonight.

I was going to tell you how I spent Sunday. Claribel and I went to church in the morning and in the afternoon Mr. and Mrs. Turner took Claribel and I over to Mpls. with them. They called on Mr. and Mrs. Keller, Mrs. Keller is leaving tomorrow for California to be gone six months. Can you ever imagine me leaving my hubby that long? Not unless he sends me away. We drove all around the lakes through Mpls. and then came and drove around St. Paul and went down to the warehouse to get a watermelon that Mrs. Turner wanted for supper. We were over to their place for supper and afterward went to church. Friday night they start regular choir practice again don't think I will start in though.

As to that dream you had or nightmare, I told Mr. Turner about it and he said that was a warning to you and I should ask if you had insurance on your house and machine. Of course you should, but he surely is superstitious and no wonder I am inclined that way, hearing so much about it.

My I hope business gets better. I will offer up another prayer tonight.

Ever so much love and kisses from

Hildred

◆

Postmark: 6 p.m. Sept. 22, 1914, Detroit, Mich.

Stamped: Missent to Spokane, Wash.

Sept. 22nd/14

Sweetheart My Dear, -

This is Tuesday so I suppose I will get a letter on the last mail this afternoon, hope you wrote a big long letter Sunday to your hubby. There is to be a meeting of the alumni Assoc. at 4 p.m. today so I am going to write early then I won't miss.

It was surely hot today nearly suffocating, wish it would cool off a little.

Made $18.00 yesterday nothing so far to day not a single red cent, are you keeping up the little prayer Hildred?

Had my suit and overcoat fitted this AM they will be finished next Saturday. You won't know me with the big long tail I am going to have. May be you will be frightened and run away will you?

Hildred I am going to ask you to be ready for all the loving in the world when we get together you better put yourself in a little form then I would be able to squeeze you to death.

By the way I had another dream last night, I am surely putting in some awful nights, I dreampt [sic] you had a great big tumor on your shoulder, I'll bet you anything I worried for two hours in my sleep last night, I could see the tumor so plain and it seemed so real that I can scarcely make myself believe you haven't one. You surely haven't one have you?

Will write you more tomorrow after I hear from you.

Just Loads and Loads of love to my sweetheart and a great big hug & kiss.

Lovingly,

Chas.

◆

Postmark: 10:30 a.m. Sept. 23, 1914, St. Paul, Minn.

Tuesday, Sept. 22, 1914

Dearest Sweetheart:

What do you eat to have such terrible dreams. I wish I had received your letter sooner, because if I am going to be killed driving an old machine, I would not have bought so many things today, and paid out so much money.

Mamma and I spent the whole day shopping and I think we accomplished a lot, but oh! the money how it went! I am not quite broke but I tell yu, pretty badly bent. I bought my suit for one thing, got it at Fields but I did not get green. I tried on lots of different shades but they really did not look a bit good on me. I was disappointed at first because I had my head so set on green but I tried on some dark brown ones and now I wouldn't have anything else. My suit is dark brown broadcloth and it has a (caracul) collar and cuffs. I don't know if that word is spelled right. It has lots of buttons down the front and a perfectly plain back, long coat and plain skirt. I am just in love with it and sure hope my dear hubby will like it. If you don't like it when you see it, I won't either. I meant to tell you that it cost $32.50. It pretty near took a piece of my heart to part with so much but I thought better pay a few dollars more and be satisfied than get something I knew I would not like. I got a hat too. I tried all over to get a hat to match but I couldn't get anything in the same shade unless I paid $20.00 and up and that was out of the question, I had limited myself to $10.00. I did the next best then, got a black velvet hat and all in the world it has on, is a brown feather the shade of my suit and it was $10.00. It is a good looking hat I think and am well pleased. Mamma sure likes my hat and suit too, she was with me of course. I like her to be along because she sure has good taste.

Oh! and I got a trunk! I didn't get such a terribly expensive one but it is good looking and about all I felt I could afford, that was $10.60, don't see why they couldn't chop off the 60-cents.

I got some bedroom slippers too, mine are about all inski [sic]. Those were $1.25. I bought a waist to wear with my suit, that was $5.00 a little lace waist. I was going to make it but there are so many things to attend to, mamma thought I better buy it. I also bought some little incidentals so I sure spent the money today, got about 50-cents to live on this week.

Tonight we went to the dressmakers, mamma planned her dress and I mine. Now we have to get the material this week. She wants to start on them next week together, so we can go for fittings at the same time. Don't you think we accomplished a lot though today. When we came home tonight we took the skins off three baskets of grapes, mamma is going to make grape jam tomorrow. I sure love that, rather like it.

Good night dear, and don't have any more bad dreams. Glad you are getting stouter, keep it up. How much do you weigh.

All my love and kisses to the best and dearest hubby ever from

Hildred

No envelope

Sept. 23, 1914.

Dearest Sweetheart: –

I sure would like to wire you but guess we better wait a few weeks, it is only four more weeks after this one passes by. Just think only four weeks. I really can't imagine it.

Now if your mother is only hesitating because she thinks it would be asking too much of me to go there in a strange house, you just pack her suitcase and tell her to come with you, because I won't mind it one bit really. I may not be such a good cook etc. but I guess we can manage for several weeks so do your best to persuade her to come. Of course it costs quite a bit to make the trip but this is the last chance she can see one of her sons married and I am sure your dad wouldn't want her to stay home because he couldn't come. We would just love to have both of them come but if your dad can't make it, hope your mother can. It sure is considerate of your mother to think of me in that way but for mercy sake don't let that interfere with her plans, and I am still in hopes of seeing her here.

Now as to the extension phone, yes sir, I agree with you in every sense and am glad you wrote about it. I told Mr. Turner I was going to write you not to put it in, that if you would give me that $1.00, I would run the steps fifty times during the night and it would still be in the family. He got awfully provoked, said it was false economy and made me promise I would not write to you but as long as you wrote first, guess I can express my opinion but don't tell him I did. I don't think so many people will be sick that it will bother us to answer the telephone all night, we surely can stand a call once in a while. Maybe sometimes you will be glad to have it ring during the night, especially if you happen to be dreaming of burning houses, stolen autos etc. Really I think it is a needless expense, and glad you think so. Stick to it now and don't have it put in for a while wait until we get a few things taken care of and can afford those luxuries. What do you say.

I surely am pleased with the samples you sent, those are simply great and I can just see my hubby in them now and that sure will be a beauty of an overcoat. Didn't you stagger when they told you the cost? I am sending the samples back, also the postcard. That sure is pretty cute, guess you kept lots of people guessing for a while. Erma Rakowsky, a girl I have known ever since I was four years old is going to be married the 12th of October. I got an invitation to her wedding today. She lives in Duluth but that is too near our wedding to go scouting around the country. I haven't seen her for an age but her father was here this spring so I saw him then.

Mrs. Turner had to go to the dentist's this morning so she stayed down for lunch and took me with her. This afternoon she went to the Orpheum. I meant to tell you that the girls were giving a "Parcel Shower" for me, meant to mention it before.

All the love in the world, kisses in the world and hugs in the world to my dear Sweetheart, from,

Hildred

◆

Postmark: 12:30 a.m. Sept. 25, 1914, Detroit, Mich.

Addressed to: Miss H.L. Cress, c/o Booth Fisheries - No dot on envelope flap

Sept. 24th/14

My Own Dear Sweetheart, -

Gully's I just don't know what I would do without my sweetheart, I could not live four months more without her. You sure are going to be loved with all your Hubby's might before very long, 33 days more, then you will be my truly wifie, don't ever worry about us getting on the outs, because your Hubby thinks too much of you for that.

Suppose Mr. Turner gave you a day off on Tuesday that is why I have not heard from you. But don't forget to write me another long letter.

In regard to your wedding ring I think you better pick it out and let me know the amount and I will send a check. I might not get one to suit you. You have to wear it therefore you ought to get a very good one while you are at it. So if that will be something more ready, get Mr. Turner or your Daddy to go along with you. Sorry I can't go.

You can tell Mr. Turner that our house is insured. By the way Mother woke us all up last night screaming in her sleep, she thought a burglar had gotten into the basement window, my Dad grabbed her and she screamed all the worse she thought the burglar had grabbed her. Some dreamers aren't we.

I send all my love to my sweetheart kisses & hugs by the millions and a great big hug & kiss.

Lovingly,

Chas.

◆

Wednesday afternoon

My Dear Hildred, -

If you do as you say not write to me for a week, I will send the Detroit police up there to investigate, possible you are getting tired of writing or may be you do not want me to write for a couple of weeks. Received your Sunday letter this AM, but did not get your answer to my letter which you should have received Monday. I thank you for sending the little note in regard to your Sunday letter.

Have gotten a derby hat, did you want me to get a soft hat, I think a derby hat is dressier than a soft hat. May say that I am going to wear my blue suit that I got last Spring to travel in. I have only worn it two or three times this summer.

As I understand it, we are to leave from Mpls. and stay at some Hotel in Minneapolis over night, I could engage the room some time Monday and take our suit cases over there. You can plan on me being in St. Paul in time enough to take care of all necessities of the occasion.

Glad to hear that you will not have a cold at the time of the wedding.

Business is slow today this would have been a good time for the wedding, that is a good time for me to get away.

All kinds of hugs & kisses to my Sweetheart and a great big hug & kiss

Lovingly

Chas.

———————◆———————

Postmark: 9 a.m. Sept. 25, 1914, St. Paul, Minn.

Thursday

My dear Sweetheart:

I waited and waited today, for the letter that never came. Didn't you write because you failed to get a letter on Tuesday? I hope that is not the reason because I meant you should have a letter Tuesday but simply forgot to take it down in the morning.

I sure have the "blues" tonight, in fact the folks asked me what was the matter with me, said they bet I didn't get a letter. I didn't tell them what good guessers they were.

Was up to have my suit fitted today, just had to have the skirt altered the least bit, it was too large around the waist and then they had to fix the length, the coat fits just as it is. I am going to get it on Monday. I got a pair of short black kid gloves to wear with my suit, couldn't get anything to match my suit but the black will go with my hat and the collar and cuffs of my suit.

I got the goods for my wedding dress today, took it to the dressmakers tonight and will have my first fitting on Monday evening. I am awfully anxious for you to see my things, wish it were next week.

Mr. Turner got home tonight so I have a good days work ahead of me but I sure will try my best to write a long letter. If I can't find time at the office, will write tomorrow night.

Now please don't miss writing to me again because when you do, my imagination gets working and I imagine all kinds of things.

The most hugs and kisses ever to my dear sweetheart,

Lovingly

Hildred

◆

Postmark: 1 a.m. Sept. 26, 1914, Detroit, Mich.

Addressed to: Miss H.L. Cress, c/o Booth Fisheries - No dot on envelope flap

Sept. 25th/14

My Dear Sweetheart, -

I am surely getting anxious, can hardly think of business anymore, although I stick around.

Note you are spending all your money and how much you hate to part with it, never mind Hildred we won't have to worry about money some day. If I can make $3,000 my first year and I expect to run over that, why I ought to make $1000 a month very easily in 6 or 7 yrs. Glad you told me all about what you bought. I surely like to know about these things, now about the wedding dress, is it bad luck to even tell me something about it. I am surely interested in these things, my suit and light overcoat together are costing me $105.00 how would you like to pay that. Not broke but just a little bent.

Hildred you say only four weeks, that seems an awfully long time to me, just four weeks too long that's all.

May say that I was just tickled to death when I read what you had to say in regard to the telephone extension, you surely expressed my sentiments, may say that it is very seldom I am ever called out or up at night. Have not made five night calls since I have been in practice. And I always hear the telephone when it does ring. Have not been called out at night since Aunt Lena was here. Once in a while may be once or twice a day the telephone will ring when I am upstairs, but that is good exercise for me, does me good, and Uncle Chas. wants me to pay $1.00 a month to get rid of something that keeps me healthy. I do not walk enough as it is. The next real busy month I have then I will get it in anyway.

Pleased to receive a copy of the invitations & announcements – I like them both immensely, only one thing I don't care so much for that is they read Oct. 26 wish it were Sept. 28th instead.

All the neighbors know that I am going to be married even my patients are finding these things out, funny thing the way the news spreads around.

The weather is quite cool today, it is commencing to feel like winter.

Mother went down to the train, [illegible] country and is passing through Detroit today on her way to Boston, [illegible] is going to join her here and go along. After mother gets back I am going out and fix up my headlights I have not used them for some time, have not had a street car ride for months just hate to think of riding on a street car now that is just the way you will feel before long.

Write me a big long letter Sunday Hildred because you know how anxious I am, believe me I look for the mail man every day. Send lots & lots of love & kisses too. Billions of hugs & kisses to my sweetheart and a great big hug & kiss.

Lovingly

Chas.

———————◆———————

Postmark: 10 a.m. Sept. 26, 1914, St. Paul, Minn.

Dearest Hubby:

Excuse me please if I do not write tonight. I have had a busy day today, cleaned up three days work. I have a few in my book but Mr. Turner wanted to get them all out of the way as Mr. Smithers will be here tomorrow and then I never get any dictation.

I envy Flora tonight, she is down to the depot to meet her hubby. Won't I be glad when I can do the same. I am getting so lonesome, if it were more than four weeks, don't know what I would do.

Loads and loads of love from

Hildred

———————◆———————

Postmark: 1 p.m. Sept. 26, 1914, St. Paul, Minn.

Saturday noon

My dear Sweetheart:

I hustled with my lunch today so I could write to you but will save my real long letter until tomorrow. No, I should say I am not tired of writing or receiving letters, the more I get the better I like it.

As to whether we stay in St. Paul or Mps. I didn't say positively, those were only my suggestions and maybe you would rather stay in St. Paul. If so it doesn't make any difference to me but why don't you ever say which you would prefer doing?

As to your hat, I didn't ask because I would rather you have a soft hat, merely my anxiety to know what you had purchased and I know you look good in a derby because I have seen you in one. I wish the style in hats for ladies would last as long as they do for the gents.

Now Charlie, as to my wedding ring, do you want me to tell you what I would rather you do? I don't think it would be any fun picking out my wedding ring alone and I would rather have something of your choice. Why not wait until you come to St. Paul and I can describe the kind I would like to you but I would rather not see it until my own dear hubby puts it on my hand at the wedding. Do you think I have some peculiar ideas? I think so. I would like a narrow ring but quite heavy but when you come I can describe it better so would you just as soon leave it until then? Let me know though what you think.

I hope business starts up a little brisker again, how do you think you will make out this month?

I am going to send a sample of some German butterscotch Mr. Turner bought for me it is made in Germany. Don't think there is any difference in the taste but I am just sending a little sample anyway so you can tasgte it.

I am busy as can be again today, Mr. Turner found a lot more to write about today, didn't think I would get many account of Mr. Smithers being here but I have more than ever, a whole book of dictation, that is the one side of the paper and I haven't written very many of them as yet. This afternoon is their main meeting. Mr. Turner, Mr. Smithers and four gentlemen from Canada. You can pretty near cut the smoke in the office with a knife and I know Mr. Turner pretty near had a fit.

All the kisses, hugs and squeezes in the world to my dear sweetheart from

Hildred

P.S. A letter came in for Mr. T. from you, suppose on the telephone business.

———— ◆ ————

Postmark: 11:30 p.m. Sept. 26, 1914, Detroit, Mich.

Addressed to: Mr. Chas. W. Turner, c/o Booth Fisheries - Envelope flap damaged

Sept. 26/14

My Dear Sweetheart, -

Sorry you did not get a letter on Thursday, but I have written every day without exception for a long, long time, in fact I don't know just when I have missed a day, I surely wrote to you on Tuesday, so if you have not received my Tuesday letter it is someplace in the Postal Dept.

Have made $15.00 so far this afternoon, only made $2.25 this AM. Think I can make $4.00 or $5.00 to night, hope so at least.

Have a little cold in my head so I am driving with an extra coat on in the machine. It is not very bad though.

Am going to get my suit tonight and give my check for $105.00 that is the way all my money goes. Supposing we had to get married every year instead of just one.

Can you give me an idea concerning what your wedding dress is going to be made of and how it is going to be made of course if you are sure that if you tell me these things it will be bad luck I do not want you to tell me.

Dr. Moon just left could not write while he was here and I want to get my letter in so that you will get it Monday. Will write more Sunday.

The most love ever all the kisses & hugs in the world to my sweetheart and a great big hug & kiss.

Lovingly, Chas.

————————◆————————

Postmark: 9:30 p.m. Sept. 27, 1914, Detroit, Mich.

Addressed to: Mr. Chas. W. Turner, c/o Booth Fisheries - Dot on envelope flap

Sept. 27th/14.

Sunday A.M.

Sweetheart Dear, -

Well we are surely getting there aren't we Hildred, I just wonder what I will be doing four weeks from today. Wish it was one week instead of four.

I now have my suit and light coat in the house, they surely look swell silk lining and silk lapels, braid etc. striped trousers, the very best the taylor [sic] had, they almost look too swell to wear, Mother says. I look like a preacher in them, wish I could show them to you.

What I would like to do Hildred is to figure how much money I will need to send you for R.R. Tickets, then I would like you to see about getting flowers for me, and anything else you may happen to think of. Have you made up your mind to leave from Mpls. If you say Mpls. that is settled and we stay at a hotel over there.

Got up early this A.M. 6:30 filled all my dope cups on our machine oiled it up well pumped up the tires a little and did some dusting, must get busy with some soap and water pretty soon, last night when I was going over to the taylor's [sic] I believe some water got into my carburetor and I had to spin my engine about a dozen times to get it started, I was so all instbei [illegible] when she started that I could not have spun it once more, I could almost taste blood from the straining, my arm feels sore this morning, in a few minutes I am going to leave to make a call about 4 miles out in the country.

I believe mother is sorry now that Katherine has been after her so much that she did not decide to go to our wedding. She intends going up to Duluth & St. Paul I know next summer. The girl living next door to us is going to be married at 7:30 a.m. tomorrow in the Catholic Church, Mother is going to the wedding. The girl on our other side is not going to be married for a year. The Dr. building across the road is going to be married as soon as his house is finished, they are plastering now. Let me know if you got the letter I wrote Tuesday.

All the love kisses & hugs in me to my Dear little Sweetheart and a great big hug & kiss.

Lovingly

Chas.

———————◆———————

Postmark: 9:30 a.m. Sept. 28, 1914, St. Paul, Minn.

Sunday evening

My dear Sweetheart:

Thanks, just "oodles" for that dandy long letter, they always make me feel good.

I should say I am spending the money but $100.00 for a suit and overcoat, my goodness, I think somebody else is spending it too. I think the first six months after we are married we will be so poor that we will have to live on love and kisses but I am so hungry for some now that I think that is all I will want. I have been thinking some of quitting work a week before the wedding as there is quite a bit I can help with at the house and I have a place for every bit of money I will get until that time. It sure goes like hot cakes.

I hope your dreams as to making $1000.00 a month will come true, the month you make that much I think we will have to go on a spree to celebrate. As to the telephone extension, I am glad you are not going to have it put in just yet, think we can stand to run the stairs *a few times.*

Now as to my wedding dress, that is always to be a surprise to the groom, he is not really supposed to know anything about it, none of the girls tell their hubbys about it, mamma didn't but I will tell you a little bit about it anyway. The skirt part is messaline and has some lace flowing on it on the order of shadow lace with a band of the messaline at the bottom of flounce or over skirt. It has a wide girdle, and the waist is to be made on the order of a little loose packet with the lace. Now that is all I can tell you about it, will have my first fitting tomorrow. I think Mrs. Turner is quite provoked with me that I have decided on a silk dress. She suggested at one time an embroidered organdie. Well, I priced that and the flouncing that looks anyway decent is $3.50 a yard but maybe I have some high ideas too. Then again, she said a voile, well they have had that for so long, and I myself don't care a great deal for it. Mamma and I figured it up and to get the organdie it would come higher than my dress will now. The messaline was $1.00 a yard and when made up I think it will be the prettiest but of course it won't wash. I am sorry she feels that way but Mamma and I both liked the messaline best. What do you think?

Well Gladys gave the shower for me Saturday night and we sure had a picnic. Shortly after the girls arrived Gladys handed me a letter which she said was enclosed in on to her that day and your name was signed to it. In it, it said you had discovered a treasure where by we would be wealthy thereafter, but it was hidden and you would wire instructions as to where to find it as soon as possible and I was not to make any mistake or we might lose all. Pretty soon the telegrams started coming, and Gladys had her brother bring them to the front door, one at a time, and quite a bit of time elapsed between each. It was quite exciting and I found little gifts all over the house, even in the attic. I got some nice things, a small doily, two mats for under hot dishes, half a dozen ice-cream dishes, hand embroidered corset cover, bath towel, linen towel, a little oblong dish for loaf sugar, big apron and I got two bean jars so be prepared for beans three times a day. Mrs. Turner gave me a dandy surprise, she gave me a pair of tan kid gloves, sent them down with Claribel. We had a dandy lunch and the place cards were awfully cute, baskets of flowers and each had two words on them, the first letter each word being your initials. Mine, H.C. was "Happy Charles". Merle Days – M.D. Medical Doctor etc. Of course each had to find their place. Going home was the best the girls got a big bunch of rice from Mrs. Porrter when I was getting up my packages and when I got on the car they just pelted me with rice. We were all on the same car because the girls live in the park. They had taken the yellow Tarleton that was on the basket of flowers in the dining room and when we got in the car they pinned that on my hat like a long veil and it was over a yard in length. Did I feel cheap, well I should say so and Claribel was bad as any of them, but what could I do against all those girls. I was sure glad to get to Fairview Ave.

Now Charles, if you want to get something for Claribel, may I offer a suggestion to you? I think she would rather have a bracelet than the beads, that is something she has wanted for a long time and has given me the hint. The bracelet I think would be more reasonably than I imagine the beads to be, and I know she would love to have a bracelet. I don't know as I should say this to you when you suggested the beads and if you would rather get the beads, I know she would be tickled to death but I am giving you a little pointer as to some hints she has been handing to me. What do you think you will get for her? It sure is dandy of you to remember her. I must get to bed now, it was after one O'clock last night, this celebrating means late hours. Will tell you tomorrow all I have done today.

Just millions ad millions of kisses and hugs. We sure have had a short honeymoon together or rather few courtship days together and I will be Oh! so glad when this next four weeks pass so I can get some more real hugs and kisses.

Lovingly, Hildred

XXXXX

OOOOO   X 1000 = ?

ⓖⓖⓖⓖⓖ

And countless numbers

Postmark: 5:30 p.m. Sept. 28, 1914

Addressed to: Miss H.L. Cress, c/o Booth Fisheries - Envelope flap missing

Sept. 28, 1914

My Dear Sweetheart, -

Received your letters & box of candy. I am enjoying them immensely it was surely good of you to send them and I appreciate your kindness beyond description, the only fault I find is that they melt too fast, and I can't take time to suck on them. I have to bite a little to.

I feel so awfully lonesome this afternoon, it just seems that the time does not go near fast enough and I have to wait 28 days more, just think of it. Just feel as though I do not care any more whether school keeps or not, just as long as the time goes, if the mail man could only bring me a letter every five minutes that would suit me fine.

Now in regards to whether we stay in Mpls. or St. Paul over night, I think we better stay in Mpls. over night, I know you would feel better leaving from Mpls. where nobody knew us and in all probability I will feel just the same, personally I would rather not meet the people, if you say Mpls. that settles it and we stay over night in Mpls. and leave from there next morning by North Western, along about 7 a.m.

We will let the wedding ring go until I arrive in St. Paul, but I surely want to get one that you like. Glad you wrote to me in regard to the ring, I always want you to speak up to me, and tell me what you do like and do not like.

In the 27 days of this month I have made $276.75 and taken in $231.75. May say I have had more new patients this month than in any one month before at least I trust so but they only have little wee ailments and in that way I do not make so much. October I believe will be rather quiet, then in November things will pick up and your hubby will be a busy man if my business increases every year the same it has this year we will not be in debt long.

By the way Mr. Tuner has not said anything about my note will you speak to him about it, I will have to have it received.

May say I got a hard hat because I thought it would look more dressy than what a soft hat would.

Will be looking for that long letter tomorrow. I wish you would send me all kinds of love because every day makes it one day nearer.

Suppose you will work two weeks more let me know. All kinds of love hugs & kisses to the best sweetheart ever.

Lovingly,

Chas.

P.S. Where is (Miss Freedy) or Mrs. Morgan now, did you go to the wedding.

C.W.H.

———————◆———————

Postmark: 9 a.m. Sept. 29, 1914, St. Paul, Minn.

Monday, Sept. 28th, 1914

Dearest Sweetheart:

Today solves the problem as to why I did not hear from you on Tuesday. I got two letters today and across the face of one it said, "missent to Spokane, Wash." How that letter ever got away out there is beyond me because it sure said St. Paul.

Don't have any more of those dreams. Do you talk in your sleep because I would like to find out some secrets. I was looking for lumps on my shoulders but fail to find any – thank goodness – so guess I have no tumor. I haven't had any dreams lately.

How do you like your suit now that it is finished? I am awfully anxious to see it and I won't be a bit scared of the tails on it either. Maybe you would be so swell though, that I won't know you or rather you won't know me. If we had to get married every year and it would cost so much every time, I think we would have to elope to get out of the expense because it is a fright the way the money goes. Had my first fitting tonight, mamma had hers this afternoon. Just think four weeks from tonight this time 10:30 and we will be married two hours. Addison said tonight that the boys want to know when we are to be married so they will have time to gather some tin pans etc. together.

We had the grandest kind of time yesterday, went to Long Meadow, Minn. in Mr. Turner's car. The Hon. Mr. Smithers from Chicago was along too, Mr. and Mrs. Turner and our family with the exception of Claribel. One of her girl friends had invited her over, their folks were going to New Brighton, Minn. in their car and wanted her to go along so we were all some sports yesterday.

I got those films from Celia tonight of the pictures we took that Sunday, as soon as I have them printed, will send them along. I think these turned out pretty good.

I am terribly sleepy tonight will write more tomorrow.

Just bushels and bushels of kisses and millions of hugs from yours,

Hildred

———————————◆———————————

Postmark: 7 p.m. Sept. 29, 1914, St. Paul, Minn.

My dear Charles:

I cannot write to you today but will surely make up for it tomorrow. Mr. Turner leaves today for Duluth, Port Arthur and Winnipeg and won't be back until Saturday.

All the love and kisses to my dear lover, from

Hildred

———————————◆———————————

Postmark: 8:30 p.m. Sept. 29, 1914, Detroit, Mich.

Addressed to: Mr. Chas. W. Turner, c/o Booth Fisheries - Dot on envelope flap

Tuesday Afternoon

My Dear Hildred, -

If you only knew how little money I have made so far to-day I am afraid you would say something to me, nevertheless I have been busy making out my monthly accounts they are getting quite numerous, I am going to get after them hot & heavy this coming month, going to call and have a little heart to heart talk with some of them.

This noon I dressed up in my wedding duds to see how I looked, well I could almost hear the mirror crack anyway the picture in the mirror laughed at me.

If business is as quiet in Oct. as what it is now, that is at the time when I am due to leave I may skip away a day or so earlier how will that be.

Another thing Hildred don't forget that your Hubby has a birthday in Nov. that will cost you a few more penneys. [sic]

I am just writing along slowly waiting for the mail man trusting that he will deliver your Sunday letter.

I have just received your Sunday letter, but it is late so that I cannot comment on it much now but will do so tomorrow.

Glad to hear concerning your wedding dress, you surely had a great time at the shower. I am surely missing a whole lot by being so many miles away. But these weeks will surely pass pretty soon.

Glad you made the suggestion in regard to getting the bracelet for Claribel, let me know the design of a bracelet you think she would like. I wish you were here to pick it out.

All the love and kisses in the world to my own Dear Sweetheart and a great big hug & kiss.

Lovingly,

Chas.

———————◆———————

Postmark: 4:30 p.m. Sept. 30, 1914, Detroit, Mich.

Addressed to: Mr. Chas. W. Turner, c/o Booth Fisheries - Dot on envelope flap

Sept. 30/14.

My Dear Hildred, -

Another month nearly all inski, [sic] tomorrow will be part of that celebrated Oct. Twenty-six more days left to get ready in. How do you like the thought of going to Detroit to live.

Little disappointed that I did not hear from you this AM, always like to get my letter in the AM so that I can write you just think in the afternoon, I am not going to wait until this afternoon's delivery as that does not give me any time to write before the mail man gets here. Then again when I get my letter in the AM I have more to write about.

We may be pretty poor even at that for a while after we are married. I surely have spent a lot of money this past year. I have been almost dead broke a number of times. Then when I get a good month it puts me on my feet again, and it seems as though there has been a away [sic] pop up to take the money every time, my automobile & garage took quite a lump and as you say we may have to live on love & kisses.

If I were you I would not feel hurt even if Aunt Lizzie does not like your wedding dress, I know your hubby will like it anyway, if I were there I bet I would coax to see it.

We surely are having some nice weather, it is really too nice for people to get sick. It seems as though times have been dull ever since I started out then again this war had to spring up. Will be glad when business spruces up again.

I think possibly Mr. Turner is working you too hard lately. You don't want to kill yourself working too hard tell him so if you think so.

Just Loads & Loads of love & kisses and a great big hug & kiss.

Lovingly,

Chas.

PS Going to get busy on my accounts this PM. Have almost $600.00 outstanding.

C.W.H.

OCTOBER 1914

◆

Newspaper Headlines

Detroit Free Press

- Truce agreed to by rival leaders in Mexican row
- Man who saved Roosevelt's life from assassin's bullet rescues woman in war zone
- Viaduct proposed to supply Detroit with lake water
- Germans fail in fierce assault at enemy's turning base; Allies' troops believed to be at border
- Detroit girl made fire captain at Wellesley
- Exhibit to predict progress of war on tuberculosis
- Oh, isn't it just like a woman! Working at unseemly hours is so characteristic
- Kaiser and Czar personally rush to Russo-German border; Allies gain on right and left in France
- Wants employers to hire Detroit residents first
- Scores of marriages made in haste
- Ty Cobb picks Athletics to win big World's Series
- Moonlight tango under [Washington] monument is Washington fad
    - Harvest moon is preferred but any old moon is welcome

- Automobile parties find new use for noted mall
- Auto headlights illuminate the ballroom floor – dancers must buy new shoes

- Rules of road should be part of school work

- U.S. expected to referee war, says Canadian paper

- Court battle holds up new traffic laws

- "Don't stop courting your wife" Pitching Parson's advice to business men at YMCA

- Tax on gasoline for motor cars killed in caucus

- War won't last much longer, is relief in London

- King Charles of Rumania, made ill by war, dies

- Japanese women making progress in social sphere

- Russian cruiser sunk by Germans all aboard lost

- Headlights on autos opposed

- Treason admitted by two assassins of Austrian leader

- "Laughing Gas" and oxygen cause new "Twilight Sleep"

- Detroit women collect clothing to aid Belgians

- First boats pass through new lock and (Panama) Canal at 500

- Great new gold field is reported found in Alaska

- Edison comes to Detroit as guest of Ford
  - "Electrical wizard" with family motors from New Jersey home
  - Travels on date of invention of carbon light 35 years ago

- Duty-free imports make great gains

- Automobile makers wear wide smiles, business is fine

- Republicans to make good gains in next Congress

- Federal banking system to begin on Nov. 16

- Detroit's gift to Belgium's relief, 23,910 garments

- Prince Maurice of Battenberg is killed in battle; Cousin of King George first member of British Royal family slain

- Actual assassin of Archduke gets term of 20 years; four plotters, however, get death

- Plan car service over double deck Belle Isle bridge
  - Traffic survey engineers offer scheme to end congestion

St. Paul Pioneer Press

- Agreement on new depot plans near

- Permanent peace of Mexico looked for in capital

- Nation's at war seek to place big orders for supplies here

- Proposed gasoline tax is eliminated

- Assessments against auto is substituted in war revenue; bill in Senate

- Shooting in Dublin is called illegal

- Get pension after 25 years' service (teachers)

- American flag will fly today to urge peace

- Third week of battle ends without decision, violent fighting continues in Roye district; front goes north, French reported in Arras

- Autos included in War Tax bill; senate committee cuts Gasoline Tax

- British and Norsk steamers sunk by mines in North Sea

- Calls (Pancho) Villa only capable Mexican

- Scenes on European Battlefields depicted by camera and brush – submarine rescues sailors off Helgoland after first naval fight

- Thousands to pray today – St. Paul will ask end of War

- War will put damper on winter's social life

- Implements of war for beauty spots – women decorate faces and veils with aeroplanes, zeppelins, battle ship, Uhlans' heads and deadly artillery types

- Army and Navy officials make effort to arrange big football game

- Crime prevention rests with schools, declare prison reform workers

- Red Cross doctor treats wounded with shells bursting above

- Titanic survivor suicide – Mrs. Annie Robinson jumps overboard while Trans-Atlantic line is running through fog

- Braves smash every record, win Series in four straight

- German advance brings war nearer to Britain; heaviest and most important fight is raging in West Flanders and across French frontline

- Headlight problem becoming serious; urgent need of solution is daily evident, says Mitchell May – travelers are in danger; glare too great for comfort of others on road at same time

- Advertisement: Fish for Beef – Protein content of meat and fish;

You housewives are familiar with the vast difference in price but be sure you get Booth Fish – direct to you from Booth; iron-clad sanitary fishing vessels – it's fresh, wholesome and delicious
Booth Fisheries Co. – Seafood - Branches in all principal cities

- Democrats are pinning their faith on Pres. Wilson

- Secluded nook at Depot mecca for sweethearts
  - They're allowed five minutes in the kissing niche

- Archduke's slayers guilty of treason

- Sir Ernest Shackleton sends farewell as he plunges into Antarctic

OCTOBER 1914

◆

LETTERS

Postmark: 12:30 a.m. Oct. 2, 1914, Detroit, Mich.

Addressed to: Mr. Chas. W. Turner, c/o Booth Fisheries - Dot on envelope flap

Oct. 1/14.

My Dear Hildred, -

Just a line as I was called out, then again I did not have time to finish washing my machine this AM and I want to get at it again so this will be about as long a letter as you sent to me on Tuesday and they say fair exchange is no robbery.

Results for Sept. are charged $295.50 took in $237.00 had a dandy no. of new patients last month, but their ailments were very minor.

Don't forget to send me those pictures, I would surely be pleased to receive them.

Well this is the big month, as to your question as to whether I talk in my sleep you will have an opportunity to find out for yourself this month. Just think I only have 25 more nights to sleep with my lonesome then I will have a little wifie to hug up to.

Will you send the announcement & the invitation to the two Miss Malins to Gladstone Ave. Detroit instead of 495 3rd. Ave. Just found out they have moved, one of these girls is going to be married in Jany. and the other a little later.

Love & Kisses to my Sweetheart

Lovingly,

Chas.

Postmark: 4:30 p.m. Oct. 2, 1914, Detroit, Mich.

Addressed to: Miss H.L. Cress, c/o Booth Fisheries - No dot on envelope flap

Oct. 2nd/14

My Dear Sweetheart, -

Did not hear from you this AM, but hope I get a nice long letter when the mail man comes again. It is so long since I have had any news to speak of from you that I hardly know what to write about, so may be my letter will be a little short today.

Business is punk so may be we will have to live on punk before long. Everybody is talking about hard times the automobile factories are only working about half time. I do not wish the Emperor any body [sic] luck but I wish some one would put him out of business for a while, so that the war would stop and business would go ahead, then in all probability instead of talking about hard times we would be talking about how good business was.

So instead of news today I am sending millions and millions of kisses & hugs and a great big hug & kiss.

Lovingly,

Chas.

(PS)

Give me some news to write about Sunday Hildred CW.H. (in your letter)

Postmark: 9 a.m. Oct. 3, 1914, St. Paul, Minn.

Friday evening

My dear Lover:

I know I will not have time to write to you tomorrow so I will try and make up for it tonight.

I am enclosing a sample of the goods I bought today, at first I thought it might be a little heavy but the folks don't think so. What do you think and do you like the shade of blue? (**Editor's Note:** *the sample did not survive*)

Claribel is up to choir practice tonight, I guess I have about deserted the ship.

I made my third attempt at baking powder biscuits last night. I vowed if they didn't turn out good I would never try again. I told mamma to stay in the kitchen to tell me if I did anything wrong but guess I managed all right and they turned out good but the other two times, oh they were awful, hard as bullets and dad said I should make these for you when I had a grudge against you so when you see baking powder biscuits look out, you know what it means.

Last evening, mamma, Claribel and I were making chrysanthemums out of yellow tissue paper, we are going to put them around the lights in the dining room, those in the ceiling. We haven't put them up to see what they look like as yet but if they do not make too dim a light, we may put them around the other lights. What do you think?

Goodbye dear until Sunday then I will write a long letter again. I don' suppose I will get much of a letter Sunday. I mean it won't be long because you did not hear from me Friday but I am not going to let that happen again.

Just loads and loads of hugs and kisses and a couple of extra big ones.

Ever lovingly,

Hildred.

———◆———

Postmark: 5 p.m. Oct. 3, 1914, Detroit, Mich.

Addressed to: Mr. Chas. W. Turner, c/o Booth Fisheries - Dot on envelope flap

Oct. 3rd/14.

My Dear Sweetheart, -

Needless to say that I was pleased to get your letter this AM. after not hearing from you yesterday, but I feel sure you would not have failed to write to me if it were at all possible for you to do so. Another thing if when you stay at home instead of not writing to me at night you will write to me in the morning and mail your letter in the afternoon, then I will get your letter in the morning. When no letter comes in the morning and I have to wait until afternoon I just can't describe how I do feel to you. I would rather be dead than feel that way very long. Yesterday I felt glad when I got to sleep and could forget my thoughts.

Thanks for the pictures, I know you are wearing your hair the latest style but honestly

I like the way you wore it last spring as in the large picture you sent a great deal better, Mother likes it better too. What do your people say, or do they say anything about it. Which way do you like best.

You did not say whether or not we were going to leave from St. Paul or Mpls.in your letter, but let me know. Will do my best about going to St. Paul a day or so earlier, would surely like to, but I will be in a better position to say more a little later on.

Am getting a number of new patients, but there isn't very much wrong with them, only see them once, next month they will have something more wrong with them, then I will be busier.

Well Hildred in three more weeks we can or will be able to give each other some truly hugs and kisses won't that be great.

Now in regard to your trunk you can buy your ticket and get your trunk checked and tell them not to call for your trunk until Tuesday Oct. 27 and then your people can pack your wedding dress and etc. in it. I did the same thing here for Aunt Lizzie. The trunk will be checked by the transfer people and when they come to get the trunk they will then put the check on.

All my love and kisses to my Dear Sweetheart.

Lovingly,

Chas.

───────────◆───────────

Postmark: Oct. 4, 1914, St. Paul, Minn.

Enclosure: Newspaper clipping – Are You a Candy Drunkard?

Oct. 1st, 1914

My dearest Sweetheart:

I am sorry I did not write to you yesterday but I fully planned on writing in the evening. Mr. Turner dictated an immense bunch of letters before he left Tuesday and it took me all yesterday morning to write them. I went to lunch with Mrs. Turner, then to the matinee and then she asked me to stay and have dinner with her. After dinner Harriet went out and I stayed with Mrs. Turner until 9:30 and was going to leave then but Mrs. Turner said she supposed she would have to sit up until twelve o'clock alone, waiting for Harriet as she was afraid to go to bed alone. I told her if she was afraid, I would stay with her and she seemed real pleased, in fact said she would be glad if I would stay but that is how I missed writing to my sweetheart.

Just think dear, this is the first day of October! If it will only be as glorious a day on the 26th as it is today, it will be great! Honestly, I don't know what I would do if it were more than three weeks, you were with me every minute last night. I dreamed of you all night. In one of my dreams we were on the train, going to Detroit and when I woke up and found myself in bed I was disappointed because I was standing still, thought the train ought to be going.

As to buying our tickets, Mr. Turner says not to bother sending any money, he will get them and you can pay him when you come, the same with the flowers, etc.

Business sure is slack compared with last month but cheer up, you are doing great anyway and we never need starve if you can keep up that good work. I keep up my prayer right along but think I will change it along about the 20th of this month so you will come a few days sooner. Don't you think you can come about Saturday or at least Sunday? Of course Saturday would be best yet, please try and make it then.

I guess there are lots of weddings in Detroit too. I thought the doctor building across the street was married, I imagined him a middle aged man. One of the boys out at the park is going to be married tonight, Kirk Hillman, Alice's brother, I know his bride to be by sight but that is all. I guess it is to be quite a swell affair from all I hear. One of the other girls I know is going to be married in about two weeks, it seems everybody is getting married.

I thought I told you about Mrs. Morgan, she just had her and his family. Her father isn't living and they just have a three room apartment so she couldn't have a wedding. Mr. Morgan couldn't get away in time to practice for a church wedding, he came Sunday and they were married Wednesday. The funniest thing, Marion used to go to the Methodist Church before Dr. Stevens was pastor and she wanted him to marry them. She gave him her name and address and if he didn't go and lose it. The night of the wedding about twenty minutes to eight Dr. Stevens called me up and said, "For goodness sake can you give me that girl's name and address I am supposed to marry tonight?" He said he had seen me with her quite often and wondered if I couldn't help him out. Luckily I could but it sure struck me funny and I told him to be sure and remember where we lived and he said he had that planted so firmly, he couldn't forget it. He is more fun than a circus, not like a minister at all.

As to your note, Mr. Turner will fix that up as soon as he returns, possibly Saturday, and send you the old notes, guess I will pay him the interest then, not I but you.

As to getting a bracelet for Claribel, mind you don't get anything so expensive now. She hasn't any idea she is going to get something so nice from her future brother-in-law to be. She would like one quite narrow and as to the pattern, just suit yourself because I would not know what to say.

You bet I remember you have a birthday in November, the 20th isn't it? I will have to get something nice for you to make up for the beautiful things you have given me.

I am sending a few pictures of yours truly, that we took that Sunday, do you think they look like me? [**Editor's Note:** *no photos are enclosed*]

Also enclosing a clipping from Mrs. Turner. She warns me every time she sees me not to let you eat so much candy. She says you are going to make me buy a box every time I go down town and she believes it. She thinks I eat too much too.

I must go to the dressmakers now, second fitting. Please write a long letter to me will you, and I won't skip another day.

All the love and kisses in the whole world to my dear hubby (26th).

Lovingly,

Hildred

XXXX

OOOO

ⒺⒺⒺⒺ

Enclosure:

Are You A Candy Drunkard?

Doctor Says That Headache is Due to Too Many Chocolates.

Indianapolis, June 17. – Dr. J.C. Mitchell of Louisville, Ky., addressing the National Eclectic Medical association today, said the matinee girl who eats a pound of chocolates and goes to a doctor the next day was merely getting over the effects of a "drunk."

"Too much sugar in the stomach will ferment as surely as in a distiller's vat," he said.

◆

Postmark: 7:30 p.m. Oct. 4, 1914, Detroit, Mich.

Addressed to: Mr. Chas. W. Turner, c/o Booth Fisheries - Dot on envelope flap

Sunday A.M.

To the Best Sweetheart Ever, -

I just wish it was the end of the week after next, glad the 26th is no farther distant anyway.

It surely is another dandy day, Don't you wish you were here to go for a ride. Going to leave in a few minutes to meet Mother and give her a ride home from Church.

Business is just keeping company with its self expect to be a little busier tomorrow.

After I get through today I am going to do some posting into my Ledger.

Don't forget to let me know what you have decided to do in regard to leaving from Mpls. Also let me know what you did on Sunday Oct. 4 suppose you had another auto ride.

This AM I got up at 6:15 AM put a little more air in my tires, oiled my car, then put a new gasket under the engine bed so that I would not lose so much oil, so far it has held alright, before I was losing ten to fifteen cents worth of oil every day. And it surely runs up into money at that rate. Anyway I got busy, are you going to let me get up early Sunday mornings to work around my car after you get here.

Will write more tomorrow. Millions and millions of hugs and kisses to my sweetheart and a great big hug & kiss.

Lovingly,

Chas.

(I hurried can you read my writing)

———————◆———————

Postmark: 10:30 a.m. Oct. 5, 1914, St. Paul, Minn.

Typed envelope – return envelope from Booth's Cold Storage

Sunday evening

My dear Hubby:

I have ransacked the house for some writing paper and this is all I can find, guess I will have to put in a new supply.

I must not forget to put the results for September down in my little book tomorrow. Congratulations, you certainly are doing fine considering the so-called "hard times." Why couldn't it have been $300.00 though, it would have looked so much larger. Just think this month you will not need to write me the results, I will be with you at the end of the month.

I have surely been lonesome for you today, lonesome as can be. Was good this morning, we all went to church with the exception of dad, he had to go to the office. This was Peace Sunday and also Fraternal Sunday. The church was decorated simply great and they had a lot of extra music, solos etc. This afternoon I tried to take a nap, had a headache but couldn't get to sleep. This afternoon about 4 P.M. two of the girls, Hazel Law and Ethel Crosby came over, stayed here a while and from here we went to call on Alice and Hattie Miles. From there we went to Ethel's for supper, then we girls done the dishes. I washed, Hazel dried them and Ethel put them away so it did not take long. After that we were playing and singing. Ethel and her brother walked as far as Fairview and Selby Ave. with us and there we met Vera and Andy. (They were married this last Spring.) Hazel took the car from there and Vera and Andy walked home with me, they live just three blocks from us on Ashland Ave. We wanted Claribel to go along with us but she was not feeling very well. She was down to see the doctor every day last week and has to go again tomorrow.

Next week or rather this week will be a busy one, Wednesday night mamma and I have to go to the dressmakers, Thursday night Elizabeth Kennedy is going to entertain for me, about ten girls and one night this week some friends of ours from Minneapolis are coming over. Their name is Erichseu, papa has known them ever since he was married, they were neighbors. Next week Ethel Crosby and Alice Miles are going to give a shower for me, that will be two nights and I suppose a couple to the dressmaker. This is some strenuous life I am leading lately, getting to be a regular "gad-about."

Say, little Marcella wants to be a flower girl. She and her mother were at the church to see Alice's wedding and when she saw the two little flower girls she wanted to do that too. She has a little white dress, and mamma will get the little basket of flower for her. You know she has always had a horror for doctors so I told her maybe she would get scared when she saw you. She said she wouldn't though, that she had seen you before and liked you, that you were different than the others. I think you are different than the others too and won't I be happy to see you, I hope three weeks from today or yesterday, would be better still.

I can't begin to tell you of all the hugs and kisses I send, just imagine all you can manage. I will be glad to get the real thing some day in place of the imaginary kind, won't you? Now goodnight dear, with an extra big "swack" from

Hildred

———————◆———————

Postmark: 12:30 a.m. Oct. 6, 1914, Detroit, Mich.

Addressed to: Mr. Chas. W. Turner, C/o Booth Fisheries - Dot on envelope flap

Monday Afternoon

Dearest Sweetheart, -

Before I forget Mother said to ask you if you would find out from Aunt Lizzie how she tints the lace curtains that is a cream color and if you will let her know as soon as convenient.

I surely think that sample of blue is just dandy, thank you for sending it, Guess I am going to have a pretty swell wifie and I certainly want you to look tip top always even if we do owe some money.

I will be glad when you leave the office think you couldn't stand that pace very long. Just going to work next week then quit aren't you? Let me know.

Amused me to read about those baking powder biscuits. By the way I think if I get indigestion you may face the same way; however I have some good indigestion medicine in the house.

I have something I would most awfully like to tell you, however you will find out pretty soon, so please do not ask me what it is, because I do not want you to know about it just yet. Just had to tell you this much anyway.

Made $12.50 this AM expect to make $4 or 5 more today anyway.

Yesterday while taking Mother over to the cemetery a big sharp stone one of those they had leveled off the road with cut into my casing and I guess I will have to have the place vulcanized, surely hate to spend money on things like that just now.

Just interrupted, as a patient came in and paid me $10.00 can't kick about that can I, have taken in $20.00 so far today.

A friend of mine came over last night and took me to church in his machine, we went to the First Baptist Church, they certainly have some preacher, at 6:30 o'clock in the evening the church is crowded and the people sit there until 7:30 that is when the service commences and it is the largest church in the city. Will take you over there and you ought to hear how they applaud when church is over, the preacher is certainly a great orator.

All the love in the world to my Dear Sweetheart and a Great big hug & kiss. Send me lots of love Hildred

Lovingly,

Chas.

———————◆———————

Postmark: 10 a.m. Oct. 6, 1914, St. Paul, Minn.

Return envelope: Booth Fisheries

Monday evening

My dear Sweetheart: –

I simply can't get time it seems to write to you during the day, there is something to do every minute, and at noon hours I am kept busy shopping. You can't accomplish much in an hour either.

Tonight we have been busy addressing the invitations and part of the announcements, guess we will mail invitations Wed.

I am enclosing a sample of goods, [sample did not survive] this is about the shade of my suit

but not the same goods. Mrs. Turner decided between this and a black silk, finally took the black.

I am going to have more than I can put in my trunk so how would it be if I packed some of my things in a box and sent them on ahead, by freight?

It is after 11:30 – don't be shocked – so I will answer your letter tomorrow, hope to be more wide awake then. Just three weeks from tonight dear and things will be exciting. I hope they go quick.

The most love ever from

Hildred

———————◆———————

Postmark: 3:30 p.m. Oct. 6, 1914, Detroit, Mich.

Addressed to: Miss H.L. Cress, c/o Booth Fisheries - No dot on envelope flap

Envelope empty

———————◆———————

Postmark: 7:30 p.m. Oct. 6, 1914, St. Paul, Minn.

Tuesday afternoon

My dear Sweetheart:

I am just stealing a little time, should really be busy as I have a big bunch of letters today but I would rather write to you.

I don't know just what to do as to staying in St. Paul or Mpls. sometimes I think we might as well stay in St. Paul. Mr. Turner of course doesn't say anything but he does say he could get us a room without registering at all here.

As to the way I wear my hair. I got tired of having it the one way all the time, but if it pleases you better the old way, I will wear it that way again, it will be just like a change again.

You surely get up early for Sunday mornings but after I get there it will be quite late, starting to get cold and it don't get light so quick, so maybe you will be willing to stay in bed a wee bit longer, six o'clock is early for Sunday don't you think so?

Mr. Gladding an oyster man from the East is here today. Mr. Turner has taken him to

Mpls. in the car for the afternoon. He surely is interesting to talk too [sic]. I know all about the oyster business now.

I am going to write more tomorrow. I forgot, I am sending a new note today, as soon as Mr. Turner gets the old one here I will forward it but in the meantime you can sign this one and return. Mister, but don't I wish I could find a couple of thousand in some corner!

All the love and kisses to my dear sweetheart, from

Hildred

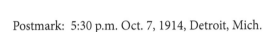

Postmark: 5:30 p.m. Oct. 7, 1914, Detroit, Mich.

Addressed to: Mr. Chas. W. Turner, c/o Booth Fisheries - Dot on envelope flap

Oct. 7th/14.

My Dear Wifie, -

Rec'd your Sunday letter today, and am still on the look out for your Monday letter, but surely hope that you wrote on Monday.

I am just half inclined to write to Mr. Turner as much as I think he is working you too hard. I surely hope you quit Saturday Oct. 17th let me know, will you.

As I said before I would most awfully like to tell you something but please don't ask me what it is until Oct. 28th/14. After we get home.

Don't believe I will make as much money this month as what I did last month in fact I just know I won't, however I will make expenses anyway, outside of the wedding etc.

Claribel is sure slow getting better, hope she improves right along.

The weather is so nice that I don't see how anybody can possibly get sick, but they will commence to quit [illegible] in 6 or 8 wks. more here's hoping Eh! Of course I do not wish anybody bad luck, but you know the way it is.

Spent $7.70 getting my car fixed had to buy a new back wheel, however had I have been insured the insurance coy [company] would not have taken care of it because the damage was under $20.00. Subrosa [sic] wifie!

All kinds of love and kisses to my sweetheart and a great big hug & kiss.

Lovingly,

Chas.

Postmark: 10:30 a.m. Oct. 8, 1914, St. Paul, Minn.

Wednesday evening

Dearest Sweetheart:

I am glad you like the goods for my blue dress but don't know as I will be what you call swell, it was a case of necessity. I think it will be pretty when it is made up. I will wear that when I go down to the train to meet you which I hope will be Saturday or Sunday.

As to how long I will work, guess I will just work until a week from Saturday but my how I hate to lose that last fifteen dollars. Mr. Turner had another application for my job today from Duluth, it makes me feel kind of funny to see them come in, guess I am kind of jealous of the position and I hate to see anybody else come to take my place. That makes about half a dozen applications so far. Mr. Turner says he doesn't know just what he will do yet, he may take Miss Oestreich (Haystack) though.

You sure have me on the anxious seat now and it is a shame to tell me not to ask any questions of you regarding your secret because I am just burning up with curiosity. What is it about? When will I find out? I think you might tell me a wee bit about it anyway.

Business surely was pretty good Monday, wish every day would be that good.

I got two letters today, one just before we went home tonight so guess I won't get any tomorrow. Mr. Lucius was in the office when it came and I didn't want to open it until after he had gone but actually I was worried for a while until I opened it, thought maybe something had happened to my sweetheart. Guess something did almost happened when you went sliding around, now do be careful Charlie so nothing happens to you because that would be terrible. Maybe you better have that back axle fixed.

Elizabeth's father – Mr. Goodjohn – is here for a couple of weeks vacation, he has been on the sick list more or less all summer. I tell you I have been teased a lot since we are engaged but that man takes the cake – to be slangy. He starts in from the time he comes in the office until he leaves and I get so rattled I hardly know where I am. He has been here about two days now.

I just wish you know how much love and kisses I send, just millions. I am storing up a big bunch to give you when I see you, maybe you will get tired of so many though.

Lovingly,

Hildred

———————◆———————

Postmark: 9 a.m. Oct. 9, 1914, St. Paul, Minn.

Return envelope from Booth Fisheries - Typed

St. Paul, Minn., October 9th, 1914

Sweetheart Dear: -

I just couldn't write yesterday afternoon and I planned on writing you a little short letter after I got home last night from Elizabeth's but we didn't get home until so late or rather early, that I thought I had better get right to bed. It was a little after one o'clock when Claribel and I got home but we did the best we could to get away earlier. I surely had a pleasant surprise, will tell you all about it in my today's letter and I will write it this afternoon no matter what happens.

I must get this into the mail or you won't get it so goodbye sweetheart and just "oodles" and "oodles" of love and kisses to you.

Lovingly,

H i l d r e d

———————◆———————

Postmark: 7 p.m. Oct. 9, 1914, St. Paul, Minn.

Return envelope: Booth Fisheries

Friday, Oct. 9, 1914

My dear Sweetheart:

I am going to try and finish this most awfully hard, before I go home tonight but don't you write Mr. Turner about working me to hard whatever you do. I admit I have had quite a bit to do by my goodness not enough that I would think of complaining. He would think I was a great one if you did such a stunt. Yesterday and today have not been quite as bad as usual because Mr. Turner has been here a week this time and he is about talked out.

Now I think you might give me just a little suggestion as to what that secret is you are going to tell me on the 28th. If you knew how my curiosity was aroused, I just know you would tell me. Why can't you tell me now, if not now please tell me when you come to St. Paul, won't you? Just think how long until the 28th.

I was going to tell you about the little affair at Elizabeth's last evening. She told me it was just a little party and when we got there, all the girls from the office were there and the two from the retail and three other girls that I know quite well that used to work here. During the course of the evening it turned out to be a shower, a regular surprise party to me. I got some dandy things, they made me sit on the floor to open them, I got six linen towels, one with crocheted lace, several with my initials and other plain. Also four heavy big bath towels, 2 painted plates, a vase, sandwich basket, butter knife, sugar-shell and a little mayonnaise dish. Really, I was so surprised I couldn't say a thing for a few minutes. The party was at Elizabeth's sister's house on Oakland Hill, you know where that is, where the Grand Ave. car runs and the way Mr. Turner usually goes home. It is about like Christmas time, getting so many pretty things.

I pretty near lost part of my heart yesterday. I found I simply had to get another pair of shoes the ones I am wearing are all inski [sic] and am actually ashamed and of course I didn't want to wear my good ones. I limited myself to $3.00 but dad wanted to go along. Well I tried on $3.00 shoes but dad didn't like them so the man tried on a $4.00 shoe and dad wanted me to take it right away said he would pay the extra dollar but I wasn't to say anything so I have the $4.00 shoes. I think they are a bit large now that I have them but better that way I guess than pinch my feet.

I have taken up ten minutes of the company's time now, it is after one so guess I must get busy again.

Oh! won't I be glad for some kisses again. I can hardly wait any more. Do try to come Sat. or Sunday won't you, we will have to start all over to learn how to spoon, so long since we have had any practice. Just millions and millions of kisses & hugs to my dear hubby,

Lovingly

Hildred

◆

Postmark: 7:30 p.m. Oct. 9, 1914, Detroit, Mich.

Addressed to: Mr. Chas. W. Turner, c/o Booth Fisheries - Dot on envelope flap

Oct. 8, 14.

My Dear Hildred, -

Just a few lines as I am closely watching after something else, but I will write more tomorrow.

Inclosed [sic] you will find the note with my John Henry on it. Glad I don't have to pay any more interest until March anyway.

Now in regard to sending the box in advance, send it right along and I will be on the look out for it, jump inside yourself, then I will be more anxious than ever.

Had a letter from Leonard, he does not think a business suit would be suitable for him to wear if he stands up with me and he does not care to buy a suit that will be of no particular after use to him hence he requests that I get somebody else to stand up with me, I surely wish you would write to him and try and persuade him different. I have written him twice, but it seems as though he will not take any heed at what I say or try to tell him.

If it is not to [sic] late and if I did not give you the name of Miss Wiehelmina Weighing St. Paul. Ave. Detroit I wish you would send her an announcement.

Just ever so much love & kisses to my Dear Sweetheart and millions more, soon see you won't I, and a great big hug & kiss.

Lovingly

Chas.

———————◆———————

Postmark: 12:30 a.m. Oct. 10, 1914, Detroit, Mich.

Addressed to: Miss H.L. Cress, c/o Booth Fisheries - No dot on envelope flap

Friday Afternoon

Dearest Sweetheart,

Have not heard from you today therefore cannot write very much, hope you have not forgotten about writing.

I suppose this coming week ends your type writing career let me know.

Meant to write you in regard to the way you were doing your hair before, but let me say this don't change your method of doing it on my account, because I too when I see you other than in a picture may like the way you are doing it at present as well as you do.

Just think that in a little over two weeks you will be my really truly wifie, does this all seem real to you, can only write you about 13 times more.

Will write you more after I hear from you. Write me about ten pages Sunday Hildred.

All kinds of love and kisses to my sweetheart and a great big hug & kiss.

Lovingly

Chas.

———————◆———————

Postmark: 11 p.m. Oct. 10, 1914, Detroit, Mich.

Addressed to: Mr. Chas. W. Turner, c/o Booth Fisheries - Dot on envelope flap

Saturday Afternoon

Dearest Sweetheart,

Seemed good to hear from you this AM after not getting a letter yesterday.

Note you are going to quit the office a week from today and that you hate to see some one else take your place, never mind you will be far, far away from that office position before long, and in time may be you will forget considerable about it.

Now Hildred you know I particularly requested you not to ask me about that secret you will surely know it in about sixteen days, and you know right well I can hardly keep from telling you. And this is one thing I do not want or would rather not let wifie know about it just yet. Now if you coax me too much I in all probability will give in but I surely want to surprise you.

This is surely one rainy day rained all morning and I made $0. How's that this afternoon so far I have made $7.00 and taken in $11.75. Don't think I will let you know my results the end of this month may be I will be ashamed to may possible make a little more tonight although it is still raining which makes business bad.

Be sure and send me lots of love Hildred, guess I could live on love.

Next week I am going to get a few more things ready not leave everything until the last minute. Just think after tomorrow only one more Sunday to spend in Detroit.

Millions & Millions of hugs & kisses to my sweetheart and a great big hug & kiss.

Lovingly,

Chas.

Postmark: 5 p.m. Oct. 11, 1914, St. Paul, Minn.

Return Envelope: Booth Fisheries

Saturday evening.

My dear Hubby:

Really I was so blue after hearing from you today, I would have given anything to have a good cry and get it over with. You don't know how that news regarding Leonard made me feel. I don't say how they can get the idea it is going to be such a swell wedding because I am sure I haven't said anything to make them think that way and it isn't either. If he has a dark business suit, that is positively all that is necessary. Of course I told Mr. Turner about it, in fact read that portion of your letter to him so he said he would write him, thought it would do more good than my writing him. He also told him it would be hard at this late date to get somebody else to stand up and that I was very much worried over it which I truly am. To cap it all, Mr. Turner said he believes the real reason your mother was not coming was account of my having a silk dress and veil and thinking it was to "swell." To have them both feel that way, it makes me feel – well, I don't know how – but mighty blue anyway. If I had had the least idea that silk dress was going to raise such unpleasant features I would have sure let the old thing go, don't think I will like it at all now anyway. I wish we had just run away and got married that's what I do, not told anybody we were engaged or anything. If we had done that we wouldn't have had to buy any new clothes, would we? I hope I feel better about this tomorrow.

Your note came today, think I will have the old one to send tomorrow or at least by Monday. We will have to get busy right away and pay up these things but it will be fun anyway, planning together where we can save a dollar, don't you think so?

Had an invitation to go to a Hayrack Party tonight, if you were here I would have liked to go but not without my sweetheart.

You can't imagine the dandy treat I had, Mr. Goodjohn bought me a box of "Smith's" today and said he didn't know what the Doctor would say but he would be out of town when you get here, so he didn't mind. It is such good candy, wish you could enjoy it with me.

I thought I was going to have such a dandy day of rest tomorrow, wasn't even going to church but now Mr. Turner wants me to come down in the morning to write the letters that come in, otherwise we are all cleaned up. He is leaving tomorrow evening for Omaha and St. Louis, suppose he will be gone most of the week. One day I will stay home, guess I can find enough to do with the rest of the time, want to straighten out his Sept. checks haven't even found time for that, transfer all letters from the files to the store room, fix up the summary of the branch house balance sheets, clear out all drawers in the office and fix everything up to the new "steno." That is the only thing I dislike about getting married, I hate to think of anybody else taking my position. I wonder who it will be! Mr. Turner says he actually hasn't given it much thought, but maybe he will give one of the girls in the office a trial, says he thinks they are in line for advancement.

I haven't packed that box as yet but will let you know when it is sent. Can't you possibly come Friday or Saturday? If business is not so rushing now you can manage to get away can't you? Please try and get here Saturday morning the latest. Then too we can practice before Monday because as mamma says, there will be so much to do the last day both for you and at the house that it will be hard to practice the last thing Monday. With Leonard it doesn't make any difference just so he knows where to stand because he won't have to come from upstairs and really all he has to do is look on.

My Milwaukee chum, Elizabeth Gregory wants us to stop off at Milwaukee on our way to Detroit or else let us know when we go through so she can come to the depot to see us when we go through. I would not think of stopping off, but should we let her know when we go through? She is not a girl that would raise a rumpus, though [sic] rice etc. but just the same maybe it would be better to go right through and say nothing. What do you think?

I felt rather "grippee" tonight so dad gave me a hot "toddy" to ward it off because I sure don't want to catch cold now, above all things. I look bad enough anyway.

I asked Claribel if she had any message for you and she said, "Sure, tell him 'good night' it is time for you to come to bed."

Just two weeks from today I am figuring on some really, truly kisses and you won't disappoint me will you? Please let me meet you Saturday morning, the earlier the better. Oh! just loads and loads and loads of kisses dear, I can't begin to tell you how many. Send me lots of them, won't you?

Lovingly

Hildred

[In margin] Don't forget, you are to tell me something of that secret, can hardly wait to hear it. H.C.

P.S.

Sent out the invitations in the city today, out of town ones on Wednesday last. Have also added Miss Weighing's name to the announcements.

"Wifie"

———————◆———————

Postmark: 8:30 p.m. Oct. 11, 1914, Detroit, Mich.

Addressed to: Miss H.L. Cress, c/o Booth Fisheries - No dot on envelope flap

Sunday A.M.

Dearest Sweetheart, -

Just two weeks from today and there will be something doing. Let me know whether or not you are going to be nervous, now supposing when the train pulls in there is another young girl down there looking for her hubby to arrive and I mistake her for you and she also in the excitement makes a mistake and you find me kissing her what will you say, you won't run away and look for her hubby, or will you? And another thing, I like to bite ears pretty well. Mother can tell you that, and supposing I get excited and bite your ear clean off, better get some ear protectors, I suppose if I bite your ears you will do what Mother does tickle my ribs.

Today is nice and shiney [sic] after our rain of yesterday, only made $2.50 this PM. But yesterday AM it was $0. In afternoon however I got busy and made up for it.

This morning I was up at 6 AM and worked on my [illegible] until 7:30. Suppose when it gets real cold I will [illegible] on this early morning business. May be my wife will kick on it too. This afternoon I don't know what I will do will think it over after dinner.

Now in regard to you sending the box on ahead if you are going to do that it would be a good idea if you would send it sometime this week then it would arrive before I leave.

You surely are late going to bed some nights, if you keep up the present pace you will be getting dark circles under your eyes and a wrinkled forehead.

Just imagine the most hugs and kisses ever sent, and a great big hug and kiss and millions more.

Lovingly,

Chas.

◆

Postmark: October 12, 1914, St. Paul, Minn.

Sunday evening.

My dear Sweetheart:

I am surely going to get to bed early enough tonight, it is only seven O'Clock and I am all ready for bed. I am awfully tired though it has been all of 11:30 and twelve every night this week and still I can't see that I have accomplished anything. Next week I won't have to keep such late hours so don't scold.

Have had a busy Sunday, really feel kind of guilty don't tell anybody when I tell you all I have done. This morning of course I was down at the office, took pretty near fifty pages of dictation so I have a nice start for tomorrow. After dinner Mamma suggested we pack my things so we could do it in daylight. I thought papa was going to send out one big box but instead he sent out two smaller ones, said they would hold together better so there will be two boxes arriving instead of one. The first day that the Boston truck comes out this far we will send them and I will let you know when to expect them. My things surely look nice when they are all together. I have two old relics that dad is going to send for me. I will never want to use them in our home but just have them as keep sakes. One is a picture of my great great grandfather and the other a picture of myself at about a year old so I would kind of like to keep track of it.

Tomorrow night I have to go to the dress makers again, honestly I pretty near live there it seems.

Tuesday Mr. Turner has given me as a day of leisure but I am going to help the housekeepers with the cleaning. They surely have been just great to me lately and nobody could expect more of them, when mama is good natured she couldn't be beat.

*I am enclosing the old note to you, wish it were all canceled but it wouldn't take us long will it? (**Editor's Note:** This note does not survive) How are you making out this month? Do try and come Friday or Saturday the latest won't you? One day can't make so terribly much difference but it does to me because I can hardly wait to see you. Just two weeks, no I can't realize it, don't suppose I will until we are really married.*

I expect to work this next week and then stay home the last week. I tell you what, write me two letters on Friday, address one to the office and one to me at the house then I will get one Monday too, if you don't write until Saturday to the house I won't get it until Tuesday morning, don't think so anyway. Of course when you are writing to the house address their [sic] to me.

As to the way I wear my hair, I change off but it doesn't make any difference to me the folks like it the later way but I will wear it which ever way you like it best.

Flora is going to mail some letters so will close so she can take this with her. Hope you wrote a long letter today. I will have to wrap all your letters up and bring them along in my trunk, I couldn't part with them. All the kisses and hugs ever to my dear hubby.

Lovingly,

Hildred.

P.S. Is your mother really not coming just on account of my having a silk dress? I can't get this out of my mind, feel awfully bad about it. H.C.

———————◆———————

Postmark: 12:30 a.m. October 13, 1914, Detroit, Mich.

Addressed to: Mr. Chas. W. Turner, c/o Booth Fisheries - Dot on envelope flap

Monday Afternoon

Dearest Sweetheart, -

Rec'd your Friday letter this a.m.

Just a few lines as I have been interrupted and am in a hurry to get away at 4 o'clock.

You surely are enjoying yourself with all those surprise parties, and I am certainly missing a whole lot by not being with you, but two weeks from today we will be enjoying ourselves together, won't that be great.

As soon as I write this letter I am going to make a trip away out in the country, Dr. Moon is going to take a ride with me. Will write more tomorrow Hildred.

Just millions of kisses and millions of hugs to my sweetheart and lots more besides.

From your Hubby.
Chas.

◆

Postmark: 9 a.m. Oct. 13, 1914, St. Paul, Minn.

Monday evening

Dearest Sweetheart:

Just two weeks from tonight dear and won't we be happy? That surely isn't very long and I can hardly imagine it to be true. I just close my eyes sometimes and try to imagine it all. I have tried on my wedding dress for the last time until I put it on for our wedding and my only wish is that it will please you because it has caused some disappointment on my part although I like the dress very much.

I packed up all your letters today and put them in a box, will bring them home the first time we come home in the machine again. I read some of the first ones over again, also some of the last ones, the first were simply "dear Friend," but now "Dearest Sweetheart." It isn't very long since I was merely a friend, is it? And it has all happened in a hurry.

I don't know as anybody will be on the scene at our wedding, after dinner tonight I made some "noodles" for chicken noodle soup tomorrow and in the morning I am going to try and make baking powder biscuits for breakfast. I am afraid if it isn't death tomorrow morning it will be at dinner time. Am preparing for the worst.

Mamma and dad were to see the caterer this afternoon, Mr. Ramsley, they know him personally and he gave them somewhat of a reduced price, don't know just how much though. They got the little boxes from him too, to wrap up the wedding cake in because he gave them such a good price. As to the two waiters, they gave me my choice of two girls or the two colored waiters but I think by all means the girls don't you? I can't go those colored people, somehow they give me the creeps, and again they make things so stiff looking I think. The refreshments are unbeknown to me so far although I know there is to be chicken salad, guess I can find out the rest too pretty soon. They sure have been great lately, doing all a person could ask.

Talk about miserable weather, it has been raining and cold all day today and yesterday, I should think it would make lots of people sick, hope it does in Detroit anyway because we need the money, don't we? Be sure and let me know what you make this month whether little or big. Maybe now you can plan on being here Friday, Saturday the latest. Please!!

Goodnight dear I must hurry to bed so I have a clear head for biscuits in the morning. Oh! ever so many hugs and kisses dear and some extra big ones. I can't describe how big but hope to show you a week from Friday or Saturday.

Lovingly,
Hildred

———————◆———————

Postmark: 5:30 p.m. Oct. 13, 1914, Detroit, Mich. Grand River Station

Addressed to: Miss H.L. Cress, c/o Booth Fisheries - Envelope flap missing

Tuesday Afternoon,

Sweetheart Dear, -

Surely pleased to receive your longer letter of Saturday eve. Sorry you had the blues in regard to what I told you about Leonard but don't worry now. I have it all fixed up. Received a letter today from Leonard to the effect that he would take his part. Now in regard to your silk dress, that is just what I wanted you to have so do not pay any attention to what anybody else has to say about it. Now don't worry everything is alright and will be better still if Oct. 26th will only hurry up.

It would be alright for you to let your Milwaukee chum know when we would be passing through as long as she will not raise a rumpus with us. I don't think we pass through Milwaukee proper but just through Milwaukee junction.

Now in regard to that secret it is to be a surprise for you, that is why I do not want to tell you.

As far as arriving in St. Paul is concerned if I had my way about it I would be there today, just why I am holding off a little is because I hate to miss anything because I know we can make use of all our money had I had been away last Saturday I would have missed an accident case, there again I have a couple of patients who come to the office every day for treatment and if I were away so long what would I do with them in all probability I would lose them whereas if I leave on Sunday I could fix them up Sunday AM. and leave Sunday noon, and fix them up Wednesday Eve. and thereby only miss two full days. I could also do the same thing with any patients I had sick at their home, however you can leave it to me Hildred if there is any possible chance of my getting there Saturday or Sunday I will do so. And as I said before I surely wish I were there now.

The weather has turned a little cool today and the leaves are commencing to fall pretty good. So I guess winter is coming alright.

Mother has gone into the city to do some shopping and no patients have called in so far this afternoon so it certainly seems awfully quiet here for your hubby this afternoon.

Hildred I have gotten so much love in store for you that really I don't know how to send it anymore. It consists of just millions & millions of hugs and kisses and more to. And besides that all the love and more than anybody could send and then some more. Now don't worry Hildred everything will come out alright. Just Loads and Loads of hugs and kisses and a great big hug & kiss.

Lovingly,

Chas.

Postmark: 10 a.m. Oct. 14, 1914, St. Paul, Minn.

Hand-written; envelope from Booth Fisheries

St. Paul, Minn.

Oct. 13, 1914

My dear Sweetheart:

I surely got a good supply of mail today, one from my sweetheart, one from your mother, one from Katherine and still another from a girl in Green Bay. I think I shall have to hire a private secretary if this keeps up because I have quite a few others to answer. I hope they keep coming though, because I like to get letters.

Well, I guess we simply can't persuade your mother to come but I sure am sorry about it all. I had so hoped she would change her mind and come anyway.

Will I be nervous in about two weeks, well I should say so. I think I will know you though and if I see you kissing some other girl, I should say I wouldn't look for her hubby b ut she and I would have a battle royal right there. I think this wifie would come out on top too. You better not make any of those kinds of mistakes though, it would be more fun if you didn't.

Some busy day today, we house-cleaned the front room and dining room have everything back in place again. You wouldn't have known your "Scrub Girl" today, sleeves all rolled up, dust cap on etc. and we made the dust fly for a while. I think it is fun when there are a few to help but of course when there is only one to do it all like your mother, it becomes a task. Why didn't she leave it until I got there, I would just love to help her.

I have just spent a good half hour talking with Claribel, she is as good as a circus. They wanted both of we girls to help serve tonight at a reception given for Dr. Stevens and his family but I have to much to attend to now. Claribel went and has been raving ever since she is home. She gets a little slangy once in a while and I wish I knew how many times she said "Gee! The dresses – good night!" She says she hardly knew where to walk, afraid somebody would leave part of their train under her feet, she says. She had to keep skipping around all night. She says most of them were real low necked, satin gowns and she simply couldn't get through talking about it. She wore a little light dress she has always cherished as a pretty nice dress but tonight when she got home she simply rolled it up and threw it in the corner. She says she is going to wash it and hopes it shrinks to the size of a necktie so she won't have to wear it again. I don't think it does her any good to go to these affaires.

Katherine has offered to bring some cedar along with her for decorations if I want her too [sic]. I think it would be great because we had planned on using the oak leaves to a great extent, for on the stairway etc. but it has been so stormy don't think there will be many nice ones left and to buy decorations it comes awfully high. We could have those banked along the rail of the stairway and around the radiator. Papa is going to make a wire arch to go from one end of the radiator to the other in the front room, right in front of the bay window and we are going to twine that with surilax and have the surilax hanging from the arch as sort of a background. These are going to rent a dozen palms and we have made white paper chrysanthemums with the green leaves for all the lights in the parlor and yellow for in the dining room. I have a black and blue spot on my knee from curling chrysanthemums, should have used a pillow but it worked better on my knee.

Well Mr. Turner lost out on his guess as to the ball games. He bet Boston would win the first three, lose the fourth and win the fifth. I was about as excited as he was over the scores. Dr. Lankester is a great fan, you couldn't find him in his office afternoons, he has been watching returns at the Dispatch office. [**Editor's Note:** The Boston Braves swept the World Series against the Philadelphia Athletics in what would be called one of the greatest of all upsets in baseball history. In July, the "miracle Braves" were in last place on July 4, then roared on to win the National League pennant by 10.5 games and sweep the stunned Athletics. Source: Wikipedia]

Well, I simply can't write with Claribel talking away here, I think of something to say and forget it again the next minute.

All the kisses and hugs in the world to the dearest hubby in the world from

Hildred

P.S. Try and come Friday or Saturday, please! H.C.

———————◆———————

Postmark: 9:30 a.m. October 15, 1914, St. Paul Minnesota

Booth Fisheries envelope

Thursday morning

My dear Hubby: -

I have all kinds of news for you but yesterday was awfully busy and after one again before I was off to dreamland. I am going to write you a great big letter today and tell you all the *happenings. I think next week I will have to set my bed time at eight o'clock to make up for all lost time. Just think dear a week from Monday and we can love each other again. I wish putting the clock ahead would hasten the day.*

Ever so many hugs and kisses and a little ear bite too.

Lovingly,
Hildred

———————◆———————

Friday Afternoon.

Dearest Sweetheart,

Rec'd your Tuesday letter last eve.

Say, Hildred – I have just thought of a new stunt that is to let my mustache grow and have one at the time of the big event, wouldn't that be funny and I am pretty sure I can grow one too, and I also think, that possibly you will like your hubby better with than with out a mustache, now let me know right away so I will have a better and longer time to grow one in.

Glad I was not out of the city this morning got two new patients, but you know where I would like to be, just 10 days more then their [sic] will be some hugging & kissing & squeezing won't there?

It has rained nearly every day for a week my car is pretty dirty must wash it up a little next week before I leave.

Now Hildred when I come to St. Paul, if anybody comes down to the train to meet me, that is with you what I would like you to do is to run away ahead of the rest to meet me, so that they will not be just there. Don't you think that would be better?

I think your sister Claribel is quite a tease and another thing when she is like that she will likely be playing some tricks on us, you better watch her pretty close.

Let me know how you felt Saturday when you left the office knowing you would not be going back there anymore to work, did it make you feel blue or did you get the blue willies.

Forgot to tell you that the Lady who came out to see us yesterday brought a half Dozen teaspoons out along with new forks.

Just Loads & Loads of love and Millions and millions of kisses and hugs to my Sweetheart.

Lovingly,
Chas.

———————◆———————

Postmark: 12:30 .m. October 16, 1914, Detroit, Mich.

Addressed to: Mr. Chas. W. Turner, c/o Booth Fisheries - Dot on envelope flap

Oct. 14th/14

My Dear Sweetheart, -

Rec'd your Sunday letter, but no Monday letter as yet.

Now in regard to the boxes you are sending can you give me an idea as to how large they are and whether or not you think I will be able to bring them out to the house in my machine. Also let me know how you are sending them and about when they will arrive.

Now in regard to that silk dress I spoke to Mother about it and she said that has absolutely nothing to do in regard to her not attending the wedding, she says Uncle Chas. imagines a whole lot of things and she seemed very much surprised that he said anything like that.

I purchased a very narrow bracelet for Claribel the inner diameter is just the same size as the hole I have cut in the inclosed [sic] piece of paper [**Editor's Note:** did not survive], it seems to me as though she might not be able to get her hand through such a small place what do you think about it, where I got it they said most any girl could get her hand through a place that size, I got a tie pin for Leonard set with two pearls and an amesthet you know what I mean.

Business is a little better today, if this weather only keeps up, things will pick up a little. Made four calls this AM and have another one to make after my afternoon office hour.

I suppose you did not work Monday in as much as I have not heard from you so far today. Two weeks from today this time I trust we will be nearly back to Detroit. St. Paul will be in the distance My Wifie.

Loads & Loads of hugs & kisses to my wifie and all the love in me.

Lovingly,

Chas.

———◆———

Postmark: 10 a.m. October 16, 1914, St. Paul, Minn.

Thursday evening.

Dearrest Sweetheart:

It is pretty near eleven o'clock again, actually I don't know where all the time goes to but it sure goes somewhere. Mrs. Turner and her brother were over tonight, had planned on ironing but couldn't anymore after they left.

I am sure glad Leonard has decided to stand up for you, actually you don't know how mean it made me feel. I just felt sick all over. I think maybe the reason you say the silk dress is just what you wanted me to have is because you are afraid you may hurt my feelings, if you say otherwise. Isn't that a fact?

As to when you will arrive in St. Paul, of course if you can't make it Saturday or Sunday, it will just have to be Monday but "jingo" I hope it will be Saturday. Cure the patients up so you can come won't you? It really would make it awfully late to practice on Monday because there are so many other things at that time. Leonard and Katherine are planning on coming Sunday so you surely can make it a day sooner. Papa's folks are coming a day sooner too. Let me know a few days ahead what you do but I am not going to coax any more, know you will do all you can to get here.

I had a little note from Marion today and guess – she is living just fifteen minute's walk from your home. Maybe you know where it is, Winslow Ave.? She says she is happy as can be, got the best hubby ever but I can't agree. I know I have. She is busy now washing windows, putting up curtains and putting her house in order. I am anxious to see her again, she is a dandy girl.

Say what do you think, Claribel is to work tomorrow, it all happened in a few minutes. Mrs. Turner told her Dr. Phillips (dentist) was looking for an office girl so off she hiked at five o'clock tonight and is going to work in the morning. His offices are on Prior Ave. so she isn't far from home. I was awfully surprised but she doesn't want to stay home anymore.

The girls had the shower for me last evening and I got some dandy things again. Do you know what they did? They wanted to see who could make the best looking groom and they had a big bunch of heads and men cut out, the heads in one box and bodys [sic] in the last and you had to draw one of each. I wondered why I was last but here they had gotten a picture of yours from Mrs. Turner and cut it in half and I drew that. It was the one where you are holding Katherine's baby, was taken a year ago this summer. You should have heard the girls kid me about that picture. I have it for keeps now, both the real and the picture.

I am beginning to see double again, think it is about time I go to bed. I wish I had you for my bed partner tonight, it is so cold and I am so tired I would just love to cuddle up to you. All the love and kisses in me to my precious sweetheart.

Lovingly,

Hildred

P.S. I forgot, I got a lovely letter from your Aunt Seleva today. H.C.

———————◆———————

Postmark: 12 p.m. October 16, 1914, Detroit, Mich.

Addressed to: Miss H.L. Cress, c/o Booth Fisheries, No dot on flap

Oct. 15th/14.

Dearest Sweetheart, -

And you surely are the best little sweetheart that ever lived. Note what you say in regard to bringing my letters to Detroit with you, count and see how many you have and let me know. Will you?

Think you did right in regard to selecting two girls instead of two chocolate drops to wait on us. Always imagine these chocolate drops stick their fingers into everything.

Just don't know whether to leave here next Friday Oct. 23rd or not, see I would have to let all my patients go and if there is anything I hate to do that is to lose a patient, then again I want to be with you in the worst way. The only thing by leaving here Sunday morning I could then take care of my patients before I would leave and they would not mind so much my being away for just two days. Another thing competition is always pretty Keen in a new neighborhood, and you know how much I need the money. Think it over sweetheart and let me know.

A Lady Friend of Mother's just came in and I am going to drive her over to the other side of the city, so will write you more tomorrow.

I surely send you loads & loads of love Hildred, and more than I can send you by writing how could I send more. Not only that but all the hugs and kisses in the world.

Lovingly,

Chas.

———————◆———————

Postmark: 9:30 a.m. October 17, 1914, St. Paul, Minn.

Friday evening.

My dear Sweetheart: -

Just think, only about half a dozen letters more to write and then I can see my dear hubby again. I am really getting excited over it now that the time is drawing so near and just wish it were next week Friday instead of this week. We are going to do some spooning aren't we, to make up for these four awful long months that have just passed.

I ironed a table cloth and dozen napkins tonight. They were not full bleached so I have had them in the wash the last two times to kind of bleach them out and ironed them so they would look at least half way respectable.

I was pretty near thunder-struck today when Mr. Turner asked me to work up to and including Wednesday. He says if I will do that, he will give me a week's pay. That sure looks good to me but really I have so much to do, I think I owe myself a week so I won't have to do it all evenings. Mr. Turner would like me to stay until all of the work is cleaned up again, he just got back this morning but he has decided on Mable Oestreich for the office and she is used to the fish line of the business so I don't see why she can't take it. I have told papa about it and he pretty near had a fit, said he would sooner give me the money himself but I wouldn't think of that for a minute. I don't know just what I will do but hardly think I will work after tomorrow.

You surely are the best hubby ever to get Claribel that bracelet, will you let me see it first? I imagine it is awfully pretty. It is plenty large enough because Claribel's hand is smaller than mine and I could get that piece of paper over my hand, just tore it the tiniest might.

Dad sent the boxes today and I will send you a copy of the freight bill tomorrow. Now I wouldn't say positively, but I think he said he sent them Northwestern Freight, c/o Michigan Central at Chicago but I will get you that freight bill tomorrow. Dad thinks you can take the both of them out to your house easy enough in your machine but I am kind of leary about the two at once, hope however you can. They should be there about Wednesday or Thursday the latest.

I'll bet that is a dandy tie pin you got for Leonard and like a youngster, can hardly wait to see the prize packages. What I am most anxious to know though is that surprise you have for me. I am pretty near burning up with curiosity but willing to wait. You must be pretty near broke after all your purchases. Of suit, coat, gifts rail fare etc. I am going to be quite an expense the first thing, such a bunch [?] of rail fare to take me home.

Mr. Turner asked me why my lips were so chapped, which they are, and I told him I was so in need of "Tulip Salve" (Two Lip) but it was a hard thing to get lately, had a supply promised in about a week. He chuckled and shook his head, guess he thinks I am hopeless.

Good night dear, just loads and loads of hugs and kisses to you.

Lovingly,

Hildred

Postmark: 8 p.m. Oct. 18, 1914, Detroit, Mich.

Addressed to: Miss H.L. Cress, Ashland Ave, St. Paul Minn.

Sunday AM.

Dearest Sweetheart, -

Rec'd your Thursday letter, note you are staying up pretty late at nights, think you better write me in the AM. Now then you can get to bed earlier.

I meant what I said in regard to the silk dress, this affair only happens once, and I think we should prepare for it in our best manner and of course keeping within our means.

As I said before I surely would like to arrive in St. Paul a day or so ahead of time, but if business is the same next Friday, Saturday & Sunday AM as it is this morning, do not think I better let things go as it will mean so much to me not only money but I would have to give up patients and they are too hard to get to give up without every reason and another thing if I arrive in St. Paul Monday AM, I will have lots of time, just got to get the ring, license, suit pressed, can do that all in the morning in the afternoon I can get shined up a little, and we can have the rehearsal at 4 o'clock, in the afternoon, as far as the wedding day itself is concerned, everything concerning it should be ready at least a day ahead of time. Another thing if I were there I would take up a lot of your time which in all probability you could use to better advantage just at this time now in regard to getting your clothes ready etc. Then there is another thing that waiting around getting anxious for the time to come if I were there two or three days ahead of time would not be good for either of us, we would both get nervous, and people would have ever so much more to talk about. As I said before Hildred, nothing would please me better than to be with you a day or so ahead of time, but I have told you exactly what I think, and I feel sure that when you study these things over you will agree with me that if I arrive in St. Paul Monday AM at 10 o'clock, leaving next Sunday AM that everything will work out better. Therefore unless you hear to the contrary I will arrive in St. Paul Monday AM at 10 o'clock that is on Oct. 26/14.

Funny thing your Friend Marion living within one mile or so from us, when she might live so many other places.

Note you would like to cuddle up to your hubby just a few more nights and you will have the opportunity. I want to have you cuddle up to me every night year in and year out. One of these nights I will lay awake to see what you talk about in your sleep.

Just millions of hugs and kisses and all the love in the world to my sweetheart.
Lovingly,
Chas.

———————◆———————

Postmark: 5 p.m. October 19, 1914, St. Paul, Minn.

Sunday evening.

My dear Sweetheart: –

I am glad you think I am the best sweetheart that ever lived and I hope you will always think so. I surely think there is only one dear hubby in the world or ever was or will be and my but won't. I will be glad to see you – next Sunday I hope.

As to when you leave, no doubt you have Mr. Turner's letter and see what he thinks. I really wanted you to come before – and from a selfish standpoint. I never thought of the rest of the folks but I know I wanted to see you myself. Of course I know it is hard to leave your patients but Mr. Turner thinks it would be better to come Sunday, that is get here then and I know Sunday is an awfully long time to wait, this past week has been longer than any I know of. Of course if you can't make it Sunday we will have to wait until Monday and will be just as happy to see you. Just think dear, a week from tomorrow, is it possible? Let me know what day you will come won't you? Of course I will meet you no matter what day it is and as you say, if I can manage it I will run ahead of the rest of them so you won't be so fussed when you kiss me. You will be won't you, now own up! I don't think anybody but Mr. Turner will go down to the depot – and myself of course – but I will sure make a bee line when I see you.

No sir, don't you grow a mustache, ish [sic], I don't like them. Just think everytime you kissed me that awful thing would be in the way and maybe get in my mouth if I had to kiss you in a hurry. Again, if you were drinking hot chocolate – not coffee – you know how that gets a little skim over the top of the cup when it stands a few minutes and then when you drank it the skin would catch on your moustache and you would be a great looking sight. No sir, dad had one and I don't like the old things so just forget all about it. Whenever I read a book and the hero had a moustache, I get disgusted right away. I know you just said this to tease me but now you know what I think of a moustache don't you? Maybe if I saw you getting off the train with one I would get cold feet and run away. No I wouldn't I would simply run the lawn mower over it some night or else better still cut half of it off when you were asleep so you would have to get rid of the rest.

I should say I did hate to leave the office. Mr. Turner left a little after five and I didn't leave until about quarter after six. I filed all the letters, sorted the balance sheets and straightened everything tip top for the new steno – Miss "Haystack." Mind you, she didn't want to take it at first, you know she is kind of afraid of Mr. "T" but I can't see why. She isn't very strong either and is afraid the work will be too hard for her, but she is gong to give it a trial. She stayed Saturday night too and I told her about different things around the office. After that I had some shopping to do and she went with me and then wanted to know if I couldn't go to a "movie" with her so I called up the folks and it was O.K. so to the "movies" we went. After I got home my new dress was here but the buttons were not on. I couldn't get them until last night so I told the dressmaker I would put them on because I wanted to wear the *dress today. That cost $4.75 to have made, that seems like throwing money away.*

Gladys went to church with me today and tomorrow has asked me to take supper with her and then go to a "movie." I sure will miss her, see her pretty near every day. Do you know we have been taken for sisters a great many times? People say we are together so much and also that there is a great resemblance too.

Tuesday night Ethel is giving her shower for me and I guess that is my last night "out," must get to bed early after that so you will know me at the depot.

Papa addressed all of the announcements today and I folded them and put them in the envelopes. Those the folks will mail the morning after hubby and I are married.

I don't think Mr. Turner likes it that I did not work until Wednesday, but actually I couldn't any more and besides the folks wouldn't hear of it. I figure Mon., Tues., Wed. and possibly Thursday I will do some of the sewing or mending I have. Mr. Turner says leave it until I get to Detroit. That is all well and good and I am leaving plenty until then because I had to but I want the few clothes I have got to look a little decent anyway. Friday and Saturday there will be plenty to do around the house and Sunday is the big event when I expect you will come and Monday the still bigger event, biggest of all.

I didn't get that freight bill yet, I asked Bob for it Sat. night after dad had gone but it was on dad's desk which was locked and he forgot too bring it today so I guess tomorrow is the best I can do.

I am going to count those letter and let you know, I know it is an awful bunch, pretty near everyone you have written. I threw away an awful bunch of letters the other week that I had, didn't care about paying freight on them. I am going to tell you what I want you to do with these letters when I see you dear.

I pretty near forgot, but that sure was dandy of that friend of your mother's to give us those spoons. Those are two other things I am anxious to see and hear about, the spoons and the surprise. I can't forget that surprise you know.

Well good night dear, I am off to dreamland now, I hope I have a dandy dream of my sweetheart. All the love I can possibly give to you dear, and some whopping big kisses and hugs.

Lovingly,

Hildred

———————◆———————

Postmark: 12:30 a.m. Oct. 20, 1914, Detroit, Mich.

Addressed to: Miss H.L. Cress, 1847 Ashland Ave., St. Paul, Minn. - No dot on envelope flap

Oct. 19th/14

Dearest Sweetheart,

Awfully busy this afternoon, will write more tomorrow.

Even if I have no news to send, I have millions and millions of hugs & kisses, will give you some real ones pretty soon.

A whole lot more hugs & kisses, and some more the largest of all.

Lovingly,

Chas.

———————◆———————

Postmark: 9 a.m. Oct. 20, 1914, St. Paul, Minn.

St. Paul – Oct. 19, 1914.

My dear Hubby:

Just a little note tonight, was quite disappointed not to hear from you today but I know you would write if you could. Maybe your letter is delayed somewhere. The folks say we have a new mail man and that he is pretty good on mixing things up.

I sewed all day today but simply couldn't accomplish a thing, it was an off day for me. You know my blue dress, it had a puff skirt and I didn't like it any more so ripped it all out and am pleating it instead and also shortening it. I just have a little hand sewing to do on that and then I made part of a dressing sack – if you know what they are.

This evening I had supper with Gladys at the Y.W.C.A. and then we went to the Starland, saw Ethel Barrymore in "The Nightingale (movies) and it was certainly great. We were out by 8:30 and then we hustled home to Gladys' and I saw her new furs. Mr. Jones but they are great, Hudson Seal and Fitch. She wanted me to stay over night with her but it would make it quite late to get home in the morning.

Celia Brown called up this morning and wants Claribel and I to come over for lunch tomorrow, one o'clock so out we go again. Tomorrow night is the shower and then I hope I am through because I have certainly been going lately. I ought to call on Alice and Vera, haven't called since they are married mind you I don't know if I can make it anymore.

My dear, I hope I get a long letter tomorrow, just think a week from tonight and you are my own dear real hubby. I am getting awfully excited now, can hardly wait any more, do a lot of day dreaming now too. Goodnight lover, just all the kisses and hugs imaginable.

Lovingly,

Hildred

P.S. I forgot to get some writing paper today, will you excuse this tablet paper until I get down town again? –H

◆

Postmark: 5:30 p.m. October 20, 1914, Detroit Mich. Grand River Station

Addressed to: Miss H.L. Cress, Ashland Ave., St. Paul, Minn.

Oct. 20th/14.

Dear Sweetheart, -

If you don't hurry up and write to me may be you will not see me next Monday, here it is Tuesday and the last letter I received was written away last week Friday, isn't that awful. What makes you so busy you can't find time to write to your hubby.

Think I will write to you Wednesday then again Thursday, then on Sunday I will send you a telegram, possibly from Chicago. If you can arrange for a rehearsal late Monday afternoon, we will have all kinds of time on Monday. In fact we do not want to have any spare moments on our hands to sit around and get nervous. May say I think we will be a pretty spoony [sic] pair alright.

Will let you see those prize packages as you call them first, but they do not amount to much.

I tell you Hildred we will be badly bent when Oct. 26th comes, better get your bread basket filled up good before you leave St. Paul the good Lord only knows whether or not you will ever get it filled up again. One thing you won't need to worry about getting too stout, no chance, we will have to live on pork & beans, along with lots of hugs & kisses. Now do you want to come to Detroit.

Business has been a little better the last few days. Would surely have missed something yesterday had I been away.

Going to tell you something else, the other morning when I woke up I found one sleeve of my nightie was ripped from the shoulder all the way down how it got that way I do not know. You surely will have to hang on to your hubby at nights or you may land out of bed on the floor.

The most love & kisses ever to my Dearie.

Lovingly,

Chas.

———◆———

Postmark: 10 a.m. Oct. 21, 1914, St. Paul, Minn.

Wednesday 12:30 A.M.

To the Dearest Sweetheart Ever:

Scandalous to be writing at this time of the morning I know, but I couldn't make it today. It has been "go" ever since we got up. Our washwoman disappointed us today and we did not want to be delayed so we all pitched in. We have two washboards so Flora and I rubbed, rinsed them etc. and then Mamma hung them out and done the housework. Claribel wasn't feeling very well so we didn't let her help much. We were all through by twelve, didn't start until pretty near nine o'clock as we expected the washwoman right along. At one o'clock Claribel and I were over to Celia's for lunch. Maybe we didn't have some dandy lunch, will tell you all about it some day but must hurry tonight. We didn't get home until three and then I done a little sewing, made my first muffins for supper and they wouldn't give you indigestion either, they were good, and tonight was the shower. Oh! this is some strenuous life dear. Tomorrow (night) Alice Crawford and Alice Hazen want me to come over, they live in a duplex, one upstairs and the other downstairs. I hardly think I ought to, think the rest would do me a lot more good.

Say you can't imagine the spiffy present I got from the office employees, it is great. It is a gold link bracelet with a gold, open faced watch, simply wonderful really it is. I am not much of an artist but it is something like this

(Goodness I didn't think it would look so awful on paper.) If I have looked at it once I have looked fifty times. Well dear, off to bed I must get, my eyes feel a little sandy.

I almost forgot, I suppose you will be answering my Saturday letter, where Mr. Turner tells you to come Sunday but dear, if you find you can't make it, why then don't come until Monday. Be sure you write Thursday and let me know when you come so I can hear from you Saturday, if it is too late to send it to the house, then send it to the office. If you come Sunday, I hope you will plan on eating your Sunday dinner with us. You will won't you? I will promise not to make biscuits.

All the love in the world dear from your sweetheart,

Hildred

Here's hoping it will be Sunday but if you can't make it, all O.K. H.C.

◆

Postmark:11:30 a.m. Oct. 21, 1914, Detroit, Michigan

Addressed to Miss H.L. Cress, c/o Booth Fisheries - No dot on envelope flap

Oct. 21st/14.

My Dear Hildred, -

Wish to write you a few lines in regard to a letter I received Yesterday from Uncle Chas.

May say that Uncle Chas. has looked over the names I sent for invitations and announcements to be sent to, Now in making out the list of names for invitations to be sent to I did not include Aunt Lizzie and he, and I surely hope you have sent them an invitation, of course he did not come right out only told me an indirect way. However the questions along that line in which he asked me made me think that he doubted me and needless to say made me feel very much hurt with myself. In fact I feel anyway but happy this morning. I surely did not mean to do wrong it was unintentional on my part.

Then again Uncle has approached me pretty strong on arriving in St. Paul on Sunday. May say if my wishes were fulfilled I would be there today. You know yourself that I would like nothing better than to be with you. May say that Uncle Chas. always reasons in my behalf with the consideration that I can afford or do not have any more than what he does his own. Of course I honor his advice but I have to consider where I spend & how I spend my time & pennies.

Competition is keen I am a beginner and have a home on my hands not only that but I have had a lot of expense this last year. I must either take care of my patients or lose them, I feel that I can put a number of them off for two days, but not for three without losing them and we surely need them all, I want to get out of debt. I am making good money but various things have taken a lot of it and I feel sure you would not want to marry me and not have me in a position to take care of you. I wouldn't want to marry you unless I felt sure I could take better care of you, than what you have had previous. I trust you will over look my arriving on Monday morning, consider that it is for the best, and think more of me for wanting to go ahead in life. If I had not have had a little stick in me all the way along, I would have nothing today.

May be I feel a little more down hearted today, in as much as I have not received a letter from you later than your Friday letter, no Saturday, no Sunday & no Monday letter has arrived so far. I know when you miss a day you feel awfully blue that is in hearing from me. I wish I had not missed more than one day and I surely hope the tide will turn before the day is out and I will hear from you.

Business has been better the last few days last evening I had my office full and people waiting outside. Another party walking around the street waiting, supposing I had been away last night.

I have talked my troubles over with mother and she says she does not see how I can be away and retain my business, that is for any length of time.

Surely would be pleased if you would or could set me right with Uncle Chas. because I surely feel bad about it, write me right back will you Hildred.

The most love ever to my dear Sweetheart loads of hubgs & kisses.

Lovingly,

Chas.

(PS) our wash woman said to mother this am. I hear the doctor is going to be married, don't know how they hear these things. CW

Postmark: 1 p.m. October 22, 1914, Detroit, Mich.

Wednesday evening

My dear Sweetheart: -

Your letter surely was short but sweet today, glad you wrote to me anyway. I think I shall have to make mine short tonight, not because I am busy though, tired as the effect of high life last night.

We got a couple of nice presents today, a beautiful cake knife from my Milwaukee friend and a dandy big bath rug from Flora. Mr. Turner says there are two packages at the office for us but instructions are that they are not to be opened until Monday. Goodness that is a long time to wait, for a curious person like I am anyway. Say guess, mamma and dad are going to give us a set of dishes isn't that great?

Tomorrow I am going down town and invest in some writing paper so tomorrow's letter will look half way decent again.

Just loads and loads of hugs and kisses to my dear sweetheart,

From Hildred

P.S. I am anxious to hear from you tomorrow, maybe you have decided to get here Sunday.

H.C.

———————◆———————

Postmark: 5:30 p.m. October 22, 1914, Detroit, Mich. Grand River Station

Addressed to: Miss H.L. Cress, 1847 Ashland Ave., St. Paul, Minn.

Oct. 22nd/14

My Own, The Dearest and Best Sweetheart Ever, -

I surely feel loads better today, may say that I received two letters from you yesterday, just wish I could have you here to hug so tight, am afraid I would never let go, could squeeze you right in two, surely wish it were Monday tomorrow, glad I did not consent to have the wedding postponed until Nov. 1st. I tell you Hildred I would not want to live like [illegible]. I am very much longer is that what you call living love sick.

May say that my working right until Sunday I have been able to secure something else pretty nice for my little wifie, but you have got to be my really, truly, dear little wife before you can get it and love me oh! so hard, and I am so anxious to give it to you, really I am so anxious to give it to you that I just know I could not help but give it to you even if you weren't going to be my dear little wifie. Then I got a surprise for you next Wednesday too. Am going to tell you this that they will be worth nearly four months of you $15.00 per week, that is all I am going to say at present, will demonstrate later.

To-morrow I will write again & address my letter in care of Booth Fisheries Coy. so you will get it Sunday, there on Sunday evening if I have time between trains in Chicago I will send you a telegram to Ashland Ave. Will probably send it about 8 o'clock so you ought to get it by 9 o'clock. Now on Monday morning as you know I plan on arriving in St. Paul at 10 o'clock. Now when you meet me, I want to kiss you twice anyway, if we know just how we are going to act then we won't seem to the people that we are a little excited, then when we get out to the house I hope we can have a few minutes to ourselves to hug & kiss each other that is away from everybody else.

Now Hildred maybe I mistook or misunderstood Uncle Chas.' little note the other day, but I surely hope you sent him an invitation.

All the love in the world, all the kisses in the world, all the hugs in the world and millions and millions more, and then some more to the best & dearest Little Girl I ever met, my Own dear little Sweetheart, Lots of Love.

Lovingly,

Chas.

◆

Postmark: 10 a.m. October 23, 1914, St. Paul, Minn.

October 22, 1914

My dear Sweetheart:

Really I was not surprised to get your letter today as to what Mr. Turner said. This all came to a climax Sunday evening and I thought best not to say anything about it until you came as you would just worry about it and possibly not understand. I did not think Mr. Turner would write to you. The first thing I want to tell you is that Mr. and Mrs. Turner got an invitation we knew you meant them to have one.

Saturday Mr. Turner was awfully provoked with me that I would not stay at the office until Wednesday, in fact did not have much to say to me at all but really dear, I had so many things to attend to, mending, packing etc. and I could not leave it all to the last because I must help mamma out a little too, turn about is fair play you know, again, dad said he wouldn't think of letting me work any longer.

Before I left, Mr. Turner asked to see your list and of course I showed it to him. Mr. Turner had already received his invitation though. He immediately remarked about your not having Mrs. Menges name down for an invitation and said as much as I should have known enough to send it anyway. To say the least I was pretty near thunderstruck. When your list came I was surprised you had so few invitations but guess you misunderstood me. When I said fifty invitations, I meant that many for the house but I sent invitations to all my relatives and close friends. I was going to write to you about it first but did not think you misunderstood me and thought as long as you knew they could not come anyway that you would sooner not send any invitation so I didn't say anything about it. That is the trouble, when you can't talk things over there is so much chance to get things mixed.

To talk about the Detroit invitation again, Mr. Turner wanted me to promise to send it and I did say I thought I would send it. When I got home I talked it over with the folks and they thought I shouldn't send it, I have my list to go by and should stick to it. I hadn't quite made up my mind though, in fact we were just talking about it early Sunday evening when Mr. Turner called up and wanted to know if I had sent the invitation and when I told him no, that is where he started in at me. I don't know when I was so hurt. I don't believe I ever heard Mr. Turner talk so cross to anybody. The folks sure didn't object to my sending the invitation and I know I didn't but the folks thought I should send invitations to only those you had on the list. It has all turned out alright, the invitation is sent and everybody friendly again but I will tell you all about it when I see you. I cried pretty near all night, felt so bad because that is the first time Mr. Turner has spoken cross to me. Be prepared for a lecture when you come but don't mind anything that is said because I have had my share too.

Now as to when you come to St. Paul, you just come when you can. If you can't make it until Monday, nobody is kicking at all, I appreciate your position and know you would come if you could. Maybe I have said too many times how well I would like to see you Sunday but I surely do not want you to come when it would be a detriment to your future so don't you come Sunday you come Monday and I will be on hand Monday to meet you. I think what I will do though, I will order my flowers before you come, then you will just have the ring, license, suit to get pressed and get our room at the hotel, that is all I know of, and you will have plenty of time for that.

I got little Marcella a comb and brush (ivory) she has everything else under the sun, rings, bracelet, locket, everything in toys, gloves etc. so that is the best I could think of.

I can't understand why you have not heard from me, I have written every day but Saturday and given the letters to dad to mail so you would get them in better time and he says he has mailed them all. I am going to take this to Prior post office, doing the best I can to hurry this to you.

This is the last letter I am writing to my sweetheart, the next will be to my sweetheart and hubby.

I hope you will send me a wire from Chicago, want to know if you get there safe you know, I will be anxious after I know you have left Detroit.

Ever and ever so much love dear and some big, big kisses. My I am glad it is not long until Monday you bet.

Lovingly,

Hildred

———————◆———————

Postmark: 5:30 p.m. October 23, 1914, Detroit, Mich. Grand River Station

Addressed to: Miss H.L. Cress, c/o Booth Fisheries

Friday Afternoon.

Sweetheart Hildred Dearest Ever, -

What do you know I purchased my ticket this a.m. Am already to go, Oh! for the time to come, could not wait one second longer, My Sweetheart to see, just think, alias my wifie, how great to think of it.

It was surely good of those office friends of yours to give you that bracelet, won't I have some stylish wifie though, I surely will take great pride in always seeing you look tip top.

Just think day after tomorrow I leave, also only have three more of these lonesome nights to put in then I can sleep with my Sweetheart and be with her all the time; and another thing you better get all the sleep you can before Monday night, as on Monday night we will be laying awake loving each other that will be great to. [sic] Because we both must look bright and fresh on Tuesday AM, if any of our people are going to see us off to Detroit.

Business has been with the last few days just because I want to go away.

Look for a telegram from me Sunday night am leaving here 12:30 noon Sunday will make Chicago 10:10 Sunday night, arriving in St. Paul 10 AM Monday.

Just Millions and Millions of hugs, Billions and Billions of Kisses, besides all the love in me, and more to [sic], to my Sweetheart the Best ever, And a great big hug & kiss, Good Bye Sweetheart until Monday at 10 AM.

Lovingly,

Chas.

EPILOGUE

◆

On the evening of what the St. Paul Pioneer Press characterized a "fair" weather day, Hildred and Charles were married in the parlor of the Cress family home on Ashland Avenue in St. Paul, Minnesota. Family minister Dr. Alex C. Stevens of Trinity Methodist Episcopal Church performed the ceremony, witnessed by Charles' brother, Leonard Husband, and Hildred's sister, Claribel Cress. Forty-six friends and family were also in attendance.

It is not known if the couple had a honeymoon, or if they made their train safely without the family teasing, which they so very much wanted to avoid.

What is known is that Charles and Hildred were married 65 years, parted only on November 4, 1979, when Charles died at the age of 92. They were able to celebrate their final wedding anniversary together with a small cake in Mount Carmel Hospital, where Charles had been admitted weeks before – the same hospital in which he served as first Chief of Staff and performed the first surgical procedure.

In those 65 years, Hildred and Charles lived a life rich in experience and accomplishment. Charles practiced medicine for 59 years, joining the staff of Mt. Carmel Mercy Hospital when it opened in 1938. During his remarkable career, Charles served as the hospital's chief of surgery, and chief of staff. He was a member of the hospital's Executive Committee, and, at the time of his death, was an emeritus member of its surgical staff. Charles was also a senior surgeon for 25 years at Providence Hospital in Southfield, Michigan.

In 1974, he received the Mount Carmel Hospital Silver Sword of Mercy award, which hung in a place of honor in the library of their Argyle Crescent home.

Hildred made a home for Charles and handled the business end of the medical practice, balancing books and other duties. She was active in charitable work and remained athletic. As a member of the Detroit Golf Club and the Detroit Athletic Club, she and Charles both played an excellent round of golf. Hildred even captured the woman's club championship at the Golf Club in the 1930's.

Together, they had three children: Raymond Charles Husband, M.D. (1916-1988); and fraternal twins Roberta Emily (1918-2003) and Hildred Loretta (1918-2002).

The pair remained active with their eight grandchildren: son Raymond's children, Nancy, Susan, Raymond and Deborah Husband; Roberta's sons, Charles and Bruce Thom; and Hildred's children, Glenn and Hildred Corbett.

The older grandsons, Charles and Bruce Thom and Glenn Corbett, accompanied their grandparents to Washington D.C., with stops at the Gettysburg battlefield. When the oldest granddaughters, Nancy and Susan Husband and Hildred Corbett were teenagers, their grandmother took them to New York City for a week-long visit. One highlight, among many, included dinner at the Waldorf which featured actress Carol Channing's cabaret show at the hotel.

Together, the couple traveled the world, always returning to their Argyle Crescent home. Charles never really gave up his medical practice. Partnering with his son Raymond, Charles continued to see patients even after he had given up surgery.

Hildred lived another six years. She still enjoyed going out and visits from her family and friends, dying peacefully in her own bed on February 2, 1985. She was 89 years old.

Perhaps the couple's greatest legacy remains their descendants. Their eight grandchildren have brought them many great-grandchildren and great-great grandchildren. Now, in the summer of 2013, a great-great-great grandchild has joined the growing list. Of those descendants, only one is no longer living: Glenn E. Corbett, the grandson who rescued the letters from the trash, died in 2008 at the age of 62. We miss him still.

And what of the rest of the people who were part of the living fabric of life described in the letters? We know more than might be expected after 100 years.

Charles' brother, Leonard, and his wife, Katherine, returned to their home in Duluth and raised their children. They visited Hildred and Charles regularly over the years.

Claribel married Ernest Groenig, who was listed as a wedding guest. It is unknown if they knew one another prior to that October evening in 1914. Perhaps he was there to assist Dr. Stevens, and they met that evening. We do know that Ernest Groenig was a Methodist minister, serving churches in the northern Middle West. In about 1952, the couple came to Michigan, where he baptized Hildred and Charles' granddaughter, Hildred Corbett, into the Methodist church.

Claribel and Ernest retired to Arizona, where she became an accomplished painter, specializing in scenes from the Painted Desert and Native American portraiture. Claribel died in Phoenix, Arizona May 10, 1987, a little more than two years after her older sister.

The fate of Hildred's father, Henry Cress, and her younger brother, Addison was, until recently, unknown. Genealogist Gail Campbell Schulte took on the search for Henry

Cress as her personal mission. She located him through the 1930 census. By then, Henry and his wife, Ellen, were employed as a butler and maid to actor Frederic March in Beverly Hills, California. There is no known record indicating when they moved there or how they came to join the March staff.

They lived in the March home until Henry's retirement in 1933. On June 29, 1933, Henry Cress died in North Bend, Coos County Oregon at the age of 65. His obituary states that he and his wife "had been residents of North Bend for only a few weeks, coming to that city from California." He was buried in Portland Oregon following a Masonic funeral.

No mention of Addison Cress is made in the 1930 census record from California. Late in her life, Hildred said she never knew what happened to her little brother, adding that when she was in California years before she unsuccessfully tried to find him through the telephone book.

Campbell Schulte launched a search for Addison. All that was known was he was born June 2, 1903 and died December 7, 1969. She found the 1930 census listing him as serving in the U.S. Army, stationed at Fort Adams in Newport, Rhode Island.

Later records indicate he was living in California in 1933, when he was 30 years old. Addison remained in Los Angeles for 36 years, and was employed as a night club manager at Billy Gray's Bandbox in Hollywood. He died in 1969 at the age of 66. It appears he was married and may have had children.

Charles Turner, Hildred's employer and Charles' uncle, has a tug boat named for him. According to a website maintained by Harvey Hadland and Bob Mackreth, it was built in 1900 for S.P. Hogstad Fish Co. in Duluth, Minnesota. The 55 ft. x 13 ft. boat was acquired by Booth Fisheries in 1912 for operation from their Bayfield, Wisconsin plant, picking up fish from the many fish camps among the Apostle Islands. Passengers were also carried. The boat last operated in 1937. It remains moored in Bayfield.

One never knows when an action will change the course of life, even in a small, nearly undetectable way. If Hildred and Charles had not decided to write a century ago; if Glenn and June had not rescued the letters, this story could not have been written.

Indeed, without the letters, Hildred and Charles might have drifted apart and all of our lives would have been very different, indeed. Luckily, it didn't happen that way. But one thing is clear: in our family, our lives began from a great love. Let us hope that, at the end of our own lives, we will have experienced at least one great love ourselves.

Made in the USA
Charleston, SC
02 June 2014